Rhetoric and Religion in Ancient Greece and Rome

Trends in Classics – Supplementary Volumes

Edited by
Franco Montanari and Antonios Rengakos

Associate Editors
Stavros Frangoulidis · Fausto Montana · Lara Pagani
Serena Perrone · Evina Sistakou · Christos Tsagalis

Scientific Committee
Alberto Bernabé · Margarethe Billerbeck
Claude Calame · Jonas Grethlein · Philip R. Hardie
Stephen J. Harrison · Stephen Hinds · Richard Hunter
Christina Kraus · Giuseppe Mastromarco
Gregory Nagy · Theodore D. Papanghelis
Giusto Picone · Alessandro Schiesaro
Tim Whitmarsh · Bernhard Zimmermann

Volume 106

Rhetoric and Religion in Ancient Greece and Rome

Edited by
Sophia Papaioannou, Andreas Serafim
and Kyriakos Demetriou

DE GRUYTER

ISBN 978-3-11-126270-3
e-ISBN (PDF) 978-3-11-069962-3
e-ISBN (EPUB) 978-3-11-069970-8
ISSN 1868-4785

Library of Congress Control Number: 2021944978

Bibliographic information published by the Deutsche Nationalbibliothek
The Deutsche Nationalbibliothek lists this publication in the Deutsche Nationalbibliografie;
detailed bibliographic data are available on the Internet at http://dnb.dnb.de.

© 2023 Walter de Gruyter GmbH, Berlin/Boston
This volume is text- and page-identical with the hardback published in 2021.
Editorial Office: Alessia Ferreccio and Katerina Zianna
Logo: Christopher Schneider, Laufen
Printing and binding: CPI books GmbH, Leck

www.degruyter.com

Contents

Acknowledgements —— VII
List of Tables —— IX

Sophia Papaioannou and Andreas Serafim
Religion and Rhetoric in Ancient Graeco-Roman Texts and Contexts —— 1

Part I: Religion, Rhetoric and Law

Edward M. Harris
Religion and the Rule of Law in the Greek *Polis* —— 17

Jakub Filonik
Speaking for the Gods: Greek Cultic Regulations and their Silent Informants —— 37

William Furley
Religious Arguments in Antiphon Rhetor —— 59

Part II: Magic and Religion

Despina Keramida
Performing the Rhetoric of Magic in Ovid's *Epistulae Heroidum* and *Metamorphoses* 10 —— 81

Panagiota Sarischouli
Transcultural Context in Graeco-Egyptian Magic: Two Case Studies from a Bilingual Theban Handbook —— 101

Part III: Religion and Rhetorical Performance

Maik Patzelt
Trends in the Rhetoric of Prayer: The *Actio* of Prayer and the *Eloquentia Popularis* —— 133

Christopher Degelmann
Between Compassion and Aggression: The Rhetoric of Mourning in Republican and Early Imperial Rome —— 153

Glenn Holland
Argument and Performance in the Creation of a Rhetorical Matrix in Paul's Congregations and Beyond —— 171

Part IV: **The Rulers' Religion**

Vasileios Liotsakis
Beloved of the Gods, Son of the Gods, Rival of the Gods: Alexander and the Rhetoric of Religion in Plutarch, Arrian and Curtius Rufus —— 193

Kelly E. Shannon-Henderson
What Makes a *Divus*? The Prospective Rhetoric of Deification in Pliny's *Panegyricus* —— 221

Hans-Friedrich Mueller
***Tua Divinitas*: Religious Self-fashioning in Tiberian Rome —— 245**

Part V: **Rhetoric and Religion in Verse Style**

Konstantinos Melidis
Biblical Epics: Intersection of Rhetoric and Religion in Greek and Latin Hexametric Paraphrases of Psalm 136 (137) —— 269

Notes on Editors and Contributors —— 291
General Index —— 293
Index Locorum —— 297

Acknowledgements

The editors would like to acknowledge a number of individuals and institutions whose help and support have been invaluable in the conception and completion of this volume. We would like to thank, first and foremost, the two editors of Trends in Classics at De Gruyter, Professors Antonios Rengakos (Aristotle University of Thessaloniki/Member of the Academy of Athens) and Franco Montanari (University of Genova), for having believed in the significance and usefulness of this volume and supported us wholeheartedly from the initial theoretical meanderings to the preparation of the final full manuscript of the volume.

The editors would also like to thank the contributors, who have been very patient and helpful throughout the process of putting together this volume, in the face of many rounds of revisions. As editors, we have been delighted to see how exchanges of initial ideas and outlines have led to the formulation of chapters that will enhance our knowledge and understanding of the features of the interconnection between rhetoric and religion in the ancient world. We are sure the contributors will forgive us for having bombarded them with countless questions and requests which placed a huge demand on their time. The fruitful and fascinating result of our smooth cooperation reimburses us all for our labours.

Andreas Serafim would like, finally, to thank the Research Centre for Greek and Latin Literature of the Academy of Athens for providing excellent research facilities that make the timely completion of this volume possible; and Millie Gall for reading and commenting on several drafts of the Introduction and of other chapters within the volume.

Abbreviations throughout this volume follow those in *L'Année philologique* or the *Oxford Classical Dictionary*. A certain level of formatting standardisation has been imposed to ensure consistency across the volume, but individual stylistic distinctiveness has been respected. The volume is intended for specialist scholars and graduate students of rhetoric, ancient religion and religious studies both in Classics and beyond. All long quotations of Greek and Latin are accompanied by English translation. Only key passages are included in the *Index Locorum*, which does not aim to provide an exhaustive list of all textual references in this volume.

Sophia Papaioannou, Andreas Serafim and Kyriakos Demetriou
Athens and Nicosia, July 2021

List of Tables

Tab. 1: Adjectives describing the cities. —— 275
Tab. 2: Adjectives inserted by Paulinus of Nola. —— 277
Tab. 3: Paulinus' direct and indirect influences. —— 279
Tab. 4: Syntactic similarity between the *Vorlage* and the paraphrases. —— 283
Tab. 5: Greek: *Vorlage* and paraphrase. —— 285
Tab. 6: Latin: *Vorlage* and paraphrase. —— 286

Sophia Papaioannou and Andreas Serafim
Religion and Rhetoric in Ancient Graeco-Roman Texts and Contexts

It is perhaps a truism to note that ancient religion and rhetoric were closely intertwined in Greek and Roman antiquity. Religion is embedded in socio-political, legal and cultural institutions and structures, while also being influenced, or even determined, by them. The notion of *polis*-religion, first coined and developed by C. Sourvinou-Inwood, encapsulates this two-cornered relation between religion and the civic/political or ethnic community in ancient Greek and Roman history.[1] Rhetoric, being the vehicle for expressing ideas and beliefs that relate to the community, is also thought to be steadily connected with religion; for, as has recently been argued, "religion intersects with social/civic institutions that are central to rhetorical processes and outcomes, thereby impacting upon political attitudes, decision-making and mass persuasion, or manipulation".[2] The interrelation between rhetoric and religion is, in a sense, both indisputable and inevitable: religion is articulated, discussed, explained and propagated verbally; in other words, rhetoric, the art of speaking, is the unavoidable vehicle through which religion takes form and is practised within the context of a community of people who espouse its beliefs and theological principles. Rhetoric is used to address the divine, to invoke the gods, to talk about the sacred, to express piety and to articulate, refer to, recite or explain the meaning of hymns, oaths, prayers, oracles and other religious matters and processes. The twelve contributions to this volume explore themes and topics that most succinctly describe the firm interrelation between religion and rhetoric mostly in, but not exclusively focused on, Greek and Roman antiquity, offering new, interdisciplinary insights into a great variety of aspects, from identity construction and performance to legal/political practices and a broad analytical approach to transcultural ritualistic customs. The volume also offers perceptive insights into oriental (i.e. Egyptian magic) texts and Christian literature.

---

[1] Sourvinou-Inwood 1988, 259–274; 1990, 295–322; 2000, 38–55. For a comprehensive survey of the most influential theories on the notion and the widespread application of *polis*-religion: Serafim 2020, esp. 1–18. The survey includes references to influential theories by British and French classicists, sociologists and anthropologists, including E. Durkheim, J.E. Harrison, W. Burkert and L.B. Zaidman.
[2] Serafim 2020, 11. On the interconnection between law, politics and religion in early Greece: Gagarin 2013, 59–78.

https://doi.org/10.1515/9783110699623-001

This Introduction comprises two parts, each of which aims to shed light on the various aspects of the relationship between rhetoric and religion in the diversified periods of time and topics that are examined in this volume. The first part, "Scholarly perspectives on the synergy between religion and rhetoric", examines the current scholarly work on the steady interconnection between religion and rhetoric both in the contemporary and in the ancient context. The second part of the Chapter, entitled "New light on the ancient intersection between rhetoric and religion", outlines the main arguments of each of the twelve chapters of this volume, clarifying the ways in which they contribute to the overall enhancement of knowledge about the interrelationship between religion and rhetoric.

1 Scholarly perspectives on the synergy between religion and rhetoric

Much has been written, in interdisciplinary and classical scholarship, in discussing a great variety of aspects of the intricate and multidimensional connection between religion and rhetoric. K. Burke, in his mighty book *The Rhetoric of Religion: Studies in Logology*, argues that language and rhetoric, what he calls *logology*, "words about words", are intertwined with religion in various ways, a line of argument that also appears in W.C. Booth's chapter to the volume of W.G. Jeanrond and J.L. Rike, *Radical Pluralism and Truth*. The contributions to the volume of W. Olmstead and W. Jost, *Rhetorical Invention and Religious Inquiry*, also offer meticulously crafted insights into the multifaceted intersection between rhetoric and religion.[3]

In classical scholarship, there are a few important full-scale studies (in contrast to the insightful and useful but fragmentary discussions in commentaries, journal articles and multi-authorial volumes) that underline the nexuses between rhetoric and religion. K. Dover, for example, discusses two aspects of rhetorical and legal processes and outcomes in Classical Athens: the first is the dicastic oath, i.e. the oath the judges in the law-court swore to abide by the laws in casting their verdict, and the second is the references of speakers to religious discourse and, specifically, their claims that their adversaries violated the rule of both secular and divine law.[4] J. Mikalson explains how and why patriotism (specifically

---

[3] Burke 1970; Booth 1991, 62–80; Olmstead and Jost 2000.
[4] Dover 1974.

the acts of treason or heroism) acquires a religious dimension,[5] while R. Parker explores the connection between patriotism, land and religion in the context of autochthony, the Athenian myth par excellence.[6]

The first, relatively recent and certainly thorough and meticulous, study that explores systematically the use, purpose and features of references to religion – what is called *religious argumentation* – in Attic oratory is offered by G. Martin, in his book *Divine Talk: Religious Argumentation in Demosthenes*. Martin focuses mostly on Demosthenes (i.e. 18–20 and 22–24), with a few glimpses of other orators, i.e. Lysias, Aeschines and Lycurgus, to examine how and why a whole range of religiously-flavoured issues, including oaths, prayers and references to the intervention of the gods in human affairs, are exploited to the best rhetorical effect. Martin's book is important not only because it examines a great pool of patterns of religious argumentation, but also because it explores their use in both public and private oratorical contexts. Martin has been the first to prove the validity, with regard to the use of religious discourse in Attic oratory, of the argument that the distinction between public and private speeches, on the one hand, and defence and prosecution, on the other, affects the use of rhetorical techniques.[7] Martin suggests that religious argumentation is used mostly in forensic and symbouleutic speeches and less in epideictic orations, more in public than in private cases, and more in logographic speeches than in the speeches that were delivered by the orator himself.[8]

The arguments of Martin are discussed and in some cases contested in the most recent, fully-fledged examination of references to the aspects of religion in Attic oratory – labelled as *religious discourse* – offered in A. Serafim's *Religious Discourse in Attic Oratory and Politics*. Serafim, offering a full-scale investigation of aspects of religious discourse in the entirety of the transmitted forensic, symbouleutic and epideictic orations of the Ten Attic Orators, a body of 151 speeches which represents the mature flourishing of the ancient art of public speaking and persuasion in Classical Athens, argues that Martin is right in the first two conclusions mentioned above, but not in the third. After surveying the persistently and recurrently used features of religious discourse in forensic, symbouleutic and epideictic orations, Serafim explains the use of specific patterns in specific oratorical contexts, examining the means and the restrictions that these contexts generate for the speaker akin to the theory of the "logic of appropriateness" that New

---

5 Mikalson 1983; Crowley 2017.
6 Parker 1997.
7 On this argument see Rubinstein 2004, 187–203; 2005, 129–145.
8 Martin 2009; cf. Martin 2016, 281–300.

Institutionalism suggests, i.e. that there are rules and practices that specify what should be expected and what makes sense within a given (institutional or textual) context. Serafim argues, unlike Martin, that instances of religious discourse are higher in number in the orations that Demosthenes delivered himself than in the three he composed for others to deliver (i.e. speech 22: *Against Androtion*; speech 23: *Against Aristocrates*; speech 24: *Against Timocrates*). *Religious Discourse in Attic Oratory and Politics* also discusses the actual reactions (i.e. those about which sources provide information) or the potential and expected reactions (i.e. those that might have happened) of both the speaker and the audience, when religious discourse is used: both physical/sensory and cognitive/emotional reactions are discussed. Finally, the book also examines how religious discourse is used for the purpose of identity construction, with a specific reference to the ways in which religion intersects with civic spirit/patriotism, an intersection that is exemplified by the paradigm of political statesmen and mythical heroes.[9]

However useful the books of Martin and Serafim are for the meticulous examination of the connections between religion and rhetoric, the high level of complexity of this connection requires more studies on a wider variety of issues covering multiple genres in both ancient Greek and Latin literature. Some studies have already been produced: the relationship between religion and rhetoric has also been manifested, and thus discussed, in historiography. In her Ph.D. thesis, *Speeches and Speechmaking in Herodotus' Histories*, I.E.M. Stone, for example, offers the first comprehensive inquiry into the role of direct speech in Herodotus' *Histories*, exploring, *inter alia*, the use of religious discourse. The examination of religion and rhetoric in historiography, however, is less studied than the general use of religion in historical works (as in "Herodotus and Religion" by J. Gould; *Divinity and History: The Religion of Herodotus* by T. Harrison; *Herodotus and Religion in the Persian Wars* by J. Mikalson; and "The Religious Dimension to the Peloponnesian War, or, What Thucydides Does Not Tell Us" by S. Hornblower).

Several other studies explore aspects of the relationship between religious discourse and rhetoric, as manifested in Latin literature. The studies of G.A. Kennedy on the reception of classical rhetoric in the Roman world from the beginning till Late Antiquity (*The Art of Rhetoric in the Roman World, 100 BC – AD 300*; *Classical Rhetoric and Its Christian and Secular Tradition from Ancient to Modern Times*; *Greek Rhetoric under the Christian Emperors*) are still reference works and the place to start on the topic. J. Pollini's book, *From Republic to Empire: Rhetoric, Religion, and Power in the Visual Culture of Ancient Rome* examines important material evidence ranging from the Late Republic to the Early Imperial period, e.g.

---

9 Serafim 2020.

the cultural, social and religious connotations of ancestral wax masks; various types of heroic and divine imagery of deified leaders; and various iconographic types of Octavian/Augustus. While there have been studies on Roman speeches more overtly concerned with religious rhetoric (e.g. *Literature and Religion at Rome: Cultures, Contexts, and Beliefs* by D. Feeney; *Religions of Rome* by M. Beard, J. North and S. Price; and *The Matter of the Gods: Religion and the Roman Empire* by C. Ando), there have been fewer studies on the speeches made in legal or political contexts. Cicero's Catilinarian speeches, for example, known for their political importance, historical value to the period and rhetorical craft receive less coverage for Cicero's often direct references to the Roman religious ideals. There have been a few interesting studies, such as the books *Cicero and the State Religion* by R. Goar; *Cicero and the Rise of Deification at Rome* by C. Spencer; and *Religiöses in der politischen Argumentation der späten römischen Republik: Ciceros Erste Catilinarische Rede – eine Fallstudie* by V. Sauer; and a few shorter studies, such as "Pollution and Ritual Impurity in Cicero's *de Domo Sua*" by J. Lennon.

A few works have also explored a range of other issues in a variety of texts, contexts and times: medicine (e.g. "Rhetoric and Faith in the Hippocratic Philosophy of Medicine" by A. Roth); drama and politics (e.g. "Drama, Political Rhetoric and the Discourse of Athenian Democracy" by J. Ober and B. Strauss); Hellenistic and Roman times (e.g. "Religious Discourse in Hellenistic and Roman Times: Content *Topoi* in Greek Epigraphic Cult Foundations and Sacred Norms" by M.P. de Hoz). There are also studies on postclassical religious rhetoric in both the pagan and Christian worlds.[10] L. Pernot, in his weighty article "The Rhetoric of Religion", explores the intersections between rhetoric and religion in Graeco-Roman antiquity, both pagan and Christian. Rhetorical forms of religious expression include discourse about the gods (narrative, eulogy, preaching, naming) and discourse addressed to the gods, especially prayers and hymns.

The high Roman Empire and Late Antiquity are periods of transition in politics and in religion alike, often in interrelation. As the political crisis of the Roman Empire in the 3rd century unraveled and Christianity gradually became a prominent religious movement with a successfully developing mechanism of expansion, rhetoric was increasingly used to signal the interlocking of religion and politics to eager audiences and the potential for employing the peculiar rhetorical concepts of the one to infuse the other into a knowing community. Classical rhetoric, already employed in the Hellenistic era to corroborate the religious foundations of the Hellenistic monarchs in order to solidify their power and guarantee public order, is adopted by the Romans, and inspires the leaders of Christianity,

---

10 Marchal 2006.

as Roman religion was evolving and assuming a hierarchy and a structure much more homogeneous and kindred to that of the political *status quo*. This tight intersection of rhetoric, religion and politics in Late Antiquity has attracted considerable attention in recent decades, and the relevant bibliography is now more than ample (notable studies include *Hellenism and Empire: Language, Classicism, and Power in the Greek World, AD 50–250* by S. Swain; *Christianity and the Rhetoric of Empire: The Development of Christian Discourse* by A. Cameron; and *Christian Origins. Theology, Rhetoric and Community* edited by L. Ayers and G. Jones). All these studies take the use of classical rhetoric as a springboard to recast religious and political institutions so as to make them new and attractive to a new era of political and religious realities.

This overview of the most fundamental trends in the study of the intermingling between religion and society indicates that much progress has been made in discussing, debating and thus more fully understanding religion as a result of civic, political and rhetorical variants. A diversity of topics has been investigated, from the links that betray the relationship between religion and rhetoric (law and politics), to the level and breadth of the authority that the latter exerts over the first. Despite this expanded gamut of investigation, however, there is a notable lack of a single and updated examination of the use of similar or kindred forms of religious discourse across genres and times, focusing specifically on how, where, why and to what effect, this wide and diverse use of religious discourse helps define a typology thereof. While it is generally true that it is easier for us to discern patterns than to explain them, it is both interesting and useful to try to explain the strategic reasoning behind the use of religious discourse in specific texts, contexts and genres. An interdisciplinary volume with chapters covering a wide range of cultures, eras, texts and contexts most suitably serves the purpose of discussing as thoroughly as possible a demanding and multifaceted topic. This is the purpose of the volume at hand: however fragmentary in approaching such a complicated issue this (and any other) multi-author volume avowedly is, or may seem to be, the stimuli that the chapters offer shed new light on features of the relationship between religion and rhetoric, as this is manifested in literature, providing the readers with ideas about further research on the matter.

2 New light on the ancient intersection between rhetoric and religion

The value of this volume lies in two distinct features. The first is that it examines the widest possible spectrum of genres in Graeco-Roman literature across the centuries from the classical period to the age of Christianity. This broad thematic latitude has the potential to provide new insights into, and open up the terms of scholarly examination of, the ways in which religious rhetoric is manifested in literature and reflects upon civic, social and cultural institutions in antiquity. The second distinct feature of this volume is that it draws on theories beyond the confines of Classics – e.g. cognitive and sociological theories, performance, sex/gender studies, linguistics and other interdisciplinary theories and topics – to approach the dynamic and multidimensional relationship between religion and rhetoric in ancient Graeco-Roman texts and contexts, as also transculturally (e.g. through references, as in P. Sarischouli's chapter, to Graeco-Egyptian magic, and through the discussion of Christian texts and contexts, as suggested in the chapters by G. Holland and K. Melidis). The volume offers, in a sense, a valuable culture lesson both by discussing and interpreting the cultural (literary, socio-political, legal and moral) workings of the interconnection between religion and rhetoric, and by examining transcultural contexts – i.e. Classical Greek, Hellenistic, Roman, Egyptian and Christian. In elucidating the features and the purposes of the use of religious discourse in diversified texts and cultural contexts in antiquity, this volume is also important for the establishment of a framework within which the components and the function of religious discourse and rhetoric might be explored by anyone working on ancient civilisations, particularly their legal institutions, on ancient rhetoric and ancient religion, politics and literature.

The volume comprises five thematic parts, which allow an incisive examination of some of the most intriguing aspects of the multidimensional relationship between religion and rhetoric: Part I – Religion, rhetoric and law; Part II – Magic and religion; Part III – Religion and rhetorical performance; Part IV – The rulers' religion; and Part V – Religion and rhetoric in verse style. All parts of the volume, apart from the second and the last, consist of three chapters. The first chapter of Part I, "Religion and the rule of law in the Greek *polis*", by Edward M. Harris, examines the relationship between the rule of law and religion in the Greek city-state. First, the chapter shows that the laws of the city-state were based on the unwritten laws of the gods and drew their legitimacy from the gods. There was no division between church and state. Second, the basic features of the rule of law (accountability of officials, enactment of rules in the Assembly, fines for infractions) were operative in public cults. Third, the ideal of the rule of law can also be seen in private religious associations.

The second chapter of the first part of the volume, "Speaking for the gods: Greek cultic regulations and their silent informants", by Jakub Filonik examines the ways in which both the city officials and common informers played a pivotal role in the Athenian administration of justice in areas crucial to the order of the state and people's identities, such as proper religious conduct. By reconstructing Athenian legal proceedings through close readings of literary and epigraphic material, the chapter deals with both the judicial procedures and the auxiliary means of prosecution that allowed a more limited involvement of the informant. This includes a discussion of the often-overlooked legal actions of φράζειν ("pointing out"), φαίνειν ("denouncing") and μηνύειν ("informing"), and an analysis of Demosthenes 22.27 and a law regulating the Eleusinian Mysteries (*SEG* 30.61). In doing so, this contribution aims to answer more general questions related to religion, enforcement of legal rules and the exercise of power in ancient Greek societies.

The third and final chapter of Part 1, "Religious arguments in Antiphon Rhetor", by William Furley, examines the particularly prominent references to religion in the speeches of Antiphon of Rhamnous (including the *Tetralogies*). By *religion* the chapter means anything referring to the gods, the sacred, rites, piety or impiety, prayers or curses etc. Although some scholars have taken Antiphon to represent an early stage in the development of Greek forensic oratory, perhaps even with touches of the archaic, in fact we find a thoroughly rationalistic approach to religion, with sophistry and probability arguments applied to the field of religion just as much as to other aspects of the case. In short, it would arguably be wrong to see in Antiphon the traces of a judicial process which relied on theodicy, divine retribution etc. as the proper way of dealing with killers. Rather Antiphon shows how 5th-century thought began to manipulate these traditional-seeming beliefs to good rhetorical effect.

Part II explores aspects of the interconnection between rhetoric, magic and religion. The first chapter, by Despina Keramida, has the title "Performing the rhetoric of magic in Ovid's *Epistulae Heroidum* and *Metamorphoses* 10". It examines Ovid's incorporation of magical practices in selected passages from the *Epistulae Heroidum* and the *Metamorphoses* that are indicative of the poet's gendered rhetoric. The discussion focuses on letters of female writers from the epistolary collection and on tales of male artists from the *Metamorphoses*. Within the boundaries of the two works, some Ovidian heroines and heroes, such as Deianira and Orpheus, introduce the rhetoric of magic with ambiguous references to *carmina*, combined more often than not with funerary lamentation, underlining the ritualistic aspect of magic. However, only Laodamia and Pygmalion introduce the practice of *simulacra* as part of their magic ritual. These passages offer an indicative overview of the categories of magical practices in the Ovidian corpus and, as the chapter suggests, the Ovidian writers and artists speak and perform magic in the two works, eager to illustrate the functionality of magical performance within the boundaries of rhetorical performance.

The second chapter of Part II, "Transcultural context in Graeco-Egyptian magic: Two case studies from a bilingual Theban handbook", by Panagiota Sarischouli, offers a stimulating inter-cultural analysis in that it discusses cultural plurality in the mythical language and in the complex system of symbols used in Late Egyptian (private) ritual texts. Taking into consideration that the rhetoric of Egyptian magic was structured on the belief that deeper foundational truths are to be expressed through mythical motifs and symbols, the chapter presents two magical recipes from a bilingual (Greek/Demotic) Theban handbook, dated to the mid-late 2nd century AD, as case studies. Though written in Greek, the two texts are believed to have been produced by Egyptian priests. The first *praxis* aims at producing an epiphany of a Greek goddess (Kore/Persephone) who is to fulfil the practitioner's wishes. The second text describes in detail an erotic *praxis*, instructing the practitioner on how to mobilise Eros (and Psyche) as his assistant(s), applying a complex three-day consecration ritual.

Part III revolves around and focuses on the rhetorical performativity of religion. Its first chapter, "Trends in the rhetoric of prayer: The *actio* of prayer and *Eloquentia Popularis*", authored by Maik Patzelt, aims to reconsider Roman public prayers as expressions of the embodied capacities of the praying agent and thus as one form of public speech that involves far more than proposing one's request in the right word order. To this end, the chapter shifts the focus from the orality of prayer (prayers that have a prescribed content) to the vocality of prayer (prayers as an accumulation of sounds) – from *logos* to *sonority*. This examination involves essential elements, such as the "double speech" through a prompting priest (*praeire*) and clear voice (*clara vox*), which are crucial elements of public speeches as well. Above all, such an approach enables us to detect similarities between trends in public speech (*eloquentia popularis*) and forms of public prayer that turn out to be the result of such trends as well.

In the second chapter of this part of the volume, "Between compassion and aggression: The rhetoric of mourning in Republican and Early Imperial Rome", Christopher Degelmann examines the connection between rhetoric and mourning, as well as its development in the Roman Republic and the Early Imperial period. In addition, the creative appropriation of funeral rhetoric for political purposes is also demonstrated. It turns out that the Romans used a wide-ranging set of signs for expressing grief, and that they also used these on other occasions not linked to deaths in the narrower sense, taking advantage of the haunting effect of the *laudatio funebris* on the emotional state of their listeners. However, this was only possible because the deep religiosity of the Romans, described by Polybius, played little, if any, part in their mourning. Grief was rather a social phenomenon, with the funeral ritual referring to beliefs in the afterlife only indirectly.

The final chapter of the third part of the volume, "Argument and performance in the creation of a rhetorical matrix in Paul's congregations and beyond", by Glenn Holland, aims to demonstrate how Paul's letters provided the rhetorical matrix in which his ideas about Jesus and the life of the faithful were understood by Paul's congregations. The letters became authoritative for other congregations beyond those founded by Paul himself through their re-performance before new audiences. In addition, each of the letters designated "deutero-Pauline" – 2 Thessalonians, Colossians and Ephesians – built on Paul's language, metaphors and rhetorical strategies to expand and develop his ideas for later audiences. The performance and re-performance of the deutero-Pauline letters as well as Paul's own letters established the authority of the apostle's terminology and theological concepts – often as they were later developed by the deutero-Pauline authors – as a normative standard for all congregations that recognised Paul's authority, and ultimately for the entire Christian movement.

The three chapters of Part IV examine aspects of the use of religion by, or in, works that refer to political rulers and magistrates. In the first chapter of this part, "Beloved of the gods, son of the gods, rival of the gods: Alexander and the rhetoric of religion in Plutarch, Arrian and Curtius Rufus", Vasileios Liotsakis explores the ways in which Alexander is presented as (ab)using religion. Liotsakis refers, specifically, to three areas of interest in the historical accounts of Plutarch, Arrian and Curtius: (a) divine favour; (b) divine origins; and (c) the king's competitiveness towards Heracles and Dionysus, trying to detect both the convergences and the divergences between the three authors in the ways in which religious rhetoric is used for the purposes of Alexander's self-fashioning and political/military propaganda.

In the second chapter, "What makes a *divus*? The prospective rhetoric of deification in Pliny's *Panegyricus*", Kelly E. Shannon-Henderson examines references to the deification of emperors in Pliny's *Panegyricus*, and interprets these references as a meditation on Trajan's future deification after his death. Pliny's *Panegyricus* is an example of pseudo-deification. Throughout the speech, Pliny describes Trajan's earthly powers as approaching or even exceeding those of the gods. Furthermore, he sets up a cause-and-effect relationship between deification and an emperor's deeds in life: those who acted well deserved to be deified (e.g. Nerva), while bad emperors suffered ignominy (e.g. Domitian). Pliny compares Trajan favourably with both *mali principes* and previously deified emperors, suggesting that he, like the existing *divi*, will earn his own place in heaven upon his death. Thus, in a speech emphasising Trajan's *civilitas*, humility and respect for the law, Pliny also prepares his audience for the fact that Trajan will ultimately become a god. Far from being in conflict, these two notions reinforce each other and are crucial to understanding Pliny's celebration of the reign of this *optimus princeps*.

The last chapter of this part of the volume, "*Tua divinitas:* Religious self-fashioning in Tiberian Rome", by Hans-Friedrich Mueller, surveys passages in which Valerius Maximus explicitly describes his personal experience (*Praef.*, 2.6.8, 4.4.11, 4.7.*ext*.1, 3.4.*ext*.1, 6.1.*init.*, 9.11.*ext*.4) in order to assess his self-representation. What is particularly striking about Valerian self-fashioning in these passages is the author's combination of traditional figures of rhetoric with traditional religious vocabulary (e.g. allusions to *auspicia*) and themes (traditional gods and other ancestral rites) in order to portray emotionally religious subjectivity that embraces not just traditional religion, but also a new imperial religion centred on the divine Caesars, including the living Tiberius (which must be put in the context of Tacitus *Ann.* 4.38). Valerius locates Rome's new religious identity in the exemplary fragments of Rome's republican past, and Valerian self-fashioning of a subjective religious experience emerges, in this wider view, as yet another paradigm for Valerius' audience to emulate.

The last part of the volume, Part V, examines the synergy between rhetoric and religion in verse literary texts and contexts. In "Biblical epics: Intersection of rhetoric and religion in Greek and Latin hexametric paraphrases of Psalm 136 (137)", specifically, Konstantinos Melidis provides a comparative examination of Pseudo-Apollinaris' *Metaphrasis Psalmorum* and Paulinus' *Carmen IX*, roughly contemporary hexametrical paraphrases of Psalm 136 (137), through the lens of traditional Greek and Latin rhetorical theories on paraphrastic procedure. This contribution examines the rhetorical strategy of amplification (*auxēsis/adiectio*) employed by both authors, stressing mainly their common amplificatory practices, in order to embellish or explain their *Vorlage*. Emphasis is placed on the ways in which their classicising epic poetry reflects early Christian theological and exegetical texts and contexts.

Bibliography

Ando, C. (2009), *The Matter of the Gods: Religion and the Roman Empire*, Berkeley/Los Angeles.
Ayers, L./Jones, G. (1998), *Christian Origins. Theology, Rhetoric and Community*, London/New York.
Beard, M./North, J./Price, S. (1998), *Religions of Rome: Volume 1, A History*, Cambridge.
Booth, W.C. (1991), 'Rhetoric and Religion: Are They Essentially Wedded?', in: W.G. Jeanrond/J.L. Rike (eds.), *Radical Pluralism and Truth*, New York, 62–80.
Burke, K. (1970), *The Rhetoric of Religion: Studies in Logology*, Los Angeles.
Burkert, W. (1985), *Greek Religion: Archaic and Classical*, Oxford.
Burkert, W. (1995), 'Greek Poleis and Civic Cults: Some Further Thoughts', in: M.H. Hansen/K. Raaflaub (eds.), *Studies in the Ancient Greek Polis*, Stuttgart, 201–210.
Burkert, W. (1996), *Creation of the Sacred: Tracks of Biology in Early Religions*, Cambridge, MA.
Cameron, A. (1991), *Christianity and the Rhetoric of Empire: The Development of Christian Discourse*, Berkeley.
Crowley, J. (2017), 'Patriotism in Ancient Greece', in: M. Sardoc (eds.), *Handbook of Patriotism*, Cham, Switzerland.
Dover, K.J. (1974), *Greek Popular Morality in the Time of Plato and Aristotle*, Oxford.
Durkheim, E. (1912), *The Elementary Forms of Religious Life*, New York.
Feeney, D. (1998), *Literature and Religion at Rome: Cultures, Contexts and Beliefs*, Cambridge.
Gagarin, M. (2013), 'Law and Religion in Early Greece', in: A.C. Hagedorn/R.G. Kratz (eds.), *Law and Religion in the Eastern Mediterranean: From Antiquity to Early Islam*, Oxford, 59–78.
Goar, R. (1972), *Cicero and the State Religion*, Amsterdam.
Gould, J. (2001), 'Herodotus and Religion', in: J. Gould (ed.), *Myth, Ritual, Memory, and Exchange: Essays in Greek Literature and Culture*, Oxford, 359–377.
Harrison, J.E. (1927), *Themis: A Study of the Social Origins of Greek Religion*, Cambridge.
Harrison, T. (2000), *Divinity and History: The Religion of Herodotus*, Oxford.
Hornblower, S. (1992), 'The Religious Dimension to the Peloponnesian War, or, What Thucydides Does Not Tell Us', in: *Harvard Studies in Classical Philology* 94, 169–197.
Hoz, M.P. de (2017), 'Religious Discourse in Hellenistic and Roman Times: Content *Topoi* in Greek Epigraphic Cult Foundations and Sacred Norms', in: *Kernos* 30, 187–220.
Kennedy, G.A. (1972), *The Art of Rhetoric in the Roman World, 100 BC – AD 300*, Princeton.
Kennedy, G.A. (1980), *Classical Rhetoric and Its Christian and Secular Tradition from Ancient to Modern Times*, Chapel Hill.
Kennedy, G.A. (1983), *Greek Rhetoric under the Christian Emperors*, Princeton.
Lennon, J. (2010), 'Pollution and Ritual Impurity in Cicero's *de Domo Sua*', in: *Classical Quarterly* 60, 427–445.
Marchal, J. (2006), *Hierarchy, Unity, and Imitation: A Feminist Rhetorical Analysis of Power Dynamics in Paul's Letter to the Philippians*, Leiden/Boston.
Martin, G. (2009), *Divine Talk: Religious Argumentation in Demosthenes*, Oxford.
Martin, G. (2016), 'The Gods in the Athenian Assembly', in: E. Eidinow/J. Kindt/R. Osborne (eds.), *Theologies of Ancient Greek Religion*, Cambridge, 281–300.
Mikalson, J.D. (1983), *Athenian Popular Religion*, Chapel Hill/London.
Mikalson, J.D. (2003), *Herodotus and Religion in the Persian Wars*, Chapel Hill.

Ober, J./Strauss, B. (1990), 'Drama, Political Rhetoric and the Discourse of Athenian Democracy', in: J. Winkler/F.I. Zeitlin (eds.), *Nothing to Do with Dionysus?* Princeton, 237–270.
Olmstead, W./Jost, W. (eds.) (2000), *Rhetorical Invention and Religious Inquiry*, New Haven, CT.
Parker, R. (1997), *Athenian Religion: A History*, Oxford.
Pernot, L. (2005), 'The Rhetoric of Religion', in: *Rhetorica: A Journal of the History of Rhetoric* 24, 235–254.
Pollini, J. (2012), *From Republic to Empire: Rhetoric, Religion, and Power in the Visual Culture of Ancient Rome*, Norman, OK.
Roth, A. (2011), 'Rhetoric and Faith in the Hippocratic Philosophy of Medicine', in: W. Krieger (ed.), *Science at the Frontiers: Perspectives on the History and Philosophy of Science*, Pittsburgh, 3–16.
Rubinstein, L. (2004), 'Stirring up Dicastic Anger', in: D.L. Cairns/R.A. Knox (eds.), *Law, Rhetoric, and Comedy in Classical Athens. Essays in Honour of Douglas M. MacDowell*, Swansea, 187–203.
Rubinstein, L. (2005), 'Differentiated Rhetorical Strategies in the Athenian Courts', in: M. Gagarin/D. Cohen (eds.), *The Cambridge Companion to Ancient Greek Law*, Cambridge, 129–145.
Sauer, V. (2012), *Religiöses in der politischen Argumentation der späten römischen Republik: Ciceros Erste Catilinarische Rede – eine Fallstudie*, Stuttgart.
Serafim, A. (2020), *Religious Discourse in Attic Oratory and Politics*, New York/London.
Sommerstein, A.H./Torrance, I.C. (2014), *Oaths and Swearing in Ancient Greece*, Berlin/Boston.
Sourvinou-Inwood, C. (1988), 'Further Aspects of Polis Religion', in: *AION* 10, 259–274.
Sourvinou-Inwood, C. (1990), 'What is Polis Religion?', in: O. Murray/S. Price (eds.), *The Greek City: from Homer to Alexander*, Oxford, 295–322.
Sourvinou-Inwood, C. (2000), 'Further Aspects of Polis Religion', in: R. Buxton (ed.), *Oxford Readings in Greek Religion*, Oxford, 38–55.
Sourvinou-Inwood, C. (2003), *Tragedy and Athenian Religion*, Lanham, MD.
Sourvinou-Inwood, C. (2005), 'Greek Tragedy and Ritual', in: R. Bushnell (ed.), *A Companion to Tragedy*, Malden/Oxford, 7–24.
Spencer, C. (2014), *Cicero and the Rise of Deification at Rome*, Cambridge.
Stone, I.E.M. (2018), *Speeches and Speechmaking in Herodotus' Histories*, Ph.D. Thesis, Sydney.
Swain, S. (1996), *Hellenism and Empire: Language, Classicism, and Power in the Greek World, AD 50–250*, Oxford.
Zaidman, L.B. (1995), *Religion in the Ancient Greek City*, Transl. by P. Cartledge, Cambridge.

Part I: Religion, Rhetoric and Law

Edward M. Harris
Religion and the Rule of Law in the Greek *Polis*

Abstract: This chapter examines the relationship between religion and the rule of law. Some scholars believe that in Sophocles' *Antigone* there is a conflict between the laws of the city championed by Creon and the laws of the gods championed by Antigone, but Antigone opposes Creon because he is a tyrant whose orders (*kērygmata*) violate both the laws of the gods and the will of the people. The Greeks saw no conflict between the two and believed that the laws of the city were based on the laws of the gods. On the other hand, the ideals of the rule of law can be seen in the law enacted by the Greek *polis* about religious matters (accountability of officials, equality before the law). One can find the same principles at work in private religious associations.

In 1992 Roy Moore was appointed as Etowah County Circuit Judge in the state of Alabama in the United States of America.[1] While serving as Circuit Judge, he placed a plaque containing the Ten Commandments on the wall behind his bench. When asked by a reporter from the *Montgomery Advertiser* why he did this, he replied that he wished to "establish the moral foundation of our law". He also started his sessions in court with a prayer asking that the jurors receive divine guidance. In June 1993 the American Civil Liberties Union sent Judge Moore a letter threatening a lawsuit if the prayers did not stop. On 20 June 1994, the ACLU sent a representative to observe and record Judge Moore's prayer in court and held a press conference after the session to criticize the practice as unconstitutional. Moore brushed off the objections and ran for election to the judgeship later that year. He won with 62% of the vote.

In March 1995 the ACLU filed a lawsuit against Judge Moore. The case was tried before Circuit Judge Charles Price, who ruled that the prayers in court must stop, but allowed the Ten Commandments to remain on the wall of the courtroom. Moore then ran for Chief Justice of the Alabama Supreme Court in 2000 and defeated three other candidates in the Republican primary (including one heavily

---

[1] This account of Roy Moore's actions draws on Bethea 2019; Beyerle 2012; Green 2005; Johnson 2003; McGrew 2003; Robertson 2006. For the decision about the Ten Commandments see Glassroth vs. Moore CV – 01 – T –1268 – N and Maddox and Howard v. Moore CV – 01 – 1269 – N F Supp. 2d 1290 (M.D. Ala. 2002).

https://doi.org/10.1515/9783110699623-002

backed by the party hierarchy and the business community). He won the election with over 60% of the vote. After being sworn into office, he stated that "my mind had been opened to the spiritual war occurring in our state and our nation that was slowly removing the knowledge of that relationship between God and law". He declared "I pledged to support not only the U.S. Constitution, but the Alabama Constitution as well, which provided in its preamble that the state 'established justice' by 'invoking the favor and guidance of Almighty God'. The connection between God and our law could not be clearer".

Acting on these convictions, Judge Moore made plans for a larger monument to the Ten Commandments to be placed in the Heflin-Torbert Judicial Building. The monument was installed on 31 July 2001 and was three feet deep and four feet tall, weighing 2,400 kilograms. On the top were two large tablets with the Ten Commandments. The day after Judge Moore announced: "today a cry has gone out across our land for the acknowledgment of that God upon whom this nation and our laws were founded... May this day mark the restoration of the moral foundation of law to our people and the return to the knowledge of God in our land".

The American Civil Liberties Union and two other groups filed a lawsuit on 30 October 2001, and on 18 November 2002 Federal District Judge Myron Thompson issued his ruling that the monument violated the First Amendment of the U.S. Constitution: "if all Chief Justice Moore had done were to emphasize the Ten Commandments' historical and educational importance... or their importance as a model code for good citizenship... this court would have a much different case before it. But the Chief Justice did not limit himself to this; he went far, far beyond. He installed a two-and-a-half-ton monument in the most prominent place in a government building, managed with dollars from all state taxpayers, with the specific purpose and effect of establishing a permanent recognition of the 'sovereignty of God', the Judeo-Christian God, over all citizens in this country, regardless of each taxpaying citizen's individual personal beliefs or lack thereof. To this, the Establishment Clause says no".

Judge Moore attempted to defy the order, but he was overruled by the eight other members of the Alabama Supreme Court and was later suspended from office. In November 2012 he was re-elected to the position of Chief Justice by a decisive majority. Yet on 6 May 2016, the Alabama Judicial Inquiry forwarded six ethics charges against Judge Moore. Despite legal challenges, Moore was found guilty of all six charges on 30 September 2016 and removed from office. This is not the place to discuss his campaign for a Senate seat in a special election that took place in 2017.

I begin with this story because it illustrates both the continuity and the differences between ancient and modern attitudes about religion and the rule of law. To start with continuity. If Judge Moore could have converted to the religion of the ancient Greeks and started to pray to Zeus, Apollo and Aphrodite (rather appropriate in his case given the later charges against him) instead of Jesus Christ the Lord and been transported to Classical Athens, he would have felt right at home. And if a time-machine could be constructed to transport Roy Moore back to Greece in this period, I am sure that the majority of those who voted in the special election in 2017 would have been glad to contribute generously to a one-way ticket for Roy Moore on such a journey. Roy Moore would have found Athenian attitudes about religion and the law very congenial. The Greeks believed that the gods were the authors of their laws and were not afraid to say so.[2] And they certainly did not have to worry about the American Civil Liberties Union. On the other hand, the ancient Greeks would have found the objections brought by the eight other members of the Alabama Supreme Court rather strange. The Athenians and other Greeks had no problem with placing the words "the gods" at the beginning of their decrees.[3] The Athenians also placed reliefs of the gods above their public decrees in the 4th century.[4] The Spartans consulted the oracle at Delphi to gain divine approval for their laws (X. *Lac. Pol.* 8.5). Cleisthenes also did so when he created the ten Attic tribes ([Arist.] *Ath. Pol.* 21.6). In the Constitution of the United States, however, there is a strict division between Church and State and the First Amendment requires that congress pass no law establishing a religion, which means that there is no national church in the United States (unlike the Church of England in the United Kingdom). The two institutions, church and state, are separate. The state does not gain its legitimacy from the approval of the Church as the representative of God on earth.

This chapter discusses the rule of law and religion, two areas that are usually not discussed together. I believe the main reason for this is that most scholars believe that the rule of law belongs to one realm, the secular and rational part of Greek society, and religion to the non-rational or what E.R. Dodds called the Irrational part of Greek society which was based not on reason but on emotional drives and what writers in the Enlightenment would call "superstitions".[5] This chapter shows that this is to a large extent a false dichotomy. The Greeks saw no

---

[2] On gods as the authors of law see Harris 2006, 48–57; Harris 2010, 124–126.
[3] Pounder 1984.
[4] See Lawton 1995.
[5] On the Greeks and the "irrational" see Dodds 1951.

clash between the two, which they thought peacefully co-existed. There were obviously tensions and perhaps even contradictions within Greek values, but this is not one area where there was any serious conflict. In modern society we often look back to the Greeks of antiquity as the source of many of our traditions, but as the Alabama Supreme Court has shown, this is one area in which one should not deny the gulf between ancient and modern attitudes.

First, however, it is important to be clear about what we mean by the rule of law.[6] There have been many discussions in legal theory about the concept, with some scholars limiting the rule of law to a set of procedural norms, while others extend the concept to include substantive norms or fundamental human rights. The latter would include rights such as a right to education, a right to health care, a right to marry and gender equality.[7] There are clearly differences between some aspects of the Greek conception of the rule of law and modern conceptions, but there are also undeniable similarities. The ideals of equality before the law, accountability of officials, accessibility to laws and legal procedures, the principle that disputes must be decided by laws and not by *ad hoc* decisions, the rule that there is no punishment without a law and the right to a fair trial were recognised by the Athenians and by the countries who are members of the European Union. The right to a fair trial includes many basic rights such as the right of the defendant to know the charges before going to court, the right to a trial before impartial judges, the right to a legal decision within a reasonable time and the right to present the evidence of documents and witnesses. These rights were at the heart of the Athenian legal system and as far as we can tell also at the heart of the legal systems of the other Greek city-states.[8] They were also extended to free foreigners who had access to the courts in Athens and other communities, but not of course to slaves.[9] For the Greeks the concept of the rule of law was probably more expansive and included the belief that laws should have the approval of the community and that officials should be selected by lot from the citizens or chosen by election. This included the view that rulers should not gain power by violent means, which was equivalent to tyranny.

But some scholars believe that there was a clash in the Greek *polis* between the laws of the gods and the laws of the people or state. One of the main works scholars have cited in support of this view is Sophocles' *Antigone*. For instance,

---

6 This section draws on Harris 2013, especially 3–18; Harris 2016.
7 See Bingham 2010.
8 For the rule of law as a widely followed ideal in the Greek world see Harris 2006, 3–28. For the accountability of officials in the Greek *poleis* see Fröhlich 2004.
9 On the access of foreigners to the courts see Gauthier 1972.

S. Goldhill has asserted that "Antigone sets the laws of the gods in opposition to the laws of the land".[10] M. Ostwald believed that the play concerns the conflict "between political obligations imposed by the state's *nomoi* and religious obligations incumbent on the family".[11] R. Thomas holds a similar view: "there is a conflict between the laws of the state (i.e. Creon) and the unwritten laws of the gods – here the right of burial – which have higher moral value".[12]

Those who interpret the conflict in this way place much emphasis on lines 450-455. Yet it is important to place the lines in context. To briefly recall the plot: Polynices has died fighting to conquer the city of Thebes. Creon had forbidden the burial of Polynices, but Antigone defies the order and buries her brother. After she is caught by the Guard, Creon asks Antigone whether she denies the Guard's report about her burial of Polynices. Antigone admits the facts of the Guard's account. Creon then asks her if she was aware that she had violated his decree. The word he uses is *kērygma* at this point (S. *Ant.* 446–447). Antigone admits that she knew that Creon had forbidden the burial of Polynices (S. *Ant.* 448). Creon then shifts his language slightly: he asks her if she has dared to violate these laws (S. *Ant.* 449: νόμους). In response she gives her famous speech:

> οὐ γάρ τί μοι Ζεὺς ἦν ὁ κηρύξας τάδε,
> οὐδ' ἡ ξύνοικος τῶν κάτω θεῶν Δίκη
> τοιούσδ' ἐν ἀνθρώποισιν ὥρισεν νόμους.
> οὐδὲ σθένειν τοσοῦτον ᾠόμην τὰ σὰ
> κηρύγμαθ', ὥστ' ἄγραπτα κἀσφαλῆ θεῶν
> νόμιμα δύνασθαι θνητὸν ὄνθ' ὑπερδραμεῖν.
> οὐ γάρ τι νῦν γε κἀχθές, ἀλλ' ἀεί ποτε
> ζῇ ταῦτα, κοὐδεὶς οἶδεν ἐξ ὅτου 'φάνη.
>
> S. *Ant.* 450–457

It was not Zeus who issued this order,
Nor did Justice, who lives with the gods below,
mark out such laws among men.
Nor do I think your orders (*kērygmath'*) are so strong
that one who is mortal can override the unwritten and
unshakable laws (*nomima*) of the gods.
For they live not just now and yesterday,
but always, and no one knows from where they came.

---

10 Goldhill 1986, 96.
11 Ostwald 1986, 149, 152.
12 Thomas 1996, 17.

It is important to have the Greek text before us because in his translation R. Fagles seriously distorts the meaning of the text by translating: "of course, I did. It wasn't Zeus/who made this proclamation".[13] One cannot, however, find any word in the Greek text which is equivalent to the English phrase "of course, I did". This is not a minor error because D. Allen in the *Cambridge Companion to Greek Law* follows this translation and bases her interpretation of the play on this misinterpretation of the text.[14] In fact, Antigone in effect answers "no" by making it clear that she does not consider Creon's decree a "law" but only the order of an official (*kērygma*), which she carefully distinguishes here from a *nomos* or law as she does elsewhere in the play (S. *Ant.* 7–8, 26–34). Now these scholars rightly observe that Antigone bases her disobedience to Creon's order partly on the unwritten laws of the gods. This would, therefore, appear to place her in opposition to the community and its leader Creon. One might get this impression if one did not read the rest of the play. Antigone also bases her disobedience on the lack of legitimacy behind Creon's order, which she argues is only a *kērygma* and not a *nomos*, which in the Greek world would require the approval of the entire community. Later in the same scene, Creon insists that his view of her conduct is shared by the other citizens and claims that "you alone of Cadmus' people see it this way" (S. *Ant.* 508). Antigone does not ignore the views of the people and does not argue that whatever the people may think, the laws of the gods take precedence. She also claims to have the support of the people, who she says would agree with her if they could speak freely: "these men do too, but to you they keep silent" (S. *Ant.* 509). This is a reasonable view given what the chorus has just stated. When the Guard reports that Polynices' body was buried, they strongly suggest that this was the work of the gods. And it would be wrong to say that Creon relies only on his position as leader of the commuity to justify his order against burying Polynices. He too claims that the gods support his order. In the first scene Creon states in response to the chorus' suggestion that they gods have buried the body of Polynices: "what you say is intolerable, claiming that the gods are showing concern for this corpse. Do they honour him as a benefactor and over the body of the man who came to burn the columns and dedications in their temples, to tear apart their land and their laws?" (S. *Ant.* 282–288). It would be a serious mistake to say that Creon's view is similar to that found in the Athenian law against traitors.[15]

---

13 Fagles 1982, 64.
14 Allen 2005, 390. Allen believes that the Athenian legal system was designed with the aim of controlling anger. This is not convincing: as a rule, accusers in Athenian legal oratory do not state that they have brought their charges because they are angry. See Harris 2017.
15 For this view see Hester 1971, 19–21; Ostwald 1986, 151 with note 41.

That law only forbade burial in Attica and permitted it elsewhere; it did not order that traitors remain unburied and without funeral rites.¹⁶ Creon does not have this law on his side. One should not invent ambiguities and uncertainties in the play where they clearly do not exist. The rule that the dead should be buried was widely accepted in Greece.¹⁷ In fact, in other plays the Athenians invaded Boeotian territory when the Thebans did not bury the Seven who had attacked the city and after a victory performed the rites over the dead.

Haemon pursues both of Antigone's arguments in the following scene. He states that the average man is intimidated by Creon's position and that the city is mourning for Antigone (S. *OT* 688–696). When Creon says that Antigone has been infected by the sickness of disobedience, Haemon counters that the people of Thebes do not agree (S. *Ant.* 732–733). When Creon asserts his power over the community, Haemon states that the city does not belong to him alone (S. *Ant.* 736–737). When Creon asks whether the city belongs to its ruler, Haemon replies sarcastically that "you would do a fine job ruling a desert by yourself" (S. *Ant.* 738–739). But Haemon not only accuses his father of defying the will of the people but also of trampling on the gods' honours (S. *Ant.* 745). Just like his fiancée, Haemon justifies his position both by citing the will of the people and by invoking the will of the gods. There is no clash between the two.

One might argue that this view that the laws of the human community ought to be based on the laws of the gods is just the view of the "conservative" Sophocles and was not shared by contemporary Athenians and other Greeks. But this argument would be a mistake. In a famous passage, the philosopher Heraclitus (fr. 253 Kirk/Raven) stated that "those who speak with sense must rely on what is common to all, as a city must rely on its laws, and with much greater reliance. For all laws of men are nourished by one law, the divine law, for it has as much power as it wishes and is sufficient for all and is still left over".¹⁸

The Attic orators who wrote speeches to be delivered in court before hundreds of judges shared this view about the laws. In *Against Macartatus* the litigant discusses the laws about inheritance and asks the court to "please read the words

---

16 See Harris 2006, 67–68. Cf. Pritchett 1985, 235–241; Parker 1983, 48: "Creon's offence is the familiar one of denying an enemy the right to burial". Griffith 1999, 28–32 does not take this evidence into account. My analysis of the *Antigone* is endorsed by Cairns 2016.
17 Cf. Parker 1983, 47 ("prolonged public exposure of the corpse, as prescribed by Creon in the *Antigone*, was not the practice of any Greek state, and when mentioned is treated as shocking"). Cf. the evidence of the funeral orations discussed by Bennett and Tyrrell 1990.
18 One finds a similar view in a fragment attributed to Archytas of Tarentum (fr. 6 Thesleff = Stobaeus 4.1.132): the νόμοι θεῶν ἄγραφοι are the πατέρες καὶ ἀγεμόνες τῶν γεγραμμένων νόμων καὶ δογμάτων ἀνθρώποις τεθέντων.

of the oracle brought from Delphi, from the shrine of the god, that you may see that it speaks in the same terms concerning relatives as do the laws of Solon" (Dem. 43.66). In *Against Aristocrates* the accuser attributes the foundation of the Areopagus to the gods (Dem. 23.81). In Plato's *Crito* (54c6–8) Socrates calls the laws in Hades the brothers of the laws of the city.

Some scholars have argued that the religious belief that murder incurred ritual pollution was an irrational view, which paid no attention to moral or legal categories.[19] For instance, A. Adkins claimed: "it must be held that certain acts *per se* engender 'pollution', and the emotions originally engendered by despair and disaster will be transferred to the act of killing in its own right. There will be a horror of the killer, but not a moral horror which will conform to moral categories".[20] There would seem to be a clash between the requirements of religion, which views all bloodshed as causing pollution, and the rule of law, which allocates different penalties according to levels of guilt and innocence. It is true that when a relative brought an accusation of murder against someone, the *basileus* banned the accused "from lustral bowls, libations, sacrifices, the *agora* at the centre of the city" and that the defendant who was convicted was considered polluted. But Adkins did not note three key facts. First, not all killing incurred pollution. There were three basic categories of homicide: deliberate homicide, involuntary homicide and just homicide or homicide according to the laws. This last category covered the following cases: first, the killing of anyone caught on top of a wife, daughter, mother, sister or concubine kept for the purpose of free children (this included cases of sexual violence and seduction); second, the killing of someone attacking from ambush; third, the killing of someone carrying off property without justification; fourth, the killing of a man convicted of murder who returned to Attica; and fifth, the killing of a tyrant or someone betraying the community.[21] Even though those convicted on the first two charges were polluted, those who killed in these circumstances were considered ritually "clean" (*katharos*; cf. Dem. 9.44; Dem. 20.158; Lycurgus, *Leoc.* 125).[22] This shows that pollution did not inhere in the act of bloodshed, but paid attention to criminal intent. If there was no criminal intent, there was no pollution. Second, those who were convicted of deliberate homicide could not remove the pollution. As a result, they

---

19 My analysis of pollution for homicide draws on Harris 2015a; Harris 2018.
20 Adkins 1960, 98.
21 On this category see Harris 2013, 50–53.
22 The document inserted into the text of Andoc. 1.96–98 also mentions the purity of those who kill tyrants but this text is a forgery. The attempt of Sommerstein 2014 to defend the authenticity of this document contains several flaws and is refuted in detail in Harris 2013/2014.

were punished with permanent exile or execution. Those who were convicted of involuntary homicide could be pardoned by the relatives of the victim and return to Attica after performing purificatory rituals. This shows that there were two levels of pollution for homicide, which differed according to the moral intent of the killer. Third, a person who attempted to commit homicide but did not succeed in killing the victim could be accused of "plotting homicide", brought to trial, and if convicted, punished with a penalty, which was probably exile.[23] As a passage from Livy (42.15–16; 45.5) indicates, the person who attempted to commit homicide was also considered polluted. Livy informs us that Evander of Crete and three Macedonians attempted to murder King Eumenes by rolling boulders on him, but did not succeed. Here there was no actual murder and possibly no bloodshed, only the intent to kill, but the criminal still incurred pollution. After Evander entered the sanctuary on Samothrace, he was denounced for entering holy ground while polluted and summoned to trial. All three facts show that Adkins' view of pollution must be rejected.

In a well-known essay, J.-P. Vernant argued that there was a clash between the laws of the gods and the laws of men in Sophocles' *Oedipus Tyrannos*. Following Dodds, Vernant believed that Oedipus in the play would have been acquitted of killing Laius in an Athenian court according to the laws of men.[24] But Vernant thought that Oedipus was considered polluted because he was a scapegoat and thus subject to punishment in the eyes of the gods. This view is untenable. First, the oracle of Apollo reported by Creon states that the pollution afflicting Thebes was caused by the murder of Laius and could be removed only by punishing the murderer with death or permanent exile (S. *OT* 96–101). The text says nothing about a scapegoat, and the Greek word for scapegoat *pharmakos* is conspicuously absent from the play.[25] Second, if Oedipus was a scapegoat and recognised to be one, Creon and the community would have driven him out of Thebes at the end of the play, which of course does not occur. Third and most important, Oedipus would have been convicted of deliberate homicide in an Athenian court because he did not kill Laius in self-defence. A. Sommerstein, followed uncritically by P. Finglass in his new commentary, has attempted to deny this, but the account given by Oedipus himself shows that Laius did not intend to kill him and that his intent in murdering Laius was not to save himself but out of anger at an insult.[26]

---

23 On the crime of plotting a homicide see Harris 2006, 391–404.
24 Vernant 1972, following Dodds 1966 on the guilt of Oedipus.
25 On the *pharmakos* see Bremer 1983.
26 Sommerstein 2011, followed by Finglass 2018, 73.

Oedipus himself states that his retaliation was out of all proportion to the treatment he had suffered. What is decisive against Sommerstein is that the gods demand that Oedipus be punished, which they would not have done if he were innocent and that Oedipus is considered polluted, which he would not have been if he were innocent as the passages mentioned above clearly demonstrate.[27] So *pace* Dodds and Vernant, there is no clash between the laws of men and the laws of the gods in this play.

It is clear that the *polis* was obligated to follow the laws of the gods and that the unwritten laws provided the foundation of legitimacy for the laws of the community. But the ideals of the rule of law were also respected in the realm of religion.[28] What is striking is that one finds the same political concern about the rule of law in regulations enacted by the *polis* about religion as one finds in other laws of the *polis*. The rule of law was not confined to the secular sphere but extended into the conduct of religious cults and rituals carried out by priests. As early as the Archaic period, laws in many Greek *poleis* aimed at restricting the powers of officials and preventing the accumulation of power in the hands of a few.[29] This was done in several ways: 1) clearly delineating the jurisdiction of officials and distributing powers to different of officials, 2) limiting terms of office to one year, 3) imposing penalties for officials who do not follow the law, 4) assigning functions to boards of officials, not one person, and 5) using entrenchment clauses to ensure permanence and stability. One finds precisely the same concerns in many of the sacred laws of the Greek *poleis*. First, the sacred laws aim to specify the jurisdiction and to limit the powers of religious officials. For instance, the earliest law from Athens about religious matters is a law about the powers of the Treasurers and the *prytanis* on the Acropolis to impose fines for specific actions and limits the amount of the fines (*LSCG* no. 3, l. 6–8, 11–13, 15–16, 22–23). A law about a festival in honour of Hephaestus and Athena at Athens limits the amount that the *hieropoioi* can impose as fines and requires that for larger amounts they bring a case in court (*LSCG* no. 13, l. 26–30). The decree proposed by Callias in the late 5th century BC creating treasurers for the Other Gods goes into obsessive detail about their duties and responsibilities (*IG* I^3 52). Regulations about religious matters from other *poleis* often specify the duties and limit the amount of fines to be imposed by religious officials. The law from Andania assigns the duties of supervising the Mysteries to several different officials, carefully delineates their duties and specifies the amounts of fines (*LSCG* no. 65. For fines see l. 9, 77, 106, 111,

---

27 For detailed refutation of Sommerstein see Harris 2018, 435–440.
28 This section draws on Harris 2015b, 67–70.
29 On these methods of preventing the accumulation of power see Harrris 2006, 14–25.

162–163). As a result, religious officials do not act on their own discretion or their own views about what is appropriate behaviour. They are to act in accordance with the laws of the *polis* like other officials (*LSCG* no. 69, l. 6–8; no. 92, l. 30–31). From a legal point of view, they are just as accountable to the *polis* as other public officials.[30] Their religious function did not give them a privileged position vis-à-vis the Assembly and the courts. Second, the sacred laws set forth penalties for religious officials who do not perform their duties. For instance, in a law from Eretria dated to the 4th or 3rd century BC the *hieropoioi* who do not perform their duties according to the written rules are to pay a fine of five hundred drachmas each (*LSCG* no. 93, l. 29–32). In a law dated to the 4th century BC from Thasos the *agoranomos* and the priest of Asclepius are threatened with a fine if they do not keep the shrine of Heracles clean (*LSCG* no. 115, l. 6–10). Third, the *polis* does not leave the policing of public officials to social pressure or to the gods, but assigns other officials to keep watch on their activities and to make them accountable just like all officials of the *polis*. At Athens the Council supervised many officials responsible for religious matters.[31] Fourth, the sacred laws show a concern for consistency and stability. Just as politicians often justified their policies by appeals to the *patrios politeia*, the people who drafted sacred laws invoked *ta patria* as the sources of authority for their proposals.[32] To ensure stability, entrenchment clauses in some cases were added to decrees to prevent them from being overturned.[33] Fifth, religious officials are often limited to one-year terms of office by appointment or election.[34] Sixth, to prevent the accumulation of power in the hands of one person, religious duties are often assigned to boards of religious officials. Several such boards are attested at Athens in general and for Eleusis in particular. For the mysteries at Andania there were several boards: the Sacred Men, the Sacred Women, the Ten and the Five, the *rhabdophoroi*.[35] Similar boards of religious officials are attested in other Greek *poleis*.[36] Seventh, to encourage average citizens to help officials enforce the law, there are often procedures encouraging "anyone who wishes" to report violations, sometimes with the promise

---

30 Mikalson 2016, 201 believes that priests were accountable only for financial matters, but this is mistaken. For a case of a priest being convicted for not carrying out his religious duties in the legal manner see [Dem.] 59.116. Cf. Harris 2015b, 69 with note 60.
31 For the Council supervising religious matters see Rhodes 1972, 92–96, 127–134.
32 For the phrase *kata ta patria* in laws and decrees about religious matters see Harris 2015b, 77–78.
33 See Harris 2015b, 69 with note 62. On the role of entrenchment clauses see Harris 2006, 23–25.
34 See Harris 2015b, 69 with note 63.
35 On the boards of officials in the Andania law see Gawlinski 2012, 22–27.
36 Harris 2015b, 69 with note 67.

of financial rewards.³⁷ Relations between the community and the gods were too important and required detailed regulations. Religion was also a potential source of power, and, as with all sources of power in the Greek *polis*, those who had responsibility for religious practices affecting the common good had to be closely monitored, and their powers carefully circumscribed.

But what about the private associations whose members joined together to worship the gods, make sacrifices and share in feasts and other rituals? In a recent volume, C. Taylor and K. Vlassopoulos have claimed that the private associations lay outside or below the *polis*, and that their members were joined only by *philia* and not by the bonds of legal obligation.³⁸ Nothing could be further from the truth. When either a citizen or a non-citizen stepped into the world of the private association, he or she did not leave the ideals of the *polis* such as the rule of law behind and enter a world outside the conceptual framework of the *polis*. On the contrary, the Greeks of Athens and other *poleis* brought these concepts and distinctions with them and used these concepts to shape their interactions with others in their networks. In fact, he or she did not leave the courts behind as the *Eikadeis* inscription reveals (*IG* II² 1258). When the members of this private association had a disagreement, they used the courts of Athens to resolve their dispute. And the member of a private association did not leave the discursive practices of the *polis* behind – even though he might leave the Assembly, the Council and the law-courts, he would still speak the language of the *polis* and its ideal of the rule of law and use its terms and standard phrases.

Let us look at the inscriptions in which the private groups recorded their affairs, none of which Taylor and Vlassopoulos actually examine in detail. First, there is a strong distinction between the officials of the association and the other members of the association. Some of the names of officials in the private associations differ from those of the *polis*, but many such as *epimelētēs* and *grammateus*, two of the most common, are the same.³⁹ In the decree about the *Eikadeis*,

---

37 See Harris 2015b, 69 with note 68.
38 Taylor and Vlassopoulos 2015, 6: "many Athenians were members of religious associations, performed political duties, borrowed money from or met in the agora, others were not part of their extended family. The boundaries of the *polis* (Athens or otherwise) did not define these networks". Cf. Vlassopoulos 2007, 15: "the concept of the network takes the form of *koinōnia* (association) in the micro-level below the *polis*".
39 *Antigrapheus* – *IG* II² 1278, line 9. *Archeranistes* – *IG* II² 1297, lines 10, 16, 23; *IG* II² 1319, lines 15–16; *IG* II² 1322, line 21; *IG* II² 1339, line 4; *IG* II² 1343, lines 13, 33, 37; *Hesperia* 14 (1945) 147, no. 19. *Tamias* – *Agora* XVI: 230, line 2; 231, line 3; *AJA* 64 (1960) 269 (= *BCH* 84 [1960] 655); *IG* II² 1271, line 3; *IG* II² 1278, lines 9, 15; *IG* II² 1291, lines 12–13; *IG* II² 1292, lines 2, 28, 31; *IG* II² 1298, lines 21-22; *IG* II² 1316, line 22; *IG* II² 1317, lines 2, 7; *IG* II² 1322, line 23; *IG* II² 1323, lines 5-6; *IG* II²

the officials are given the responsibility for having the honorary decree inscribed and placed in a shrine. It also appears that like the officials of the *polis*, the officials of the *koinon* also have strict term-limits and serve for a year.[40] Second, like the *polis* the associations are obsessed with keeping written records of their members.[41] There is a strict distinction between the private property of the association, which is designated as *koina*, and the private property of members. Third, officials as at Athens are appointed by lot or by election.[42] Fourth, the decrees of the associations start with enactment formulas that borrow the language of the Council and Assembly (see Appendix). As we can see from the *Eikadeis* decree, they are also structured in the same way as decrees of the Council and Assembly, starting with a clause of justification with *epeidē*, followed by an enactment phrase and a verb in the infinitive. Sixth, the decrees of the associations also use entrenchment clauses similar to those found in decrees from Athens and from other Greek *poleis*, which reflect a concern for keeping the laws fixed and stable.[43] Seventh, the associations do not rely on friendship and good will to regulate ties between members, but formulate written laws and include penalties for violations.[44] V. Gabrielsen has recently claimed that we should question the view that the associations did "possess the means to effectuate a rigorous enforcement of their rule so as to deter possible transgressors" and claims that this view "has

---

1324, line 32; *IG* II² 1326, lines 20, 32; *IG* II² 1325, line 51; *IG* II² 1335, line 10. *Grammateus* – *AJA* 64 (1960) 269 (= *BCH* 84 [1960] 655); *IG* II² 1263, lines 5–6; *IG* II² 1277, lines 4; *IG* II² 1278, line 9; *IG* II² 1284, line 22; *IG* II² 1292, lines 3, 33; *IG* II² 1298, line 22; *IG* II² 1317, line 8; *IG* II² 1322, line 22; *IG* II² 1323, line 12; *IG* II² 1328, lines 44; *IG* II² 1335, line 11. *Grammatophylax* – *IG* II² 1278, line 10. *Epimelētēs* – *IG* II² 1256, line 3; *IG* II² 1261, lines 12, 27; *IG* II² 1262, line 5; *IG* II² 1277, line 3, 24; *IG* II² 1278, line 9; *IG* II² 1282, lines 5–6; *IG* II' 1291, lines 21-22; *IG* II² 1292, lines 3–4; *IG* II² 1301, line 2; *IG* II² 1316, line 23; *IG* II² 1317, lines 2, 7–8 (see also the crowns); *IG* II² 1327, lines 27, 30; *IG* II² 1335, line 13. *Hieropoios* – *IG* II² 1261, lines 37, 45–46; *IG* II² 1263, line 36; *IG* II² 1265, line 5; *IG* II² 1291, line 22; *IG* II² 1292, line 14; *IG* II² 1297, line 12.
40 See Arnaoutoglou 2003, 104–105. For an explicit ban on iteration in office see *IG* II² 1328, lines 16–20.
41 Lists of Members: *IG* II² 1297; *IG* II² 1298; *IG* II² 1325; *IG* II² 2343; *IG* II² 2345; *IG* II² 2346 (?); *IG* II² 2348 (?); *IG* II² 2349 (?); *IG* II² 2351 (?); *IG* II² 2352 (?); *IG* II² 2354; *IG* II² 2356 (?); *IG* II² 2358; *IG* II² 2359 (?); *IG* II² 2361; *IG* II² 2481; *IG* II² 4817; *Rhamnous* 203; *SEG* 36.228 (list of people admitted); *SEG* 41:84. For lists of citizens in Archaic Greece see Faraguna 2015.
42 Appointment of officials by election or by lot: *IG* II² 1271, line 3; *IG* II² 1273, lines 5–6; *IG* II² 1282, line 5; *IG* II² 1284, line 22; *IG* II² 1315, lines 5–6 (term of office one year); *IG* II² 1334, lines 4–6 (appointment for one year).
43 *Agora* XVI: 202[3], lines 4–6.
44 *Syll.*³ 921; *IG* II² 123; *Agora* XVI: 202[3], lines 6-7 (*eranistai*); *IG* II² 1263, lines 43–45 (for officials failing to do their duty); *IG* II² 1273, lines 21–26; *IG* II² 1275, lines 14–17; *IG* II² 1292, lines 15–17; *IG* II² 1297, lines 17–18; *IG* II² 1328, lines 11–19; *IG* II² 1339, lines 12–15.

never been proven".[45] According to Gabrielsen, "rules seem to have been there less for their legal use and more for the commitment they were broadcasting for that code". As a result, Gabrielsen asserts that the main sources of trust in associations were "their strong adherence to the ethics of friendship and their pronounced religious devotion". This makes little sense. If the rules were there only for advertising purposes, why did the associations often go to great lengths to specify penalties to be imposed and give their officials the power to seize goods if fines were not paid? When we read that an association granted a crown to a benefactor, we see no reason to doubt that an actual crown was awarded and that this was not just a way of advertising the members' gratitude. By the same token, there was little point to setting rules and penalties and assigning powers to officials unless the members expected fines to be imposed for infractions. In the worst case, the members could exclude a member who did not abide by the rules as several inscriptions reveal. This was one of the reasons why the associations maintained lists and updated them. *Pace* Gabrielsen, the associations did have the means to enforce the rules. Moreover, in the honorary decrees passed by associations, we never find the honorand praised for the ethics of friendship – the term *philia* is never found in such decrees. And when their internal mechanisms were not adequate to deal with disputes, an association like the *Eikadeis* might use the courts to deal with members who were disruptive. Finally, one should note that even though most Greeks were pious, the *polis* still set rules about religious matters and imposed penalties for *asebeia*.[46] It did not rely solely on everyone's religious devotion to see that these rules were respected. There is no reason to believe that the situation with the associations was any different. Eighth, the associations use the same kinds of incentives for good conduct, rewarding benefactors with honorary decrees and crowns.[47] We, therefore, find the same relationship between benefactor and community as we witness in the *polis*. Ninth,

---

45 Gabrielsen 2015.
46 On *asebeia* see Filonik 2013 and his chapter in this volume.
47 The use of clauses in honorary decrees about the use of honours to motivate others to show *philotimia* and confer benefits: *IG* II² 1252, lines 18–22 (*orgeons*); *IG* II² 1259, lines 7–9; *IG* II² 1261, lines 53–55; *IG* II² 1262, lines 12–15; *IG* II² 1263, lines 27–31; *IG* II² 1265, lines 10–12; *IG* II² 1271, lines 18–21; *IG* II² 1277, lines 29–33; *IG* II² 1278, lines 5–8; *IG* II² 1284, lines 7–11; *IG* II² 1293, lines 8–11; *IG* II² 1301, lines 8–10; *IG* II² 1314, lines 9–11; *IG* II² 1316, lines 18–20; *IG* II² 1318, lines 9–13; *IG* II² 1319, lines 7–11; *IG* II² 1324, lines 10–12, 19–25; *IG* II² 1327, lines 20–23; *IG* II² 1329, lines 19–22; *IG* II² 1333, lines 11–13; *IG* II² 1334, lines 11–13; *IG* II² 1337, lines 9–11. For an example in a decree of the Assembly see *IG* II² 509, lines 8–11: εἰδότες ὅτι χάριτας ἀπολήψονται παρὰ τ[οῦ δήμου ἀξίας τῶν εὐ]εργετημάτων. On these phrases see Henry 1996; Hedrick 1999 (claiming that they are democratic); and Sickinger 2009 (showing that they are not necessarily democratic).

the associations also use the *epidosis* as a way of raising money for common funds just as the *polis* does. Tenth, the officials of the associations undergo *euthynai* for their conduct in office, and as in the laws of Athens, officials are not allowed to receive honours for their overall conduct in office until they have passed their *euthynai* (although they can receive honours for individual acts of generosity before this).⁴⁸ The language and procedures of the associations are virtually identical with those of the *polis*. They also share the view that the business of the religious association should be conducted by fixed rules, which they often call *nomoi*, and that their officials should be accountable.⁴⁹ These are key features of the rule of law.⁵⁰

All this evidence shows that the world of the associations was not a completely separate universe, which conceptually lay outside or below the *polis* but fully within the conceptual universe of the *polis* whose institutions provided the language and procedures that individuals used to shape their interactions within these associations. The behaviours that the *polis* created by its rules and system of incentives for compliance and disincentives for violations of those rules structured the actions of individuals (though of course it did not determine them). The ideology of the rule of law and the tools created by the *polis* to implement the rule of law were too effective and too beneficial to be abandoned by individuals in private life. As O. Van Nijf has observed about professional associations in the Roman Near East: "honorific inscriptions thus open a door for us upon the concerns and aspirations of the craftsmen and traders of the cities of the Roman East, and upon their view of their own place in society. It is obvious that they used their honorific inscriptions not as public declarations of autonomy, separating themselves from the general populace, but rather as demonstrations of conformity, consciously adopting public models of euergetism".⁵¹

---

48 Officials undergo *euthynai* after their term of office – *IG* II² 1277, lines 16–17 (δεδώκασιν δὲ λόγον καὶ εὐθύνας πάντων ὧν διωικήκασιν); *IG* II² 1282, lines 9–10 (λόγον ἀπέδω[καν τοῦ ἀναλ]ώματος); *IG* II² 1284, lines 26–27 ([περὶ] ὧν οἰκονόμηκεν λόγον καὶ [εὐθύ]ν[α]ς δέδωκεν); *IG* II² 1292, lines 6–7 (τὰς] εὐ[θύνας] δεδώκα[σιν] περὶ [πάντ]ων παρὰ τὸν [εὔθυνον]); *IG* II² 1318, lines 6–9 (δεδώκασιν δὲ καὶ λό[γον καὶ] εὐθύνα[ς ἁπά]ντων τ[ῶν ὠικο]νομημένων αὐτοῖ[ς ἐν τῶι][ἐν]ιαυτῶι).

49 *IG* II² 1275, line 12–17; *IG* II² 1361, lines 13–14; *SEG* 44.60.

50 One must not make the mistake of Kierstead 2013, 174–225, who believes that the associations declined as the Athenians became less democratic. The associations continued to flourish in the 3rd century BC and into following period. See the more convincing analysis of Steinhauer 2014. There is no reason to believe that there was a correlation between the number of associations and democracy because many associations were found in Asia Minor during the Roman Empire. See Van Nif 1997.

51 Van Nijf 1997, 128.

Now one might argue that all these rules and officials and formal language were the product of Athenian obsessions and that the Athenian evidence is not characteristic of associations in general. Now for the Hellenistic period, there is not much evidence for associations in other *poleis* aside from Rhodes (there is more for Asia Minor in the Roman period), but in the few cases in which we do have documents, the pattern is the same.[52] Let us look at the so-called "Testament of Epicteta" which was found on the island of Thera and has been dated to the 210–195 BC.[53] The word "Testament" is misleading because only the first part of the inscription contains the will of Epicteta (lines 1–108). The larger part of the document contains rules about a religious association founded by Epicteta's husband (lines 109–287). One finds the same basic features one encounters in the Athenian documents about associations. First, there is the same distinction between officials and regular members. The association has *epimenieuontes* (lines 138–139, 155, 171, 178, 225, 239), and *artutēr* (lines 144–145, 148, 159, 163, 166, 169, 173, 194, 221), who collects fines, and *epissophos* (lines 203, 209, 234, 250). Second, the document uses an enactment formula to give a formal air (line 126: ἀγαθᾶι τύχαι δεδόχθαι) and specifies what actions are authoritative and what are not. Third, the activities of the members are not regulated by some common understanding or oral knowledge, but governed by written rules, which are mentioned in several places. Fourth, if anyone violates these written rules, there are stiff penalties and exclusion from the group. Now Vlassopoulos and Gabrielsen would have us believe that these associations were held together by *philia*, which implies that the members of the association all trusted each other and had no need for legal procedures or penalties to go about their business. On the contrary, the members of this association seem to have had an almost pathological distrust of their peers, especially those whom they elected as officials. One finds no mention of *philia* in this inscription. In fact, almost one third of this part of the document is taken up with penalties for officials who do not carry out their duties and goes into considerable detail about how to collect these fines. Let us take one of these clauses: "but if there are no sacrificial priests any longer serving at their own expense, the members will assume the charge in turn in order of seniority, as it has been prescribed for those who assumed the charge at their own expense, and they will receive from the administrator fifty drachmas ten days before the Assembly takes place. If he shall not assume the charge although he has received

---

[52] On the Rhodian associations see Maillot 2015 and Thomsen 2020. Cf. Maillot 2015, 146: the Rhodian associations "imitate the organisation and institutions of the city-state". For the terms *psēphismata* and *nomoi* used by the Rhodian associations see Maillot 2015, 147–148.
[53] For text and translations see Wittenberg 1990.

(the money), he shall pay a hundred and fifty drachmas, and the administrator shall make him pay and his property will be subject to forfeiture according to the laws; until he has paid, he shall have no part in the association" (lines 155–165). Far from being peaceful, patient and forgiving, the members come across as rather vindictive. Instead of performing their duties out of the goodness of their hearts and their warm and fuzzy feelings toward their fellow members, they have to be coerced with the threat of penalties. So much for this being a "friendly society". Fifth, another indication that the group's cohesion did not rest on a tacit understanding of codes of behaviour is the requirement for keeping extensive records.

One should be under no illusions about this association being held together only by religious bonds and friendly feelings. To keep the association in existence, there is a long clause threatening penalties and exclusion against anyone who proposes to dissolve the association (lines 254–267). What is striking is that this clause resembles the entrenchment clauses found not only in formal decrees in Athens, but in decrees from all over the Greek world.[54]

As we can now see, the world of the associations relied on many of the same procedures and methods as the *polis* and its subdivisions. The *polis* created not just a set of institutions with rules that operated in certain restricted contexts. It created a set of behaviours and a form of discourse that penetrated all aspects of social life, both religious and non-religious. On the other hand, the beliefs and practices of religion were not kept separate from the world of law and politics. The Greeks based the legitimacy of their laws on the approval of the gods and drew on religious beliefs about pollution when formulating and enforcing their laws about homicide. Finally, the interpenetration of religion and the rule of law existed not only at the level of the *polis* but also at the level of private associations.

Appendix: Enactment formulas in decrees of private associations

Agora XVI: 161, line 2 ([δεδόχθαι] τοῖς ὁ[ρ]γεῶσιν); *Agora* XVI: 223, lines 3–4 ([δεδό|χ]θαι τῶι κοινῶι [τῶν θιασωτῶν); *IG* II² 1252, line 2 (δεδόχθαι τοῖς ὀργεῶσι. Cf. lines 13–14); *IG* II² 1253, line 2 (ἔδοξε τοῖς [ὀργεῶσι]); *IG* II² 1255, lines 1, 6–7 ([ἔδοξεν τοῖς ὀ]ργεῶσι; ἐψ[η]||[φίσθαι τοῖς ὀργ]εῶσι); *IG* II² 1261, line 2 (ἔδοξεν τοῖς

---

54 On entrenchment clauses see Harris 2006, 23–25 and Sickinger 2008.

θιασώταις. Cf. lines 10–12, 25–26, 34–35, 47–48); *IG* II² 1263, lines 3–4 (ἔδοξεν τοῖς θιασώταις); *IG* II² 1265, line 1 (δεδόχθαι τοῖ]ς ἐρανισταῖς); *IG* II² 1271, lines 14–15; *IG* II² 1273, line 9 (δεδόχθαι τοῖς θιασώταις. Cf. line 33); *IG* II² 1278, line 8 (δεδόχθαι τοῖς θ[ιασώταις); *IG* II² 1283, line 13 (δεδόχθαι τοῖς ὀργεῶσιν); *IG* II² 1284, lines 11, 27–28 (δεδόχ[θαι τ]οῖς ὀργεῶσιν); *IG* II² 1291, lines 10–11 (δεδ[όχθαι] τοῖς ἐρανισταῖς); *IG* II² 1293, line 12 (δεδόχθαι [τοῖς Ἀσκ]ληπιασ[ταῖς]); *IG* II² 1297, lines 2–3 ([ἔδοξ]εν τῶι κοινῶι. Cf. line 9); *IG* II² 1298, lines 8–9 (δεδόχθαι τῶι κοινῶι τῶν θι[ασω]τῶν); *IG* II² 1301, line 11 (δεδόχθαι τοῖς [θιασώταις]); *IG* II² 1314, line 13 (δεδόχθαι τοῖς ὀργεῶσιν); *IG* II² 1315, line 19 (δ[ε]δόχθαι τοῖς ὀργεῶσιν); *IG* II² 1316, lines 13–14 ([δεδόχ]θαι το[ῖς ὀργεῶσιν); *IG* II² 1317, line 5 (δεδόχθαι τοῖς θιασ[ώταις); *IG* II² 1317b, line 3 (ἔδοξεν τῶι κοινῶι. Cf. line 6); *IG* II² 1319, lines 1–2 (δεδό]χθαι [τοῖς θι][ασώταις); *IG* II² 1322, lines 10–11 (δεδόχθαι τοῖς Ἀμφιεραϊσταῖς); *IG* II² 1323, lines 3–4 (ἔδοξεν τοῖς θι[α]σώταις); *IG* II² 1324, lines 13–14 (δεδόχθαι τοῖς ὀργεῶσιν); *IG* II² 1325, lines 18–19 (ἔδοξεν τοῖς [Διον]υσιασταῖς. Cf. line 34); *IG* II² 1326, line 33 (δεδόχθαι τοῖς ὀργεῶσιν); *IG* II² 1327, line 17 (δεδόχθαι τοῖς ὀργεῶσιν); *IG* II² 1328, lines 8 and 37 (δεδόχθαι τοῖς ὀργεῶσιν); *IG* II² 1329, line 22 (δεδόχθαι τοῖς ὀργεῶσιν); *IG* II² 1334, line 14 (δεδόχθαι τῶι κοινῶι τῶν ὀρ]γεώνων); *IG* II² 1335, line 4 (ἔδοξεν τοῖς Σαβαζιασταῖς); *IG* II² 1337, line 3 (ἔδοξεν τοῖς ὀργεῶσιν). Almost all enactment formulas are preceded by ἀγαθῆ τύχῃ.

Bibliography

Adkins, A.R.H. (1960), *Merit and Responsibility: A Study in Greek Values*, Oxford.
Allen, D. (2005), 'Greek Tragedy and Law', in: M. Gagarin/D. Cohen (eds.), *The Cambridge Companion to Ancient Greek Law*, Cambridge, 374–393.
Arnaoutoglou, I. (2003), *Thusias heneka kai sunousias: Private Religious Associations in Hellenistic Athens*, Athens.
Bethea, C. (2019), 'Roy Moore is Running for the Senate Again and Alabama Republicans are not Happy', in: *New Yorker*, June 20, 2019.
Beyerle, D. (2012), 'Moore Wins GOP Nomination for Chief Justice', in: *Gadsden Times*, March 4, 2012.
Bingham, T. (2010), *The Rule of Law*, London.
Bremer, J. (1983), 'Scapegoat Rituals in Ancient Greece', in: *Harvard Studies in Classical Philology* 87, 299–330.
Cairns, D. (2016), *Sophocles: Antigone*, London.
Dodds, E.R. (1951), *The Greeks and the Irrational*, Berkeley/Los Angeles.
Dodds, E.R. (1966), 'On Misunderstanding the *Oedipus Rex*', in: *Greece and Rome* 13, 37–49.
Fagles, R. (tr.) (1982), *The Three Theban Plays. Antigone, Oedipus the King, Oedipus at Colonus*, New York.

Faraguna, M. (2015), 'Citizen Registers in Archaic Greece: The Evidence Reconsidered', in: A. Matthaiou/N. Papazarkadas (eds.), *ΑΞΩΝ: Studies in Honour of Ronald S. Stroud*, Athens, 649–667.

Filonik, J. (2013), 'Athenian Impiety Trials: A Reappraisal', in: *Dikē* 16, 11–96.

Finglass, P. (2018), *Sophocles: Oedipus the King*, Cambridge.

Fröhlich, P. (2004), *Les cités grecques et le contrôle des magistrats (IVe - Ie avant J.-C.)*, Geneva.

Gabrielsen, V. (2015), 'Be Faithful and Prosper: Associations, Trust and the Economy of Security', in: V. Gabrielsen/C.A. Thomsen (eds.), *Private Associations and the Public Sphere: Proceedings of a Symposium held at the Royal Danish Academy of Sciences and Letters, 9-11 September 2010*, Copenhagen, 87–111.

Goldhill, S. (1986), *Reading Greek Tragedy*, Cambridge.

Green, J. (2005), 'Roy and His Rock', in: *The Atlantic*, October 2005.

Harris, E.M. (2006), *Democracy and the Rule of Law in Classical Athens: Essays on Law Society and Politics*, Cambridge.

Harris, E.M. (2010), 'Is Oedipus Guilty?', in: E.M. Harris/D. Leao/P.J. Rhodes (eds.), *Law and Drama in Ancient Greece*, London, 122–146.

Harris, E.M. (2013), *The Rule of Law in Action in Democratic Athens*, Oxford.

Harris, E.M. (2013/2014 [2015]), 'The Document at Andocides 1.96–98', in: *Tekmēria* 12, 121–153.

Harris, E.M. (2015a), 'The Family, the Community and Murder: The Role of Pollution in Athenian Homicide Law', in: C. Ando/J. Rüpke (eds.), *Public and Private in Ancien Mediterranean Law and Religion*, Berlin/Munich/Boston, 11–35.

Harris, E.M. (2015b), 'Toward a Typology of Greek Regulations about Religious Matters: A Legal Approach', in: *Kernos* 28, 53–83.

Harris, E.M. (2016), 'From Democracy to the Rule of Law? Constitutional Change during the Fifth and Fourth Centuries BCE', in: C. Tiersche (ed.), *Die Athenische Demokratie im 4. Jahrhundert: Zwischen Modernisierung und Tradition*, Stuttgart, 73–87.

Harris, E.M. (2017), 'How to "Act" in An Athenian Court', in: S. Papaioannou/A. Serafim/B. de Vela (eds.), *Aspects of Performance in Greco-Roman Oratory and Rhetoric*, Leiden/Boston, 223–242.

Harris, E.M. (2018), 'Pollution for Homicide in Athenian Law and Attic Tragedy: Parallels or Divergences?', in: S. Bigliazzi/F. Lupi/G. Ugolini (eds.), *Συναγωνίζεσθαι. Essays in Honour of Guido Avezzù*, Skenè (Skenè Studies I - 1), Verona, 419–454.

Hedrick, C.W. (1999), 'Democracy and the Athenian Epigraphical Habit', in: *Hesperia* 87, 387–439.

Henry, A.S. (1996), 'The Hortatory Intention in Athenian State Decrees', in: *Zeitschrift für Papyrologie und Epigraphik* 112, 105–119.

Ismard, P. (2010), *La cité des réseaux: Athènes et ses associations, VIe-1er siècle av. J.-C.*, Paris.

Johnson, B. (2003), 'Court Rules against Moore', in: *Tuscaloosa News*, July 2, 2003.

Kierstead, J. (2013), *A Community of Communities: Associations and Democracy in Classical Athens*, Ph.D. Thesis, Stanford University.

Lawton, C. (1995), *Attic Document Reliefs: Art and Politics in Ancient Athens*, Oxford.

Maillot, S. (2015), 'Foreigners' Associations and the Rhodian State', in: V. Gabrielsen/C. Thomsen (eds.), *Private Associations and the Public Sphere*, Copenhagen, 136–182.

McGrew, J. (2003), 'Moore Suspended', in: *Montgomery Advertiser*, August 23, 2003.

Migeotte, L. (1992), *Les souscriptions publiques dans les cités grecques*, Geneva/Québec.
Mikalson, J. (2016), *New Aspects of Religion in Ancient Athens: Honors, Authorities, Esthetics and Society*, Boston/Leiden.
Ostwald, M. (1986), *From Popular Sovereignty to the Sovereignty of Law*, Berkeley/Los Angeles.
Poland, F. (1909), *Geschichte des griechischen Vereinswesens*, Leipzig.
Parker, R. (1983), *Miasma. Pollution and Purification in Early Greek Religion*, Oxford.
Pounder, R.L. (1984), 'The Origins of ΘΕΟΙ as an Inscription Heading', in: K. Rigsby (ed.), *Studies Presented to S. Dow*, Durham, NC, 243–250.
Rigsby, K.J. (ed.) (1984), Pritchett, W.K. (1985), *The Greek State at War. Part IV*, Berkeley/Los Angeles.
Robertson, C. (2016), 'Roy Moore, Alabama Judge, Suspended on Gay Marriage Stance', in: *New York Times*, May 6, 2016.
Sickinger, J.P. (2008), 'Indeterminacy in Greek Laws: Statutory Gaps and Conflicts', in: E.M. Harris/G. Thür (eds.), *Symposion* 2007, Vienna, 99–112.
Sickinger, J. (2009), 'Nothing to do with Democracy: Formulae of Disclosure and the Athenian Epigraphic Habit', in: L. Mitchell/L. Rubinstein (eds.), *Greek History and Epigraphy: Essays in Honour of P.J. Rhodes*, Swansea/Oakville CT, 87–102.
Sommerstein, A.H. (2011), 'Sophocles and the Guilt of Oedipus', in: *Estudios griegos e indoeuropeos* 21, 103–117.
Steinhauer, J. (2014), *Religious Associations in the Post-Classical Polis*, Stuttgart.
Taylor, C./Vlassopoulos, K. (eds.) (2015), *Communities and Networks in the Ancient Greek World*, Oxford.
Thomas, R. (1996), 'Written in Stone? Liberty, Equality, Orality and the Codification of Law', in: L. Foxhall/A.D.E. Lewis (eds.), *Greek Law in its Political Setting*, Oxford, 19–31.
Thomsen, C.A. (2020), *The Politics of Associations in Hellenistic Rhodes*, Edinburgh.
Van Hove, R. (2018), *Divining the Gods: Religion and Authority in Attic Oratory*, Ph.D. Thesis, King's College, London.
Van Nijf, O.M. (1997), *The Civic World of Professional Associations in the Roman East*, Amsterdam.
Vernant, J.-P. (1972), 'Ambiguité et renversement: Sur la structure énigmatique d' *Œdipe Roi*', in: J.-P. Vernant/P. Vidal-Naquet, *Mythe et tragédie en Grèce ancienne*, Paris, 99–131.
Vlassopoulos, K. (2007), 'Free Spaces: Identity, Experience, and Democracy in Classical Athens', in: *Classical Quarterly* 57.1, 33–52.
Wittenberg, A. (1990), *Il testamento di Epikteta*, Trieste.

Jakub Filonik
Speaking for the Gods: Greek Cultic Regulations and their Silent Informants

Abstract: This chapter discusses procedures used in the Greek world to denounce transgression in religious activities. It starts with the passage from Demosthenes (22.27) about modes of prosecuting theft and impiety in Classical Athens, and sets out to assess its claims about Athenian procedural variety (including the *apagōgē, ephēgēsis, graphē* and *dikē*). It pays special attention to the legal parlance of *phrazein, phainein, mēnyein* and *eisangellein*, used for describing general acts of "denouncing", and includes a textual analysis of the Demosthenic passage and inscriptions where these terms appear (in particular, the regulation of orderly conduct in the Eleusinian Mysteries in Classical Attica) together with parallels from several periods, regions and sources in the Greek world. The chapter also aims to reconsider the assumptions often made about the Greek legal system and its dependence on citizen prosecutors and politicians, and suggests a wider participation of free non-citizens and slaves in supplementary legal proceedings in several crucial socio-political domains.

1 Introduction

Whenever ancient impiety trials are mentioned, students of Classical Athens immediately recall the *graphē asebeias*, the procedure used for cases similar to the famous one against Socrates. This focal point certainly does not reflect the entire scholarly discussion on the topic, but it shows where attention tends to shift in the general debate.[1] In this chapter, I would like to focus on a more neglected aspect of Greek laws, namely the involvement of both city officials and ordinary people, including non-citizens, in the parts of Athenian legal system concerned with religion, as opposed to the role well-known public figures played in it as

---

My sincere thanks go to Ilias Arnaoutoglou, Edward Harris, Janek Kucharski, Peter Liddel, Lene Rubinstein and Rachel Zelnick-Abramovitz, as well as to the audience of the "Symposionaki" conference (University of Athens, 2016) and the anonymous reviewer, for all the helpful notes on earlier versions of this chapter.

1 See Filonik 2013 for a detailed discussion of all – alleged and historical – Athenian impiety trials and the problems we now face in studying them.

either prosecutors or defendants. While the broad topics of Greek cultic regulations and the capacities of religious officials have been given considerable attention in recent scholarship,² this chapter aims to single out and analyse several variants of supplementary legal procedures that could be used in such contexts, in particular those overlooked in our handbooks of ancient Greek law, in order to offer a more comprehensive model in this matter.

2 Procedural variety in Athens

An often quoted but problematic passage recurring in the discussions of procedural flexibility in Athens comes from Demosthenes' speech *Against Androtion* (§§26–28). In a prosecution speech from the 350s BC concerned with bringing an illegal proposal, Demosthenes used the authority of the lawgiver Solon to claim that Athenian laws were developed in such a way that the system would promote fairness and justice by allowing various individuals to participate in it according to their skills and confidence. The speaker's primary examples are based on the procedures available in cases of theft. He provides a series of conditional clauses:

> ἔρρωσαι καὶ σαυτῷ πιστεύεις· ἄπαγε· ἐν χιλίαις δ' ὁ κίνδυνος. ἀσθενέστερος εἶ· τοῖς ἄρχουσιν ἐφηγοῦ· τοῦτο ποιήσουσιν ἐκεῖνοι. φοβῇ καὶ τοῦτο· γράφου. καταμέμφει σεαυτὸν καὶ πένης ὢν οὐκ ἂν ἔχοις χιλίας ἐκτεῖσαι· δικάζου κλοπῆς πρὸς διαιτητὴν καὶ οὐ κινδυνεύσεις. ... τῆς ἀσεβείας κατὰ ταῦτ' ἔστιν ἀπάγειν, γράφεσθαι, δικάζεσθαι πρὸς Εὐμολπίδας, φράζειν πρὸς τὸν βασιλέα. περὶ τῶν ἄλλων ἁπάντων τὸν αὐτὸν τρόπον σχεδόν.
>
> Dem. 22.26–27

φράζειν Mss SAFY : φαίνειν Weil³

You are [physically] strong and confident [in your own ability in court]: arrest him (by *apagōgē*) and risk a fine of 1,000 drachmas. You are [physically] weaker: lead the magistrates to him (by *ephēgēsis*), and they will do it. You are also afraid of this: bring a public charge (*graphē*). You do not feel confident, and since you are poor, you would not be able to pay the fine of 1,000 drachmas; bring a private action (*dikē*) before the arbitrator, and you will run no risk. ... The situation is the same with cases of impiety: someone can make an arrest [*apagōgē*], bring a public charge [*graphē*], bring a *dikē* before the Eumolpidai or

---

2 On ancient Greek "sacred laws" see recently Parker 2004; Lupu 2009; Carbon and Pirenne-Delforge 2012; Harris 2015; Clinton 2005; 2008. See Rhodes 2009; Harris 2013a on religious officials.
3 All four manuscripts read φράζειν, which Weil in his 19th-century AD edition corrected to φαίνειν. See the discussion below.

make a "denunciation" to the Basileus. And it is more or less the same for all other procedures.

tr. Harris 2008, modified

What Demosthenes presents here is a "decreasing risk" order of procedures,[4] from high-profile to low-profile, with *dikē* in the first case and denunciation before the Basileus in the second, being the least risky way of reporting crime, due to there being no danger of penalties for not securing enough votes in the trial. The orator's model, presented for the sake of his immediate rhetorical goals, has been rightly criticised by scholars as an inaccurate description of litigants' actual capabilities in most cases covered by Athenian law, since the speaker wants his audience to believe that such cherry-picking was available to every litigant, rather than strictly limited by circumstances and the substance of the law.[5] What is important here, however, is that there might have been a common perception of the Athenian legal system as allowing the more and less confident individuals to take part in the administration of justice by reporting an offence, with the city officials then taking over at the following stages of that process. Let us briefly review this paradigm before discussing its possible variations.

The *apagōgē* opens both Demosthenic lists. It would involve dragging the perpetrator caught ἐπ' αὐτοφώρῳ, that is one whose guilt was evident, to the Eleven, who were the magistrates responsible for such cases.[6] This would presumably involve dealing with the so-called *kakourgoi* ("malefactors"),[7] and thus one cannot help to think that in addition to actual trials for *asebeia* (as in the festival violations described below), Demosthenes is extending here the meaning of impiety (*asebeia*) to also cover cases of sacrilege (*hierosylia*) normally tried as a separate offence, and so chooses not to be specific.[8] The *ephēgēsis*, a sister procedure of *apagōgē*, which we should thus assume for *asebeia* as well (but which was not explicitly mentioned on the second list), meant that the denunciator would not need to make an arrest himself, but would lead the magistrates to the perpetrator – hence Demosthenes' remarks on physical strength. In both of these procedures, however, the denunciator would need to prove that the offender was caught ἐπ' αὐτοφώρῳ, meaning that the guilt would need to be evident. This was

---

[4] See Carey 2004.
[5] See Harris 2000; 2008, 179–181; Carey 2004 arguing against the interpretation of Osborne 1985 (= Osborne 2010, 171–204, with afterthoughts) and his interpretation of "procedural flexibility" based on this passage.
[6] Cf. Harris 2006, 373–390; 2013a, 53–54.
[7] On *kakourgoi* see Hansen 1976; Gagarin 2003; Harris 2006, 291–293.
[8] Cf. Carey 2004, 126–127. On the differences between *asebeia* and *hierosylia* see Filonik 2013, 62.

presumably easier when the person was caught in the act, rather than with the stolen property later, but the phrase seems to have covered both possibilities.[9] The *graphē*, a public trial in a *dikastērion*, was apparently the most common procedure used in impiety cases. *Graphai* could be brought by "anyone who wished", not necessarily the victim, and thus also on behalf of the state or, in a sense, of the gods. Similarly, in the cases of theft, *graphē* could concern stolen public property. This would not involve a direct confrontation the way *apagōgē* and *ephēgēsis* did, and the prosecutor was not required to demonstrate that the offender was caught ἐπ' αὐτοφώρῳ.

Up to this point, the relation between both lists is quite straightforward.[10] It should be also safe to assume that the *dikē klopēs* before a public arbitrator, that is a "regular" private trial for theft, was in Demosthenes' own order of risk in a place similar to the *dikē asebeias* before the Eumolpidai. The process is initiated in the presence of these officials, with the *diaitētai* leading the arbitration and the Eumolpidai giving interpretation of the sacred rules, and with both groups of officials presumably having the right to either dismiss the case on the basis of formal requirements or admit it to court as relevant to the offence in the charge.[11] The name within the list of specific procedures seems to be used in opposition to the *graphē*, but it is possible that *dikazesthai* in this case should be understood as a generic term, meaning "to bring a case to court", without specifying the procedure. From the extant sources we learn that the Eumolpidai had the right of giving the *exēgēsis*,[12] a non-binding interpretation of the proper conduct – especially of sacrifices – in the Eleusinian Mysteries, and thus customarily presided over some of the court proceedings, so their place at the initial stage of crime reporting and before the actual court trial is understandable as long as it concerned the Mysteries (regardless of their possible involvement in the trial later).

---

9 See Harris 2006, 373–390 on this expression.

10 Theft: 1. *apagōgē*, 2. *ephēgēsis*, 3. *graphē*, 4. *dikē* brought before the arbitrator. Impiety: 1. *apagōgē*, (2. *ephēgēsis*?), 3. *graphē*, 4. *dikē* brought before the Eumolpidai.

11 Cf. Schol. 83 Dilts ad Dem. 22.27: ἱερὸν δὲ γένος οἱ Εὐμολπίδαι, ἱερᾶται δὲ Ἐλευσῖνι, καὶ ἐπὶ τούτου πολλάκις ἐδικάζοντο ἀσεβείας οἱ βουλόμενοι ("the hallowed family of Eumolpidai that performs the priestly service at Eleusis and before whom volunteer prosecutors often brought cases for impiety", tr. JF); the scholiast probably did not have a detailed knowledge of the Athenian legal system but might not be far from the truth here. See the discussion below on the scholia to Demosthenes.

12 See Clinton 1974; Pepe 2018 on the *exēgēsis* and *exēgētai* in Athens; cf. Filonik 2013, 44 n. 129.

Irrespective of naming, the trial brought *pros Eumolpidas* in the 4th century[13] would place the priests in the same position as the public arbitrator from the *dikē pros diaitētēn*,[14] which is as someone who would initially accept and try to resolve the dispute, and refer it to the court or relevant board of officials if unsuccessful.[15] Presumably, this would involve cases directly linked to the Eleusinian Mysteries, perhaps shortly after the festival, similarly to the way *probolē* was initiated after the Dionysia or sometimes the Mysteries (Dem. 21.175–182; cf. below).[16] This stage probably would not incur any penalties for providing false information, as was the case with other types of arbitration in Athens, but such acts could increase the risk of taking the case to trial, and if the case was treated as a public one rather than a private *dikē*, documents presented to the Eumolpidai would be sealed in the *echinos* and false testimony would be subject to a separate court trial (*dikē pseudomartyriōn*).[17] There is also some debatable evidence for a regular *dikē* for impiety in Pseudo-Lysias, where a private trial for damaging someone else's Herm is briefly mentioned, which could – but does not need to – influence the way we interpret *dikazesthai pros Eumolpidas* from Demosthenes' list (not least because Ps.-Lys. 6 might be a later forgery). In the case of the *Against Androtion*, *dikē* in a religious context might thus point to a quite general or more archaic, conservative usage of the term (as the verb *dikazesthai* was indeed often used), without opposing it to a public trial, even though Demosthenes seems to be consciously implying such an opposition by listing it among other specific procedures for the purpose of his paradigm.

3 *Eleusis*: Informers of the two goddesses

From there, the list gets more obscure but also more interesting from the vantage point of this chapter, where the original *phrazein* or the emended *phainein* appears. First, *phainein* (or *phasis*) in other types of cases was a property-related

---

13 All dates will be BC, unless otherwise stated.
14 On public and private arbitration see Harris 2018; cf. Rhodes 1981, 589–596 on *dikē pros diaitētēn*.
15 On boards of officials and their penalisation for misconduct, cf. Rubinstein 2018.
16 On the procedure of *probolē* see a summary of the traditional view in MacDowell 1990, 13–23 (a single two-step procedure); for another, convincing interpretation see Harris 2008, 79–80; 2013b, 211–223 (an initial procedure at the Assembly against those who committed an offence against the festival, after which the prosecutor could move to court with a separate procedure).
17 See Harris 2018, 224–226.

and high-risk procedure but also one with a financial reward (probably because it was concerned with property, which could be divided and partly given to the prosecutor), and second, we do not find in our sources any impiety cases where it was used. But, as Robert Wallace has convincingly shown, there was clearly more than one legal procedure known under this generic name ("showing").[18] A larger problem, and one usually omitted by scholars, is that all manuscripts for this passage simply read φράζειν, while φαίνειν is Henri Weil's emendation based on a remark by a late scholiast (preserved in two manuscripts); the issue is discussed further below.[19]

There is an interesting 4th-century parallel for *phainein* in a law regulating the Eleusinian Mysteries, probably from the 360s or 350s,[20] so incidentally around the time of delivery of Dem. 22 (dated ca. 357–354). It might have been enacted because of the growing popularity of the Mysteries and large numbers of people willing to be initiated and joining the procession to the temple in Eleusis.[21] It reads:

ἐὰν δέ τις μυῆ[ι Ε]ὐμολ[πιδῶν ἢ Κηρύκων οὐκ ὢν ε]ἰδώς, ἢ ἐὰν προσάγηι τις μυησόμε[νον ....23............ τοῖ]-
[ν] Θεοῖν, **φαίνεν** δὲ τὸμ βολόμεγο[ν Ἀθηναίων, καὶ ὁ βασι]λεὺς εἰσαγέτω εἰς τὴν Ἡλιαίαν κα[.............26............. αὐ]-
[τ]ὸ βολευέτω ἡ βολὴ ὡς ἀδικõντος.[22]

Before proposing a translation, let us focus on the terminology: the act of "pointing out" the transgression appears here, again, as general rather than specific.[23] But more importantly, even though "anyone who wishes" (*ho boulomenos*) can initiate the denunciation, it is the Basileus who introduces the case before the Assembly (pointedly called "Heliaia"). The *protasis* in l. 27 is more problematic. Kevin Clinton explains his own conjectures in the commentary as "it is illegal for

---

18 See Wallace 2003; Arnaoutoglou 2017, 455–456 on *phasis* (or *phainein*); both rightly note its general aspect of reporting the kinds of information not available to the officials themselves by those who could attest what has happened, reflected in the generic wording of denunciation procedures. On the financial reward for volunteers in Greek laws see Rubinstein 2016 (with pp. 423–424 and 428 on *phainein*), with a reply by Arnaoutoglou 2017.
19 To be discussed in more detail in a forthcoming paper.
20 Dated more broadly to 380–350 or more specifically to 367–ca. 350, cf. *SEG* 30.61; Clinton 2008, 117 = Clinton 1980, 272.
21 See Clinton 1980, 274–275; 2008, 117.
22 *I.Eleusis* 138 (= *SEG* 30.61), 27–29.
23 Cf. *phainen* in a religious context: *IG* XII.5, 2.A, 6–7 (*LSCG* 105) from 4th-century Ios; *IG* I² 4, 24–25 (*LSCG* 3) from 5th-century Athens and *IG* II² 30, 6 from 4th-century Athens.

a person who knows that he is not a member of the Eumolpidai or Kerykes to perform *myēsis* and for anyone to introduce someone seeking initiation to such a non-member" (the phrases "who knows that he is not a member of" and "to such a non-member" are the author's conjectures). He describes a situation from the 2nd-century AD, in which Valerius Mamertinus believed he was a member of the Kerykes and was elected *dadouchos* but was later removed from priesthood through a legal challenge.[24] However, this parallel does not really seem applicable to 4th-century Athens, and this translation of the law and interpretation of the legislation's real purpose – while not impossible – remains problematic. In fact, a better alternative can be offered, since a direct equivalent of the Eleusinian inscription's use of εἰδώς (l. 27) comes from the gymnasiarchal law of Beroia, which speaks of similar provisions (*I.Beroia* 1.B.26–35 = *SEG* 27.261):[25]

...οἷς οὐ δεῖ μετεῖ-
ναι τοῦ γυμνασίου· μὴ ἐγδυέσθω δὲ εἰς τὸ γυμνάσιον δ[ο]ῦ[λ]ος μηδὲ ἀπε-
[λ]εύθερος μηδὲ οἱ τούτων υἱοὶ μηδὲ ἀπάλαιστρος μηδὲ ἡταιρευκὼς μη-
[δ]ὲ τῶν ἀγοραίαι τέχνῃ κεχρημένων μηδὲ μεθύων μηδὲ μαινόμενος· **ἐὰν**
[δ]έ τινα ὁ γυμνασίαρχος ἐάσῃ ἀλείφεσθαι τῶν διασαφουμένων **εἰδώς**,
[ἢ] ἐνφανίζοντός τινος αὐτῶι καὶ παραδείξαντος, ἀποτινέτω δραχμὰς
χιλίας, ἵνα δὲ καὶ εἰσπραχθῆι, δότω ὁ προσαγγέλλων ἀπογραφὴν τοῖς ἐξε-ᵛ
[τ]ᾳσταῖς τῆς πόλεως, οὗτοι δὲ παραγραψάτωσαν τῶι πολιτικῶι πράκτορι· ἐ-ᵛ
[ὰ]ν δὲ μὴ παραγράψωσιν ἢ ὁ πράκτωρ μὴ πράξῃ, ἀποτινέτωσαν καὶ οὗτοι τὸ ἴσον
[ἐ]πίτιμον καὶ τῶι ἐγδικασαμένωι διδόσθω τὸ τρίτον μέρος ... κ.τ.λ. (tr. in n. 25 below)

According to the Hellenistic regulations of this oligarchic Macedonian town, all social groups listed in the inscription are to be excluded from entering the gymnasia, while the gymnasiarch is forbidden to either *knowingly* (B.30: εἰδώς, cf. A.32)[26] allow them to enter, or to neglect to act if anyone *reports* (ἐνφανίζοντος)

---

24 Clinton 2008, 119, cf. Clinton 1980, 278.
25 Eran Lupu has translated this correctly in his edition of new Greek sacred laws (*NGSL* 14): "those who ought not to share the gymnasium: the following shall not strip off (to exercise) in the gymnasium: a slave, a freedman and their sons, an *apalaistros*, a prostitute, anyone of those who have business at the marketplace, a drunk, and an insane person. If the gymnasiarch knowingly allows any of those specified to anoint himself or after someone has reported or indicated (this) to him, he shall pay a thousand drachmas. To ensure collection (of the fine), the informer shall hand a (written) charge to the *exetastai* of the city, and they shall submit his name to the civic *praktōr*. If they do not submit his name or the *praktōr* does not collect (the fine), they too shall pay the same penalty, and a third shall be given to the prosecutor". I would like to thank Lene Rubinstein for pointing out this similarity.
26 Cf. a similar use in *IG* II² 1368.96–99 (*LSCG* 51) and *IG* IX 2, 1109.a.28 (*LSCG* 83).

or *indicates* (παραδείξαντος) such an offence to him, under the penalty of a thousand drachmas. If a gymnasiarch ever transgresses this rule, the written charge (*apographē*)[27] should be prepared and passed on to the city officials (*exetastai*).[28] The *exetastai* shall in turn introduce the case before the "civic *praktōr*" for him to collect the fine: a markedly similar procedure and language to the Eleusinian law (*enphanizein* for *phainein*; *exetastai* for the Basileus; civic *praktōr* possibly for all collective Athenian institutions: the *praktores*, mentioned in l. 34 of the Eleusinian law, the Council and the courts).

Similarly, in the law regulating the Mysteries, εἰδώς – which could appear without an object – should be understood as "knowingly" or "deliberately", while the text in the lacuna could speak of a group – such as *atimoi*, as in Andocides' case, or others convicted of grave crimes[29] – to be excluded by law from initiation and other rites. In fact, at least one such group seems to be mentioned in l. 25 (ἐξ ὧν οὐκ ἔξεστι μυεῖσθα[ι). The quoted extract from the law would thus read: "and if someone knowingly performs initiation [without being one of?][30] the Eumol[pidai or the Kerykes], or if someone introduces a would-be initiate... the Two Goddesses, anyone who wishes [of the Athenians?][31] shall denounce him (*phainein*), and the [Basi]leus shall bring the matter before the Heliaia... and the Council shall deliberate on this, treating it as a case of wrongdoing" (tr. JF).

Phainein here could refer to denouncing to the Basileus those who knowingly initiate a member of one of the previously mentioned groups excluded from the rites. It would not need to be done by someone "not being" a member of the Eumolpidai or Kerykes ("not being" was Clinton's conjecture) but actually by a priest from one of the two families yet in violation of the regulations. As suggested in the discussion above, the procedure could be initiated before the whole Assembly soon after the festival, similarly to the way *probolē* was brought before the case was referred further to courts or dismissed. In 4th-century Athens, the word "Heliaia" used in the inscription was an archaising term for a judicial meeting of the Assembly, which points to a more conservative language of the law.[32]

---

27 Cf. Lys. 9.3, 29.1 in the sense "written denunciation"; in And. 1.23 mentioned together with *mēnysis*. *Apographai* were commonly given before the Assembly or the Council see And. 1.12–13, Lys. 13.30.
28 See Gauthier and Hatzopoulos 1993 on the Beroia law and the city's constitution. See Rubinstein 2016, 424–426 on rewards for denunciations in the *apographē* procedure.
29 Cf. *Ath. Pol.* 57.4.
30 This reading is itself problematic but a better one would still need to be proposed.
31 On this assumption and expression see the discussion further below; the text could speak of a group allowed to participate in the Mysteries rather than of Athenian citizens specifically.
32 Cf. Scafuro 2011.

This archaising language suggests that *phainein* might have been a similarly generic rather than specific term in this context, but regardless of its exact meaning, "showing" or "pointing out" is semantically broad enough to suggest some initial "reporting" of the crime to the people and be understood as an act of letting the official know about the apparent transgression.

An interesting parallel for regulating the conduct of those involved in the Mysteries may be found in Apollodoros' *Against Neaira* from the late 340s, in the case of Archias of the Eumolpidai, a hierophant who was convicted of impiety for not performing the rites in accordance with tradition.[33] Accordingly, the Eleusinian law could regulate the conduct of the Eumolpidai themselves and allow anyone to denounce *them* to the presiding official, the Basileus. Similar regulations of priests' conduct were widespread both in Athens and in other poleis. For example, Aeschines in his *Against Ctesiphon* of 330 BC claims that "the law requires that priests and priestesses be subjected to audit (*hypeuthynoi*)... and they are not just audited individually but also by whole clans, the Eumolpidae, the Ceryces, and all the rest" (3.18, tr. Carey 2000). Other Athenian laws had similar provisions for the scrutiny (*euthynai*) of the *hieropoioi*.[34] It is significant in this context that part of the fragmentarily preserved inscription on the Mysteries is concerned with regulating the duties of the Basileus and the *exēgētai* (A.*ab*.29–40, B.*a*.23–24).[35] Yet based on Aeschines' remarks, we might assume that the Athenians did not see the role of such priests as endowed with particularly significant legal powers, since in the quoted passage they are rather degraded by being described as "people who merely receive the relevant privileges and offer prayers to the gods on your [sc. the people's] behalf". Their proper conduct needed to be regulated just like any other aspect of the ever-growing Mysteries.

According to ll. 29–38, the Basileus and some other officials named in the lacuna, perhaps the newly appointed *epimelētai*, also had the power to levy small fines on disorderly initiates (*akosmountas*; cf. [Lys.] 6.4, *Ath. Pol.* 57.1), and larger

---

33 [Dem.] 59.116–117; cf. Filonik 2013, 66–67.
34 In the Eleusinia: *IG* I³ 5; cf. Clinton *IE* 28a (*CGRN* 31); on other officials undergoing *euthynai* in the Eleusinian Mysteries see *IG* II² 1078, Clinton *IE* 638; see also an earlier inscription on the Mysteries (ca. 470–460) which forbade the Eumolpidai and Kerykes to initiate candidates in groups, rather than individually (*I.Eleusis* 19, C. 26–30). The scrutiny (*euthyna*) of "religious" officials was very common in the Greek world, cf. Fröhlich 2004 and the collection of inscriptions in Lupu 2009. On some prerogatives of the *hieropoioi* in Athens see *IG* II³, 447 B (*CGRN* 92), cf. Rhodes 1981, 605 for details.
35 The officials called *exēgētai* were probably a post-403 invention see Clinton 1974, 90–93; Gagné 2009, 225.

fines required a trial in court.³⁶ If this was the case with *phainein* before the Basileus from the Demosthenic list, it is difficult to see why the Eumolpidai would also impose summary fines, and it helps us to understand the Demosthenic *dikē* as proceedings over which they would simply preside with a customary right of interpretation of the sacred rites and laws regulating the conduct of initiates (cf. *IG* I³ 6), rather than a proper court trial held before them (in line with the meaning of *pros* mentioned with an official in other inscriptions). But at the same time we learn about the involvement of some priests in religious trials in Athens, including a hierophant Eurymedon who apparently supported the prosecution of Aristotle by *graphē asebeias*, and we hear of involvement of another hierophant, Eurykleides, in the prosecution of Theodoros "the Atheist"; and finally, Kallias, a member of the Kerykes, could have been behind the *endeixis* brought on the charge of impiety against Andocides (And. 1.112–132).³⁷ However, all of these cases seem to show the support for prosecution or defence given by priests as private individuals, sometimes acting as *synēgoroi* for one party, and not *ex officio*.³⁸

4 How to report: *Phrazein* vs *phainein*

Let us now briefly consider the textual tradition of the *Against Androtion*. Both Demosthenic manuscripts with the scholion *vetus* mentioning *phasis* are dated to around the 9–10th century AD, and the information they include most likely goes back to antiquity.³⁹ In both, the scholion occurs as a comment on the word *phrazein*, which seems to treat it as a preliminary action, leading to a fully-fledged *phasis* before the Basileus, who should refer the case to the Thesmothetai.⁴⁰ One objection we might have to this is that the scholiast appears to be explaining the term *phasis* in the bracketed section of the scholion (see n. 40 above).

---

36 Cf. Clinton 1980, 280–283; Harris 2013a, 32–33.
37 Cf. Filonik 2013, 44–46, 72, 75.
38 On *synēgoria* see Rubinstein 2000.
39 Codd. Y (Parisinus graecus 2935) and L (Laurentianus 59, 9) in Dilts's edition, both from the same ancestor, from around the time of codd. S, A and F with Demosthenic speeches.
40 Schol. 84 ad Dem. 22.27: φράζειν πρὸς τὸν βασιλέα] ἵνα ὁ βασιλεὺς τὴν φάσιν λαβὼν (φάσις δὲ κατηγορίας ὄνομα) τοῖς θεσμοθέταις φανερὰν καταστήσῃ καὶ παρὰ τῶν θεσμοθετῶν γνωρισθῇ τοῖς δικάζουσι τὰ ἐγκλήματα. ὁ δὲ βασιλεὺς εἷς καὶ αὐτὸς ἄρχων κατ' ἐνιαυτὸν τῶν ἐννέα καλουμένων, ὃς καὶ αὐτὸς ἐπιμελεῖται τῶν ἱερῶν ("*pointing out to the Basileus*] so that the Basileus, having accepted the *phasis* (for *phasis* is a name of prosecution), might reveal it to the Thesmothetai and in the presence of the Thesmothetai make known the written charges to the

However, the surviving scholia agree with the Demosthenic manuscripts and read *phrazein* when trying to explain the meaning of the procedure. One reason the scholiast might be doing this was that *phrazein* was comprehensible to his contemporary readers as a general term, regardless of its legal connotations in the Classical period, while *phasis* needed a more detailed explanation.

First and foremost, what has been overlooked in scholarship is that we have good parallels for *phrazein* as both an act of denunciation and a specific legal action that followed. From Plato's *Laws* (XII, 955a), we learn about the regulation of proper conduct of the participants in athletic, musical or other contests, where in the case of illegal competition anyone who wishes (ὁ ἐθέλων) shall report (φραζέτω) the issue to the relevant officials, namely the patrons of the games (τοῖς ἀθλοθέταις). And although it may prove risky to cite Plato in discussing the law of democratic Athens, one needs to keep in mind that his *Laws* drew heavily on Athenian and other contemporary legal regulations.[41] In his dialogue, *ho ethelōn* may qualify as a Cretan technical term, but it seems to be a direct counterpart of the Athenian *ho boulomenos* both in Plato (cf. 707e) and in legal parlance of those *poleis* that preferred to use the former, such as Thasos and some Aegean and Peloponnesian cities in the Classical period.[42]

Moreover, the Epistatai Decree (*IG* I³ 32 = *I.Eleusis* 30, 6–22), usually dated to the 430s, similarly speaks of the overseers of the treasury at Eleusis who are required to report (*phrazein*) and collect any debts owed to the treasury. The main difference here is that it is the officials, not private individuals, who need to make the report before the board of magistrates responsible for the matter.[43] *Phrazein* also appears as a term perfectly recognisable to Aristophanes' 5th-century audience in a legal context of "reporting" an offence, in both the *Clouds* (844–846) and *Thesmophoriazusae* (764, report to the Prytaneis), used similarly to *endeiknynai* and *phainein* elsewhere in comedy (*Eq.* 278–279; *Ach.* 819–820, 823–826, 911–914, 917; *Eq.* 300–302 alluding to temple debts in unpaid tithe), and requiring the officials to intervene and act in their legal capacity following the report.[44]

Perhaps *phrazein* in impiety cases, similarly to Plato's law on sporting competitions, would be open to any participant of the festival, citizen or not, who

---

judges. The Basileus is a single Arkhon appointed for a year and he himself is one of the so-called Nine, who himself is responsible for managing the sacred rites", tr. JF).
41 See Saunders 1994.
42 Cf. Rubinstein 2003 on the variants of "volunteer" terminology.
43 See Cavanaugh 1996, 2–3 for an overview, pp. 20–21 for a translation.
44 Cf. Olson 2002, 277–279.

wished to report something *during* the festival to the relevant official, such as the Basileus, who would then take over without further involvement of the informer – one possible example out of many showing the role of officials in running the Athenian legal system and one of the procedures pointing to the role of informers in this process among many unknown to us. We know that domestic slaves also participated in the rites in Athens (Antiph. 1.17), sometimes even when they were not formally allowed to participate, for example, during certain closed stages of the ritual after the public procession (Isae. 6.49–50). Whether in such contexts they would be denunciators more often than persons denounced as transgressors is more problematic and remains an open question.

In the trials arising from the mutilation of the Herms and the profanation of the Mysteries in 415, many denunciations (*mēnyseis*) came from citizens, metics and slaves who did not need to take part in the rest of the prosecution themselves (And. 1.17). Perhaps the forms of reporting mentioned by both Demosthenes and the Eleusinian law could reflect this pattern, probably also with some form of initial public statement. In 415, an entire set of denunciations was in fact initiated by reports coming from a slave, Andromachos, who received immunity as a result of laying information in public (And. 1.11, 27). Both terms also appear surprisingly close to each other in Book XI of Plato's *Laws* (XI, 932d; cf. 932a–b), in a law about mistreatment of one's parents, where the act of reporting is described as *phrazein*, while slave testimony rewarded with freedom as *mēnyein*, thus with one clearly distinguished from the other (and with *exangellein* used as another general term for "reporting"). Elsewhere in Book XI (914a), *mēnyein* describes denunciations by both free men and slaves without any distinction.

5 The volunteer denunciator

This brings us to one more interesting question: how should we read the technical term *ho boulomenos* in places such as the Eleusinian law discussed above. The genitive Ἀθηναίων that follows it in the inscription is part of the conjecture. The actual legal term might not have been that exclusive and could have encompassed non-citizens, in this case all those who could participate in the festival, including foreign guests. In the surviving inscriptions, *ho boulomenos* is not always followed by citizens' *ethnikon* (such as Ἀθηναίων) or a variant of the customary phrase οἷς ἔξεστι ("to whom it is allowed").⁴⁵ Each such case needs to be investigated separately, as scholars may have been too eager to assume that such volunteers had to come from the citizen body. This assumption could be particularly problematic in the cases where being a volunteer would not lead to a fully fledged legal procedure but rather a simple act of denouncing. The suggestion does not seem too far-fetched considering that we even hear of some free non-citizens who could bring not just private cases but also *graphai* to Athenian courts ([Dem.] 59.66; cf. a general statement in Lys. 12.4). This process could be even better grounded in the case of religious festivals. In Athenian religion, various groups of non-citizens were allowed to take part in the Eleusinian rites, while Athenian metics were present at the Panathenaic processions and at the dramatic festivals such as the Rural Dionysia and the Lenaia. They were also allowed at the Hephaisteia by the time of Demosthenes' speech, while public slaves (*dēmosioi*) are recorded in the regulations concerning the Khoes festival.⁴⁶ Their inclusion in denunciation procedures through relevant city officials could be similar to the inclusion in regular court cases through the Polemarch at earlier times (cf. Isoc. 17.12–14; Lys. 23.2–5, 13).⁴⁷

Thus, the term *ho boulomenos* in the case of denunciations might include all individuals present at the festival, since all of them could help preserve the order of the rites. In fact, we learn from Demosthenes' *Against Meidias* (21.175) that a man from Karia accused a man from Thespiai of an offence that took place during the Mysteries in Athens. What is striking here is that this was done through a *probolē*, which had to be brought before the Assembly at a special meeting after the festival and could include complaints by foreigners, as did the denunciations in a trial for religious transgressions in 415, including slave testimony presented there (And. 1.14; cf. 1.27).⁴⁸ We hear little about how this was made possible in practice in the "citizen bodies" of the Assembly and the Council, but their regulations provided for hearing speeches from foreign envoys or foreigners pleading for Athenian citizenship, and such models could easily offer ad hoc solutions at the special meetings that took place after major festivals, which could later make their way into proper legal procedures (and indeed, such special provisions were

---

45 For example, *IK.Priene* 145.25 (*CGRN* 175); cf. ὁ χρῄζων in the context of *phasis* in *IG* XII.4 100.28 (*CGRN* 197) and *IG* XII.4 319.35 (*CRGN* 220).
46 See Parker 2005, 169–171; Kamen 2013, 16, 30; Wijma 2014.
47 On the Polemarch and changes in this respect during the Classical period see MacDowell 1978, 221–224, 257.
48 See Filonik 2013, 40–45 on the details of the events of 415.

sometimes made at the special Assembly meetings concerned with religious matters, *meta ta hiera*).⁴⁹

Another possibility is that *phrazein* was limited to free citizens and non-citizens, while slaves would report offences through a *mēnysis*, as outlined in the passage from Plato's *Laws* discussed above (XI, 932a–d). Moreover, our sources are highly selective in discussing the importance of metics, foreigners and slaves to Athenian political, military and social developments, which means we should not expect more explicit statements about this than the ones already discussed.⁵⁰ Denunciations such as those brought through *mēnysis* were markedly different from the regular testimonies (*martyriai*), and as such were probably allowed only in very specific circumstances. Nevertheless, those circumstances might be broader than scholars usually allow.⁵¹

At the end of the 4th century, in three cities of the Aegean island of Keos both free people and slaves were encouraged by the law (*IG* II² 1128 = *RO* 40) to inform about those instances of the export of red ochre (*miltos*) that did not agree with Athenian ordinances, particularly if conducted on ships other than those selected by Athens.⁵² The procedures for informing mentioned there are *phasis* and *endeixis* in one city, and *phasis* and *mēnysis* in another (with *endeixis* probably correctly restored in the lacuna). The law was apparently based on Athenian laws and in some way imposed on the Kean cities by Athens already in the past, though we cannot be sure if the same names for procedures in different cities are not just "false friends", as Lene Rubinstein once called them.⁵³ But whether there is any relation to the Athenian *phasis* or not, it is nevertheless worth noting that in Keos the denunciations were not limited to citizens or free men but included slaves, who were offered freedom and substantial financial rewards for providing information (the latter somewhat similar to the regular property-related *phasis* known from Athens, since it dealt with actual measurable goods).

One might also wonder if it bears any significance that although *phasis* appears in the laws concerning both Kean cities, slaves are each time mentioned in connection with another procedure, both denoting an act of "pointing out" –

---

49 For the details on the right of *prosodos* see Henry 1983, 191–203; Zelnick-Abramovitz 1998, 556–557 with notes.
50 See, e.g., van Wees 1995, on the military and political contexts (arguing that most of the extant sources remain silent on non-citizens' participation in the Athenian fleet).
51 In particular, Osborne 2010, 229–243, who limits this to religious sphere, treats the Kean regulations (*RO* 40) as void exercise of imperial power (cf. below) and argues that Athenians consciously tried to keep slave informers out of the courts, *contra* Hunter 1994, 70–95.
52 Cf. Harrison 1968, 182 n. 1.
53 See Rubinstein 2003.

endeixis in Koresia, *mēnysis* in Ioulis – even though all procedures are mentioned in one breath. This is, again, similar to Plato's usage, so even though slaves were allowed to report in many instances where the free would inform through *phrazein* or *phainein*, the terminology could differ depending on the legal status of the denunciator. And while all these enactments use the language of "informing" in such a way that the parts about slave evidence are not markedly distinguished, slaves were not required by the law to do anything further after "pointing out" the crime to the officials, who would themselves act on the information acquired from slave denunciators.

Scholars were mistaken in the past about the nature of the law regulating the export of *miltos* when they claimed that this was an impractical and symbolic form of exercise of Athenian power. Ephraim Lytle has persuasively argued in a recent paper against such readings,[54] showing that the Athenians considered ochre to be essential in maintaining their navy as a way of preventing ships from being destroyed by shipworms, and the one acquired from Keos was considered particularly valuable. This means that trade regulations, especially those involving military matters, could be considered in some respects a sphere equally important to the Athenians as the sacred rites and thus require similar measures in terms of acquiring information. Yet it is interesting that we do not hear about such actions being encouraged in Athenian laws about tyranny, unlike their 5th-century equivalent in Thasos, which allowed slave denunciations through *phainein* and *kateipein*, with a reward for truthful information and without further involvement of the informer (Körner no. 70).[55]

A slightly different example from Athens comes from Nikophon's law on approvers of silver coinage of 375/374 (*RO* 25), which introduces *phasis* to *sitophylakes* in the case of offences concerning the corn-market and to the board of the overseers when involving the imports. Yet this kind of *phasis* seems to be different from the kind of reports discussed previously, and appears as a variant of the property-related procedure that in Athens involved the risks of a regular public procedure coupled with rewards for the public prosecutor. And even though a considerable number of slaves had to be present in such situations of everyday trade, they appear in this particular inscription either as shopkeepers, who could be publicly beaten if they refused to accept the approved coins, or as public slaves acting as their approvers. They played a role not only in maritime trade but also

---

54 Lytle 2013.
55 Cf. Rubinstein 2003, 103; Osborne 2010, 236–237. A deposit was needed, which was presumably lost if the information was not considered truthful.

in small everyday transactions in local shops.⁵⁶ It is thus surprising that we do not find them in such regulations as individuals allowed to make reports. Similarly, we would expect slaves – ever-present in the Athenian *agora* – to be able to report market offences to the *agoranomoi* and *sitophylakes* by simple informal denunciations, in order to make the system of market control more efficient.⁵⁷ It is now rather enigmatic what called for their inclusion or exclusion in such circumstances, considering that the extant laws tend to be inconsistent in this matter. Many such generically expressed procedures of "reporting" are attested in Hellenistic inscriptions from a variety of Greek cities, and although their wider legal context is often unclear, the known cases from the 2nd century include provisions for denouncing those who owe money to the sanctuary that use *phainein* and its compounds as the term for "reporting".⁵⁸

6 Conclusion: Initiators of legal actions

Considering how much the image of Athenian legal system changes when we make space for a variety of reports of this nature, it might not even be crucial to the Demosthenic model if we prefer *phrazein* or *phainein* as the proper reading. In both cases, it would form similarly low-risk measures, rather than a fully-fledged one such as the property-related *phasis*, even though the latter could also be carried out further by the relevant officials in various Greek cities.⁵⁹ The distinction might be important, however, in deciding whether we are dealing with an actual procedure that had to be taken all the way to court or just its germ in the act of denunciation without involving the denunciator further and with the legal framework of the city taking over as soon as the transgression was officially reported. In the latter case, we might wonder if there were any status distinctions with respect to individuals allowed to perform such acts of "pointing out" the

---

56 Cf. Vlassopoulos 2007.
57 On these officials in Athens and their equivalents in other cities see Bresson 2015, 225–259.
58 *IG* IV² 1.45 (Epidauros, l. 7: ἐμ]φανιζέσθω), *IG* XII.4, 1.319 = *CGRN* 220 (Kos, l. 35: φαινέτω δὲ ὁ χρῄζων), *IK.Priene* 145 = *CGRN* 175 (Priene, l. 26: φαινέτω δὲ ὁ βουλόμενος). See Rubinstein 2016, 428–429 (mostly variants of *deiknyein* and *phainein*), cf. cat. nos. 27, 46, 62 for the inscriptions listed above, and the Collection of Greek Ritual Norms website for the text, translation and commentary. For *mēnyein* in 3rd-century Delphi see *CID* IV 14, 6–7; IV 15, 5–6; IV 22, 8; IV 23, 6–7; IV 25, 5–6.
59 See, e.g., *I.Magnesia* 99.12–15 (*CGRN* 187), *IK.Priene* 145.25–27 (*CGRN* 175).

crime to an official at – or after – a religious festival in which they were otherwise allowed to participate.

As to the reports concerning religious festivals specifically, such cases in Athens would indeed fall into the jurisdiction of the Basileus (*Ath. Pol.* 57.1–2, cf. [Lys.] 6.4), and thus might be brought by him personally to the relevant bodies after the initial report by the denunciator. Given his other duties, reports of this kind could also include matters concerning the sacred land.[60] It was also the Basileus who conducted the preliminary examination before choosing to take *graphai asebeias* to court (Pl. *Ap.* 19b, 24b). A likely parallel for such denunciations is given by Andocides (1.111), who speaks of an *endeixis* brought by the Basileus before the Council, which is only later referred to the courts, possibly with a different presiding magistrate.[61] Also in the 5th-century First-Fruits Decree (*IG* I³ 78), it was the Basileus who would initiate legal actions before the Council. There were many cases in Athenian and other Greek legal regulations where the officials were responsible for carrying out the law, while individuals were only meant to report the offence to them, a practice sometimes compared to reports made to the police in modern states.[62] As in the case of *ephēgēsis* described by Demosthenes, officials in Athens at various stages of legal proceedings could have taken the lead in the pursuit of justice, perhaps without later even involving the denunciators, who in this case did not even have to come from the citizen body.

Thus, a crucial appendix to the Demosthenic list would be *mēnysis*, best known from Andocides 1 and, to a lesser degree, Lysias 5 and 7 and Thucydides (6.27–29, 53–61), as well as some scattered inscriptions, some of them already cited. It was a procedure allowing everyone, that is men and women, citizens and non-citizens, free and slaves, to give supporting evidence in the ongoing proceedings. At least in 415, denunciators were given immunity (*adeia*) and rewards (And. 1.27–28, 45), while slaves – unlike under normal circumstances – could provide evidence without testifying under torture, and could gain freedom in return (Th. 6.27.2, Lys. 5.3–5, 7.16). Some of this could be exceptional to unusual circumstances such as those surrounding the cases of 415, but the frequent mention of denunciation procedures in our sources is something that cannot be easily dismissed.

Slaves were also allowed to present some kind of evidence in homicide trials when the victim was a free person (Ant. 5.48), but this issue is far from clear, as well as Antiphon's suggestion that a *mēnytēs* in such a trial could be tortured

---

60 See, e.g., *Ath. Pol.* 47.4, with Rhodes 1981, 556.
61 Cf. Harrison 1971, 6–7.
62 Harris 2013a, 21–59 on Athens; see Rubinstein 2003 and 2018 on officials in other *poleis*.

(5.46), but his use of the term might either not be technical or not reflect later usage. In the trials of 415 there was a risk of losing one's life for giving false evidence, but this was apparently either exceptional to that case or simply abandoned later. Informants were known to the public, since denunciations were made before the Assembly or the Council (cf. Lys. 12.48), but they did not have to participate in further court proceedings.

Slaves could have detailed knowledge about the lives of their masters and might provide valuable information (Isae. 6.49–50, 64–65), not least when the reward was freedom (Lys. 5.5).[63] Their presence might have been encouraged, just like that of women of various legal statuses (And. 1.16; [Dem.] 59.46), whenever they could provide information crucial to the case, even if they would not otherwise be expected to actively participate in the Athenian legal system. There might have been many more similar procedures named after the general terms "to inform" or "to denounce", including the verb *eisangellein*, used in Andocides 1 in the general sense "to lay information", similarly to its use in some other *poleis* (cf. the Arkesinian *IG* XII.7, 4), and in the cases of 415 used about a denunciation given before the Assembly by a slave (And. 1.14; cf. 1.27). Some of these might have been specific legal procedures, while others could be treated as general terms for an act of denouncing needed to initiate or advance a proper trial, in the cases where regular citizen or metic testimony under oath (*martyria*) was not possible or preferred.[64]

What is equally important in this reconstruction is that no known denunciations in Athens seem to have been anonymous: the names of informers were publicly known and most denunciations had to be made before the collective political bodies, then written down and publicly read by the clerks during court proceedings as evidence.[65] Whether anything can be deduced from this in regard to the links between the Athenian constitution and its legal system, is a separate issue. Perhaps anonymous denunciations were considered unfitting for a "civic" system as more appropriate for the subjects of a tyrant, a presumption apparently shared by some oligarchic regimes. They do not seem to be employable in states such as Athens, since evidence had to be presented before one of the collective

---

[63] See Hunter 1994, 70–95.
[64] Scholars have sometimes suggested that witness testimony coming from a citizen was more valuable to the dikasts than metic testimony. Perhaps in denunciations the person's legal status would have a similar effect, considering the panic caused by one citizen testimony in 415 and the harsh reaction to it when it was proved untrue (And. 1.43–45, 66). However, errors in recognising one's status were probably far from uncommon in the society without national IDs (see [Dem.] 59.9, Isoc. 17.14, Lys. 23.2 ff.; cf. Lys. 4.14, 23.15).
[65] In 415, this included a body of specially appointed "commissioners" (*zētētai*, And. 1.14).

political bodies, even if through a magistrate, and those bodies would conduct proper examination before taking action. The question of personal responsibility is rather vague, since we hear of a death penalty for false information only in 415, eventually carried through just in the case of a single citizen (And. 1.20, 66). We are also unaware of both earlier and later similar examples in Athens, which suggests the practice could have been abandoned soon after these prosecutions.[66] The speaker in Lys. 5, written probably not much later, clearly states that the slaves acting as *mēnytai* run no considerable risk (Lys. 5.4–5). Reporting to the Basileus in religious cases, however, is a puzzle in terms of (1) prospective rewards (freedom for reporting a serious offence, also one committed by the slave's master?), (2) risks involved, and (3) whether the name of the informer would be passed on to subsequent institutions by the Basileus if he was able to confirm the offence, himself being present at the ceremony.

As rightly observed by Chris Carey, it was often just one or a limited number of these "fallback" procedures that would be available to someone wishing to prosecute impiety or give evidence in such cases, and the choice would be limited by the substantive aspects of the laws and the offence in question.[67] In other words, contrary to what Demosthenes suggests when he overemphasises the prosecutor's free choice based on his social standing and personal confidence, the model of the Athenian legal system that assumes free choice of procedure irrespective of offence and particular context does not hold ground. But the consequences of the procedural variation independent from that model are significant.

It is crucial for our understanding of the Athenian legal system and political practice – yet usually overlooked in modern studies – that some of these procedures, sometimes in very limited circumstances, allowed or, indeed, encouraged the participation of non-politicians and, more strikingly, even non-citizens in the Greek "administration of justice", however inhospitable it was to the latter in many respects;[68] and it was often the city officials, not just the judges or volunteers, that helped the laws to be enforced. The image that emerges from closer readings of the extant evidence is quite different from the simplistic model often presented in our handbooks of Athenian democracy and political history, with just the famous figures of the Athenian political scene involved – on equal terms – in the Assembly and in the courts, not least in matters of religion, without the inclusion of ordinary members of the democratic polity.

---

[66] Similarly, *synēgoroi* were exempt from a fine and *atimia* (incidentally a risk-reducing institution omitted by Demosthenes in his *Against Androtion*), on which see Rubinstein 2000.
[67] Carey 2004.
[68] Cf. Patterson 2000.

The diversification of means available in prosecuting religious misconduct, or "impiety", is probably a trait that we should not extrapolate to the entire legal system of Classical Athens. However, it does show the importance of normative religious behaviour to those responsible for the development of that system, as it reached its mature state around the time of Demosthenes. This can be seen not just in the wide variety of procedures, but also in allowing a number of state officials and individuals of different legal statuses to take part in it. Such a wide range of measures was available at least where the community's concern about its fundamental well-being was considered particularly urgent, as was the case with religion or warfare. Whether Demosthenes' civic audience was prone to think of this system and of regulating the orderly religious conduct in the terms the speaker and the laws proposed, is a question that requires further consideration.

Bibliography

Arnaoutoglou, I. (2017), 'Rewards to Informers. Response to Lene Rubinstein', in: D.F. Leão/ G. Thür (eds.), *Symposion 2015: Vorträge zur griechischen und hellenistischen Rechtsgeschichte (Coimbra, 1.-4. September 2015)*, Wien, 451–459.

Bresson, A. (2015), *The Making of the Ancient Greek Economy: Institutions, Markets, and Growth in the City-States*, Princeton/Oxford.

Carbon, J.-M./Pirenne-Delforge, V. (2012), 'Beyond Greek "Sacred Laws"', in: *Kernos* 25, 163–182.

Carey, C. (tr.) (2000), *Aeschines*, Austin.

Carey, C. (2004), 'Offence and Procedure in Athenian Law', in: E.M. Harris/L. Rubinstein (eds.), *The Law and the Courts in Ancient Greece*, London, 111–136.

Cavanaugh, M.B. (1996), *Eleusis and Athens: Documents in Finance, Religion, and Politics in the Fifth Century BC*, Atlanta.

Clinton, K. (1974), 'The Sacred Officials of the Eleusinian Mysteries', in: *Transactions of the American Philosophical Society* 64, 1–143.

Clinton, K. (1980), 'A Law in the City Eleusinion Concerning the Mysteries', in: *Hesperia: The Journal of the American School of Classical Studies at Athens* 49, 258–288.

Clinton, K. (2005), *Eleusis, the Inscriptions on Stone: Documents of the Sanctuary of the Two Goddesses and Public Documents of the Deme. Volume Ia: Text*, Athens.

Clinton, K. (2008), *Eleusis, the Inscriptions on Stone: Documents of the Sanctuary of the Two Goddesses and Public Documents of the Deme. Volume II: Commentary*, Athens.

Filonik, J. (2013), 'Athenian Impiety Trials: A Reappraisal', in: *Dikē* 16, 11–96.

Fröhlich, P. (2004), *Les cités grecques et le contrôle des magistrats (IVe-Ier siècle avant J.-C.)*, Geneva/Paris.

Gagarin, M. (2003), 'Who were the *Kakourgoi*? Career Criminals in Athenian Law', in: F.J.F. Nieto/G. Thür (eds.), *Symposion 1999: Vorträge zur griechischen und hellenistischen Rechtsgeschichte (Pazo de Mariñán, La Coruña, 6.-9. September 1999)*, Köln, 183–191.

Gagné, R. (2009), 'Mystery Inquisitors: Performance, Authority, and Sacrilege at Eleusis', in: *Classical Antiquity* 28, 211–247.
Gauthier, P./Hatzopoulos, M.B. (1993), *La loi gymnasiarchique de Beroia*, Athenes.
Hansen, M.H. (1976), *Apagoge, Endeixis and Ephegesis Against Kakourgoi, Atimoi and Pheugontes: A Study in the Athenian Administration of Justice in the Fourth Century BC*, Odense.
Harris, E.M. (2000), 'Open Texture in Athenian Law', in: *Dikē* 3, 27–79.
Harris, E.M. (2006), *Democracy and the Rule of Law in Classical Athens: Essays on Law, Society, and Politics*, Cambridge.
Harris, E.M. (2008), *Demosthenes, Speeches 20-22*, Austin.
Harris, E.M. (2013a), *The Rule of Law in Action in Democratic Athens*, Oxford/New York.
Harris, E.M. (2013b), 'The *Against Meidias* (Dem. 21)', in: M. Canevaro, *The Documents in the Attic Orators: Laws and Decrees in the Public Speeches of the Demosthenic Corpus*, Oxford, 209–236.
Harris, E.M. (2015), 'Toward a Typology of Greek Regulations about Religious Matters: A Legal Approach', in: *Kernos* 28, 53–83.
Harris, E.M. (2018), 'Trials, Private Arbitration, and Public Arbitration in Classical Athens or the Background to [Arist.] *Ath. Pol.* 53, 1-7', in: C. Bearzot et al. (eds.), *Athenaion Politeiai tra storia, politica e sociologia: Aristotele e Pseudo-Senofonte*, Milano, 213–230.
Harrison, A.R.W. (1968), *The Law of Athens: The Family and Property*, Oxford.
Harrison, A.R.W. (1971), *The Law of Athens: Procedure*, Oxford.
Henry, A.S. (1983), *Honours and Privileges in Athenian Decrees: The Principal Formulae of Athenian Honorary Decrees*, Hildesheim.
Hunter, V. (1994), *Policing Athens: Social Control in the Attic Lawsuits, 420-320 BC*, Princeton.
Kamen, D. (2013), *Status in Classical Athens*, Princeton.
Lupu, E. (2009), *Greek Sacred Law: A Collection of New Documents (NGSL)*, 2nd ed., Leiden/Boston.
Lytle, E. (2013), 'Farmers into Sailors: Ship Maintenance, Greek Agriculture, and the Athenian Monopoly on Kean Ruddle (*IG* II^2 1128)', in: *Greek, Roman, and Byzantine Studies* 53, 520–550.
MacDowell, D.M. (1978), *The Law in Classical Athens*, London.
MacDowell, D.M. (1990), *Demosthenes, Against Meidias (Oration 21)*, Oxford.
Olson, S.D. (2002), *Aristophanes: Acharnians*, Oxford/New York.
Osborne, R. (1985), 'Law in Action in Classical Athens', in: *Journal of Hellenic Studies* 105, 40–58.
Osborne, R. (2010), *Athens and Athenian Democracy*, Cambridge/New York.
Parker, R. (2004), 'What are Sacred Laws?', in: E.M. Harris/L. Rubinstein (eds.), *The Law and the Courts in Ancient Greece*, London, 57–70.
Parker, R. (2005), *Polytheism and Society at Athens*, Oxford/New York.
Patterson, C. (2000), 'The Hospitality of Athenian Justice: The Metic in Court', in: V. Hunter/J. Edmondson (eds.), *Law and Social Status in Classical Athens*, Oxford/New York, 93–112.
Pepe, L. (2018), 'Athenian "Interpreters" and the Law', in: G. Thür/R. Zelnick-Abramovitz/U. Yiftach (eds.), *Symposion 2017: Vorträge zur griechischen und hellenistischen Rechtsgeschichte (Tel Aviv, 20.-23. August 2017)*, Wien, 105–128.
Rhodes, P.J. (1981), *A Commentary on the Aristotelian Athenaion Politeia*, Oxford.
Rhodes, P.J. (2009), 'State and Religion in Athenian Inscriptions', in: *Greece and Rome* 56, 1–13.

Rubinstein, L. (2000), *Litigation and Cooperation: Supporting Speakers in the Courts of Classical Athens*, Stuttgart.
Rubinstein, L. (2003), 'Volunteer Prosecutors in the Greek World', in: *Dikē* 6, 87–113.
Rubinstein, L. (2016), 'Reward and Deterrence in Classical and Hellenistic Enactments', in: D.F. Leão/G. Thür (eds.), *Symposion 2015: Vorträge zur griechischen und hellenistischen Rechtsgeschichte (Coimbra, 1.-4. September 2015)*, Wien, 419–449.
Rubinstein, L. (2018), 'Summary Fines in Greek Inscriptions and the Question of "Greek Law"', in: P. Perlman (ed.), *Ancient Greek Law in the 21st Century*, Austin, 104–143.
Saunders, T.J. (1994), *Plato's Penal Code: Tradition, Controversy, and Reform in Greek Penology*, Oxford.
Scafuro, A.C. (2011), 'Conservative Trends in Athenian Law: IE 138, a Law Concerning the Mysteries', in: G. Thür (ed.), *Symposion 2009: Vorträge zur griechischen und hellenistischen Rechtsgeschichte (Seggau, 25.-30. August 2009)*, Wien, 23–46.
van Wees, H. (1995), 'Politics and the Battlefield: Ideology in Greek Warfare', in: A. Powell (ed.), *The Greek World*, London/New York, 153–178.
Vlassopoulos, K. (2007), 'Free Spaces: Identity, Experience and Democracy in Classical Athens', in: *Classical Quarterly* 57, 33–52.
Wallace, R.W. (2003), '*Phainein* in Athenian laws and legal procedures', in: F.J.F. Nieto/G. Thür (eds.), *Symposion 1999: Vorträge zur griechischen und hellenistischen Rechtsgeschichte (Pazo de Mariñân, La Coruña, 6.-9. September 1999)*, Köln, 167–181.
Wijma, S.M. (2014), *Embracing the Immigrant: The Participation of Metics in Athenian Polis Religion (5th-4th century BC)*, Stuttgart.
Zelnick-Abramovitz, R. (1998), 'Supplication and Request: Application by Foreigners to the Athenian *Polis*', in: *Mnemosyne* 51, 554–573.

William Furley
Religious Arguments in Antiphon Rhetor

Abstract: This chapter examines the occurrences and nature of references to religion in the extant speeches of Antiphon Rhetor. The term religion is meant to cover references to the gods, their worship and their influence on humanity. It is found that such references are not rare and by no means trivial. Particularly in homicide cases the gods were thought to take particular interest, as life was (at least in the moral structure of Attic forensic oratory) sacrosanct and its unlawful taking constituted a religious crime which involved the gods and their regard for justice. A murderer was not just a wicked person, but an offender against the divine order. However, whilst we might think such a position was at odds with a purely rational regard for the facts of the case that establish a person's guilt, we find that the gods' position on a certain case was subject to the same sophistic vying for the rhetorical advantage as were other aspects of the case. In other words, religion was not "the other" but rather a key factor in weighing arguments from probability. In this sense, the forensic rhetoric of Antiphon reflects Athens' intellectual history at a point where respect for the gods coalesced with thought experiments of the sophistic movement.

In Antiphon's second *Tetralogy*, a case of a boy accidentally killed by a flying javelin in the gymnasium, the prosecutor asserts a remarkable point about the role of divine judgement (theodicy) in the case.[1] If, on the one hand, he says, the misfortune (ἀτυχία) happened without the god's guiding hand (ὑπὸ μηδεμιᾶς ἐπιμελείας τοῦ θεοῦ), then the youthful perpetrator deserves to be punished because it was his fault (ἁμάρτημα). If, on the other hand, the god had placed a curse (κηλίς) on the boy because of his godlessness (ἀσεβοῦντι), then it is hardly right to stand in the way of divine intervention (τὰς θείας προσβολάς). I say remarkable because it shows that at this juncture of rhetorical history, some time in the second half of the 5th century,[2] a speaker could still operate with the Homeric concept of a god's steering hand behind the throw of a lance. Essentially, it shows

---

1 It is of some interest that Perikles and Protagoras had apparently debated just such a case: Plutarch, *Perikles* 36. See Carawan 1993, 238–239, who suggests that the debate, if real, may be placed in the forties, or somewhat later, of the 5th century.
2 Many have thought the *Tetralogies* are earlier than the extant court speeches: thirties, perhaps, of the 5th century? Edwards 2000 has argued that Antiphon's work as *logographos* may

that the belief in, or possibility of belief in, theodicy along epic lines was relevant in an Athenian court of law, where "reasoned" argumentation (*entechnoi pisteis*) from logical probabilities was already far advanced. Life still had a divine superstructure. Behind a homicide case divine will was still a relevant factor, or at least a concept which had to be reckoned with by a speaker.[3]

I do not mean to imply that there is anything "primitive" about this. It is not as if we are dealing with a relic of superstition in the otherwise rational and legal structure of Athenian legislation. Far rather, as we shall see, litigants applied the same logic of rational probability to what we would call "religious arguments" as they did to profane aspects of the case. However, there is something elevated, or perhaps sanctimonious, about litigants' references to the gods in Antiphon. Their speech slips easily from "justice" to "the divine"; from "just" to "god-fearing", from "wicked" to "impious". The religious terminology is a kind of higher register, with perhaps greater rhetorical impact, drawn upon by a speaker for effect and for the rhetorical capital to be made through a "bow to the gods".[4] Nor do I want to imply that the religious arguments we shall be considering here are hypocritical in any way. As I have argued elsewhere (and still believe)[5] it is simply that the intellectually brilliant Athenians had by no means given up their "belief" in the gods by this time; an ἄθεος, atheist (we might think), was, at this time, someone who believed in unconventional gods, like Socrates, not a denier of gods *tout court*. Conversely, the "man in the street" was still deeply involved in, and influenced by, the whole apparatus of state religion. The question of "belief" is hardly relevant. One does not conduct an elaborate and expensive state ritual such as the Great Dionysia unless one "believes" in the great god in whose honour it was performed.

The extant speeches of Antiphon (excluding the fragments) all concern cases of homicide, murder or death by misadventure.[6] The first speech is the prosecution of the speaker's stepmother for the murder of his father by poisoning. Then, in the traditional order, come three tetralogies, that is, two pairs of speeches for

---

have begun earlier than previously thought: again perhaps in the thirties rather than the twenties of the 5th century?

3 This is not the place to consider whether the *Tetralogies* might not be genuine works of Antiphon, as has been argued by e.g. Sealey 1984 and Carawan 1993.

4 King 1955, 371 concludes his paper with the words: "thus, it is clear that Greek rhetoricians used the appeal to religion extensively and effectively as a means of persuasion. The examples cited show that it formed part of the customary pattern of rhetorical practice".

5 Furley 1996.

6 There are fragments extant from his other speeches, for example the speech in his own defence. Unfortunately the new OCT, Dilts and Murphy 2018, has chosen not to include fragments.

the defence and the prosecution respectively. The first concerns the death of a man and his servant while out walking at night. The second concerns the accidental killing of a boy in the gymnasium who was struck by a flying javelin thrown in practice. The third concerns an elderly man who died as a result of becoming embroiled in a brawl while both parties were under the influence of alcohol. The tetralogies have been considered to be theoretical, or didactic, or perhaps protreptic in purpose ("model speeches"), showing Antiphon's ability to argue both sides of a case with sophistic logic.[7] Then come two further "real" speeches. First, the defence of Euxitheos, accused of murdering Herodes while they were both travelling by boat from Mytilene. This is a cloak-and-dagger piece whereby the *corpus delicti* was never discovered. Finally, the defence of a wealthy gentleman accused of poisoning a boy member of a chorus while they were practising on his premises.

1 The gods and homicide

The character of all these speeches concerning as they do the loss of human life is very important for the religious dimension of the lawsuits. For, as Antiphon states, "the homicide laws come to us from the gods and the ancestors".[8] The sentiment is echoed in 6.2: "and all men would praise the laws which exist concerning these matters (sc. homicide) as being the finest of all our laws and the most holy".[9] Such cases were heard, as a rule, in the court of the Areopagus, although *On the Murder of Herodes* was heard in the agora,[10] as the prosecution had chosen the trick of accusing Euxitheos of *kakourgia*, malpractice, possibly with a view to earning money from him and leaving the way open for a murder trial later.[11] Of great importance is the concept of *miasma* or religious pollution which arises

---

7 See Eucken 1996, who argues for the theoretical nature of *Tetr.* 2, at least.
8 1.3: τιμωρῆσαι πρῶτον μὲν τοῖς νόμοις τοῖς ὑμετέροις, οὓς παρὰ τῶν θεῶν καὶ τῶν προγόνων διαδεξάμενοι κατὰ τὸ αὐτὸ ἐκείνοις περὶ τῆς καταψηφίσεως δικάζετε.
9 The full passage runs (6.2): Καὶ τοὺς μὲν νόμους οἳ κεῖνται περὶ τῶν τοιούτων πάντες ἂν ἐπαινέσειαν κάλλιστα νόμων (ἁπάντων) κεῖσθαι καὶ ὁσιώτατα. Ὑπάρχει μὲν γὰρ αὐτοῖς ἀρχαιοτάτοις εἶναι ἐν τῇ γῇ ταύτῃ, ἔπειτα τοὺς αὐτοὺς αἰεὶ περὶ τῶν αὐτῶν, ὅπερ μέγιστον σημεῖον νόμων καλῶς κειμένων. Following the first sentence, the second translates "for it is a fact that they are the oldest [laws] in this country, further that they remain unaltered with the same content, which is the strongest sign of laws which are well formulated".
10 Perhaps in the court of the Palladion.
11 The accusation was by *apagōgē*: Carawan 1993, 245.

when a human life is taken. The court case is seen as a kind of purification rite for this pollution, which can affect an entire community.¹²

The *Third Tetralogy* opens with interesting remarks on the religious underpinning of homicide cases.¹³ Let us first look at these in some detail, as they provide a framework for understanding most of the other religious remarks in Antiphon's speeches. As stated, the hypothetical speech concerns the death of an older man through blows from a younger man. The first speech for the prosecution outlines his view of the sanctity of human life:

> For the god, through a desire to create the human race, engendered our earliest ancestors, and gave them as foster-parents the earth and the sea, so that we would not die out before reaching old age through a lack of the necessities of life. Now whoever, after our life has been held in esteem by the god, kills any one of us unlawfully, he sins with regard to the gods and he overturns the institutions of men. (*Tetr.* 3a2)¹⁴

A generalised and impersonal god is mentioned, not any specific deity such as Zeus.¹⁵ The description of the origin of man is hardly mythical but rather a highly condensed, almost shorthand, account of man's divine origin and the anthropocentric view of the environment: earth and sea are there to feed us.¹⁶ Because of this "esteem" which the gods have granted humanity (ὑπὸ τοῦ θεοῦ ἀξιωθέντος τοῦ βίου ἡμῶν), it is an offence to take human life unlawfully.¹⁷

---

12 See generally Parker 1983. Carawan 1993, 249–254 is quite a detailed treatment of this subject in Antiphon's *Tetralogies*, but the tendency of his argument is that the *Tetralogies* differ in some fundamental ways from the court speeches in this matter, whilst I will suppose that the former provide the basis for understanding the latter.
13 Cf. Eucken 1996, 80–81.
14 Ὅ τε γὰρ θεὸς βουλόμενος ποιῆσαι τὸ ἀνθρώπινον φῦλον τοὺς πρῶτον γενομένους ἔφυσεν ἡμῶν, τροφέας τε παρέδωκε τὴν γῆν καὶ τὴν θάλασσαν, ἵνα μὴ σπάνει τῶν ἀναγκαίων προαποθνήσκοιμεν τῆς γηραιοῦ τελευτῆς. Ὅστις οὖν, τούτων ὑπὸ τοῦ θεοῦ ἀξιωθέντος τοῦ βίου ἡμῶν, ἀνόμως τινὰ ἀποκτείνει, ἀσεβεῖ μὲν περὶ τοὺς θεούς, συγχεῖ δὲ τὰ νόμιμα τῶν ἀνθρώπων.
15 Gagarin makes the point against Latte 1920, that there is no one overarching god responsible for justice in Greek rhetoric, unlike the one authoritative god in early German justice. Against that one might point to Hesiod's equation in the *Theogony* of the rule of Zeus with justice on earth, but it is true that references to the god(s) in rhetoric tend to be of this generalising, anonymous type.
16 Eucken 1996, 80: "in aller Knappheit ist hier eine naturrechtliche Theorie entworfen, wie sie uns in der Sophistik auch in anderen Ausprägungen begegnet".
17 See Eucken 1996 for a discussion of a basic discrepancy between this fundamental principle – it is always a crime against humanity and religion to take a human life – and the obvious fact that some "Tötungsdelikte" are condoned in real life (and at Athens) as being justifiable, e.g. in self-defence.

To this one may add a passage from the sixth speech (*On the Choreutes*) which elaborates upon the fate of the culprit who is accursed. Such a person is "excluded by law from the divine services of the city, from festival meetings and sacrifices, which are the most important and most venerable of human institutions".[18] A man guilty of manslaughter, even if there is no one to bring the matter to trial, "purifies himself out of respect of custom and divine law, and keeps away from the (institutions) mentioned in the law, hoping thereby to act most correctly".[19]

To return to the exposition in the *Third Tetralogy*: it follows that homicide, having deprived a human of his god-given life, causes an imbalance in the natural (or rather, divine) order:

> For the deceased person, having been deprived of that which the god granted him, understandably leaves behind him, as the god's instrument of vengeance, malignant avenging spirits; those who judge wrongly or bear false witness, join with the perpetrator in sin and introduce an alien pollution into their own houses. (*Tetr.* 3a3)[20]

It is not just that a trial is likely to follow a violent death, as still happens nowadays, too. Rather, the death has set in motion a process of divine retribution. Malign spirits roam the earth as agents of the god's vengeance, just as the Erinyes pursue the matricide Orestes on the tragic stage.[21] Then the speaker draws the judges and witnesses in the case into the scope of divine powers. If they fail to judge and testify justly they will incur a share in the killer's guilt.[22] The *miasma* spreads like a contagion. Actually this might seem to go against the precautions

---

18 *On the Choreutes* 4: καὶ νόμῳ εἴργεσθαι πόλεως ἱερῶν ἀγώνων θυσιῶν, ἅπερ μέγιστα καὶ παλαιότατα τοῖς ἀνθρώποις. Cf. 5.10 where it is said that those convicted of murder were excluded from the Agora. And 5.62: this banishment from public institutions "deprives the person of the sacred and profane (sc. institutions) and other things which are of greatest moment to men, and rated most highly" (ἀπεστέρει δὲ αὐτὸν ἱερῶν καὶ ὁσίων καὶ τῶν ἄλλων ἅπερ μέγιστα καὶ περὶ πλείστου ἐστὶν ἀνθρώποις).
19 *On the Choreutes* 4: ὥστε καὶ ἄν τις κτείνῃ τινὰ ὧν αὐτὸς κρατεῖ καὶ μὴ ἔστιν ὁ τιμωρήσων, τὸ νομιζόμενον καὶ τὸ θεῖον δεδιὼς ἁγνεύει τε ἑαυτὸν καὶ ἀφέξεται ὧν εἴρηται ἐν τῷ νόμῳ, ἐλπίζων οὕτως ἂν ἄριστα πράξειν. An ancient form of "self-isolation"!
20 Ὅ τε γὰρ ἀποθανών, στερόμενος ὧν ὁ θεὸς ἔδωκεν αὐτῷ, εἰκότως θεοῦ τιμωρίαν ὑπολείπει τὴν τῶν ἀλιτηρίων δυσμένειαν, ἣν οἱ παρὰ τὸ δίκαιον κρίνοντες ἢ μαρτυροῦντες, συνασεβοῦντες τῷ ταῦτα δρῶντι, οὐ προσῆκον μίασμα εἰς τοὺς ἰδίους οἴκους εἰσάγονται.
21 Eucken 1996, 80 adds the cases of Alkmaion and Oedipus in this context.
22 Judges cannot shirk their responsibility to convict and punish a miscreant just because the gods are angry at the crime; as Demosthenes 19.71 reminds them, it is the job of the judges to punish wrongdoing *on behalf of the gods* when they catch a criminal; it is up to the gods when the criminal escapes detection.

taken in a homicide case to avoid this spread of pollution by holding session under an open sky.²³ But perhaps the point here is not the contagion through proximity (as we catch viruses in crowded public spaces) but rather the guilt incurred by convicting, or testifying against, the wrong man.²⁴

Finally, the prosecution is liable to the contagion if it prosecutes unjustly:

> And we, the prosecutors on behalf of the deceased, if we pursue the innocent through some unrelated enmity, by failing to avenge the deceased person, we too will incur the frightful spirits of the deceased who demand vengeance; and if we unjustly bring conviction upon the innocent, we are subject to the penalties for killing. By persuading you (sc. the judges) to act unjustly, we become responsible for your error (sc. of judgement). (*Tetr.* 3a4)

Here we encounter a new term, *prostropaios*, a word of almost pure tragic pedigree, which derives from προστρέπω (-ομαι), supplicate, or "turn to for help".²⁵ Here the *alitērioi* stirred into action by killing are represented as supplicating the members of court for justice. Only by just punishment of the truly guilty man will their thirst for vengeance on behalf of the dead man be stilled.

Both the second and third sections quoted here read somewhat like oaths: the judges and witnesses on the one hand, and the prosecution on the other, are said to be bound by the terms of their office to *act justly*, otherwise they too will incur their own *alitērioi*. In an oath, the typical form was to swear (ἦ μήν) by a certain god or gods who are called upon to destroy the oath-taker and his family if he commits perjury. We know that all the parties at a homicide trial took such oaths prior to hearing the case.²⁶ Euxitheos in the Herodes murder case is incensed that the prosecution has avoided taking such oaths by making his trial one of *kakourgia* rather than *phonos*.²⁷

This scheme – murder leads to *miasma* of the perpetrator and stirs avenging spirits of the victim which can only be appeased by just punishment of the guilty

---

23 Ant. 5.11. The aim is not to ὁμωρόφιος γίγνεσθαι (5.11), to be under the same roof, as the criminal(s).
24 Zinsmaier 1998, 418, points to an interesting passage in Gorgias' *Palamedes* 34 ff., with similar sentiments.
25 On tragedy and early Attic rhetoric see Riedweg 2000. Carawan 1993, 253 finds Antiphon's treatment of religion in the *Tetralogies* to be "borrowed from drama, not from the courts".
26 6.6: "For precisely these reasons (there are) these rituals, oaths, sacrifices and proclamations" (Αὐτῶν δὲ τούτων ἕνεκα οἵ τε νόμοι καὶ αἱ διωμοσίαι καὶ τὰ τόμια καὶ αἱ προρρήσεις). See King 1955, 367; MacDowell 1963, 90–100.
27 See 5.12; and cf. 1.8 and 1.28 for the διωμοσία sworn by defendant and prosecutor; 6.14 for the *horkōtēs* responsible for administering the oaths at a homicide trial. On oaths sworn before impiety trials cf. And. 1.31–32. Kurt Latte, *Heiliges Recht* concentrates on oaths in early Greek justice for their religious component.

party[28] – is glimpsed, or becomes explicit, throughout Antiphon's extant works. Above all it allows the rhetorical shift in register from just to holy, unjust to sinful, a shift which is omnipresent, but most prevalent in the introduction to and peroration of a speech.[29] The guilty party is a sinner, not just a criminal. All parties in the court case may be said to εὐσεβεῖν, act according to divine law, if they act justly, and conversely to sin, ἀσεβεῖν, if they act unjustly. Crimes are not just ἄδικα but also ἀνόσια, ἄθεα, ἀθέμιτα.

Let us look at one example in more detail. In the *Stepmother* speech (1), the crime allegedly committed by the stepmother of the plaintiff is presented in an extended peroration in a religious light. The plaintiff asks the judges to become the "avengers" of the dead man "for all eternity" (1.21: τὸν ἀΐδιον χρόνον τιμωροὺς γενέσθαι). Conversely, the brother (defending the stepmother) shows no pity for the victim, who "deserves to receive the pity of the judges, their support and avenging action, as he died in a godless, pitiable way before his allotted time at the hands of the least appropriate people" (1.21: ὃς ἄξιος καὶ ἐλέου καὶ βοηθείας καὶ τιμωρίας παρ' ὑμῶν τυχεῖν, ἀθέως καὶ ἀκλεῶς πρὸ τῆς εἱμαρμένης ὑφ' ὧν ἥκιστα ἐχρῆν τὸν βίον ἐκλιπών). The conviction of the accused will be "more just and more god-fearing in the eyes of both gods and men" for the judges (1.25: καὶ γὰρ (ἂν) δικαιότερον καὶ ὁσιώτερον καὶ πρὸς θεῶν καὶ πρὸς ἀνθρώπων γίγνοιτο ὑμῖν). The stepmother herself "respected neither gods nor heroes nor men" (1.27: αὕτη οὔτε θεοὺς οὔθ' ἥρωας οὔτ' ἀνθρώπους αἰσχυνθεῖσα). And finally the speaker makes a dark reference to the "underworld gods" who will "take care of those wronged" (1.31: οἶμαι δὲ καὶ θεοῖς τοῖς κάτω μέλειν οἳ ἠδίκηνται). These passages show how the speaker peppers his closing remarks with references to the "justice of the gods", the "impiety of the guilty party" and the necessity for

---

28 For the religious register of the passage see Eucken 1996, 79: "welcher Rechtswelt dieses wichtige nicht-staatliche Gesetz angehört, wird aus den Tetralogien selbst ersichtlich. Sie geben alle drei in ungewöhnlicher Dichte und Eindrücklichkeit der religiösen Vorstellung Ausdruck, dass Mord befleckt und die Getöteten, die ohne Sühnung bleiben, sich rächen. Anklage und Verteidigung verweisen in allen Plädoyers in je verschiedener, ihren Zwecken entsprechender Weise auf ein solches Walten höherer Mächte, im Fall des vorsätzlichen Mordes ebenso wie in dem der unbeabsichtigten Tötung. Es betrifft den Täter sowie alle, die die Aufgabe der Vergeltung nicht wahrnehmen, und schliesslich die ganze Gemeinde, so dass, wenn ein Unschuldiger bestraft oder der wahre Täter nicht bestraft wird, ein allgemeines Unheil droht".

29 King 1955, 365. King sees in the appeal to "holy justice" at beginnings and ends of speeches an attempt by the speaker to portray himself as a pious man and his opponent, conversely, as a scoundrel. This type of language is designed, according to King, to show the "good character" of the speaker. This is plausible.

"vengeance" on behalf of the dead father. These remarks are fully in accord with the long theoretical passage of *Tetr.* 3, with which I started.³⁰

2 Proofs and the divine

But how was the court to know what the gods' will *was* in these lawsuits? The conceptual framework sketched above appears to have been generally accepted by all parties; at any rate there is no attempt to contest it in extant speeches. That a man guilty of manslaughter acquired a *miasma*, and that the "spirits of revenge" of the dead required appeasement through the just conviction of the guilty party, were facts of life, or society. But how to tell the guilty and the innocent apart? For an accused person did not go down without a struggle.³¹ He fought with all possible arguments for an acquittal, particularly if he had Antiphon as his *logographos*. I think we can recognise, broadly, two possible answers, or partial answers to this question. On the one hand, there was the whole panoply of divine signs, from extispicy at sacrifice to presumed divine intervention in cases such as ships sinking. On the other, we observe the speakers of Antiphon's logographic speeches and the *Tetralogies* applying logical reasoning to the *likelihood* of the god's possible intervention (theodicy).

One might align these two approaches with Aristotle's *atechnoi pisteis*, "unreasoned proofs" and *entechnoi pisteis*, "reasoned proofs", as I would like to translate these terms.³² Unreasoned proofs are those which apply without any interpretation or reasoning, such as laws themselves, contracts, the evidence of witnesses, tortured slaves, material evidence etc. Reasoned proofs are those

---

30 Further examples abound, e.g.: 5.88: to convict the wrong man is an "error and a sin towards the gods and the laws" (ἁμαρτία καὶ ἀσέβειά ἐστιν εἴς τε τοὺς θεοὺς καὶ εἰς τοὺς νόμους); 6.3: judges' interest in deciding a murder charge is "mainly for the sake of the gods and piety" (μάλιστα μὲν τῶν θεῶν ἕνεκα καὶ τοῦ εὐσεβοῦς); 6.7: corrupt motives of prosecution despite professed piety (οὗτοι (μὲν) γὰρ τὴν μὲν δίωξιν εὐσεβείας ἕνεκά φασι ποιεῖσθαι καὶ τοῦ δικαίου, τὴν δὲ κατηγορίαν ἅπασαν πεποίηνται διαβολῆς ἕνεκα καὶ ἀπάτης).
31 Although it is interesting that the defendant in the *Third Tetralogy* leaves the second defence speech to his friends, as he has "withdrawn" (ὑπαπέστη = run away? Thus Eucken 1996, 81).
32 They are usually translated "artistic" and "nonartistic" proofs; see Gagarin 1990. Somehow these words give the wrong impression. On p. 24 Gagarin says that πίστις should not be translated "proof", but "evidentiary material". That is such a circumlocution, however, that I will stick to "proof". In essence πίστις is something which lends credibility to a person or thought. The mutilation of the Herms was a *pistis* for the participants, proving their loyalty to a cause (And. 1.67.5).

which apply the principle of "probability" (εἰκός or τὰ εἰκότα) to the available facts of the case:³³ "is it probable that the older man would, of his own accord, have attacked the younger and stronger man in the street?" (a point in the *Third Tetralogy*). Accordingly, one might say arguments from religious signs are "unreasoned proofs", as they simply say what the signs appear to signify, whilst the arguments concerning the *interpretation* of divine will are clearly (as we shall see) "reasoned proofs".³⁴ In fact, there are hardly any divine signs, pure and simple, cited by Antiphon's speakers. Rather they are all "contaminated" by reasoned argument. That is to say, they are treated as evidence no differently to other types of evidence, including slaves' testimony under torture. The only real *atechnoi pisteis* to appear are witnesses who are called forward to testify. Mostly, their testimony is simply left to stand on its own merit, although there is argument in the *First Tetralogy* about the merit of the evidence of the servant who died alongside his master when they were both attacked in the street at night (*Tetr.* 1c4).

On the first class, those of signs, the speaker of 5.81 says:

> Furthermore, it is obligatory to cast your (the judges') vote not least on the strength of the signs from the gods concerning these matters. For you govern the community of the city reliably when you place greatest trust in these (signs), whether it be with regard to external dangers, or to matters outside such dangers (Ant. 5.81).³⁵

Not so many divine signs are mentioned overtly in the extant speeches. Euxitheos in the fifth speech on the murder of Herodes says the prosecution would certainly have cited all the ships which had sunk with Euxitheos on board, all the sacrifices

---

33 Hoffman 2008 sees the primary sense of εἰκός in rhetoric as "verisimilitude", through the word's derivation from ἔοικα, "I look like" or "resemble" something: "an account has the quality of verisimilitude when it resembles or is similar to what is known to be true" (p. 3). Actually that definition is problematic because *eikos*-arguments are used by orators precisely because it is *not* known what is true! The point is clearly made by Zinsmaier 1998. Other aspects of Hoffman's paper are questionable, too, in my opinion: that ancient *eikos* has no similarity to the modern statistical sense of "probability" does not require arguing.
34 King 1955, 363, opts for a different approach, saying that appeals to religion could fall in all of Aristotle's three types of persuasion, viz. "(1) appeals to the direct evidence of the gods as manifested in events, or by the gods in person, or by oracles; (2) appeals to precedents established by the gods; (3) a more general class of appeals varying with the particular circumstances of the case". He then proceeds to scour the Greek orators for examples of all three. I am not sure the *dihaeresis* really works, as most references to religion in the orators fall into more than one, or all three, categories.
35 χρὴ δὲ καὶ τοῖς ἀπὸ τῶν θεῶν σημείοις εἰς τὰ τοιαῦτα οὐχ ἥκιστα τεκμηραμένους ψηφίζεσθαι. Καὶ γὰρ τὰ τῆς πόλεως κοινὰ τούτοις μάλιστα πιστεύοντες ἀσφαλῶς διαπράσσεσθε, τοῦτο μὲν τὰ εἰς τοὺς κινδύνους ἥκοντα, τοῦτο δὲ [εἰς] τὰ ἔξω τῶν κινδύνων. See King 1955, 363–364.

he had attended which had failed to obtain appropriate omens, if there had been any. In this case, however, reasons Euxitheos, he had sailed on many ships without mishap and attended many sacrifices which had obtained quite satisfactory signs (sc. from examination of the entrails). So, surely this *absence* of negative divine signs works in his favour. The argument can be closely paralleled with Andocides *De mysteriis*, in the passage where Andocides refutes the prosecution's case that the gods had led him to Athens now where trial and punishment await him. He says that when they (the gods) had him at their mercy on the ship sailing to Athens, surely they would have punished him by sinking the ship if they had so wished (*De mysteriis* 137). Again, an argument from a negative sign: no sinking ship, no divine anger.[36]

One or two other passages show the speaker basing an argument on the *miasma* topos. In 6.40 (*On the Choreutes*), for example, the defendant says it was strange that his present accuser, Philokrates, touched his arm and addressed him by name in the Bouleutērion before many witnesses *after* the death of the choreut. Clearly Philokrates did not consider him polluted by the death then.[37] The religious motif of *miasma* is again used in an argument from probability to prove the speaker's innocence: "is it likely these men would have associated with me in the *Bouleutērion*, if they had thought me guilty?" (i.e. it was all a plot when they accused him later of the poisoning of the choreut).

We can imagine, then, that the prosecution may have cast around for signs that *miasma* attached to the accused person, or that a *kēlis* from the gods had

---

36 Another clear use of a religious sign occurs 5.110–116. Andocides is accused of laying a suppliant branch on the altar of the Eleusinion at Athens during the Mysteries, which is illegal. His accusers say he did this in ignorance of the law: clearly the gods led him astray so that he could be punished. Andocides retorts with the sophistic deployment of logic which we find in Antiphon, too. He points out that, when the *kēryx* asked who had placed the branch on the altar, he had not answered. Now, if his enemies were right that he had *placed* the branch in ignorance of the law, then surely the gods had *saved* him when he did not own up. It turned out that not Andocides had placed the branch on the altar, but Kallias, his enemy, wishing to implicate Andocides in an impious act. A clear case of the dastardly manipulation of divine signs!

37 "Finally, O Zeus and all you gods, this very same Philokrates, standing beside me on the stage in the *Bouleutērion* before the Council, took my arm and spoke to me, addressing me by name, and I him. So it seemed strange to the Council, when it heard that I had been forbidden access to the civic institutions by the very men whom they had seen associating with me on the previous day and conversing with me" (Τὸ τελευταῖον, ὦ Ζεῦ καὶ θεοὶ πάντες, Φιλοκράτης αὐτὸς οὑτοσὶ ἐν τῷ βουλευτηρίῳ ἐναντίον τῆς βουλῆς, ἑστὼς μετ' ἐμοῦ ἐπὶ τοῦ βήματος, ἁπτόμενος ἐμοῦ διελέγετο, ὀνόματι οὗτος ἐμὲ προσαγορεύων, καὶ ἐγὼ τοῦτον, ὥστε δεινὸν δόξαι εἶναι τῇ βουλῇ, ἐπειδὴ ἐπύθετο προειρημένον μοι εἴργεσθαι τῶν νομίμων ὑπὸ τούτων οὓς ἑώρων μοι τῇ προτεραίᾳ συνόντας καὶ διαλεγομένους).

struck him, as a way of arguing for the man's guilt. Conversely, the defendant was obliged to argue that events showed rather that *miasma* did not attach to him, nor were any *alitērioi* out to get him.[38] In a way such jockeying for position in the field of religious status might be compared to modern "character" assessments in trials. A person of otherwise exemplary character might be viewed differently by the judge and the jury compared to one with a history of crime or misconduct. Let us look again at the passage from the second speech for the prosecution in the *Second Tetralogy* with which I began, and its context.

3 *Tychē* and theodicy in the *Second Tetralogy*

The speech follows on from the emotive appeal of the defendant's father in the first speech for the defence: "so, respecting the piety of the deeds done and their justice, acquit us both piously and justly, and do not inflict untimely disaster on this most miserable pair of us, father and son".[39] The plaintiff (the father of the boy killed in the gymnasium) addresses the judges in matching fashion: "gentlemen of the jury, punishers of godless deeds, discerners of the god-fearing" (2c3: ὦ ἄνδρες ἀνοσίων ἔργων τιμωροί, ὁσίων δὲ διαγνώμονες). Although the speaker asserts his trust in justice, yet he admits to a doubt about the workings of the supernatural: "and yet, having no faith in the relentless workings of Fate" (τῆι σκληρότητι τοῦ δαίμονος ἀπιστῶν), I fear that I will not only lose the company of my son, but will live to see him convicted by you of having caused his own death" (2c4). We note the anonymous force named by the speaker as ὁ δαίμων, a force which can appear cruel and relentless and is probably to be equated with "Fate" here.

These remarks in the religious register lead up to the passage we have already seen (2c8) but which here should be reconsidered.

---

38 King 1955, 364 cites further appeals to the gods as witnesses: Aeschines 1.128–130, with Demosthenes' riposte in 19.243; Demosthenes, *On the False Embassy* 297. Carawan 1993, 250, argues that the *Tetralogies* differ from the court speeches in extending the threat of pollution from the culprit to the judges themselves (if they find the wrong man guilty). On p. 252 Carawan seems to imply that the author of the *Tetralogies* may have been influenced in this matter by Lysias 12.99–100, delivered after the fall of the Thirty. I am not sure what to make of that.

39 *Tetr.* 2b12: Τήν τε οὖν εὐσέβειαν τούτων τῶν πραχθέντων καὶ τὸ δίκαιον αἰδούμενοι ὁσίως καὶ δικαίως ἀπολύετε ἡμᾶς, καὶ μὴ ἀθλιωτάτω δύο πατέρα καὶ παῖδα ἀώροις συμφοραῖς περιβάλητε. We note again the point made above that the register of a speaker can slip easily from mundane justice to heavenly piety.

> He (sc. the defendant = father of the spear-thrower) does not deserve to be acquitted through the unlucky nature of his (boy's) error. For if misfortune occurs through no will of the god, it is right and proper that misfortune befalls the aberrant person as it was a mistaken action. If, however, divine anger strikes the agent because of his impiety, it is not right to hinder divine retribution from running its course. (*Tetr.* 2c8)[40]

The defendant has argued that it was simply bad luck that his boy's spear struck the other boy.[41] Now the plaintiff focuses attention on the question of luck, or rather bad luck, in the case. Using the technique of *dihaeresis*, making a distinction, he argues that if it was pure bad luck that the spear of the defendant's son struck the other boy, nevertheless he deserves to suffer the consequences as it was *his mistake* (*hamartēma*) which led to the death. If, on the other hand, he had been struck by a divine *kēlis* because he was impious, then who are we, he says, to stand in the way of the gods' will?

Conceptually, the argument depends on belief in "god's punishment", what has been termed theodicy. If a person is struck by lightning, or a flying javelin, one possible interpretation is that god willed it because the victim was impious. An argument impossible to prove, but no less compelling for that reason, granted shared belief in the conceptual framework.[42] What is clever, and a reflection upon Antiphon's *deinotēs* (skill in argument), is the distinction of two possible interpretations of the javelin thrower's guilt, to the exclusion of all else: either (1) pure bad luck, but still the miscreant's fault, so deserving of punishment or (2) an impious victim of divine justice, so obviously deserving of punishment. The religious belief underlying *kēlis* is manipulated by the speaker to work in his favour. Divine will is not ascertained by a medium, or some form of divination, but rather intellectual analysis.[43] In this age of developing sophistry, religion is grist to the rhetor's mill. Such manipulation of divine signs works both ways. In the speech

---

[40] Οὐ δίκαιος δὲ ἀποφυγεῖν ἐστι διὰ τὴν ἀτυχίαν τῆς ἁμαρτίας. Εἰ μὲν γὰρ ὑπὸ μηδεμιᾶς ἐπιμελείας τοῦ θεοῦ ἡ ἀτυχία γίγνεται, ἁμάρτημα οὖσα τῷ ἁμαρτόντι συμφορὰ δικαία γενέσθαι ἐστίν· εἰ δὲ δὴ θεία κηλὶς τῷ δράσαντι προσπίπτει ἀσεβοῦντι, οὐ δίκαιον τὰς θείας προσβολὰς διακωλύειν γίγνεσθαι.

[41] By the way, the victim had run into the javelin track on the bidding of the *paidotribēs*, sport teacher, to collect up the fallen javelins. It is strange that this man's role does not come under further scrutiny in the *Tetralogy* as it was clearly the reason for the victim's unlucky death.

[42] One recalls Euthyphro's observation, on hearing of the charge against Socrates, that religious accusations are "easy to make among the general public" (εὐδιάβολα τὰ τοιαῦτα πρὸς τοὺς πολλούς), *Euthyphr.* 3b8–9.

[43] Gagarin 1990, 25 points out that oaths, too, in themselves belonging to *atechnoi pisteis* were in fact manipulated this way and that by the skilled logographer; on p. 27 *ditto* for the *basanos*, interrogation under torture.

delivered by Euxitheos, he uses the *absence* of negative divine signs (sinking ships, ineffective sacrifices) as proof of his innocence. In the *Tetralogy* examined here, the plaintiff uses the hypothesis of a *kēlis* to demand the punishment of the defendant's son. Such arguments would, of course, be totally inadmissible in a modern European court of law. Their presence here does not point to the primitive level of Athenian law, but rather to the skill of the logographer (Antiphon) in manipulating the divine tokens which still had popular currency.[44]

4 The case of Herodes

It is probably significant that the one speech which was *not* delivered in a homicide case (δίκη φόνου), the fifth, *On the Murder of Herodes*, is significantly more free of appeals to the impiety of killing, avenging spirits, theodicy and such like.[45] As was mentioned above, the speaker laments the fact that his opponents have chosen a charge of *kakourgia*, malpractice, to pursue. This means they did not have to take the customary oaths prior to the trial or to participate in the usual sacrifices.

> Further, although you were required to swear the greatest and most powerful oath, calling destruction upon yourself and your family should you accuse me of other matters outside the killing itself, that I was the culprit; the point of this is so that I should not be convicted of anything beyond the deed itself, nor should I be saved if I had done many good works. (Ant. 5.11)[46]
>
> All these things you circumvented, inventing laws for yourself, so that that you could accuse me without being bound by an oath, the witnesses likewise, whereby it is required of them that, in giving testimony against me, they swear the same oath as you with their hands upon the sacrifices. Then you demand of the jury that they pass judgement in a case of

---

44 Xenophon's historical works, written in the 4th century, for example, are full of references to the omens taken by military commanders before entering upon a course of action. Victor Gysembergh and I have edited the papyri which deal in minute detail with the significance of liver omens in extispicy: Furley and Gysembergh 2015.
45 For a detailed study of this speech see Scheidweiler 1966; Ferrante 1972; Erbse 1977; Schindel 1979.
46 τοῦτο δὲ δέον σε διομόσασθαι ὅρκον τὸν μέγιστον καὶ ἰσχυρότατον, ἐξώλειαν σαυτῷ καὶ γένει καὶ οἰκίᾳ τῇ σῇ ἐπαρώμενον, ἦ μὴν μὴ ἄλλα κατηγορήσειν ἐμοῦ ἢ εἰς αὐτὸν τὸν φόνον, ὡς ἔκτεινα, ἐν ᾧ οὔτ' ἂν κακὰ πολλὰ εἰργασμένος ἡλισκόμην ἄλλῳ ἢ αὐτῷ τῷ πράγματι, οὔτ' ἂν πολλὰ ἀγαθὰ εἰργασμένος τούτοις ἂν ἐσῳζόμην τοῖς ἀγαθοῖς·

homicide by believing witnesses who are not bound by oath! You have made them untrustworthy by disregarding the statutory laws, and you believe your lawlessness should count for more than the laws themselves! (Ant. 5.12)[47]

This lack of oaths invoking the gods' wrath on perjurors and false accusations is probably the reason for the relative absence of the divine register in this speech. Whereas, in a normal *dikē phonou* the divinity is invoked in the course of the preliminary *sphagia* and the oaths, so that this apparatus can be appealed to by prosecution and defence in their speeches. The attention of the gods has, as it were, not been attracted in this case through the absence of ritual preliminaries. It is probably also significant that at the beginning (5.6) Euxitheos says that it is understandable that he is nervous as the outcome of the trial depends on τύχη, chance or fortune.[48] As we have seen in the case of the boy killed by a flying spear (*Tetr.* 2) τύχη represents a kind of alternative to theodicy. Here, then, Euxitheos does not appeal to the god to vindicate him in his innocence, but concedes that the hand of chance may go against him.

On the Murder of Herodes reads in fact rather like an ancient murder mystery story. Euxitheos and Herodes had been travelling from Mytilene to Ainos in the same ship. This had been forced to put into harbour off Methymna on Lesbos by bad weather. Rain had forced the men to transfer from their undecked vessel to a decked ship which was lying alongside. There had been drinking on board and, at some point, Herodes had apparently left the ship and gone ashore, and never returned. A slave under torture by the friends of Herodes had, apparently, denounced Euxitheos as the murderer, but when his tormentors failed to release him and he realised he was going to die anyway, although he had given them the testimony they wanted, he recanted and said Euxitheos was innocent. There was some blood found on board the ship but that was probably the blood of sheep victims from the pre-departure sacrifices (5.29).

There is no way for us of knowing whether Euxitheos was guilty or innocent. The speech is cleverly argued, by Antiphon, who may have had an interest in (1)

---

47 ἃ σὺ παρελθών, αὐτὸς σεαυτῷ νόμους ἐξευρών, ἀνώμοτος μὲν αὐτὸς ἐμοῦ κατηγορεῖς, ἀνώμοτοι δὲ οἱ μάρτυρες καταμαρτυροῦσι, δέον αὐτοὺς τὸν αὐτὸν ὅρκον σοὶ διομοσαμένους καὶ ἁπτομένους τῶν σφαγίων καταμαρτυρεῖν ἐμοῦ. Ἔπειτα κελεύεις τοὺς δικαστὰς ἀνωμότοις πιστεύσαντας τοῖς μαρτυροῦσι φόνου δίκην καταγνῶναι, οὓς σὺ αὐτὸς ἀπίστους κατέστησας παρελθὼν τοὺς κειμένους νόμους, καὶ ἡγῇ χρῆναι αὖθις τὴν σὴν παρανομίαν κρείσσω γενέσθαι αὐτῶν τῶν νόμων.
48 See Zinsmaier 1998, 403 with n. 20.

defending a seemingly hopeless case to advertise his *deinotēs*,⁴⁹ and/or (2) defending a Mytilenean and his father, who had been implicated in the revolt of Mytilene (427 BC). Antiphon may have wanted to thumb his nose at the Athenian democracy. Anyway, the speech is replete with arguments κατὰ τὰ εἰκότα, and, as we have seen, the mention of divine signs in this speech occurs only to show Antiphon's skill in employing them in the service of the probable: if there *had* been negative signs in Euxitheos' life following the death of Herodes, the prosecution would, no doubt, have jumped on these as (*atechnos*) evidence for his guilt. Conversely, since such signs are conspicuously absent from Euxitheos' subsequent life, it is probable that he is innocent.

5 The modern debate

5.1 Antiphon: Archaic or progressive?

Michael Gagarin's 1990 paper on the "Nature of proofs in Antiphon" was a rebuttal of Friedrich Solmsen's monograph arguing that Antiphon can be seen as standing at an intermediate stage of Athenian forensic rhetoric. Early Greek law, according to Solmsen (1931),⁵⁰ was decided chiefly by *atechnoi pisteis* such as *basanos*, witness statements, oaths, laws and so on, and the *entechnoi pisteis* were quite undeveloped. He argued that since *basanos* is quite prominent in Antiphon, and relatively under-represented in later 4th-century trials, this shows Antiphon at a transition between an archaic period of justice and the developing art of sophistry in rhetoric.⁵¹ Gagarin seeks to counter this position by showing (1) that there is little evidence that *atechnoi pisteis* were dominant and decisive by themselves in early disputes. Rather, from Homer onwards, Gagarin points out, disputes were decided rationally by reasoned argument. (2) The analogy of early Germanic law used by Solmsen, and, before him, Kurt Latte (1920), is inapplicable to

---

49 Thuc. 8.68. Cf. [Plutarch], *Vitae decem oratorum* 832 E; in Philostratus, *Vitae sophistarum* p. 499 we hear that "comedy" "took Antiphon to task for being cunning in lawsuits and writing speeches for defendants in a precarious position which ran counter to justice for high fees" (καθάπτεται δὲ ἡ κωμῳδία τοῦ Ἀντιφῶντος ὡς δεινοῦ τὰ δικανικὰ καὶ λόγους κατὰ τοῦ δικαίου ξυγκειμένους ἀποδιδομένου πολλῶν χρημάτων αὐτοῖς μάλιστα τοῖς κινδυνεύουσιν). Was Euxitheos one of those defendants "in a precarious position"?
50 And see the review by Zucker 1936, 442–444.
51 On the treatment and torture of slaves in Antiphon from an historical point of view see Suarez 2019.

archaic Greek trials because there is only minimal evidence of reaching a verdict then through ordeal, "supporting" oaths, divine ordinance and such like. (3) Antiphon's speeches are by no means dominated by *atechnoi pisteis*. True, the fifth speech *On the Murder of Herodes* does indeed make much of the slave's evidence obtained under torture (*basanos*) which implicated Euxitheos, but this fact reflects the nature of the prosecution's case, relying heavily as it did on this slave's testimony, rather than any "archaic" tradition still influencing Antiphon.[52] In short, Gagarin disputes the nature of archaic Greek law, maintaining that *logos* always played as important a part as witness-statements, oaths and the like: "I shall argue that Solmsen's thesis is based on a mistaken understanding of early Greek legal procedure compounded by a mistaken application of Aristotle's categories of proofs, and that he thus situates Antiphon in a falsely conceived legal tradition" (p. 23). Since Solmsen's monograph had the effect of limiting Antiphon's achievement compared to the 4th-century masters of oratory, Gagarin's corrective has the effect of "acquitting" Antiphon of a primitive or archaic bent.[53]

In my examination of the religious arguments in Antiphon's logographic speeches and the *Tetralogies*, it has become clear that religious "signs" were just as much subject to the orator's keen analytic mind and rational analysis as any other type of evidence. Religion is not cited as a form of unreasoned proof capable of deciding a case outright, but is rather subject to just the same criterion of probability as other aspects of the case. Divine signs are only cited for their *probable* implication, not as any kind of gold standard. Now this conclusion can be squared with both Solmsen's thesis and Gagarin's, depending on one's vantage point. It was precisely Solmsen's contention that the "unreasoned proofs" (including, we may assume, divine signs) are more in evidence in Antiphon than at a later stage of oratory, but are subject to the new sophistic reasoning. That is exactly what we have found in Antiphon's treatment of religious motifs in the extant speeches. They are prominent, but they are argued both ways. This might

---

[52] But slaves' evidence under torture is also important in the first speech.
[53] Carawan 1993, 242 takes on board Gagarin's criticism of Solmsen, but argues that Solmsen's case at least in speeches 1 and 6 is "strikingly apt": "thus in the extant court speeches in *dikai phonou* Solmsen's finding largely holds true, that arguments from probability and circumstantial evidence tend to center upon the 'nonartificial' or evidentiary proofs". Carawan's main argument is weakened, in my opinion, by his failure to grasp the reason why ancient murder trials were, apparently, little concerned with the facts: e.g. p. 244: "in any event, in Antiphon 1 the question of fact, whether the stepmother was implicated, does not appear to be the issue". The reason is simply that facts were rarely obtainable through lack of forensic evidence. Modern trials are of course dominated by forensic evidence, down to the last hair and drop of sweat. The ancient logographos *could* only argue from – to our minds – hair-raising (im)probabilities.

mean (with Solmsen) that religious motifs dominated trials at an earlier, more primitive stage to which Antiphon was still beholden, or we could argue, with Gagarin, that the mix of archaic-seeming religious elements and their logical deconstruction, *had always been* present in Athenian trials and does not constitute a "transitional stage" from the archaic to the sophistic. In other words, is our analysis to be read synchronically, with Gagarin, or diachronically, with Solmsen? I cannot give a definitive answer as the evidence is simply lacking, but non-forensic evidence from earlier poetic texts tends to show that the Greeks debated the meaning of divine signs from their earliest literature.

This is too large a topic to be dealt with here in detail, but let us consider a couple of examples. In Aeschylus' *Agamemnon*, Agamemnon is said to accept Calchas' interpretation of the omen of two eagles (that Artemis demanded the sacrifice of his daughter) "uncritically", implying that it could have been challenged (186: μάντιν οὔτινα ψέγων). Clearly "challenging a seer" was considered an option if his pronouncement offended. Even earlier, in the *Iliad*, the portent of the eagle and snake is interpreted in contrary ways by Poulydamas and Hektor (12.200 ff.). I would rather suggest that whilst apparent divine signs did inspire awe and fear generally, they did not *ever* prevent the logos-oriented Greeks from interpreting them according to their own agenda. There was no central Church with power to impose its own will on the laïty to the exclusion of argument.

5.2 Religion in Antiphon: Relevant or irrelevant?

A second topic: Christoph Eucken has argued that the *Tetralogies* are not so much exhibition pieces, or didactic in purpose, but are rather theoretical works much in line with the philosophical bent of Antiphon the Sophist. He places much emphasis on the religious material in the *Tetralogies*, in particular the opening paragraphs of the *Third Tetralogy*, as I have done. However, he pursues a quite different line of reasoning. Whilst I have sought to argue that this passage provides a theoretical basis enabling us to understand the rationale of the religious appeals and statements in the court speeches, he comes to a quite different conclusion. For Eucken, the paired speeches for the prosecution and defence are antinomic in purpose, essentially showing the reader that the matter at hand is quite simply aporetic and not permitting of a true verdict. All three tetralogies point in this direction: the man found killed by night on a highway without witnesses, the poor boy killed accidentally by a javelin during athletics practice, or, thirdly, the elderly man who died after being struck by a younger man in a brawl, then treated by an incompetent doctor. All these cases do indeed show how both sides of a case can be argued, as any good sophist was supposed to be able to do. But

Eucken argues that this tendency contradicts the absolute injunction of religious law which says that the guilty party in a homicide case must be punished in order to remove the *miasma* and lay to rest the unquiet spirits of revenge. Since the truth cannot be established finally, this divine law about avenging the dead is shown to be "realitätsfremd", not applicable in a real court of law. Perhaps it is valid on a higher, religious level, but it serves no real purpose in a human court of law as this must operate with fallible *doxa*.[54]

Clearly, I cannot follow Eucken in this. As he himself admits, there are many religious appeals and references in the court speeches which converge in sense with the analysis of *Tetralogy* 3. This has been the gist of my remarks. I cannot believe that the religious analyses of the *Tetralogies*, as I have outlined them, are a kind of red herring and that the purpose of all the *eikos*-arguments is to show the meaninglessness of the absolute religious prohibition on taking a human life. I would prefer to see in these passages of the *Tetralogies* not something incompatible with real legal practice, but rather the underlying belief system of the real murder cases treated by Antiphon. True, human reasoning has its limitations and *eikos* will not always be right, but that does not diminish the religious import of a murder trial.

I would suggest in conclusion that the religious elements we find primarily but not exclusively in Antiphon's *Tetralogies* are neither irrelevant to real court procedure (Eucken) nor evidence of Antiphon's pandering to the "superstitious among his audience" (Carawan). When we encounter ancient Greek *miasma*-beliefs associated with murder and manslaughter, and the idea that chthonic spirits may take revenge if the culprit is not brought to justice, we must use our imaginations appropriately. Now as then, killing is perhaps the most emotive act committed in society. It is the breaking of a taboo, the act most disturbing to a family or community. Guilt in the perpetrator, vindictive rage among the victim's relatives and friends: the emotions stirred by a killing are intense and instinctive. I would prefer to see in the religious concepts we have examined here in Athenian homicide trials a way of conceptualising, within a framework of religious belief, phenomena which we prefer to psychologise and label with scientific-sounding names such as PTSD.

---

54 Carawan 1993, 254 f. takes a similar line.

Bibliography

Carawan, E. (1993), 'The Tetralogies and Athenian Homicide Trials', in: *American Journal of Philology* 114, 235–270.
Dilts, M.R/Murphy, D.J. (eds.) (2018), *Antiphon and Andocides: Speeches (Antiphontis et Andocidis Orationes)*, Oxford.
Edwards, M.J. (2000), 'Antiphon and the Beginnings of Athenian Literary Oratory', in: *Rhetorica: A Journal of the History of Rhetoric* 18, 227–242.
Erbse, H. (1977), 'Antiphons Rede über die Ermordung des Herodes', in: *Rheinisches Museum für Philologie* 120, 209–227.
Eucken, Chr. (1996), 'Das Tötungsgesetz des Antiphon und der Sinn seiner Tetralogien', in: *Museum Helveticum* 53, 73–82.
Ferrante, D. (1972), *Antifonte 'Περὶ τοῦ Ἡρῴδου φόνου'*, Naples.
Furley, W./Gysembergh, V. (2015), *Reading the Liver. Papyrological Texts on Ancient Greek Extispicy*, Tübingen.
Furley, W. (1996), *Andokides and the Herms. A Study of Crisis in Fifth-century Athenian Religion*, London.
Gagarin, M. (1990), 'The Nature of Proofs in Antiphon', in: *Classical Philology* 85.1, 22–32.
Gagarin, M. (ed.) (1997), *Antiphon: The Speeches*, Cambridge.
Gagarin, M. (tr.) (1998), *Antiphon and Andocides*, Austin.
Hoffman, D.C. (2008), 'Concerning Eikos: Social Expectation and Verisimilitude in Early Attic Rhetoric', in: *Rhetorica: A Journal of the History of Rhetoric* 26, 1–29.
King, D.B. (1955), 'The Appeal to Religion in Greek Rhetoric', in: *Classical Journal* 50, 363–371, 376.
Latte, K. (1920), *Heiliges Recht*, Tübingen.
MacDowell, D.M. (1963), *Athenian Homicide Law*, Manchester.
Parker, R. (1983), *Miasma*, Oxford.
Riedweg, Chr. (2000), 'Der Tragödiendichter als Rhetor? Redestrategien in Euripides' Hekabe und ihr Verhältnis zur zeitgenössischen Rhetoriktheorie', in: *Rheinisches Museum für Philologie* 143, 1–32.
Scheidweiler, F. (1966), 'Antiphons Rede über den Mord an Herodes', in: *Rheinisches Museum für Philologie* 110, 319–338.
Schindel, U. (1979), 'Der Mordfall Herodes', in: *Nachr. der Akad. der Wiss. in Göttingen* 8, 1–41.
Sealey, R. (1984), 'The Tetralogies Ascribed to Antiphon', in: *Transactions of the American Philological Association* 114, 71–85.
Solmsen, F. (1931), *Antiphonstudien*, Berlin.
Suarez, D. Placido (2019), *Index thématique de l'esclavage: Antiphon*, Besançon.
Zinsmaier, Th. (1998), 'Wahrheit, Gerechtigkeit und Rhetorik in den Reden Antiphons. Zur Genese einiger Topoi', in: *Hermes* 126.4, 398–422.
Zuntz, G. (1949), 'Once again the Antiphontean Tetralogies', in: *Museum Helveticum* 6, 100–104.

Part II: **Magic and Religion**

Despina Keramida
Performing the Rhetoric of Magic in Ovid's *Epistulae Heroidum* and *Metamorphoses* 10

Abstract: This chapter aims to examine the rhetorical function of magical practices in selected Ovidian passages. The exploration of the gendered dynamics between male and female writers of *carmina* (*Her.* 9 and *Met.* 10.1–85) and sculptors of *simulacra* (*Her.* 13 and *Met.* 10.243–297) suggests that magic ritual is crucial for the poet's gendered rhetoric. Speech and sculpture, two stereotypically male means of artistic expression, become the main components of the rhetorical performance of Ovidian women. At the same time, men are seemingly absolved of any wrong-doing, as their preoccupation with magic is presented as part of their religious practices. Intention and misinterpretation are central in understanding gendered rhetoric in Ovid. The reader is encouraged to read behind the lines: this poetic juxtaposition between the unconvincing male rhetoric and the compelling multi-faceted female rhetoric illuminates the Ovidian perception of the dichotomy between male bias and female agency.

1 Introduction

Ovidian rhetoric has been a popular topic of discussion,[1] a trend that has re-surfaced in 20th century scholarship. It has been interpreted as the result of the poet's rhetorical training during his youth and has been labelled as another example of the "empty rhetoric" of early imperial literature.[2] In the last twenty years the scholarly approach towards Ovidian rhetoric has evolved into a multi-layered

---

[1] For example, Ovidian rhetoric (in the *Metamorphoses*) is the subject of Quintilian's criticism at *Inst.* 4.1.7. Curtius 1953, 66 even suggests that the use of rhetoric in Latin poetry in particular can be accredited to Ovid.
[2] On Ovid's training in declamatory rhetoric see Fantham 2009, 27–29; Kennedy 1972, 406–408; Kenney 1969, 241–263. On Ovid and declamation see Bonner 1949, 149–160; Clarke 1953, 85–99; Higham 1958, 32–48; Fränkel 1945, 5–8; Wilkinson 1955, 7. On the negative connotations attributed to the early imperial tradition see Hardie 2002a, 36 who explains that it is often labelled "rhetorical", meaning "literature of empty verbal display, as opposed to one seriously engaged with issues in the extratextual world".

https://doi.org/10.1515/9783110699623-005

interpretation through a variety of lenses, such as amatory persuasion, humour, aesthetics, the body and sexuality.³

Despite these multi-faceted readings, the importance of magical practices for the writers' and artists' rhetoric in Ovid has gone un-detected and, therefore, has remained un-explored so far. In fact, the poet's approach to rituals is generally treated as humorous, omitting from the discussion its rhetorical functionality.⁴ This chapter aims to address this issue and fill in the gap in Ovidian scholarship. To that end, the discussion will draw attention to the incorporation of magical practices in selected passages from the *Epistulae Heroidum* and the *Metamorphoses*. These two works are indicative of the poet's gendered rhetoric, as the former is comprised of rhetorical speeches in character (*prosōpopoeia*) uttered by female speakers in the single letters in particular,⁵ whereas the latter displays various rhetorical features, of which perhaps the most prominent, are the extended speeches of characters from the sphere of myth.⁶ What is more, magic rites are abundant in both works, amplifying their perception as a kind of "performative" theatre aiming to impress the audience.⁷

This chapter offers a comparative reading of female letter-writing and male artistry, in order to examine the complex Ovidian rhetoric of magic.⁸ The selected passages offer a glimpse into the categories of magical practices within the Ovidian corpus: the female letter-writers and male artists employ two main magical practices, underlining the two main manifestations of magic (love magic and curse magic) that, as it will be suggested, become crucial components of their rhetorical performance. The discussion is divided into two sections, as the selected passages are explored thematically. Section 2 studies the rhetorical func-

---

3 On the relationship between humour and the rhetorical tradition in Ovid's love poetry see Gross 1979, 305–318 who discusses three indicative examples (*Am.* 3.14, *Her.* 7, *Met.* 1.504–524) and reaches the conclusion that Ovid's witty use of common rhetorical features is integral for these passages, underlining the importance of amatory persuasion for Ovidian poetics. On the interconnection between rhetoric, sexuality and the aesthetics of the body in Ovid see Enterline 2004, 1–90.
4 Graf 1997, 30 explains that magic is an "autonomous domain within religious practice" in the Graeco-Roman world.
5 On rhetorical speech in the *Heroides* see Fantham 2009, 32–34.
6 On the rhetorical unity of the *Metamorphoses* see DuRocher 1985, 41–55.
7 Graff 1997, 65–88. Cf. Dickie 2003, 135 on the cultural and religious function of magic in Augustan Rome. On the connection between religious discourse and performative enactment see Serafim 2017, 117–118.
8 On the Ovidian relation between male and female within an epistolary framework see Lindheim 2002.

tion of the magical *carmen*, as it is illustrated both in Deianira's *Letter* 9 and Orpheus' tale at *Metamorphoses* 10.1–85. Section 3 draws attention to the use of *simulacra*, in Laodamia's Letter (*Her.* 13) and Pygmalion's tale at *Metamorphoses* 10.243–297, as means of persuasion that reveal the complexity of the Ovidian approach to magic.

This chapter puts forth the claim that the poet employs in these passages what is perceived by the modern Ovidian reader as the gendered rhetoric of magic. Ovid's awareness "of rhetoric as an art of verbal display and as performance" is reflected in these characters' stories, informing their rhetoric within a ritualistic context.[9] In these Ovidian tales the objective is the same: *carmina* are meant to be read and to be heard by their audience, whereas *simulacra* are meant to be seen by their spectators, as part of the Ovidian persuasive strategy.[10] This chapter suggests that the Ovidian writers and artists speak and perform magic in the two works, illustrating the gendered functionality of a magical performance within the boundaries of a rhetorical performance.

2 The art of magical *carmina* in *Heroides* 9 and *Metamorphoses* 10.1–85

This section of the chapter explores the Ovidian perception of *carmen*, as it is illustrated in two passages that are connected thematically, despite the chronological gap between their composition dates.[11] The term *carmen* has many definitions in Latin poetry, including the meanings of "a magical chant, spell or incantation",[12] "a song" and more generally "poetry",[13] that this chapter will explore within the framework of both the epistolary collection and the epic.

Even from its first appearances in written Latin the word *carmen* is associated with magic and, specifically, the utterance of spells through the medium of song

---

[9] Hardie 2002a, 38. On the importance of "verbal and visual displays" in early imperial culture see Hardie 2002a, 38–40.
[10] The terms reader(s) and audience are used in this discussion, as I consider them interchangeable in Ovidian poetry.
[11] On the dating of the *Heroides* see Knox 1995, 3–5. On the dating of the *Metamorphoses* see Anderson 1972, 3–6. For the Latin text of the *Heroides* I follow the Loeb edition by Showerman as revised by Goold (= Showerman 1977); the English translations quoted throughout are: Showerman 1977 for the *Heroides*; Mozley 1985 for the *Ars Amatoria*; and Miller 1984 for the *Metamorphoses*.
[12] *OLD* s.v. *carmen* 1b.
[13] *OLD* s.v. *carmen* 2a and 3 respectively.

with negative connotations.[14] Gradually the term also acquires positive implications while being associated with ritual ceremonies.[15] Its effectiveness, in fact, depends on the "ritual precision" by which the words are uttered within this religious context.[16] By the end of the 2nd century BC the word takes on the general meaning of "poetry", but still maintains the original sense of uttering a spell for ritualistic purposes.[17] However, it is the Vergilian approach to *carmina* that establishes the two meanings attributed to it throughout Augustan poetry: *carmina* ("compositions in verse, poems, songs") are the climax of a literary tradition beginning with Homer and, at the same time, the means by which the bard charms the audience and displays the power of speech.[18] Additionally, the term transcends the boundaries between literature and ritual, with the explicit connection of *carmen* with magic (*magico carmine*) evident throughout the Propertian and Horatian corpus.[19] So, when Ovid's poetic career begins, the term's importance is already established in his readers' minds.

As one of the Augustan poet's earlier works, the epistolary collection becomes a suitable playground for him to shape his poetics that are, in essence, proposing a systematic blending of literary genres.[20] The collection is comprised of fifteen single letters composed by female heroines (introducing the novel form of the female lamenting speaker), whereas the remaining six letters (the so-called double letters) are composed of mythological couples (with each female letter-

---

14 Putnam 2001, 132 explains that the term first appears in the "Laws of the Twelve Tables" with negative connotations, and specifically in the eighth table there is reference to those who use songs with evil intentions. The scholar also underlines the negative connotations of songs that brought about legal consequences by reminding us that "we hear of those who might be brought to justice for using 'song' to lure someone else's crops, presumably into their own possession". For a detailed discussion of magic in the Twelve Tables see Rives 2002, 270–290.
15 Putnam 2001, 132. On the distinction between *mala* and *bona carmina* at Hor. *Sat.* 2.1.80-85 see LaFleur 1981, 1816–1817.
16 Putnam 2001, 133.
17 Putnam 2001, 133.
18 Putnam 2001, 135.
19 Putnam 2001, 136 offers a brief list of the occurrences of the word with the meaning "poetry" in various literary genres (Lucil. 567M; Verg. *Ecl.* 8.10; Verg. *Georg.* 4.565; Prop. 1.1.24, 1.18.9, 2.28.35). On the importance of Propertian poetics for Ovidian poetry see Morgan 1977, 1–25. On the connection between witches and *carmina* see Prince 2013, 609–620 who explores Horace's Canidia (*Ep.* 5) channeling Medea.
20 For a discussion of the generic complexity and of the possible models of the collection see Jacobson 1974, 319–348; Knox 1995, 14–18; Knox 2002, 123–127. On the epistolarity of the collection see Spentzou 2003, 123–159.

writer responding to the male letter-writer).[21] Additionally, this collection becomes Ovid's first attempt at portraying mythological characters based on the medium of an extended speech. Hence, the poet himself underlines the novelty of this work in his *Ars Amatoria* with the use of the verb *novavit* (3.346).[22] More importantly for the purposes of this discussion, Ovid draws attention to the fact that the letters are meant to be sung, as established with the use of *cantentur* (3.345), implying that his reader(s) should perceive them as *carmina* intended to be heard and, thus, performed to an audience.

Heroides 9, the first passage under discussion, is the first lengthy Roman version of Hercules' and Deianira's love story, which is often read and interpreted intertextually in relation to Sophocles' *Trachiniae*.[23] This letter follows the thematic framework of the collection: Deianira has been abandoned by her husband, whose absence, both physical and emotional, prompts her letter-writing, with the specific aim of persuading him to return to her. In the core of her argumentation lies the concept of fame and its dual nature, positive and negative.

This bipolarity is reflected in the structure and the deliberative rhetoric of the letter.[24] The female letter-writer begins her speech by setting the framework for her first argument: Hercules' perception as a lover undermines his fame. To support this, she offers two examples: the hero's amatory indiscretions with Iole (9.1–26) and Omphale (9.47–118). In general, one of the rules of deliberative rhetoric is to argue that the recommended path is the most honorable, safe and advantageous.[25] So, Deianira applies this rule by arguing that Hercules' return to her is his best choice because the alternative will lead to his perception by others as effeminate, which poses a threat to Hercules' *fama*.

The second argument uttered by Deianira does not reflect so well on Hercules' portrayal. It becomes increasingly clear that she is not only trying to persuade him, but rather another recipient, establishing a more judicial environment. At lines 27–46 she casts herself in the role of the dutiful wife, subtly undermining

---

21 For a concise discussion of the narrator's perspective in the *Heroides* (i.e. the letter-writers as internal narrators and Ovid as the external narrator) see Armstrong 2005, 48–52.
22 Knox 1995, 14–15. See Ov. *Ars am.* 3.345–346: *vel tibi composita cantentur Epistula voce: / ignotum hoc aliis ille novavit opus* ("or let some Letter be read by you with practised utterance; / he first invented this art, unknown to others").
23 On this intertextual relationship see Casali 1995a, 11; Casali 1995b, 505–511; Jolivet 2001, 152–191.
24 On the three categories of speech delivered by Roman orators (judicial, deliberative, funeral) see Cic. *Inv. Rhet.* 1.7. For a discussion see Kennedy 1994, 102–106 and 121.
25 For similar argumentation in other Ovidian letters (*Her.* 5, *Her.* 16, *Her.* 17) see Fantham 2009, 33.

Hercules as he takes on the role of the absent husband. She begins her self-portrait with the impending loss of the title *uxor* being presented as the cause of her letter-writing. Deianira tells her readers that she is considered to have married well because she is called the wife of Hercules (9.27), a notion that she attempts to challenge. As she informs us, Hercules' absence is so constant (underlined with the use of *semper* at 9.33) that he is more of a guest than a husband. His absence has precipitated her religious preoccupations, a major example used to support Deianira's self-portrayal as pious.

As the Ovidian reader learns, Deianira spends her time "praying" (9.35: *votis*),[26] performing animal sacrifices (9.39), being plagued by "idle dreams" (9.39: *simulacraque inania somni*) and "omens" (9.39: *ominaque*) that take place during nighttime (9.40). The use of the adjective *arcana* at line 40 implies the magical nature of this preoccupation since one of its meanings associated with rituals is "mysterious, magical".[27] The choice of this type of language, as well as the use of the word *simulacra* (*simulacrum* means "ghost" or "image of a god", amongst others) could hint at magical practices such as performing sacrifices and evoking gods or phantoms in the pursue of love.[28] So, up to this point of the letter, Deianira is trying to convince her current internal reader (Hercules) and her external readers that she displays the socially accepted behaviour of the dutiful wife, who is concerned about her husband's life. By listing factual details of her behaviour, she is supplying her reader(s) with necessary background information that reinforces her rhetorical strategy.

Deianira's portraiture draws attention to her status as a pious wife who indulges in magical practices and rituals, to secure Hercules' safe physical return from his heroic travels. In fact, the heroine's prayers and her magical practices have been successful to a degree and here lies the irony: Hercules has, indeed, returned from his last heroic labour, but he has brought with him Iole, whom Deianira rightfully perceives as her rival. Deianira is forced, by circumstances, to use a variety of means of persuasion. She writes a letter, dominated by her voice and perspective, that aims to convince her reader(s) that Hercules' love affairs are damaging to his *fama* and only if he returns to her will that *fama* be restored, which is why she reminds the reader(s) of her role in achieving his fame: two of his labours are associated directly with the heroine, as established at lines 139–

---

26 *OLD*, s.v. *votum*.
27 *OLD*, s.v. *arcanus* 3. Also see Dickie 2003, 135 who suggests a ritualistic allusion: "the expression *sacra arcana*, is in fact used by Ovid in the *Heroides* to translate the Greek term *orgia* employed by Medea in the prayer in the *Argonautica* in which she invokes the mysteries of Hecate".
28 *OLD*, s.v. *simulacrum* 4.b.

142 (with the narration of the Achelous and Nessus episodes). Thus, her argumentation is seemingly strengthened: not only has she acted as any dutiful wife should during her husband's absence, but she has also been instrumental in the creation of the persona of the heroic Hercules in the first place.

However, the dual core of her argumentation (*fama* and ritual) is undermined. At lines 143–144 Deianira hears the rumour (*fama*) that Hercules is dying, which changes the storytelling and the heroine's rhetoric: a novel writing approach within the collection. She is no longer trying to convince Hercules to return to her, as this is now pointless. On the contrary, the heroine is attempting to persuade the reader(s) that she did not intend for her actions and specifically her use of magic to lead to Hercules' death and hence she should be redeemed in the eyes of her audience. The rhetoric of magic takes centre stage for the rest of the letter.

Deianira's association with magic is not an Ovidian novelty.[29] Ovid attributes negative connotations to the use of magic (manifesting as curse magic this time), as the letter-writer associates magical potions with deception and misinterpretation. As Deianira implies, she had not interpreted Nessus' words correctly. She assumed that the magical potion was a love potion that would ensure Hercules' love, misinterpreting completely Nessus' dubious speech at line 162: [Nessus] said, "This blood has power over love" (*"hic", dixit, "vires sanguis amoris habet"*). The reference to blood (*sanguis*) is not peculiar as it is often incorporated in literary descriptions of magical practices.[30] Furthermore, its combination with the verb *deprecor* at line 159 that has a dual meaning ("to pray" and "to ask for pardon")[31] not only re-enforces the religious tone of the heroine's argumentation, but also establishes the heroine's bid for exoneration. The rhetoric of magic is illustrated further as the heroine imagines herself as a wife accused of poisoning her husband by his son, a notion that already appears in Antiphon's legal speech Περὶ τοῦ Ἡρῴδου φόνου.[32] The fact that this kind of speech exists in the pre-Ovidian rhetorical tradition suggests that the interweaving of curse magic (poison) and rhetorical speech aimed at persuading Hercules' son, Hyllus (9.168) is not

---

[29] Previous sources portray the heroine as a witch, already from Hesiod's account of Heracles' apotheosis. On Deianira as a witch in pre-Ovidian tradition see Fulkerson 2005, 109. On the Ovidian portrayal of women as witches see Dickie 2003, 175–183.
[30] See Segal 2002, 6 and 32 n. 28 for examples of blood magic in Ovid.
[31] *OLD*, s.v. *deprecor* 1 and 2.
[32] I would like to thank Andreas Serafim for drawing attention to this intertextual relation. Wohl 2010, 33–70 argues in favour of a parallel between Antiphon's speech and Sophocles' *Trachiniae*, so it would not be unreasonable to compare it with the Ovidian version of Deianira's tale.

coincidental. Ovid's knowledge of rhetoric has provided him with a suitable persuasive strategy that he has embedded in the letter as part of the heroine's performance as a victim of magic.

The emphasis on curse magic is strengthened with the repetition of the verse, *impia quid dubitas Deianira mori?* ("wicked Deianira why do you wait to die?") four times at lines 146, 152, 158, 164. On the one hand, this refrain recalls funerary epitaphs and reminds us of the myth's tragic origins. On the other hand, this kind of a refrain is often used in magical practices. But, in the Ovidian corpus there are only two such examples, of which the first appears at *Amores* 1.6, where the poet explores the theme of magic, and the second at *Heroides* 9.[33] In Roman elegy the elegiac lover can resort to various means of persuasion, in his effort to conquer the *puella*: speech (*blanditiae*), verse (*carmen*), physical violence and magic ritual.[34] Similarly, the female letter-writer illuminates *her* means of persuasion: she writes and speaks her *carmen*, meaning both the poem and the magical spell, aiming to convince the reader(s) of her innocence and to exonerate herself. She acknowledges her use of magic, but she argues that Hercules was not the only victim. She, too, has been victimised by this magical practice, not once but twice. Her initial preoccupation with magical practices does not have the desired result, as Hercules has indeed returned, but not alone. Her second endeavour (the deceptive love potion)[35] aiming to secure Hercules' *amor* has been successful only to a degree: Hercules' death means that Deianira will retain her title as his *uxor*, thus semi-accomplishing the purpose of her letter-writing. The combined reference to the love potion and the refrain creates the notion of not simply a magical *carmen*, but also of a rhetorical *carmen*.[36] *Carmen*, thus, is perceived as a central concept in the collection as it highlights the different aspects of the heroines' letter-writing and storytelling, whose *carmina* are meant to be read and to be heard, aiming to persuade their audience.

In addition to its magical connotations, the refrain should also be interpreted as a rhetorical question that draws attention to Deianira's main self-characterisation as the dutiful wife, re-affirms it and allows her to illustrate her female agency through her funeral oration. Before hearing of Hercules' impending death, Deia-

---

[33] Bolton 1997, 434 n. 36.
[34] Cf. Dickie 2003, 135–136 on magical practices in *Ars am.* 2.
[35] On "love magic" in the Graeco-Roman world see Dickie 2000, 563–583.
[36] Fulkerson 2005, 116 notes that this type of refrain is often found in magical rituals. Also, Fulkerson 2005, 111 suggests that the heroine's association with magic reveals their desire for authorship.

nira bases her argumentation on Hercules' fame and her contribution to it, wittingly subverting the male ego. Once the story changes trajectory, the heroine, who initially presents herself as the catalyst in the creation of the heroic Hercules persona, now also assumes responsibility for his end. By doing so, she too lays claim to immortality, as her own death is interwoven with his demise.

Both deaths create the impression of a ritual sacrifice, which is foreshadowed from the superficial reference to animal sacrifice by the heroine. Hercules is burned on the pyre literally because of *amor*, hence his ritualistic sacrifice has amatory implications, whereas Deianira assumes the role of the sacrificed victim knowingly and performs a ritual sacrifice as part of her rhetorical performance: this magical performance within her rhetorical performance is meant to function as her exoneration. Her final argument focuses on the concept of intent. Although her role in Hercules' death is acknowledged, her intention was not to harm the hero. So, if her intention is not murderous and she is in fact willing to accept the consequences of her actions, albeit misguided, then why shouldn't the reader(s) perceive her as a heroine who, despite her flaws, deserves exoneration?

Accepting (or not) responsibility for one's actions is a notion implied as well in Orpheus' tale at *Metamorphoses* 10.1–85, who is cast in the role of the narrator of its Cypriot tales.[37] In contrast to the female heroines of the epistolary collection, whose preoccupation with the magical arts is seemingly viewed in a negative light, Orpheus is initially portrayed as a renowned bard and bewitcher of audiences, mourning the loss of his beloved Eurydice. However, his mourning leads to an explicit display of misogyny expressed through his *carmina* ("songs").[38] But before assuming that role, Orpheus is presented as a lamenting husband who takes matters into his own hands, travels to the Underground and pleads his case. Unlike Deianira's speech that displays elements of both deliberative rhetoric (as she extols the benefits of the most suitable choice for Hercules by attacking at the same time her rival – a typical rhetorical strategy), judicial rhetoric (as she defends herself) and funeral oration meant not for Hercules, but for herself (as she refers to her own lineage, her character, her piety), Orpheus' speech is considered more judicial with Hades functioning as the judge.[39]

---

[37] On the importance of Orpheus' tale in Book 10 see Young 2008, 1–31. On Orpheus as a storyteller in Book 10 see Anderson 1989, 1–11; Barchiesi 2006, 284–294.

[38] For a detailed discussion of Orpheus' condemnation of female passion and agency compared to his celebration of divine pederasty see Janan 1988, 110–137.

[39] Versteeg/Barclay 2003, 402. On the distinctive legal aspect of Orpheus' speech see Versteeg/Barclay 2003, 400–409 who put forth the claim that "Ovid infuses a parodic legitimacy to Orpheus' legal position" (402) by using Roman legal principles concerning marriage law, property law and theft law. For a different interpretation see LaFleur 1995, 55; Mack 1995, 282.

Although the rhetorical aspect of this speech has been discussed in depth, its relation to magic ritual has remained rather unexplored.[40] The power of one's speech, and specifically Orpheus' speech, is indicated already from the opening lines of the story (10.3), a theme that dominates Book 10. Orpheus is portrayed as a "bard" (10.12: *vates*) "singing to the music of his lyre" (10.16: *pulsisque ad carmina nervis*), creating the impression of a performance. At lines 17–39 Orpheus displays his persuasive abilities and lays out his rhetoric. He first addresses the recipients of his speech (10.17–18), respectfully asks permission to speak (10.19–20), explains that his journey has not a heroic (10.21–22) but rather an amatory motive (10.23–24). This is the first time in the passage that the word *venenum* (10.23) is used, since as noted earlier it has negative connotations due to its use in curse magic.[41] Its inclusion here has a rhetorical effect: Orpheus is creating the rhetoric of the dutiful, yet wronged husband, who has lost his wife in her prime. Although he has tried to move on, he has not been able due to the power of Love (10.26). This reference is also not coincidental as it enables the speaker to use Hades' and Proserpina's own amatory story as an argument in his favour (10.29). After having unfolded his initial argument, Orpheus states explicitly his request, i.e. that his wife is allowed to return to the upper world (10.31). To strengthen his case, he argues that since everyone ends up in the underworld anyway, so will the heroine even if he is granted this request. And, surprisingly, utters an empty, and rather comical, threat: if his prayer is not answered, he too will remain in the underworld (10.38–39).

His *carmen* is successful (10.45–48), but there is one stipulation that functions as a magical spell (10.51–52: *ne flectat retro sua lumina, donec Avernas / exierit valles; aut irrita dona futura*, "that he should not turn his eyes backward until he had gone forth from the valley of Avernus, or else the gift would be in vain"),[42] revealing once again the intrinsic connection between rhetoric and magic ritual

---

40 Cicero in his *De Inventione*, lists six parts of a rhetorical speech: *exordium* (introduction), *narratio* (narration), *partitio* (partition), *confirmatio* (confirmation), *reprehensio* (refutation) and *conclusio* (conclusion). On Ovid's use of the Ciceronian rhetorical model for the formation of Orpheus' argument see Versteeg/Barclay 2003, 409–410.

41 There are numerous references to *venenum* in the Ovidian corpus. See, for example, *Am.* 1.8.104, 1.14.44, 2.14.28, 3.7.27; *Her.* 2.139, 6.101, 6.131, 9.115, 9.163, 12.181; *Met.* 1.444, 2.198, 2.777, 3.33, 3.49, 4.500, 4.506, 7.123, 7.209, 7.394, 7.535, 9.130, 9.694, 10.23, 14.55, 14.403, 15.359. Interestingly enough for the purposes of this discussion, the occurrences in *Her.* 9 and *Met.* 9 are linked with Deianira's usage of curse magic, whereas the occurrences in *Her.* 12 and *Met.* 7 are associated with Medea's portrayal as a witch.

42 Versteeg/Barclay 2003, 396.

in Ovidian poetry.⁴³ Despite the clear warning, Orpheus does not obey and driven by his fear (10.56) during the journey back to the world of the living he turns to see Eurydice, thus sealing her fate (10.57: *flexit amans oculos et protinus illa relapsa est*, "eager for sight of her, turned back his longing eyes; and instantly she slipped into the depths"). Her second death (10.60) is now an inescapable fact, but, as the external narrator poses the rhetorical question at line 61 (*quid nisi se quereretur amatam?* "for of what could she complain save that she was beloved?") within a parenthesis, the story should be viewed under a different lens.

A gendered reading of this mythos brings to the surface the notion of the male ego: we are told that Orpheus has tried everything in his power to re-claim his beloved. Can Eurydice or even the audience really blame him for his one mistake? Apparently, the heroine does not as she cannot complain of being loved, as expressed by the rhetorical question, a strategy that the Ovidian reader has already experienced at *Heroides* 9. It becomes evident that Ovid is questioning once again the notion of accepting responsibility for actions that might lead to a loved one's death. Eurydice's attitude seems to exonerate him from any wrong-doing, but it has the exact opposite result in the eyes of a modern audience. Orpheus himself wishes to be seen as guilty of this crime (10.68–69), with the term *videri* implying that he does not fully accept responsibility. This is reinforced by his transference of blame to the cruel gods of the underworld, who have not allowed him to rectify his mistake (10.76). Orpheus' avoidance of assuming responsibility reaches a climax with his rejection of women (10.79–82), as if women are the cause of his loss and not his own lack of self-control.

The parallel reading of these two Ovidian artists leads to a gendered interpretation of their shared journey. Poison has been the common agent for their loss. The loss of a beloved triggers their *carmina* that function as means of persuasion, with a major difference that is rooted in male bias.⁴⁴ Orpheus relies on his magic *carmen* as part of his semi-funereal prayer, aiming to reverse Eurydice's status. Yet Deianira uses her *carmen* as part of her own funeral rhetoric, hoping to convince her reader(s) of her innocence. Foreshadowing and informing Orpheus' speech, Deianira's speech resembles not only a deliberative and funeral oration, but also a judicial oration, as the heroine is trying to exonerate herself in front of

---

43 Segal 1989, 54–55 and Cooke 1997, 33 underline that the Ovidian version of Orpheus' speech has divided scholars, with many questioning its tone and persuasive effectiveness.
44 On gendered reading in the *Metamorphoses* from the perspective of the "female reader" see Liveley 1999, 197–213 and in particular p. 200 explaining the two current scholarly approaches regarding Ovidian treatment of women, with the first painting the poet as sympathetic towards women and the second as misogynistic.

a judge, who in her case is Hyllus (the new internal reader) or the Ovidian reader. Her letter echoes the four basic parts of judicial oratory, namely introduction, narration, proof and conclusion.[45] The letter itself can be divided into four parts, with part one addressing the recipient of her supplication, Hercules. Part two creates a self-portrait of the heroine and offers facts regarding her relationship with her husband. Part three returns to the male hero's description by focusing on his most dangerous amatory liaison, whereas part four aims to defend the heroine by first underlining her crucial role in Hercules' heroics and secondly focusing on her misinterpretation of another male's duplicitous words. Deianira casts herself in the role of the defendant in a court of law who depends on the rhetoric of magic in order to create a line of defence: she is deceived into using what she thinks is love magic, but it is actually curse magic.

In contrast to the heroine, Orpheus is clearly aware of the stipulation imposed with the reversal of his wife's death. Yet, he breaks the one rule he has to obey. His disobedience leads to the fulfilment of the magic-like stipulation. But, this manifestation of curse magic affects only the female protagonist. Despite Orpheus' declarations of love and lament, he does not choose death. And this is where Deianira's persuasive rhetoric succeeds and outdoes Orpheus' rhetoric: the heroine has explained in detail how she is also the victim of love and of the misinterpretation of words, has expressed remorse and has chosen death as her punishment. She only wishes to be exonerated in the eyes of her reader(s), which makes her case, based on the rhetoric of magic, more compelling and convincing.

3 The rhetoric of sculpture in *Heroides* 13 and *Metamorphoses* 10.243–297

The rhetoric of magic has various manifestations in Ovidian poetry, among which the art of life-like sculptures stands out and, thus, becomes the focus of this section of the chapter. Statuesque figures, as objects of desire, are dominant in Ovidian poetry. Sculpture itself combines some of Ovid's favourite themes – love, art and transformation – hence it occupies a major role in his corpus, especially in

---

45 According to Kennedy 1994, 120–121 the first part "aims at securing the interest and goodwill of the audience". The second part is "the exposition of the background and factual details". The third part "supplies logical arguments in support of the speaker's position and also seeks to refute objections that might be made against it; the [conclusion] is often divided into a recapitulation and an emotional appeal to the audience".

the *Metamorphoses*.⁴⁶ As the comparative discussion of the two most notable Ovidian tales of agalmatophilia will show,⁴⁷ the poet introduces a new visual form of the rhetoric of magic that calls attention to the gendered dynamics between female and male artists.

Out of the heroines of the collection, only Laodamia describes in detail the practice of *simulacra* ("statues") as part of her magic ritual. She faces a slightly different predicament to Deianira: she too has been abandoned by her husband, not because of a rival, but because of the Trojan war. This desertion prompts her letter-writing which establishes her as both an artist and a practitioner of magic. In fact, she is the only heroine of the collection to admit to constructing a wax statue that substitutes the real hero. The rhetoric of magic is first detected in this letter with the reference to an omen, which functions as a curse. The heroine, foreshadowing her husband's death, warns him that the first Greek to set foot on Trojan soil will die (13.93–94). By simply uttering this omen, Laodamia seals Protesilaus' fate, as speech becomes the vehicle for curse magic, albeit unintentional.⁴⁸

At lines 109–114 this heroine, echoing Deianira who has preceded her in the collection, lists her preoccupations. The affinity between the two heroines and their letters is strengthened by intratextual verbal allusion: the verb *aucupor* is only used at *Her.* 9.41 and 13.107 in the collection.⁴⁹ In fact, these are the only two letters that contain dreams with *simulacra*. Laodamia's list includes the appearance of Protesilaus' pale face in her dreams – with *pallens imago* (13.109) foreshadowing his death, as well as the heroine's preoccupation with rituals. She also portrays herself as the dutiful wife preoccupied with rituals to ensure her husband's safe return. So, she prays to the *simulacra noctis* (the "phantoms" / "gods of night") and she pours incense on every altar in Thessaly, a place traditionally connected with magical events.⁵⁰ These ritual practices reinforce the heroine's portraiture as a woman whose superstition leads to the composition and performance of a curse-like *carmen*.

This unintended *written curse* (the letter) is solidified with the construction of a wax statue of Protesilaus. Whereas in other versions, she creates the statue *after* she hears of Protesilaus' death, in Ovid she makes the statue while the hero

---

46 On petrification in the epic see Wheeler 1999, 154.
47 On agalmatophilia see O'Bryhim 2015, 419–429.
48 Fulkerson 2005, 113.
49 Fulkerson 2005, 118.
50 Fulkerson 2005, 114.

is still at Aulis at lines 149–158.⁵¹ Fear of losing her husband is the cause of her art (13.150). So, while Protesilaus is away, she becomes the sculptor of his waxen replica (13.152: *vultus... cera*). The statue initially functions as a reminder of the absent Protesilaus whom she does not expect to see again, and becomes the focus of her amatory affections (13.153–154). The rhetoric of magic is in full effect when she proclaims that if one were to "add only a voice to the wax" (13.156: *adde sonum cerae*) then it would not be a replica of Protesilaus' image, but rather Protesilaus himself (13.156: *Protesilaus erit*). Laodamia's curse magic reaches its climax: she is aware that the statue is a lifeless substitute for her real husband (13.157), yet she does not express any remorse for creating a funerary monument for Protesilaus *before* his demise.

This lack of remorse allows for a different reading of this tale. The rhetoric of Ovidian women is manifold and may be expressed by specific verbal and visual means, such as letter-writing, song-writing and weaving. But, Laodamia is the only woman who adds another weapon in her arsenal: sculpture. Not only does she become the first and only female sculptor in Ovidian poetry, but also, she is the first female artist who controls her own narrative unapologetically by employing the masculine medium of artistic expression. This differentiation from the distinctively apologetic Deianira is heightened by the fact that this letter reflects the rhetorical structure of *Heroides* 9, with part one addressing the recipient, part two narrating the preceding events, part three exposing the speaker's argumentation and part four making an emotional appeal to the reader(s). Yet, Laodamia uses her two arguments (the omen and the statue) not to atone, but rather to empower herself.

A male reader would assume that either naivety or malevolence has led to her mistakes, which would imply that women should engage only in feminine activities, otherwise calamity ensues.⁵² But, from a female perspective Laodamia establishes her authority as a writer and sculptor, which allows her to demonstrate female agency. She is aware, that despite her protestations, Protesilaus has chosen war over love. She is equally aware of her magic *carmen* working as a curse, rather than a loving warning, which explains the creation of the statue. She knows that she will be permanently abandoned and, thus, chooses another outlet for her amatory desires. She attempts to justify her use of sculpture, that

---

51 Fulkerson 2002, 77.
52 Ripat 2016, 104–128 and in particular at p. 105 underlines that "witches of Roman literature are now generally accepted as representing reality only insofar as they serve as negative examples and so cautionary tales about proper female behaviour, or as projections of real anxieties, often men's anxieties, about women's economic, social, or religious power".

has ended up functioning as another kind of curse (i.e. a visual curse) that not only foreshadows but also cements the deadly outcome of the story. She has learned from her preceding letter-writers and in particular, Deianira, who her line of defense emphasises the misinterpretation of a male's words. Laodamia adjusts this argument, but the core clearly remains the same: she has misinterpreted Protesilaus' waxen *imago*, rather than his words.[53] Laodamia suggests that she has confused the actual Protesilaus with the life-like image of the hero, thus condemning him and herself to death, as she connects her life to his existence. This almost speaking statue becomes part of the heroine's magical performance, implicitly urging her readers to exonerate her by implying that she has been deceived by her own misinterpretation of a *simulacrum*.

Another *simulacrum* captures readers' attention at *Metamorphoses* 10. Out of the Cypriot tales narrated by Orpheus, only one explores in detail the importance of *statues* in Ovidian storytelling and associates it with ritual, the Pygmalion tale.[54] Pygmalion is another sculptor whose art is stimulated by a feeling of loneliness.[55] The Paphian artist, like another Orpheus, rejects female companionship because of the sexual promiscuity of the Amathusian Propoetides (10.244–245), creating a parallel to Orpheus' display of misogyny. However, his decision to remain celibate is undermined by his male nature as his need for companionship results in the carving of a statue made of ivory (10.248).[56] In fact, he is so enamoured with his woman-statue that he cannot distinguish between reality and fiction.[57]

During the festival of Venus, Pygmalion takes matters into his own hands and attempts to reverse his ideal woman's status, functioning as a parallel to Orpheus. The narrator sets the scene of the supplication, foreshadowing Venus' benevolence towards the sculptor: the faithful are sacrificing female heifers to the

---

[53] Fulkerson 2005, 114.
[54] On the Cypriot tales of Book 10 see Petrides 2011, 17–26, especially 4–5 on the Ovidian Pygmalion. On the poetic connotations of the Pygmalion tale see Lateiner 1984, 1–30; Elsner/ Sharrock 1991, 149–182; Sprahlinger 1996, 50–62 and 130–150.
[55] Bauer 1962, 15 notes the connection between Laodamia and Pygmalion, without exploring it further.
[56] Ov. *Met.* 10.247–253: *interea niveum mira feliciter arte / sculpsit ebur formamque dedit, qua femina nasci / nulla potest, operisque sui concepit amorem* ("Meanwhile, with wondrous art he successfully carves a figure out of snowy ivory, giving it a beauty more perfect than that of any woman ever born. And with his own work he falls in love"). On Pygmalion's ivory statue see Salzman-Mitchell 2008, 291–311.
[57] On Ovidian illusion within this tale see Hardie 2002b, 173–226.

goddess (10.271–272), incense is burning at the altar (10.273) and Pygmalion displays his piety by first offering a gift (10.273) and then stating his supplication at lines 274–276. Even though the readers would have expected for Pygmalion to request the statue as his wife, driven by fear not to invoke the goddess' wrath (10.274), Pygmalion compromises and asks for someone that would resemble the statue (10.276).[58] This compromise illuminates his awareness of the unnaturalness of his erotic desire. Yet, his tactic seems to be successful, as Venus is satisfied and demonstrates her divine benevolence with an auspicious omen, that leads to transformation (10.277–279).

Within a religious framework, the sculptor achieves the transformation of the lifeless statue into a living woman with his duplicitous words. Like his female predecessor, he is also aware that honesty is not always beneficial and uses wordplay to carefully express a supplication that conveys his request implicitly. His persuasive strategy is based on the power of male bias: in spite of his hubristic love for the statue, he performs all the necessary steps of a religious supplication and projects the persona of the pious male. And for that reason alone, he is rewarded.

This gendered prejudice is even more evident if one's juxtaposes the two Ovidian sculptors. From a male perspective the Pygmalion tale can be read as a visual display of an artist's love for his creation,[59] whereas from a female perspective the story highlights the artist's control over his creation. Laodamia, on the other hand, is casted in the role of the lamenting, but dangerous, woman relying on magical arts and whose statue-making becomes a monument of flawed feminine behaviour, if one assumes a male perspective. From a female point of view this heroine is a pro-active woman who is in control of her narrative and her rhetoric. In fact, her rhetoric of magic is more persuasive than Pygmalion's rather bland rhetoric. Both stories include omens (one negative and one positive respectively) that are connected with the art of creation in a ritual context. Pygmalion may be the image-maker, but Laodamia is the successful practitioner of magic and sculptor. The heroine, aware of the unhappy ending of her love story, creates the foundation for her defence: Protesilaus' knowledge of the omen does not discourage him; hence, it is his choice that leads him to death. But her *art* immortalises him with the creation of a visual monument.

---

58 Ov. *Met*. 10.274–276: ... 'si, di, dare cuncta potestis, / sit coniunx, opto', non ausus 'eburnea virgo' / dicere, Pygmalion 'similis mea' dixit 'eburnae' ("'If ye, O gods, can give all things, I pray to have as wife' he did not dare add 'my ivory maid', but said, 'one like my ivory maid'").
59 See Anderson 1972, 497 at Ov. *Met*. 10.254–255 who suggests that "Ovid views Pygmalion as the sinless artist; he will be rewarded by a marvelous granting of prayer".

4 Conclusion

As this chapter has suggested, the rhetoric of magic plays an integral role in Ovidian poetry. Magical practices (often within a religious context) are a central component for both the letter-writers' and artists' rhetoric, as well as the external readers' perception of written rhetoric in both the *Epistulae Heroidum* and the *Metamorphoses*. Male bias leads to a negative perception of feminine magic and a positive portrayal of men associated with magic under the guise of religious practices. Yet, female agency is illustrated through the heroines' rhetoric of magic. Their interconnected rhetorical strategy is carefully constructed so that the reader is inundated with doubt, especially once compared with the equivalent male version of the rhetoric of magic. Intent and misinterpretation are the two keywords for understanding the Ovidian heroines' performative rhetoric, smartly implied by both of them. The lines between truth and fiction are expertly blurred, so that the reader is not only encouraged to question the reliability of what (s)he is reading, but also to view magic ritual as an integral component of Ovidian rhetoric.[60]

Bibliography

Anderson, W.S. (1972), *Ovid's Metamorphoses, Books 6–10. Edited with Introduction and Commentary*, Norman, OK.

Anderson, W.S. (1989), 'The Artist's Limits in Ovid: Orpheus, Pygmalion, and Daedalus', in: *Syllecta Classica* 1, 1–11.

Armstrong, R. (2005), *Ovid and his Love Poetry*, London.

Barchiesi, A. (2006), 'Voices and Narrative 'Instances' in the *Metamorphoses*', in: P.E. Knox (ed.), *Oxford Readings in Ovid*, Oxford, 274–319.

Bauer, D.F. (1962), 'The Function of Pygmalion in the *Metamorphoses* of Ovid', in: *Transactions of the American Philological Association* 93, 1–21.

Bolton, M.C. (1997), 'In Defense of *Heroides* 9', in: *Mnemosyne* 50.4, 424–435.

Bonner, S.F. (1949), *Roman Declamation*, Liverpool.

Casali, S. (ed. and comm.) (1995a), *Heroidum Epistula IX: Deianira Herculi*, Florence.

Casali, S. (1995b), 'Tragic Irony in Ovid, *Heroides* 9 and 11', in: *Classical Quarterly* 45.2, 505–511.

Clarke, M.L. (1953), *Rhetoric at Rome*, London.

---

60 This work was co-funded by the European Regional Development Fund and the Republic of Cyprus through the Research and Innovation Foundation (Project: EXCELLENCE/1216/0525).

Cooke, D. (1997), *Refuge and Regret in the Song of Orpheus in Ovid's Metamorphoses*, M.A. Thesis, Buffalo.
Curtius, E.R. (1953), *European Literature and the Latin Middle Ages*, tr. W.R. Trask, Princeton.
Dickie, M.W. (2003), *Magic and Magicians in the Greco-Roman World*, London.
Dickie, M.W. (2000), 'Who Practised Love-Magic in Classical Antiquity and in the Late Roman World?', in: *Classical Quarterly* 50.2, 563–583.
DuRocher, R.J. (1985), 'Perpetual Rhapsody: The Rhetorical Unity of Ovid's *Metamorphoses*', in: *CEA Critic* 48.2, 41–55.
Elsner, J./Sharrock, A. (1991), 'Reviewing Pygmalion', in: *Ramus* 20, 149–182.
Enterline, L. (2004), *The Rhetoric of the Body from Ovid to Shakespeare*, Cambridge.
Fantham, E. (2009), 'Rhetoric and Ovid's Poetry', in: P.E. Knox (ed.), *A Companion to Ovid*, Chichester, 26–44.
Fränkel, H. (1945), *Ovid: A Poet Between Two Worlds*, Berkeley.
Fulkerson, L. (2002), '(Un)Sympathetic Magic: A Study of *Heroides* 13', in: *American Journal of Philology* 123.1, 61–87.
Fulkerson, L. (2005), *The Ovidian Heroine as Author: Reading, Writing and Community in the Heroides*, Cambridge.
Graf, F. (1997), *Magic in the Ancient World*, Cambridge, MA.
Gross, N.P. (1979), 'Rhetorical Wit and Amatory Persuasion in Ovid', in: *Classical Journal* 74.4, 305–318.
Hardie, P.R. (2002a), 'Ovid and Early Imperial Literature', in: P.R. Hardie (ed.), *The Cambridge Companion to Ovid*, Cambridge, 34–45.
Hardie, P.R. (2002b), *Ovid's Poetics of Illusion*, Cambridge.
Higham, T.F. (1958), 'Rhetoric in Ovid', in: N.I. Herescu (ed.), *Ovidiana. Recherches sur Ovide*, Paris, 32–48.
Jacobson, H. (1974), *Ovid's Heroides*, Princeton.
Janan, M. (1988), 'The Book of Good Love? Design Versus Desire in *Metamorphoses* 10', in: *Ramus* 17.2, 110–137.
Jolivet, J.C. (2001), *Allusion et Fiction Épistolaire dans les Héroïdes: Recherches sur l'intertextualité Ovidienne*, Rome.
Kennedy, G.A. (1972), *The Art of Rhetoric in the Roman World*, Princeton.
Kennedy, G.A. (1994), *A New History of Classical Rhetoric*, Princeton.
Kenney, E.J. (1969), 'Ovid and the Law', in: *Yale Classical Studies* 21, 241–263.
Knox, P.E. (ed. and comm.) (1995), *Ovid Heroides: Select Epistles*, Cambridge.
Knox, P.E. (2002), 'The *Heroides*: Elegiac Voices', in: B. Weiden Boyd (ed.), *Brill's Companion to Ovid*, Leiden/Boston, 117–139.
LaFleur, R. (1981), 'Horace and *Onomasti Komodein*: The Law of Satire', in: *Aufstieg und Niedergang der Römischen Welt* 2.31.3, 1790–1826.
LaFleur, R. (1995), *Love and Transformation: An Ovid Reader*, Reading, MA.
Lateiner, D. (1984), 'Mythic and Non-mythic artists in Ovid's *Metamorphoses*', in: *Ramus* 13, 1–30.
Lindheim, S.H. (2002), *Mail and Female: Epistolary Narrative and Desire in Ovid's Heroides*, Madison.
Liveley, G. (1999), 'Reading Resistance in Ovid's *Metamorphoses*', in: P.R. Hardie/A. Barchiesi/S. Hinds (eds.), *Ovidian Transformations. Essays on the Metamorphoses and its Reception*, Cambridge, 197–213.
Mack, S. (1995), 'Teaching Ovid's Orpheus to Beginners', in: *Classical Journal* 90.3, 279–285.

Miller, J.F. (tr.) (1984), *Ovid. Metamorphoses, Volume II: Books 9–15*. Revised edition by G.P. Goold, Cambridge, MA/London.

Morgan, K. (1977), 'Ovid's Art of Imitation: Propertius in the *Amores*', in: *Mnemosyne* suppl. 46–48, 1–107.

Mozley, J.H. (tr.) (1985), *Ovid. Art of Love. Cosmetics. Remedies for Love. Ibis. Walnut-tree. Sea Fishing. Consolation*. Revised edition by G.P. Goold, Cambridge, MA/London.

O'Bryhim, S. (2015), 'The Economics of Agalmatophilia', in: *Classical Journal* 110, 419–429.

Petrides, A.K. (2011), 'Οι 'Κυπριακές Ιστορίες' στις *Μεταμορφώσεις* του Οβιδίου (*Μετ.* 10.220-502)', in: *Κυπριακαί Σπουδαί* 75, 17–26.

Prince, M. (2013), 'Canidia Channels Medea: Rereading Horace's *Epode* 5', in: *Classical World* 106.4, 609–620.

Putnam, M.C.J. (2001), *Horace's Carmen Saeculare. Ritual Magic and the Poet's Art*, New Haven.

Ripat, P. (2016), 'Roman Women, Wise Women, and Witches', in: *Phoenix* 70.1/2, 104–128.

Rives, J.B. (2002), 'Magic in the XII Tables Revisited', in: *Classical Quarterly* 52.1, 270–290.

Salzman-Mitchell, P. (2008), 'A Whole-out of Pieces: Pygmalion's Ivory Statue in the *Metamorphoses*', in: *Arethusa* 41.2, 291–311.

Segal, C. (1989), *Orpheus: The Myth of the Poet*, Baltimore.

Segal, C. (2002), 'Black and White Magic in Ovid's *Metamorphoses*: Passion, Love and Art', in: *Arion* 9.3, 1–34.

Serafim, A. (2017), *Attic Oratory and Performance*, London/New York.

Showerman, G. (tr.) (1977), *Ovid. Heroides. Amores*. Revised edition by G.P. Goold, Cambridge, MA/London.

Spentzou, E. (2003), *Readers and Writers in Ovid's Heroides: Transgressions of Genre and Gender*, Oxford.

Sprahlinger, L. (1996), *Ars latet arte sua: Untersuchungen zur Poetologie in den Metamorphosen Ovids*, Stuttgart.

Versteeg, R./Barclay, N. (2003), 'Rhetoric and Law in Ovid's Orpheus', in: *Law and Literature* 15.3, 395–420.

Wheeler, S.M. (1999), *A Discourse of Wonders. Audience and Performance in Ovid's Metamorphoses*, Philadelphia.

Wilkinson, L.P. (1955), *Ovid Recalled*, Cambridge.

Wolf, V. (2010), 'A Tragic Case of Poisoning: Intention Between Tragedy and the Law', in: *Transactions of the American Philological Association* 140.1, 33–70.

Young, E.M. (2008), 'Inscribing Orpheus: Ovid and the Invention of a Greco-Roman Corpus', in: *Representations* 101.1, 1–31.

Panagiota Sarischouli
Transcultural Context in Graeco-Egyptian Magic: Two Case Studies from a Bilingual Theban Handbook

Abstract: The rhetoric of Egyptian magic is hardly comparable to classical rhetoric because (both temple and private) rituals were not believed to be in need of human listeners to produce a certain outcome. In Pharaonic times, the rhetoric of magic was mainly structured on the belief that a ritual's main function was to reconnect the practitioner to a kind of sacred truth rather than truth itself, while a highly figurative, mythical language combined with a complex system of symbols were the keys to unlocking the power of magic. Therefore, rather than focusing on the use of classical rhetorical devices in Late Egyptian ritual texts, this chapter examines the multifaceted perception of ancient Egyptian private rituals in Graeco-Roman Egypt, presenting two magical recipes from the "Theban Magical Library" as case studies. The texts reflect a striking plurality of cultural and religious traditions, motivated by both syncretic and monotheistic tendencies.

1 Magic and religion in Pharaonic Egypt

In ancient Egyptian thought, magic and religion were indistinguishable concepts, as Egyptians believed that *heka* (usually labelled in modern studies as "magic")[1] was a primordial force, which the creator god applied to bring the world into existence. *Heka* was, moreover, believed to continue to affect the created world in many ways, for the notion of cosmos in ancient Egypt was not bound up with its harmonious and stable order (as in, e.g., Platonic thought); the created world was rather believed to be in a process of continuous regeneration and, therefore, in constant change. But, while gods could use *heka* at will, humans (i.e. the king and the priests) were able to manipulate this force only through a series of complex magico-religious rituals, which may be roughly categorised in the following two strands: first, temple rituals, which were mostly performed hidden from the general population, in order to sustain the regeneration of the cycles of nature, to provide for the gods and to protect the cosmos, the

---

[1] *Heka* is a complex term with a broader sense than that of the word "magic"; for an extensive discussion on the concept of *heka* see Dieleman 2019b, 87–93.

king, the state and the temples from *daimonic* intrusion or other potential enemies. Second, private rituals, which – though significantly narrower in scope than the temple rituals – were also thought to be important in maintaining the balance in nature, as they aimed at protecting households and their members from harm, at healing injuries and diseases, and at providing for the spirits of the dead.[2] It is interesting to note, at this point, that evidence supports the assumption that temple and private rituals were both performed by the same (temple) priests when these were off-duty from temple service.[3] The boundaries, therefore, between state and private ritual are often indistinct and overlapping.[4]

Egyptian priests went through a prolonged period of apprenticeship in order to learn how to perform complex state rituals, but also to obtain the knowledge required to conduct the duties of a physician, a healer or an astrologer. Thus, the priests had a prominent role in state ceremonies related to divine kingship (such as the Coronation Ritual), performed temple cultic rituals (such as the daily Offering Ritual or the ceremonies of the Khoiak festival), but also prepared drugs, potions and ointments to treat various ailments, performed exorcisms and (malevolent) curse rituals, created amulets to provide therapeutic or preventive protection for their owner, and interpreted dreams, creating an important link between the Egyptian priesthood and the laity. Since *heka* was thought of as a morally neutral force, the intentions of the ritualist were decisive in determining whether *heka* was mobilised to protect, heal or harm.

Language was thought of as the key to unlocking the power of magic: the ritualists used incantations and magical utterances to appeal to the gods and *daimones* and, therefore, the power of *heka* was encoded in the "metaphysics" of the Egyptian language.[5] Modern scholarship has, nonetheless, paid little attention to how Egyptians employed rhetoric (or – more accurately – rhetorical devices) in their magico-religious practices.[6] And yet, although any effort to compare the ancient Egyptian

---

[2] See the discussions in Ritner 1992 and 1995a; cf. also Assmann 1984.
[3] See Dieleman 2019b, 95 n. 20.
[4] A recent overview of the nature, functions and perceptions of ritual and ritualists in ancient Egypt can be found in Dieleman 2019b.
[5] See Karshner 2011, 56–58; cf. David 2002, 86: "the two divine principles of 'perception' [*sia*] and creative speech [*hu*] are the rational forces by which creation is achieved, when the creator god first perceives the world as a concept and then brings it into being through this first utterance. To achieve this, the creator uses the principle of magic [*heka*], a force that, according to Egyptian belief, could transform a spoken command into reality".
[6] Although there are no ancient Egyptian treatises on rhetoric, those interested in the Egyptians' approach to rhetoric (as a balance between eloquence and wise silence) may consult: Fox 1983; Kennedy 1998; Hutto 2002; Lipson 2004.

rhetoric of magic to classical rhetoric is most likely to prove futile,[7] there can be little doubt that magic shares parallel roles with rhetorical discourse. In the latter, a set of utterances is directed toward a particular audience that the speaker hopes to persuade. Speaker and audience share a set of religious, philosophical and political beliefs about a foundational order of the cosmos, which allows speakers to express themselves and to be understood, as the art of rhetoric is heavily reliant on a language-entrenched interpretation of reality or truth, although speakers occasionally use other (nonverbal) communication techniques to affect, win over or manipulate their audience.[8] Similarly (yet not identically), the Egyptian ritualists and their audience share the same beliefs of a perceived cosmic order, which allows the first to use symbolic expression – verbal or nonverbal – in order to establish an encoded communication system with the gods and spirits, which their audience is familiar with and can relate to. But, while the aim of rhetoric is to convince or to persuade, a ritual is invariably designed to directly affect the created world, and does not need human listeners to produce a certain outcome.[9] Therefore, the rhetoric of Egyptian magic was structured on the belief that deeper foundational truths are to be expressed "in a highly figurative, mythical language", while rituals sought to reconnect the practitioner – through a complex system of symbols and mythical motifs – to sacred truth (*maat*), not truth itself.[10] And, although a ritual may possibly have motivated or affected its audience in various ways, that was not its principal aim.[11]

Having taken all these peculiarities into consideration, this chapter discusses the perception of ancient Egyptian private rituals in Graeco-Roman Egypt, presenting two magical recipes from the "Theban Magical Library" as case studies, and exploring cultural plurality in their mythical language and ritual symbols.[12]

---

7 On which see mainly Karshner 2011.
8 Rhetoric, as also indicated in ancient sources and modern scholarship, is closely associated with images: mainly those conjured up by language-entrenched descriptions (through alliteration, metaphors etc.), but also those created by the body language of the speaker (hand gestures, tone of voice etc.). Therefore, rhetoric can be seen as referring to the multifaceted uses of written, spoken and visual language.
9 For the differences between the rhetoric of ritual and the rhetoric of politics or law see Podemann Sørensen 2003; cf. also Watts 2009.
10 See Karshner 2011, 53.
11 Therefore, a rhetoric of efficacy is best evidenced in the advertising introductions to magical recipes written in Greek: see n. 64 below.
12 I would like to thank Christopher A. Faraone and Andreas Serafim for their valuable comments on drafts of this chapter.

2 Late Egyptian ritual texts

In post-Pharaonic times, the most prominent aspect of religion outside temples (private ritual) has been preserved in the "Late Egyptian Ritual Texts mainly in Greek and Demotic",[13] to which modern scholarship usually refers with the oversimplistic labels *PGM* (Papyri Graecae Magicae) and *PDM* (Papyri Demoticae Magicae). The *PGM/PDM* labels are used to identify c. 400 individual prescriptions to perform magical rituals of various types, which are found in instructional handbooks (also known as magical formularies or grimoires).[14] In addition to these formulary texts, the arid climate of Egypt has also preserved an albeit smaller number of activated texts: thus, the *PGM/PDM* labels are also used to refer to the magical objects created in the course of a ritual (applied magic), such as protective or healing amulets and binding-curses; the latter differ from the formularies mainly in that they are clearly personalised, as they regularly name their owners and/or victims.

The more fragmentarily preserved, earlier magical formularies (written exclusively in Hellenistic Koinē Greek) begin to appear in the Augustan age and are derived from various sites in Middle and Lower Egypt, while the longest and most complete manuscripts date from the mid-2nd/early 3rd up to the 4th/5th centuries AD, and come mainly from the Theban area in Upper Egypt: the Theban handbooks are written predominantly in Greek, but occasionally also in Demotic – sometimes mixed with hieratic signs – or Old Coptic. Some (yet not all) of the Theban manuscripts are believed to form a coherent magical "library", which recent research associates with the collecting needs of a particular patron or group of patrons.[15] Modern scholarship usually refers to this ancient "library" as the "Theban Magical Library" or the "Anastasi Handbooks" (comprising altogether ten formularies: *PGM/PDM* XII and XIV; *PDM Suppl.*; *PGM* I; VI+II; IV; V; XIII; *P. Holm.* + *PGM* Va; *P. Leiden* I 397).[16]

---

13 This designation has been suggested by Gordon/Gasparini 2014, 40 to describe the complex nature of the manuscripts.
14 A new edition of all known magical formularies unearthed from Egypt is currently being prepared through an international project lead by Christopher A. Faraone and Sofía Torallas Tovar (University of Chicago); thereby, the conventional *PGM/PDM* labels are replaced by the generic *G(reek and)E(gyptian)M(agical)F(ormularies)*-label; see also n. 33 below.
15 Cf. Sarischouli 2022; Moyer 2011; Dieleman 2005; Frankfurter 2000.
16 The texts came to be known in recent times as belonging to Giovanni (Jean) d'Anastasi (1765–1860), the Consul-General of Sweden and Norway in Egypt from 1828 to 1857, who purchased large amounts of papyri on behalf of various European collections. The purchase history of the

In addition to the Theban Magical Library, which is considered the most important ancient archive of magical handbooks, a few smaller magical archives have also been recovered in Egypt: the Fayum Magical Archive (*PGM* XXXVI, XXXVIII; 4th century AD), the Hermonthis Magical Archive (*PGM* VII, VIII, XIa; 4th century AD), the Kellis Magical Archive (*Kellis* I, 82–88; *Kellis Copt.* 35; late 4th century AD) and another multilingual magical archive (*SM* II, 96–98; 5th/6th century AD, without provenance).[17]

Let us first turn our attention to the much-debated origins of the Graeco-Egyptian magical formularies. Remarkably, although the sands of Egypt have preserved many magical handbooks written entirely in Greek, there are no extant magical handbooks written exclusively in Demotic: the surviving five Demotic manuscripts embed Greek incantations or even include significant Greek sections, while a few handbooks whose base language is Greek are found to contain short or long Old-Coptic sections.[18] Even so, there can be little doubt that earlier classicists erred in dogmatically ignoring the obviously Egyptian character of many of the Greek magical texts. On the other hand, Egyptologists – based primarily on the Theban book-rolls – have also erroneously assumed that nearly all Graeco-Egyptian magical texts (irrespective of script, date or place of origin) were produced (by the native priesthood) as close descendants of a tradition that stemmed from Pharaonic times, and were – almost exclusively – concerned with an Egyptian audience or clientele.[19]

Recent research has shown that the short incantations on one of the earliest Greek manuscripts (the so-called Philinna Papyrus) are drawn from a long Greek tradition of metrical charms and reveal no obvious signs of Egyptian influence.[20] And, although these hexametrical incantations represent an isolated category, which does not seem to constitute an innovative trend of Graeco-Egyptian private ritual, we cannot totally ignore these texts in drawing our conclusions. Yet, more decisive in tracing the origins of Graeco-Egyptian magic is another surprising fact: some of the Demotic texts in the Theban handbooks appear to have been

---

Theban Magical Library has been thoroughly discussed in recent literature: see Dosoo 2016; De Haro Sanchez 2008; Dieleman 2005, 11–21; Tait 1995.
17 See Dieleman 2019a, 292–295.
18 See Dieleman 2019a, 283.
19 To name but one example: in an otherwise helpful overview of the extant Demotic spells and their religious context, Ritner 1995b, 3361–3363 comes to the unfounded conclusion that "it is highly possible that few of the preserved Greek magical papyri were ever intended for a Greek ethnic audience".
20 See Faraone 2000, 197–202.

translated from a Greek rather than an Egyptian source.[21] Contrary to the commonly held opinions, Jacco Dieleman has cogently argued that the Demotic spells incorporated into the earlier book-rolls "did not develop organically from Pharaonic magic over a long stretch of time", but may, in fact, have "originated sometime after the Greek spells". Thus, we have good reason to believe that the Demotic spells "were written against a background of Greek spells, which were composed by Egyptian priests and circulated throughout the country, starting in the Hellenistic period".[22]

The matter becomes even more obscure when we consider that, even though the Theban handbooks comprise the most important magical archive regarding the number, length and contents of its manuscripts, these handbooks cannot be considered as typical, but rather as a special case in the production of late antique magical handbooks.[23] Yet most of our knowledge of magical practices in Graeco-Roman Egypt is actually based upon the formularies of the Theban Magical Library.

Let us try to put things into perspective: the evidence of the preserved recipes indicates that at least the late Ptolemaic and early Roman formularies, originating from the upper reaches of the Nile (that is, the more Hellenised areas of Egypt), differed from the Theban handbooks in that they were more deeply affected by Greek influences and were, therefore, more clearly concerned with a Greek audience or clientele. Although the authorship of these earlier formularies may also be hypothesised to be associated with the native priesthood, the Augustan texts display a strong Hellenistic character, thus testifying to a productive encounter of Greek immigrant society with ancient Egyptian religious practices. There can be little doubt that the production of the Late Egyptian ritual texts was the result of various initiatives linked to Egyptian priestly circles but was also affected by the major geopolitical changes of that era. To all appearances, as early as the late Hellenistic period, the temple priests became interested in building a kind of cultural "bridge" to transfer their religious wisdom and technical expertise to Hellenic cultivated circles. Their motives were complex, but probably more spiritual than material, for this effort seems to reflect their desire to demonstrate their moral superiority as part of a process of cultural confrontation. It seems safe to assume that this practice must have first emerged in the cosmopolitan *metropoleis* of late Ptolemaic Egypt.[24]

---

[21] See Dieleman 2005, 127–130.
[22] See Dieleman 2005, 293.
[23] See mainly Faraone 2000; cf. also Faraone 2012, 106–108; 2019, 171.
[24] Cf. Suárez de la Torre 2012.

The situation changed substantially with the occupation of Egypt by the Romans, which is known to have imposed a serious threat to the financial status of Egyptian temples:[25] the priests were now forced to accommodate to the new circumstances and, thereby, find a supplement to their other income. Although they never lost sight of their local clients (as we have seen above, priests performed rituals concerned with the health and well-being of private households and their members since Pharaonic times), the new challenge was to widen the diffusion of the ritual texts. The expansion of Greek-speaking populations in the numerous *metropoleis* along the Nile valley (through intermarriage and other socio-cultural interactions) appears to have led the native priesthood to choose the Greek language as a kind of "lingua franca" to make magical tradition widely accessible.[26] Yet the choice of the Greek language, as innovative as it may have been, was not the most significant change: the ritual practices themselves had to be drastically adapted to meet the demands for new types of instrumental religion, as the priests were now confronted with a new clientele who were interested in acquiring practical assistance in their lives, rather than feeling the need to be protected from *daimonic* attacks which may have jeopardised the stability of the created world (see above). Although they continued to perform rituals firmly rooted in ancient Egyptian religious thought (such as protective and healing rituals), the ritualists were now preoccupied with issues, which were previously considered completely marginal (divination, forcible erotic rituals, *praxeis* to resolve matters of interpersonal conflict etc.).[27] To package their knowledge for international consumption, they combined older (local) ritual techniques and textual forms with mythological references of various origins (not only Egyptian or Greek). At the same time, they had also developed new techniques to mobilise ritual power, which were foreign to ancient Egyptian language and culture, such as the addition of metrical sections,[28] the use of long strings of *voces magicae*,[29] of "alphabetic" verses,[30] *charaktēres*[31] and palindromes, or of the seven Greek vowels.[32] The authors (or the redactors) of the texts now employed Egyptian, Greek, Latin, Semitic, Persian, Nubian, Babylonian (and later also Christian) elements in wild combinations, and attached little importance to invoking Zeus, Iaō, Adonai, Seth,

---

25 Cf. Dijkstra 2011.
26 See Frankfurter 1998, 250.
27 See Dieleman 2012.
28 Cf. Bortolani 2016.
29 See n. 44 below.
30 See Maravela 2015; Fournet 2000.
31 Cf. Gordon 2011b.
32 Cf. Dieleman 2005, 64–69.

Pakerbeth, Isis, Horus, Osiris, Abraham, the archangels Michael and Gabriel (or Jesus Christ, for that matter) all in one breath.

3 Kore, Eros and Psyche in *GEMF* 15 (= *PGM/PDM* XII)

The development of cultural plurality in the magical formularies of the Imperial period is best evidenced by the recipes compiled into one of the most famous, bilingual (Greek/Demotic) handbooks of the Theban Magical Library, hitherto known as *PGM/PDM* XII, and now as *GEMF* 15.[33] This mid-late 2nd century magical formulary[34] contains an assortment of at least 29 individual recipes of unequal length and various magical contents,[35] written mainly in Greek and Demotic, or in a combination thereof,[36] and divided over 19 columns[37] on the verso-side of a papyrus roll (*P. Leiden* I 384 v; *AMS* 75; also *P. Leid. Greek* II, no. V). In 1828, the scroll was purchased as part of a large collection of Egyptian antiquities from Giovanni (Jean) d'Anastasi on behalf of the Dutch government,[38] and is nowadays housed in the National Museum of Antiquities in Leiden.

The multilingual and multicultural nature of the compiled texts offers a vivid testimony to the several layers of redaction involved in the production of a manuscript in a far-off corner of the Greek-speaking world; that is, the far reaches of Upper Egypt. To all appearances, the formulary was produced in an Egyptian temple scriptorium (called *pr 'nḫ*, the "House of life"), located in Thebes, by a

---

[33] The following discussion is based upon the re-edition of *PGM/PDM* XII, which will appear as *GEMF* 15 in Faraone/Torallas Tovar 2021.

[34] Although previous editors date the hand of the Greek sections to the first half of the 4th century AD, the script is more likely to be dated to the middle (or second) part of the 2nd century: see Dieleman/Sarischouli, *GEMF* 15 introduction.

[35] As not strictly magical we may consider a short procedure concerned with an alchemical tincture of gold (col. ix 18–26 = *PGM* XII 193–201), and another that provides a numerological prognostication (col. xiv 1–14 = *PGM* XII 351–364). The formulary also includes a quite unique "translation key" (cols. xv 17 to xvi 30 = *PGM* XII 401–444), enumerating code names of magical ingredients with their proper meaning.

[36] Next to Greek and Demotic, alphabetic Demotic, Hieratic and cipher are also used in this manuscript: see Dieleman 2006 and 2005, 47–101.

[37] Six badly damaged fragments remain of what was an additional column (written in Demotic) at the left end of the scroll. For the unusual layout of the manuscript see Dieleman/Sarischouli, *GEMF* 15 introduction.

[38] For the history of its acquisition see Dieleman/Sarischouli, *GEMF* 15 introduction.

single (bilingual) scribe who may have belonged to the inner-circle of Egyptian priests;[39] this individual consulted earlier Graeco-Egyptian formularies in order to copy and/or adapt older Greek texts, reworked older Egyptian ritual texts into Demotic, transcribed long strings of *voces magicae* from Greek into alphabetic Demotic signs, but also incorporated Greek incantations into Demotic recipes.[40]

Two texts, in which a striking interchange between Greek and Egyptian notions and practices can be most explicitly observed, are meticulously examined in what follows. Both are copied at the beginning of the Greek section of the scroll. The first text seems to be primarily related to ancient Greek mystical tradition, while the second features a distinct mélange of Greek, Egyptian and Jewish inspirations. Nonetheless, both magical recipes have an indisputable Egyptian methodological and structural character. The texts are introduced by short rubrics and separated from one another by a *paragraphus* line:[41] their scriptural appearance and thematic inspirations seem to indicate that these two recipes once belonged to a pre-existing exemplar, perhaps a late Hellenistic anthology of Graeco-Egyptian ritual texts.

3.1 Epiphany of Kore

The relatively short, first recipe (*GEMF* 15 col. iv 1–13 = *PGM/PDM* XII 1–13) is fully preserved, although the ink traces are very indistinct at the upper part of the column. The recipe is preceded by a laconic title indicating that the following text is a *praxis* (i.e. a "procedure" or "process"); the title is set in *eisthesis* at the top of the page and is separated from the main text by a small blank space. The text aims at producing an epiphany of Kore: to invoke the goddess, the practitioner is instructed to carry "some beeswax at night"[42] and also "hold a sword" (ἔχων

---

39 See Dieleman 2005, 285–294; cf. Sarischouli 2022.
40 For the compilation of *GEMF* 15 (= *PGM/PDM* XII) and its "sister-manuscript" *GEMF* 16 (= *PGM/PDM* XIV) see mainly Dieleman 2005 and 2019a, 320. For *GEMF* 15, cf. also Sarischouli 2022, discussing the manuscript collation, exploring the social and cultural milieu of the handbook's compiler/editor, and speculating about its implied readers.
41 A simple παράγραφος (a horizontal stroke written below the first letters of a line) was commonly used to mark text divisions. For the use of παράγραφος (and its various forms) in the papyri see e.g. Barbis Lupi 1994; Johnson 1994.
42 Beeswax seems to have been intended as an offering to the goddess: cf., e.g., *IC* III iv 38. This is not at all surprising since at Theoc. *Id.* 15.94 Persephone is referred to as Μελιτώδης; that is, as "Honey-sweet Lady". An ancient scholion to this passage comments that this euphemistic title was given to Persephone because her priestesses were known as μέλισσαι, "bees". Note, however, that the name *melissai* is mostly associated with the priestesses of Demeter (Call. *Hymn.*

κηρία μελιττῶν νυκτὸς κ[αὶ λαβ]ὼν ξίφο[c); he is then to utter a long string of *voces magicae*, many of which are completely incomprehensible while others derive etymologically from Egyptian or Greek divine epithets or fixed phrases, but appear garbled in their Greek transcription.[43] Chanting these mostly untranslatable "barbaric" names was a common technique of Graeco-Egyptian magic:[44] the *voces* were believed to serve as a code to establish communication with the gods "in a language akin to them".[45] Indeed, the text assures the practitioner: "when you say these things, Kore will come carrying torches" (ταῦτά cου [ε]ἰπόντ[ο]c ἐλεύcεται Κόρη λαμπάδας ἔχουcα). Should the practitioner utter two further magical words, the torches that she holds will be extinguished, much to the goddess' disappointment. By promising to rekindle the torches, the practitioner will be able to mobilise Kore (via *heka*, see above) to send (probably violent) dreams to his victim; what is more, if he wishes that the goddess commits a murder on his behalf, he should give her the sword, and she will return with stains of blood on it.[46] It is worth noting that similar imagery is employed in the tale of Cupid and Psyche, as narrated in Apuleius' *Metamorphoses* (see the discussion of the following procedure in this chapter): Psyche is here advised by her envious sisters, who persuade her that her husband (Cupid) is a serpentine monster, to sneak a lamp and a dagger into their bedchamber at night, and kill him while he sleeps. If not coincidental, the imagery of Kore holding a flaming torch and a sword could be reflective of an association between the current and the following procedure, which may have emerged at the time they were originally authored (see also above), even though the texts were subsequently diversified, perhaps due to corruption during transmission.

2.110–112; Apollodorus of Athens *FGrH* 244 F 89; Hsch. μ 719; Porph. *Antr. nymph.* 18.6–7; Sch. Pind. *P.* 4.106c). On the topic see Gagarin 2001, 147 nn. 50 and 51. Though dated, Cook 1895 remains valuable for his extensive discussion of bees in Greek mythology.

43 See Dieleman 2019a, 285; Brashear 1995, 3429–3438 and 3576–3603.

44 The so-called *voces magicae* (or *nomina barbara*) represent one of the most recognisable features of late antique magic. Although foreign or strange-sounding words are attested in Egyptian magical texts already from the 2nd millennium BC, *voces magicae* are absent from the earliest Greek magical papyri; in the *PGM* corpus, they first appear in the 1st century AD and by the 3rd century they are practically everywhere: a helpful overview can be found in Brashear 1995, 3429–3438 and 3576–3603.

45 Cf. Iambl. *Myst.* 7.4.256.

46 It is no surprise that the whole procedure was thought to be so dangerous that the practitioner was advised to wear a protective amulet fastened to his hand while performing the ritual (another technique which is often applied in the corpus of Late Egyptian ritual texts).

It is a commonplace that the Epiphany of Kore[47] was central to the Mystery Rites at Eleusis.[48] In fact, the fifth day of the Rites appears to have been called "Day of Torches", for at nightfall the *mustai* ("initiates") were led by a *Dadouchos* ("Torchbearer") to walk in pairs around the temple of Demeter at Eleusis, while the waving torches were changed from hand to hand to light the participants' way through the darkness.[49] The whole ritual aimed at mimicking Demeter's search for her daughter, which is said to have been conducted by the light of a torch kindled in the flames of Mount Etna. Therefore, torches, along with stalks of grain and sceptres, often appear in Kore/Persephone's iconography as her cultic attributes.

Persephone and Kore may have originally been two distinct goddesses.[50] Nonetheless, in mainstream Greek literature, the name Kore (meaning "daughter", "young bride", but also "maiden": see *LSJ*) is regularly (though not exclusively)[51] used to emphasise Persephone's tender role as Demeter's daughter, whereas the goddess takes her ominous name (i.e. Persephone), or is simply called *Thea*, "Goddess", when she appears in her chthonic role[52] as the wife of Hades and Queen of the Underworld.[53] It is also worth noting that in the Greek mythic tradition Demeter and her daughter became inextricably identified with each other quite early[54] and thus, in Egypt, Persephone (similarly with her

---

47 For epiphany as a crucial mode in Greek religious thought and practice see Petridou 2016. For divine epiphanies in the Greek magical papyri see Pachoumi 2011b.
48 For the Eleusinian Mysteries see Bremmer 2014, 1–20; Bowden 2010, 26–48; Larson 2007, 73–76; Sourvinou-Inwood 2003; Clinton 1992.
49 See Patera 2010; cf. Sourvinou-Inwood 2003, 34.
50 Cf. Zuntz 1971, 75–83.
51 See, e.g., Hom. *h. Dem.* 439; Lasus *PMG* 702; but, cf. Eur. *HF* 608 (Ἅιδου Κόρης).
52 Persephone initially belonged to the Olympian realm, but her abduction by Hades seems to have transformed her into a chthonic deity. Note, however, that the distinction between Olympian and chthonic in Greek religion has been disputed by modern scholars: see mainly Scullion 1994; Schlesier 1991/1992.
53 For example, in the Orphic Gold Tablets: see Bremmer 2019, 61–84; Bernabé/Jiménez San Cristóbal 2001 and 2008.
54 Both goddesses symbolised the power of vegetation, and many festivals of Demeter and Kore were associated with the annual cycle of grain cultivation. Persephone was seen as the power of earth manifested in the grain, while Demeter personified a more abstract concept of that same power: see Larson 2007, 69–85; Tobin 1991.

mother)⁵⁵ was closely linked to Isis.⁵⁶ Therefore, keeping in mind that assimilation between gods of different origins was a common feature of Graeco-Egyptian magic, Kore in our text may also be understood to refer to Isis (in the form of her Greek counterpart),⁵⁷ a reasonable hypothesis that jibes well with the syncretic character of the whole manuscript. Torches are known to have played a significant role in the Isiac cult in Roman times,⁵⁸ but this feature may also be rooted in Pharaonic religious practice, since flaming torches were widely used in temple rituals (occasionally, to keep away *daimones* or other enemies).

The invocation to Kore (and not to Egyptian, Semitic or Babylonian divinities) seems to indicate that the current ritual text was copied, and, most likely, adapted (to all appearances, together with the following procedure) from an older, perhaps late Hellenistic, exemplar: as discussed above, the earliest Graeco-Egyptian magical texts have a distinct Greek character, being almost exclusively linked to home-grown divinities, such as Selene, Hecate, Kronos, Pluto, Kore, Hades, the Furies, the Moirai etc.⁵⁹

Unlike Greek cult contexts, in the Graeco-Egyptian ritual texts, the name of Kore or that of the ominous Persephone are not found to be respectively associated with the positive daughter-role or the chthonic character of the goddess: both Kore and Persephone are interchangeably invoked as chthonic divinities (sometimes, even being addressed as distinct deities) in rites concerned with inflicting harm, much like the current text. A fine example can be found in a 3rd-century AD lead curse-tablet from Alexandria, in which Kore is identified with the Sumero-Babylonian goddess of the Underworld Ereshkigal, while Persephone is viewed as a different chthonic goddess.⁶⁰ Also worth mentioning, in this context,

---

55 On the identification of Demeter with Isis as symbols of divine motherhood see Tobin 1991. In Greek literature, Demeter is also known to have been assimilated with the Phrygian Cybele, another goddess whose cult was associated with mystical aspects: see Eur. *Hel.* 1301–1345 and Melanippid. *PMG* 764.
56 There is a famous passage in Plutarch's *On Isis and Osiris* (361 E), in which Isis is identified with Persephone and Sarapis with Pluto, while the Greek author also notes the similarities between the Isiac rites and the Greek Thesmophoria.
57 A fine example of the assimilation between Kore and Isis is found in a 1st/2nd-century AD procedure to make an unattractive person attractive (and thus desirable), in which Isis is referred to as ἁγνὴ Κούρα: see *GEMF* 8 = *PGM* LXXII+LVII col. ii 16.
58 For torches as a common priestly attribute in Isiac cult scenes see Griffiths 1975, 278 and 314; Heyob 1975, 104. Isis herself is also often depicted holding a torch in her right hand; e.g. on coins dated to the reign of Trajan: see Metcalf 2011, 405–408.
59 Cf. Brashear 1995, 3430.
60 More related examples can be found in Gager 1992, nos. 38, 53, 70, 84, 89, 104, 105, 110, 115, and 134.

are the references to Kore/Persephone found in another Theban magical handbook (*GEMF* 57/*PGM* IV, dated to the 4th century AD), which contains a series of syncretistic hymns written in dactylic hexameters (frequently interrupted by *voces magicae* and other magical formulae). In these hymns, Kore/Persephone appears three times in a group of four related goddesses of Greek origins, being invoked along with Hecate, Selene and Artemis (who, in other texts, appear also acting as members of a triad, without Kore/Persephone).[61]

3.2 Eros and Psyche in an attraction-procedure

The next lengthy recipe is spread over three columns (*GEMF* 15 cols. iv 14–39, v 1–34, vi 1–22 = *PGM* XII 14–95);[62] the text is introduced by a brief title (πάρεδροc Ἔρωc)[63] set in the middle of an empty line, while the main text begins with a longer, explanatory subtitle: "a rite of Eros, both consecration and preparation" (Ἔρωτοc τελετή, καὶ ἀφιέρω[c]ιc κα̣ὶ̣ κ[α]ταcκευή). It seems plausible to assume that the subtitle indicates some sort of effort on the part of the redactor of the text to adapt (in this case, to elucidate) the manuscript's immediate predecessor(s) to meet the needs of his intended readership.

The current recipe seems to originate from a religio-cultural background similar to the one that produced the former recipe, but has a more obvious Egyptianising structure. In the introduction to the procedure (col. iv 15–17), the author or the redactor of the text applies a "marketing" strategy that was very common in Late Egyptian ritual texts written in Greek (and to a lesser extent, also in those written in Demotic),[64] enumerating its many qualities: if one uses the ritual properly and in purity, "it sends dreams, induces insomnia and also changes the fate of ill-starred people" (καὶ ὀνειρ[ο]πομπείαν, ἀγρυπνίαν ποιεῖ κα̣ὶ̣ διαλλάccει

---

61 *GEMF* 57 = *PGM* IV 2522–2567 (Hymn 20, Preisendanz, vol. II, pp. 257–259); 2714–2783 (Hymn 21, Preisendanz, vol. II, pp. 259–260); 2786–2870 (Hymn 18, Preisendanz, vol. II, pp. 253–255); for the hymns see Bortolani 2016, 280–297, 309–336. For the magical Tetrad (Hecate-Selene-Artemis-Persephone) or Triad (Hecate-Selene-Artemis) cf. Petrovic 2007, 4–11. For the metrical invocations to the gods in the *PGM* corpus see Petrovic 2015.
62 The recipe is also discussed in Pachoumi 2017, 86–88; Collins 2008, 98–103; Merkelbach/Totti 1990, 65–80.
63 In Graeco-Egyptian magic, the term *parhedros* (lit. "the one who sits nearby") is used to refer to a supernatural being (a deity, a *daimon*, one's shadow or a material object) that collaborates with the ritualist as his assistant assuming different forms: see Pachoumi 2017, 35–61, 2013 and 2011b; Scibilia 2002.
64 The various types of advertising strategies used in the introductions to the Greek magical recipes are categorised and discussed in Dieleman 2005, 254–280.

κακοδαί(μο[να]c). Although these accomplishments sound too general to understand the exact nature of the procedure, it is not until the last third of the next column that the text becomes more specific: the dream sending, the infliction of insomnia and the resulting fate-change are actually linked to an attraction-procedure expected to work through touch (col. v 23: ἐν τούτῳ τῷ παραψίμῳ).[65]

At the beginning of the recipe, the practitioner is instructed to prepare two wax statuettes (each about 15cm high), one of Eros (lifting a torch in his right hand while grasping a bow and arrow in his left) and one of Psyche (with no further description), which he is to present with various offerings (fruits, cakes, pine-cones, sweetmeats, lamps not painted red, pickled food, votive tablets, sour palm fruits and a bowl of wine flavoured with honey). He is then to consecrate the divine statuettes so that they can be mobilised as his assistants in order to attract the victim.

Before we proceed with an analysis of the complex three-day consecration of the statuettes (a procedure deemed to attract a part of the divine power into the image of the god), which is the main focus of the text, let us first turn our attention to the involvement of Eros and Psyche in a Graeco-Egyptian erotic ritual. As is well known, the love story of Eros and Psyche refers to a mythological couple of divinities who – after first being seriously tormented – finally managed to overcome obstacles and enjoy their love. Similar to the happy ending in the Tale of Eros and Psyche, the consecration of their small images in the current ritual signifies the anticipation that the agent will manage to attract his/her target (the procedure can be used by both genders).[66]

Although the mythological couple of Eros and Psyche appears in Greek art as early as the 4th/3rd century BC,[67] the most extended literary source of their tale is found in Apuleius' *Metamorphoses* (4.28–6.24), a Latin novel believed to have been written about 160 AD, which makes it an almost exact contemporary of the formulary written on *P. Leiden* I 384 verso. The close chronological proximity of the two texts is, however, to be treated with some reservation, considering that even though all the recipes compiled in this handbook were copied (and/or adapted) onto the verso side of the scroll in about the mid-late 2nd century, some

---

[65] The term παράψιμον applies to forcible erotic rituals that act by contact. Other examples can be found in *GEMF* 74 = *PGM* VII 973–980 and *GEMF* 38 = *SM* II, 82 at 2–3; cf. also *GEMF* 57 = *PGM* IV 2145–2240 at 2173–2174.

[66] See n. 87 below.

[67] An early example is a 4th/3rd-century BC terracotta statuette of Eros and Psyche, which was probably found in the Boeotian town of Tanagra and is now held in the Metropolitan Museum of Art in New York (accession number: 06.1062).

of them (if not all) must have been originally produced several decades, or perhaps even a century or more earlier.

In Apuleius' novel, the tale of Eros and Psyche is presented as an allegory of love overcoming death, charged with various philosophical and mystic influences: the "fable recapitulates in miniature the experiences of Lucius",[68] the protagonist of the novel who, in consequence of a foolish curiosity, is unwillingly transformed into an ass, and then undergoes several ordeals that resemble those of Psyche (some of which seem also to be related to the Eleusinian rituals). By being initiated into the Isiac mysteries and through the intervention of Isis, Lucius finally manages to regain his human form.

There can be little doubt that the tale has a sacred origin. Reinhold Merkelbach initiated a major interpretative tradition, which emphasised the Isiac resonances in the tale, and even saw the whole novel as a piece of Isiac propaganda.[69] However, even though this interpretation still continues to have currency with many modern scholars, the mythological and philosophical background of the Apuleian fable is surely far more complex than that, since parallels to Apuleius' story can be found in Eastern (Mesopotamian and Egyptian) mythic traditions, in Gnostic and Valentinian thought, and of course in Platonic allegory.[70]

As the current magical recipe is also part and parcel of a similar intercultural milieu, it comes as no surprise that the first invocation formula (col. v 1–19) begins with a phrase (ἐπικαλοῦμαί σε τὸν ἐν τῇ καλῇ κοίτῃ, τ[ὸν] ἐν τῷ ποθεινῷ οἴκῳ, "I invoke you, who are on the beautiful bed, who are in the desirable house"), which is undoubtedly reminiscent of the description of the gorgeous palace of Cupid at the beginning of the fifth book of Apuleius' *Metamorphoses*.[71] This similarity seems to indicate the use of a common source with regard to the fable. The author (or the redactor) of the magical recipe seems, however, to have been (consciously or unconsciously) unfaithful to his source material, for, in what follows, the procedure focuses on the assistance of Eros only, while Psyche is mentioned only once at the beginning of the text and then is forgotten. Although this variation permits us to ferret out some corruption in the transmission of the original recipe, the adaptation of the source material to the needs of each individual prescription is not unusual in the corpus of magical formularies. Thus, this fable adaptation may have also occurred during the original composition,

---

[68] Thus Edwards 1992, 78. For the fable as a mythic variant of the novel see Frangoulidis 2008, 108–129.
[69] See mainly Merkelbach 1953.
[70] A helpful overview can be found in Edwards 1992.
[71] As already suggested by Merkelbach/Totti 1990, 76 n. 40.

and is probably to be compared to the use of the extremely compressed *historiolae* in the Late Egyptian ritual texts.[72]

It is, nonetheless, worth noting that references to the tale of Eros and Psyche are generally uncommon in Graeco-Egyptian forcible erotic rituals, in which the mythical *topos* of Isis' love for Osiris is regularly compared to the erotic desire that the (male) principal aimed at arousing in his victim. This *topos* is found in many ancient (or later) Egyptian hymns, mortuary and ritual texts, since Isis became associated with human erotic behaviour already in the early Dynastic period. A fine example from Roman times is a forcible erotic ritual written in Demotic (*GEMF* 18 col. viii recto 1–16 = *PDM/PGM* LXI 112–127), in which a wax figurine of Osiris is used to help the principal gain the love of the beloved woman; here, Isis is identified with the spell's target as the beloved of Osiris.

A single (albeit much later) parallel for the involvement of Eros and Psyche in Graeco-Egyptian erotic magic can be found in the so-called "Sword of Dardanus"[73] (*GEMF* 57 = *PGM* IV 1716–1870), a 4th-century AD prescription to attract and bind a female target.[74] In this text, the practitioner is instructed to prepare a wooden figure of a winged Eros, and also engrave, on one side of a magnetic stone, Aphrodite "sitting astride Psyche" (ἱππιστὶ καθημένην ἐπὶ Ψυχῆc) and, below them, Eros holding a blazing torch and burning Psyche (at 1722–1725) while, on the other side of the stone, Psyche and Eros are to be engraved embracing one another (at 1737–1739). While performing a burnt offering, the practitioner is to invoke Eros to become his assistant and sender of dreams to the victim; Eros will assume the form of a god or *daimon*[75] that the woman worships (at 1858: ὁμοιωθεὶc ᾧ cέβεται θεῷ ἢ δαίμονι), present himself in front of her, and thus manage to bend her to the agent's will. Although it follows a different ritual methodology, the "Sword of Dardanus" bears surprising similarities to our text, in which Eros is also to relay whatever message the agent may give him and wherever he/she

---

72 The *historiolae* represent a very marked feature of Pharaonic magical practice that has survived not only in Late Egyptian ritual texts, but also in Christian magic: see Frankfurter 1995; Podemann Sørensen 1984.
73 The authorship of the text is attributed to Dardanus, a famous ancient *magus* mentioned by Pliny (*NH* 30.9) and later authors, such as Apuleius (*Apol.* 90.6): see Costantini 2019, 242–245. The attribution of a magical text to a famous author was a common mystifying motif (see n. 64 above). For the presence of pseudepigraphy in the Greek magical papyri, cf. also Suárez de la Torre 2014, 251.
74 The recipe is also discussed in Faraone 2022, 294–301; Pachoumi 2017, 88–95 and 2011a.
75 Note that, in his *Symposium* (202a5–9), Plato narrates (through the priestess Diotima) that Eros is not a god but a *daimōn* and, therefore, functions as a mediator (whose function is to interpret and transmit) between God and man.

may send him, "assuming whatever form of god or goddess men and women may revere" (*GEMF* 15 col. v 2–3: παρομοιούμενος θεῷ ἢ θεᾷ οἵῳ ἂν cέβωνται οἱ ἄνδρεc καὶ οἱ γυναῖ[κ]εc, or col. vi 10: παρομοιωθείc, ᾧ cέβεται θεῷ ἢ θεᾷ). The resemblances cannot be coincidental; they strongly suggest the use of a common source.

Let us now examine more carefully the multicultural influences that are reflected in the ritual actions that are to be performed during the complex three-day consecration of the Eros statuette in our text. The practitioner is first instructed to place Eros on an offering table covered with fruits, and prepare an altar. On the first day of the consecration, he is to strangle seven birds offering them to Eros, and thus allowing their breath to enter the Eros-statuette.[76] On the second day, the practitioner is to sacrifice a young male chick as a burnt offering and, on the third day, to eat up by himself (allowing no one else to join in) another young chick, while performing the rite on the altar. The utterance of three magical formulae, in which the practitioner is to invoke a series of Egyptian, Greek and Jewish divinities to serve him as his minister against both men and women, accompanies the ritual acts; the practitioner is to utter the first one during the strangulation of the birds, and the other two over the burnt offerings.

The first invocation formula (col. v 1–19) is addressed to Eros. Although in this part of the text we find the allusion to the palace of Cupid, which associates Eros with the Greek god of love (see above), the rest of the mythological references are heavily Egyptian-themed: the text insinuates an assimilation of Eros to the sun god (Helios), but also to Osiris and to Horus.[77] All three gods are to be understood as forms of Eros, whom the text clearly describes as being capable of "assuming whatever form of god or goddess men and women may revere" (see also above). Thus, the text first refers (col. v 6–8) to the story of the sacred scarab

---

[76] Sacred animals, birds and insects were "reverently" drowned (cf. Porph. *Abst.* 4.9; Iambl. *Myst.* 5.24) or strangled (Porph. *Vit. Plot.* 10.57–59) during rituals intended to deify them (*apotheōsis*) while allowing the practitioner to absorb their supernatural power; on the topic see Moyer 2003, 221; Merkelbach/Totti 1990, 76 n. 30. In the present case, the strangulation of the birds was meant to mark them as divine emanations; the Eros statuette was then to absorb their spirits (col. iv 33–34: μέχρις οὗ ἕκαcτον τῶν ζῴων ἀποπνιγῇ καὶ τ[ὸ] πν[εῦ]μα αὐτῶν εἰc α[ὐ]τὸν ἔλθῃ, "until each of the animals is strangled and their breath enters him") so that it would become elevated to divine status.

[77] Similar assimilations can be found in Plutarch's *On Isis and Osiris* (374 C–E): the Greek writer argues that the Hesiodic Eros calls to mind Osiris, but also likens the Eros in the *Symposium* by Plato to Horus. Although the assimilation between Osiris and Eros is not common (see mainly Reitzenstein 1930), the identification of Eros with Horus-the-Child is well attested in the Roman period: see Merkelbach 1995, 87–93, and plates 122–124.

called PHŌREI.⁷⁸ In Egyptian thought, the sacred beetle represents the sun god who travels through the netherworld at night to make his daily ascent to heaven. Here, the scarab is syncretically related to Osiris, as the text next alludes to the murder and dismemberment of the god by his brother Seth (κάνθαρος, ὁ πτεροφυὴς μεcουρανῶν τύραννος, ἀπεκεφαλίcθη, ἐμελίcθη, "[the] scarab, the winged ruler of the middle-heavens was beheaded [and] dismembered").

An allusion to the loss of Osiris' phallus, which is totally missing from the Egyptian tradition but can be found in later Greek sources,⁷⁹ is also carefully embedded in the text (τὸ μέγιcτον καὶ ἔνδοξον αὐτοῦ κατεχρήcατο, "his mightiest and most glorious [member] was consumed") while the author prefers to refer only vaguely to the confinement of Osiris in the chest which led to his death (καὶ δεcπότην τοῦ οὐρανοῦ cυνκατακλείcαντες ἤλλαξαν, "they locked up the Lord of Heaven and changed his status"). In what follows (col. v 9–10), Eros is identified with Horus-Harpocrates, the personification of the young sun and is thus addressed as "Lord of Heaven, the one who illuminates the inhabited world" (ὁ δεcπότης τοῦ οὐρανοῦ, ἐπιλάμπων τῇ οἰκουμένῃ).⁸⁰ At the end of the first invocation formula (col. v 11–12), Eros is addressed as the "Lord of forms" (ὁ δεcπότης τῶν μορφῶν), which seems to correspond to the Egyptian nb ḫprw, an epithet used of Re, Osiris, Horus and other solar deities,⁸¹ testifying to the rich religious syncretism of the era. The first invocation is concluded with threats of destruction (col. v 16–18), if the invoked divine being does not perform the required service.⁸²

Religious pluralism becomes even more evident in the second invocation formula (col. v 20–27), which is to be spoken over the burnt offering: the practitioner adjures Eros by the (unnamed) god "who holds the cosmos (in his power), the one who laid the four foundations, and mixed together the four winds" (ἐξορκίζω cε κατὰ τοῦ κατέχοντος τὸν κ[ό]cμ[ο]ν καὶ ποιήcαντ[ο]c τὰ τέccαρα θεμέλια καὶ μείξαντος τοὺς δ ἀνέμους; see also below). The following explanations of the nature of this *agnōstos theos* (col. v 21–22: cὺ εἶ ὁ ἀcτράπτων, cὺ εἶ ὁ βροντῶν, cὺ εἶ

---

78 Although the interpretation of the name remains problematic, a misspelling of <χ>φωρει (l. Χφωρι), a Coptic variant to Chepri, the two-winged Egyptian sun beetle who was believed to bring forth the sun each morning seems plausible: see Merkelbach/Totti 1990, 77 n. 45.
79 The loss of Osiris' phallus is recorded by Diod. Sic. 1.22.6–7; Plut. *De Is. et Os.* 358 B (who adds that it had been devoured by the fish of the Nile); Hippol. *Haer.* 5.7.22–23. See the discussion in Sarischouli 2019, 321–322.
80 Cf. also col. vi 14–15: ὁ ἐπὶ τοῦ λωτοῦ καθήμενος καὶ λαμπυρίδων τὴν ὅλην οἰκουμένην.
81 See Maltomini 1996, 140.
82 This is another motif, commonly found in Late Egyptian ritual texts, which is believed to be rooted in ancient Egyptian prototypes. Essential literature on the topic can be found in Brashear 1995, 3392 n. 7; Merkelbach/Totti 1991, 83–88.

ὁ cείων, cὺ εἶ ὁ πάντα cτρέψαc καὶ ἐπανορθώcαc πάλιν, "you are the one who hurls lightning, you are the one who thunders, you are the one who shakes, you are the one who overturned all things and [i.e. then] set them right again") have close parallels[83] in various other magical texts with Jewish attributes.[84] The hypothesis of Jewish inspiration in this part of the text is confirmed, as the text now (col. v 24) explains that Eros is explicitly ordered "by the command of the highest god, IAŌ, ADŌNEAI, ABLANATHANALBA" (κατ' ἐπιταγὴν τοῦ ὑψίcτου θεοῦ Ἰάω Ἀδωνεαὶ αβλαναθαναλβα).[85]

Quite unexpectedly, the next phrase connects Eros with the Greek *Charites* (Graces), which were regularly seen as companions of the Olympian gods; the scene referred to in the text is particularly interesting, albeit difficult to understand (col. v 24–25: cὺ εἶ ὁ περιέχων τὰc Χάριταc ἐν τῇ κορυφῇ, "you are the one who wears the Graces around your head [i.e. like a garland?]").[86] Eros is then (col. v 25–26) imagined to hold (an image of?) Necessity in his right hand (cὺ εἶ ὁ ἔχων ἐν τῇ δεξιᾷ τὴν Ἀνάγκην), and addressed as the one "who unbinds and binds"

---

83 Cf. *GEMF* 57 = *PGM* IV 1160: ὁ βροντάζων [...], ὁ ἀcτράπτων [...], ὁ cείων [...], ὁ ζωογονῶν; 1324: ὁ cείcαc καὶ cείων τὴν οἰκουμένην; *GEMF* 58 = *PGM* V 149–150: ὁ ἀcτράπτων καὶ βροντῶν; 442–443: Ἰάω, ὁ cείcαc τὴν οἰκουμένην; *GEMF* 74 = *PGM* VII 234–235: ὁ ἀcτράπ<τ>ων, ὁ βροντάζων; 994–996: cὺ εἶ ὁ βρο]ντῶν, ὁ βρέχων καὶ ἀcτράπτων κατὰ τὸν καιρὸν καὶ καταξηράναc ὡcαύτωc; *GEMF* 72 = *PGM* VIII 91–93: ἐπικαλοῦμαί cε, τὸν ἀκέφαλον θεόν, [...] τὸν ἀcτράπτοντα καὶ βροντάζοντα. Although not exact parallels, similar phrasings occur also in *GEMF* 57 = *PGM* IV 1275–1330 at 1283–1284 (prayer to Helios-Prē, ὁ τὰ ὅλα cυνέχων καὶ ζωογονῶν τὸν cύμπαντα κόcμον) and at 1324–1325: (variant prayer: ὁ cείcαc καὶ cείων τὴν οἰκουμένην, ὁ καταπεπωκὼc τὸν ἀείζωον ὄφιν); *GEMF* 74 = *PGM* VII 284–300 at 300: ὁ βροντῶν, ὁ cείων τὸν οὐρανὸν καὶ τὴν γῆν, ὁ καταπεπωκὼc τὸν ὄφιν; 359–369 at 366: ὁ cείων, ὁ βροντῶν, ὁ καταπεπωκὼc τὸν ὄφιν. See also the discussion in Merkelbach/Totti 1990, 78, commentary to l. 60.
84 Note that a similar phrasing (ὁ ἀcτράπτων καὶ βροντῶν καὶ γνόφου καὶ ἀνέμων κύριοc) is engraved on the back of a magical gem depicting a lion-headed god (Museum Brooklyn inv. 37.1755h). The gem was found in Leontopolis, where in the early Hellenistic times a Jewish temple (in imitation of the temple at Jerusalem) is believed to have been built by a priest named Onias on the site of a ruined temple of Bubastis: see Merkelbach 1996, 123–144.
85 The Hebrew palindromic acronym ABLANATHANALBA (Atta Barouch Leolam Adonai + nathan + alba) is often found in magical formularies, but also on *defixiones* and amulets: see Brashear 1995, 3577 (with further literature); Martinez 1991, 108–110.
86 Could this be a corrupted allusion to an almost completely forgotten detail of the legend of the Cretan king Minos, which was, however, known to the Greek élite of Alexandria? According to the legend, Minos was offering a sacrifice to the Graces on the island of Paros when he learned of his son's death in Athens. The description of Minos' reaction to the terrible news is preserved in the ancient scholia on Book 1 of Callimachus' *Aitia* (F 7 Pfeiffer i): the king ripped the garland from his head and stopped the music; therefore, ritual law decreed that the sacrifices henceforth be conducted with neither garland nor flute: see Larson 2007, 163; Mori 2014, 233.

(cὺ εἶ ὁ διαλύων καὶ δεςμεύων). In Greek thought, *Ananke* ("Necessity") was often linked to Aphrodite *Ourania* ("Heavenly") who personified the higher, celestial qualities of love. The reference in our text seems, however, to be rather interspersed with philosophical or mystical ideas, in which *Ananke* appears as an inexorable force lying behind all physical or metaphysical constraints or bindings, including love. Although the references to the Graces and Necessity undoubtedly point to a Greek source, the recipe in its present form betrays several layers of redaction, which often disrupt the original flow of the text, resulting in themes isolated from their initial context.

The third invocation formula (col. v 27 to vi 3) is addressed to the heavenly, terrestrial and aerial gods, who remain unnamed (ἐπικαλοῦμαι ὑμᾶς, θεοὶ οὐράνιοι καὶ ἐπίγ<ε>ιοι καὶ ἀέρ<ι>οι καὶ ἐπιχθόνιοι). Once again, the practitioner adjures Eros by the (unnamed) god "who controls the four foundations" (see also above) to accomplish the agent's wishes.[87] He then identifies himself as a "slave of the highest god, the almighty one who holds the cosmos (in his power)" (ὅτι δοῦλός εἰμι τοῦ ὑψίστου θεοῦ τοῦ κατέχοντο[ς] τὸν κόσμον καὶ παντοκρ[ά]τορος).[88] It seems safe to assume that no Greek (or Egyptian, for that matter) would ever have referred to himself as a "slave of the highest god"; thus, although the (common) late antique concept of the Highest God may also be seen as referring to a monotheistic expression of the divine (such as the one found in another recipe of this scroll: see below), this particular reference seems to be rather linked to the Jewish concept of the creator god.[89] It is important to note that the phrasing is followed by a Jewish (Aramaic) *vox*: that is, μαρμαριωθ, meaning "Lord of lights". What is more, in the next column, the Highest God identifies himself (col. vi 1) as the "god of all gods, ιαōn sabaōth adōnai" (ὅτι εἰμὶ θεὸς θεῶν ἁπάντων Ἰάων Cαβαὼθ Ἀδωναί).

The consecration of the Eros statuette is now complete. Yet, the recipe continues: whenever the practitioner wishes to send Eros as his messenger to the beloved one, he is to lift the Eros statuette from the table and utter another magical

---

87 The agent may be a man or a woman (col. v 29–32: ἐπιτελέςαι μοι, τῷ δ(εῖνα) ἢ τῇ δ(εῖνα), τόδε πρᾶγμα καὶ δοῦναί μοι χάριν, ἡδυγλωςςίαν, ἐπ[αφ]ροδιςίαν πρὸς πάντας ἀνθρώπους καὶ πάςας γυναῖκας τὰς ὑπὸ τὴν κτίςι[ν], "to accomplish for me, the man NN or the woman NN, the following deed, and to give me favour, sweet speech, sex appeal before all men and all women under creation").

88 Note that, in the early centuries AD, Helios is often described as κοςμοκράτωρ, while the Christians usually use the epithet παντοκράτωρ to refer to their God: see Pachoumi 2017, 71.

89 Thus also Pachoumi 2017, 87. The concept of the *Hypsistos Theos* was generally – though not exclusively – associated with the Jewish god: see mainly Mitchell 1999 and 2010; but, cf. Belayche 2011, and Brenk 2014.

formula, which he is instructed to write on a papyrus strip. The magical formula (col. vi 5–22) is addressed to the young sun god Harpocrates (here identified with Eros), who is referred to as "an infant"[90] and as "the living god"[91] (cὺ εἶ ὁ νήπιος, ὁ ζῶν θεός), but is also described as "the one who has the shape" (ὁ ἔχων μορφὴν) of several Egyptian or Semitic divinities.[92] The practitioner adjures Horus-Harpocrates "by the [holy] and valuable name to which all creation is subject" (ὁρκίζω cε κατὰ τοῦ <ἁγίου> καὶ κατ' ἐπιτίμου ὀνόματος, ᾧ ἡ πᾶca κτίcιc ὑπόκειται). Though the name of this almighty God is never uttered, he is revealed as an amalgam of many different divine aspects, which signify the totality of cosmos in terms of ancient Egyptian religious thought: he is "[the one] of the Red Sea, the one who makes tremble the winds from the four regions, the one who sits upon the lily and illuminates the whole inhabited world. For in the form of a crocodile you take your seat (on the throne?), while in southerly regions you are a winged serpent, for thus were you in truth born".[93]

Close parallels of this passage are found in two slightly later magical recipes,[94] while a depiction of the described scene is engraved on a magical gemstone (CBd-497) dated to the 2nd/3rd century AD.[95] Reinhold Merkelbach and Maria Totti have convincingly argued that the text in all three versions is actually a Greek adaptation of an Egyptian prayer to the Phoenix, who is the "God of the Red Sea".[96] The myth of the Phoenix is found in many ancient cultures;[97] it was

---

90 Cf. *GEMF* 31 = *PGM* I 33; 74 = VII 516; 68 = XXXVI 218–219; see also n. 102 below.
91 A common Egyptian epithet of Osiris who is often referred to as *ntr 'nḫ* ("living god"): see Ritner, *GMPT* 156 n. 19.
92 Note that, in the first invocation formula, Eros is addressed to as the "Lord of forms": see n. 81 above.
93 *GEMF* 15 col. vi 14–17 (= *PGM/PDM* XII 87–90): <ὁ ἐκ?> ἐρυθρᾶ<c> θαλάccηc, ὁ ἐκ τῶν δ μερῶν τοὺc ἀνέμουc cυνcείων, ὁ ἐπὶ τοῦ λωτοῦ καθήμενοc καὶ λαμπυρίδων τὴν ὅλην οἰκουμένην. καθέζῃ γὰρ κορκοδειλοειδήc, ἐν δὲ τοῖc πρὸc νότον μέρεc[ι]ν δράκων εἶ πτεροειδήc, ὣc γὰρ ἔφυc τῇ ἀληθείᾳ.
94 The prayer appears (in a longer variation) in *GEMF* 30 col. iii 55 to col. iv 20 (= *PGM* II 64–184 at 103–122), dated to the 2nd/3rd century AD and, very briefly, also in *GEMF* 55 = *PGM* III 1–164 at 153–154, dated to the 3rd/4th century AD.
95 The surface of the gemstone is divided into four sections; in the middle, there is an oval field in which a phoenix is depicted. Harpocrates upon a lotus flower is engraved on the top right section; a winged snake flying upwards is engraved on the top left section; a crowned falcon on the bottom left section, while on the bottom right section the remnants of belly and feet of a crocodile are still visible. On the gem see Michel 2001, 63–64, no. 97; cf. Gordon 2011a, 44 (with pl. 10). The significance of the directions is discussed in Harrauer 1987, 36–39. Two amuletic parallels are discussed in Barb 1957, 81–86.
96 See Merkelbach/Totti 1990, 20–34.
97 See Nigg 2016.

known already to Hesiod (fr. 304 M–W), but also to later mystico-religious traditions.[98] Thus, Herodotus informs us (2.73) that the Phoenix was a sacred bird of Eastern origins related to the worship of the sun god in Egypt: this unique bird, says Herodotus, comes to Egypt once in five hundred years, when his father dies, and carries his father's remains encased in an egg made of myrrh to be buried at the temple of the Sun. Herodotus' account is related to the myth of the Egyptian *bennu*, a cosmogonic creature associated with solar theology and figured already in the Heliopolitan creation myth. In ancient Egyptian prayers and iconography, this sacred bird was linked to Atum, the sun god Ra, but also Osiris, as a symbol of the rising sun and resurrection.[99]

A not so close parallel (albeit revolving around similar themes) may also be found in another recipe of the current manuscript, which prescribes an elaborate procedure for consecrating a ring that is expected to provide its bearer with success in every operation (*GEMF* 15 = *PGM/PDM* XII 201-269). The recipe includes (col. x 5 to xi 20 = *PGM/PDM* XII 216–267) a lengthy prayer addressed to the powerful All-Lord, a pantheistic deity whose name is never explicitly mentioned in the text. The prayer begins with an address to the "three suns" (identified as gods in heaven, under the earth and in the realm in-between, similar to our text), who are mostly referred to by Egyptian epithets that underline their power over the physical world, but are also portrayed as governors of Fate and of *Nemeseis* (the text contains no further Greek mythological inspirations). The prayer continues with imagery derived from Egyptian theology, such as the Osiris myth, the daily birth of the sun god out of the watery abyss, the Phoenix myth (associated with the sun god, similar to our text) and the genealogy of the Heliopolitan Ennead. It is also worth noting that the prayer incorporates a prose hymn addressed to the "pantocrator" (col. x 27 to xi 10 = *PGM/PDM* XII 238–257) who is referred to as "the one from the four winds (similar to our text: see below), the almighty god, the one who blew into mortals the breath of life, master of the beautiful things of the cosmos.[100] The prose hymn is interrupted by a hexametric hymn of approximately eight verses (col. x 33 to xi 5 = *PGM/PDM* XII 244–252), whose form and contents are, once again, suggestive of Greek origins.

---

98 Cf. Van den Broek 1972, 76–145.
99 See Van den Broek 1972, 261–304; Lecocq 2016.
100 *GEMF* 15 col. x 27–28 (= *PGM/PDM* XII 238–239): δεῦρό μοι, ὁ ἐκ τῶν δ ἀν[έ]μων, ὁ παντοκράτωρ θεός, ὁ ἐνφυσήσας πνεύματα ἀνθρώποις εἰς ζωήν, δέσποτα τῶν ἐν κόσμῳ καλῶν. Part of the pantocrator hymn is also found (in variations) in *GEMF* 43 = *PGM* XXI 1–28, and *GEMF* 60 = *PGM* XIII 732–1056 at 761–794: see Merkelbach/Totti 1990, 127–222.

To return to our text: the Phoenix (the "God of the Red Sea") is addressed as having various aspects, each of which is associated with a different (cardinal) direction[101] ("the winds from the four regions"). In one direction, he appears as Harpocrates upon the lotus illuminating the whole inhabited world (the young sun god);[102] in another direction, he appears as a crocodile (a form of Sobek-Ra); in the south, he appears as a winged serpent (that is, Agathos Daimon, a multifaceted deity that took on solar attributes and became conflated with Prē and Helios).[103] One of the four aspects of the god is, however, missing from our text (betraying corruption in the process of transmission). Luckily, we can find it in one of the other versions of the prayer, and also on the magical gem: the missing aspect is that of Horus the falcon.[104] There can be little doubt that in all extant versions of the prayer (textual or iconographic) the sacred *bnw* of Egyptian theology is associated with different aspects of the sun god.[105]

It is plausible to assume, as suggested by Reinhold Merkelbach and Maria Totti,[106] that the prayer may have originally been part of a ritual drama, enacted by the Egyptian priests,[107] remnants of which survive in col. vi 19–20 and explain the sharp stylistic turn into the first person singular; a priest would have addressed the Highest God with the following words: "I am the one whom you met at the base of the holy hill and to whom you gave as a gift the knowledge of your most great na[me]".[108] The genuine Egyptian roots of the text are clearly visible in

---

101 Cf. Assmann 1975, nos. 128.50 (on p. 292) and 129.140–145 (on pp. 298–299).
102 See also *GEMF* 15 col. v 9–10 and vi 6. Similar phrasings can also be found in *GEMF* 57 = *PGM* IV 1110–1111, 1684; *GEMF* 18 col. iv verso 13 = *PGM* LXI 32. Note that Plutarch (*De Is. et Os.* 355 B) also associates the rising sun with Harpocrates seated upon the lotus. An explanation of the symbolism behind this image can be found in Iamblichus (*Myst.* 7.2.251–252): see Pachoumi 2015, 391–392, and 2017, 64–65. The rising sun is also often depicted on magical gems (dating from the late Ptolemaic and Roman periods) as a naked child (Harpocrates) seated on a lotus flower or a boat: see El-Kachab 1971.
103 Note that the Greek Eros was often depicted as a winged infant, while in Sappho (fr. 130 L–P) he is referred to as γλυκύπικρον, ἀμάχανον ὄρπετον: cf. Merkelbach/Totti 1990, 28–29.
104 See *GEMF* 30 = *PGM* II 64–184 at 108–110: ἐν δὲ τοῖς πρὸς νότον μέρεϲι μορφὴν ἔχειϲ τοῦ ἁγίου ἱέρακοϲ, δι' ἧϲ πέμπειϲ τὴν εἰϲ ἀέρα πύρωϲιν. A crowned falcon is also engraved on the bottom left section of the amuletic parallel (CBd-497): see n. 95 above.
105 Cf. Horap. 1. 34 (p. 78.3 Sbordone): ἡλίου ἐϲτὶν ὁ φοῖνιξ ϲύμβολον.
106 See Merkelbach/Totti 1990, 20.
107 For dramatic reenactments of mythical stories (as part of religious ceremonies) in ancient Egypt see Leprohon 2007. For the long-standing debate over the use of the terms "theatre", "drama" or even "performance" in Egyptology see Mikhail 1984.
108 *GEMF* 15 col. vi 19–20 (= *PGM/PDM* XII 92–93): ἐγώ εἰμι ᾧ ϲυνήντηϲαϲ ὑπὸ τὸ ἱερὸν ὄροϲ καὶ ἐδωρήϲω τὴν τοῦ μεγίϲτου ὀν<όματόϲ> ϲου γνῶϲιν. The phrase (in variations) is also found in the parallel texts: see *GEMF* 30 col. iv 24–26 (= *PGM* II 126–128): ἐγώ εἰμι ὁ δ(εῖνα), ὅϲτιϲ ϲοι

this part of the recipe. The prayer ends with a common motif of Egyptian religion: the promise to keep secrecy from laity, but share the secret knowledge with those initiated into the sacred rites, while worshipping the god in cultic purity.[109]

Conclusions

The two magical recipes discussed in this chapter belong to a mid-late 2nd century AD Theban handbook. Although they cannot be seen as typical representatives of the whole corpus of late antique magic, the recipes are provided here as élite examples of Late Egyptian ritual texts (private ritual), being produced by professional ritual specialists (probably, Egyptian priests).

Both prescribed *praxeis* were meant for purely private ends: that is, to resolve matters of interpersonal conflict. The first *praxis* is methodologically simple: it mainly aims at mobilising through ritual actions (utterances and offerings) a Greek goddess (Kore) to send (probably violent) dreams to the victim (but also allows the agent the possibility of killing the victim, if he/she does not comply with his/her wishes). The relation between the agent and the victim remains unknown, although it would not be implausible to assume an erotic dimension. The transition from incantations linked exclusively to Greek divinities to those in which Greek influence is mingled with Egyptian or Jewish mythological notions and ritual practices is best evidenced in the second text which describes in detail an erotic *praxis*: the practitioner is instructed on how to mobilise Eros (and Psyche) as his assistant(s) applying a complex three-day consecration ritual.

The original author(s) of the texts appears to have been well versed in the religious literature of his (or their) times, and thus found cross-cultural inspiration in Egyptian, Greek, but also in Jewish (Aramaic) ritual texts and authoritative traditions. What is more, although many of the ritual techniques used in the two procedures point back to their traditional Egyptian roots, both recipes also include techniques that are rooted in Greek phonemics (such as the use of *voces magicae* and palindromes) and are thus considered as foreign to Egyptian language and culture.

ἀπήντηcα, καὶ δῶρόν μοι ἐδωρήcω τὴν τοῦ μεγίcτου cου ὀνόματοc γνῶcιν, and *GEMF* 55 (= *PGM* III 157): ἐγώ εἰμι ᾧ ὑπήντηcαc [καὶ ἐ]δωρήcω τὴν τοῦ cοῦ μεγίcτου ὀνόμα<τοc> γνῶcιν.

109 For secrecy as a major component of Egyptian religion see mainly Assmann 1995. For secrecy in Graeco-Egyptian magic see Dieleman 2005, 80–101. It is, of course, a commonplace that the Greeks also limited the secrets of the mysteries to the initiates.

Both rituals demonstrate that the rhetoric of Graeco-Egyptian magic was, similar to that of Pharaonic times, structured on the belief that religious truths are to be expressed through a complex system of symbols and mythical motifs. Nonetheless, each of the two texts chosen as case studies mirrors a long process initiated in the late Hellenistic period and developed throughout the Roman period. During this process, various concepts firmly embedded in Pharaonic magico-religious tradition were reworked into a different realisation (shaped by syncretic and monotheistic tendencies) to meet the needs of a new multicultural audience whose main interest was focused on acquiring divine assistance in everyday life.

Bibliography

Assmann, J. (1975), *Ägyptische Hymnen und Gebete*, Zurich/Munich.
Assmann, J. (1984), *Ägypten, Theologie und Frömmigkeit einer frühen Hochkultur*, Stuttgart.
Assmann, J. (1995), 'Unio Liturgica. Die kultische Einstimmung in götterweltlichen Lobpreis als Grundmotiv "esoterischer" Überlieferung im alten Ägypten', in: H.G. Kippenberg/G.G. Stroumsa (eds.), *Secrecy and Concealment. Studies in the History of Mediterranean and Near Eastern Religions*, Leiden, 37–60 (Studies in the History of Religions 65).
Barb, A. (1957), 'Abraxas-Studien', in: M. Amand et al. (eds.), *Hommages à Waldemar Deonna*, Brussels, 67–86 (Coll. Latomus 28).
Barbis Lupi, R. (1994), 'La *paragraphos*: analisi di un segno di lettura', in: A. Bülow-Jacobsen (ed.), *Proceedings of the 20th International Congress of Papyrologists*, Copenhagen, 414–417.
Belayche, N. (2011), 'Hypsistos: A Way of Exalting the Gods in Graeco-Roman Polytheism', in: J.A. North/S.R.F. Price (eds.), *The Religious History of the Roman Empire: Pagans, Jews, and Christians*, Oxford/New York, 139–174.
Bernabé, A./Jiménez San Cristóbal, A.I. (2001), *Instrucciones para el más allá: Las laminillas órficas de oro*, Madrid.
Bernabé, A./Jiménez San Cristóbal, A.I. (2008), 'Las laminillas órficas de oro', in: A. Bernabé/F. Casadesús (eds.), *Orfeo y la tradición órfica: un reencuentro*, Madrid, 495–535.
Bortolani, L.M. (2016), *Magical Hymns from Roman Egypt: A Study of Greek and Egyptian Traditions of Divinity*, Cambridge.
Bowden, H. (2010), *Mystery Cults of the Ancient World*, London.
Brashear, W.M. (1995), 'The Greek Magical Papyri: An Introduction and Survey; Annotated Bibliography (1928–1994)', in: W. Haase/H. Temporini (eds.), *Aufstieg und Niedergang der Römischen Welt* 2.18.5, Berlin/New York, 3380–3684.
Bremmer, J.N. (2014), *Initiation into the Mysteries of the Ancient World*, Berlin/Boston (MVAW 1).
Bremmer, J.N. (2019), *The World of Greek Religion and Mythology*, Tübingen (WUNT 433).
Brenk, F.E. (2014), 'Philo and Plutarch on the Nature of God', in: *The Studia Philonica Annual* 26, 79–92.
Clinton, K. (1992), *Myth and Cult: The Iconography of the Eleusinian Mysteries*, Stockholm.
Collins, D. (2008), *Magic in the Ancient Greek World*, Malden, MA/Oxford.

Cook, A.B. (1895), 'The Bee in Greek mythology', in: *The Journal of Hellenic Studies* 15, 1–24.
Costantini, L. (2019), *Magic in Apuleius' 'Apologia': Understanding the Charges and the Forensic Strategies in Apuleius' Speech*, Berlin (BzA 373).
David, R. (2002), *Religion and Magic in Ancient Egypt*, New York.
De Haro Sanchez, M. (2008), 'Les papyrus iatromagiques grecs et la region thébaine', in: A. Delattre/P. Heilporn (eds.), *"Et maintenant ne sont plus que des villages...": Thèbes et sa région aux époques hellénistique, romaine et byzantine. Actes du colloque tenu à Bruxelles les 2 et 3 décembre 2005*, Brussels, 97–102 (Papyrologica Bruxellensia 34).
Dickie, M.W. (2001), *Magic and Magicians in the Greco-Roman World*, London.
Dieleman, J. (2005), *Priests, Tongues, and Rites: The London-Leiden Magical Manuscripts and Translation in Egyptian Ritual (100-300 CE)*, Leiden (Religions in the Graeco-Roman World 153).
Dieleman, J. (2006), 'Abundance in the Margins — Multiplicity of Script in the Demotic Magical Papyri', in: S. Sanders (ed.), *Margins of Writing, Origins of Culture. New Approaches to Writing and Reading in the Ancient Near East*, Chicago, 67–81 (Oriental Institute Seminars 2).
Dieleman, J. (2012), 'Coping with a Difficult Life: Magic, Healing, and Sacred Knowledge', in: C. Riggs (ed.), *The Oxford Handbook of Roman Egypt*, Oxford, 337–361.
Dieleman, J. (2019a), 'The Greco-Egyptian Magical Papyri', in: D. Frankfurter (ed.), *Guide to the Study of Ancient Magic*, Leiden, 283–321 (Religions in the Graeco-Roman World 189).
Dieleman, J. (2019b), 'Egypt', in: D. Frankfurter (ed.), *Guide to the Study of Ancient Magic*, Leiden, 87–114 (Religions in the Graeco-Roman World 189).
Dijkstra, J.H.F. (2011), 'The Fate of the Temples in Late Antique Egypt', in: L.A. Lavan/M. Mulryan (eds.), *The Archaeology of Late Antique 'Paganism'*, Leiden, 389–436 (Late Antique Archaeology 7).
Dosoo, K. (2014), *Rituals of Apparition in the Theban Magical Library*, PhD Thesis, Macquarie University, Sidney.
Dosoo, K. (2016), 'A History of the Theban Magical Library', in: *Bulletin of the American Society of Papyrologists* 53, 251–274.
Edwards, M.J. (1992), 'The Tale of Cupid and Psyche', in: *Zeitschrift für Papyrologie und Epigraphik* 94, 77–94.
El-Kachab, A.M. (1971), 'Some Gem-Amulets Depicting Harpocrates Seated on a Lotus Flower', in: *The Journal of Egyptian Archaeology* 57, 132–145.
Faraone, C.A. (2000), 'Handbooks and Anthologies: The Collection of Greek and Egyptian Incantations in Late Hellenistic Egypt', in: *Archiv für Religionsgeschichte* 2, 195–214.
Faraone, C.A. (2012), 'The Problem of Dense Concentrations of Data for Cartographers (and Chronographers) of Ancient Mediterranean Magic: Some Illustrative Case Studies from the East', in: M. Piranomante/F. Marco Simón (eds.), *Contesti Magici / Contextos Mágicos*, Rome, 103–110.
Faraone, C.A. (2019), 'Cultural Plurality in Magical Recipes for Oracular and Protective Statues', in: L.M. Bortolani/W.D. Furley/S. Nagel/J.F. Quack (eds.), *Cultural Plurality in Ancient Magical Texts and Practices: Graeco-Egyptian Handbooks and Related Traditions*, Tübingen, 171–187.
Faraone, C.A. (2022), 'The Composite Recipes in *GEMF* 57 (= *PGM* IV) and How They Grew', in: C.A. Faraone/S. Torallas Tovar (eds.), *The Greco-Egyptian Magical Formularies: Libraries, Books and Individual Recipes*, Ann Arbor, 282–303 (New Texts from Ancient Cultures).
Faraone, C.A./Torallas Tovar, S. (eds.) (2021), *Greek and Egyptian Magical Formularies: Text and Translation*, vol. I, Atlanta (Writings from the Greco-Roman World Supplement series).

Frangoulidis, S. (2008), *Witches, Isis and Narrative: Approaches to Magic in Apuleius' Metamorphoses*, Berlin/New York (Trends in Classics Supplementary Volumes 2).

Frankfurter, D. (1995), 'Narrating Power: The Theory and Practice of the Magical *Historiola* in Ritual Spells', in: M.W. Meyer/P.A. Mirecki (eds.), *Ancient Magic and Ritual Power*, Leiden, 457–476 (Religions in the Graeco-Roman World 129).

Frankfurter, D. (1998), *Religion in Roman Egypt: Assimilation and Resistance*, Princeton.

Frankfurter, D. (2000), 'The Consequences of Hellenism in Late Antique Egypt: Religious Worlds and Actors', in: *Archiv für Religionsgeschichte* 2, 162–194.

Fournet, J.-L. (2000), 'Au sujet du plus ancien chalinos scolaire: chalinoi et vers alphabétiques grecs', in: *Revue de Philologie, de Littérature et d'Histoire Anciennes* 74, 61–82.

Fox, M.V (1983), 'Ancient Egyptian Rhetoric', in: *Rhetorica: A Journal of the History of Rhetoric* 1, 9–22.

Gagarin, M. (2001), 'Women's Voices in Attic Oratory', in: A. Lardinois/L. McClure (eds.), *Making Silence Speak: Women's Voices in Greek Literature and Society*, Princeton, 161–176.

Gager, J.G. (1992), *Curse Tablets and Binding Spells from the Ancient World*, New York/Oxford.

Gordon, R.L. (2011a), 'Archaeologies of Magical Gems', in: C. Entwistle/N. Adams (eds.), *"Gems of Heaven": Recent Research on Engraved Gemstones in Late Antiquity, c. AD 200–600*, London, 39–49 (British Museum Research Publication no. 177).

Gordon, R.L. (2011b), '*Signa nova et inaudita*: The Theory and Practice of Invented Signs (*charaktēres*) in Graeco-Egyptian Magical Texts', in: *MHNH* 11, 15–44.

Gordon, R.L./Gasparini, V. (2014), 'Looking for Isis 'the Magician' (ḥk3y.t) in the Graeco-Roman World', in: L. Bricault/R. Veymiers (eds.), *Bibliotheca Isiaca* III, Bordeaux, 39–53.

Griffiths, J.G. (1975), *Apuleius of Madauros. The Isis-book (Metamorphoses, Book XI)*, Leiden (Études préliminaires aux religions orientales dans l'Empire romain 39).

Harrauer, C. (1987), *Meliouchos: Studien zur Entwicklung religiöser Vorstellungen in griechischen synkretistischen Zaubertexten*, Vienna (Wiener Studien, Beiheft 11).

Heyob, S.K. (1975), *The Cult of Isis among Women in the Graeco-Roman World*, Leiden (Études préliminaires aux Religions orientales dans l'Empire romain 51).

Hutto, D. (2002), 'Ancient Egyptian Rhetoric in the Old and New Kingdoms', in: *Rhetorica: A Journal of the History of Rhetoric* 20, 213–233.

Johnson, W.A. (1994), 'The Function of the Paragraphus in Greek Literary Prose Texts', in: *Zeitschrift für Papyrologie und Epigraphik* 100, 65–68.

Karshner, E. (2011), 'Thought, Utterance, Power: Toward a Rhetoric of Magic', in: *Philosophy and Rhetoric* 44, 52–71.

Kennedy, G. (1998), *Comparative Rhetoric*, New York.

Larson, J. (2007), *Ancient Greek Cults: A Guide*, New York/London.

Lecocq, F. (2016), 'Inventing the Phoenix: A Myth in the Making Through Words and Images', in: P.A. Johnston/A. Mastrocinque/S. Papaioannou (eds.), *Animals in Greek and Roman Religion and Myth*, Newcastle upon Tyne, 449–478.

Leprohon, R.J. (2007), 'Ritual Drama in Ancient Egypt', in: E. Csapo/M.C. Miller (eds.), *The Origins of Theater in Ancient Greece and Beyond: From Ritual to Drama*, Cambridge, 259–292.

Lipson, C.S. (2004), 'Ancient Egyptian Rhetoric: It All Comes Down to Maat', in: C.S. Lipson/R.A. Binkley (eds.), *Rhetoric Before and Beyond the Greeks*, Albany, 79–98.

Maltomini, F. (1996), 'PGM XII 50–51: Ο ΔΕΣΠΟΤΗΣ ΤΩΝ ΜΟΡΦΩΝ', in: *Zeitschrift für Papyrologie und Epigraphik* 111, 140.

Maravela, A. (2015), 'Alphabetic Verses and Cipher Alphabets from Western Theban Monasteries: Perspectives on Monastic Literacy in Late Antique Egypt', in: E. Juhász (ed.), *Byzanz und das Abendland III: Studia Byzantino-Occidentalia*, Budapest, 67–83.

Martinez, D.G. (1991), *Michigan Papyri XVI: A Greek Love Charm from Egypt (P. Mich. 757)*, Atlanta (American Studies in Papyrology 30).

Merkelbach, R. (1953), 'Eros und Psyche', in: *Philologus* 102, 103–116.

Merkelbach, R. (1995), *Isis Regina-Zeus Serapis*, Stuttgart.

Merkelbach, R. (1996), *Abrasax: Ausgewählte Papyri religiösen und magischen Inhalts*, vol. 4: *Exorzismen und jüdisch/christlich beeinflusste Texte*, Opladen (Papyrologica Coloniensia 17.4).

Merkelbach, R./Totti, M. (1990), *Abrasax: Ausgewählte Papyri religiösen und magischen Inhalts*, vol. 1: *Gebete*, Opladen (Papyrologica Coloniensia 17.1).

Merkelbach, R./Totti, M. (1991), *Abrasax: Ausgewählte Papyri religiösen und magischen Inhalts*, vol. 2: *Gebete (Fortsetzung)*, Opladen (Papyrologica Coloniensia 17.2).

Metcalf, W.E. (2011), *The Oxford Handbook of Greek and Roman Coinage*, Oxford.

Michel, S. (2001), *Die magischen Gemmen im Britischen Museum*, 2 vols., London.

Mikhail, L. (1984), 'The Egyptological Attitude to Drama in Ancient Egypt: Is it Time for a Revision? (Part II)', in: *Göttinger Miszellen* 77, 25–33.

Mitchell, S. (1999), 'The Cult of Theos Hypsistos between Pagans, Jews, and Christians', in: P. Athanassiadi/M. Frede (eds.), *Pagan Monotheism in Late Antiquity*, Oxford, 81–148.

Mitchell, S. (2010), 'Further Thoughts on the Cult of Theos Hypsistos', in: S. Mitchell/P. van Nuffeen (eds.), *One God: Pagan Monotheism in the Roman Empire*, Cambridge, 167–208.

Mori, A. (2011), 'Names and Places: Myths in Alexandria', in: K. Dowden/N. Livingstone (eds.), *A Companion to Greek Mythology*, Malden, MA/Oxford, 227–241.

Moyer, I.S. (2003), 'The Initiation of the Magician: Transition and Power in Graeco-Egyptian Ritual', in: D.B. Dodd/C.A. Faraone (eds.), *Initiation in the Ancient Greek Rituals and Narratives*, London, 220–230.

Moyer, I.S. (2011), *Egypt and the Limits of Hellenism*, Cambridge.

Nigg, J. (2016), *The Phoenix: An Unnatural Biography of a Mythical Beast*, Chicago/London.

Pachoumi, E. (2011a), 'Eros and Psyche in Erotic Magic', in: *Classica et Mediaevalia* 62, 39–49.

Pachoumi, E. (2011b), 'Divine Epiphanies of Paredroi in the Greek Magical Papyri', in: *Greek, Roman and Byzantine Studies* 51, 155–165.

Pachoumi, E. (2013), 'The Religious-Philosophical Concept of Personal Daimon and the Magico-Theurgic Ritual of Systasis in the Greek Magical Papyri', in: *Philologus* 157, 47–48.

Pachoumi, E. (2017), *The Concepts of the Divine in the Greek Magical Papyri*, Tübingen.

Patera, I. (2010), 'Light and Lighting Equipment in the Eleusinian Mysteries: Symbolism and Ritual Use', in: M. Christopoulos/E.D. Karakantza/O. Levaniouk (eds.), *Light and Darkness in Ancient Greek Myth and Religion*, Lanham, MD, 261–275.

Petridou, G. (2016), *Divine Epiphany in Greek Literature and Culture*, Oxford.

Petrovic, I. (2007), *Von den Toren des Hades zu den Hallen des Olymp: Artemiskult bei Theokrit und Kallimachos*, Leiden/Boston (Mnemosyne Supplement 281).

Petrovic, I. (2015), 'Hymns in the Papyri Graecae Magicae', in: A. Faulkner/O. Hodkinson (eds.), *Hymnic Narrative and the Narratology of Greek Hymns*, Leiden/Boston, 244–267 (Mnemosyne Supplement 384).

Podemann Sørensen, J. (1984), 'The Argument in Ancient Egyptian Magical Formulae', in: *Acta Orientalia* 45, 5–19.

Podemann Sørensen, J. (2003), 'The Rhetoric of Ritual', in: T. Ahlbäck/B. Dahla (eds.), *Ritualistics*, Åbo, 149–161 (Scripta Instituti Donneriani Aboensis 18).

Reitzenstein, R. (1930), 'Eros als Osiris: Ein Nachtrag', in: *Nachrichten von der königlichen Gesellschaft der Wissenschaften zu Göttingen aus dem Jahre 1930, phil.-hist. Klasse*, 396–406.

Ritner, R.K. (1992), 'Egyptian Magic: Questions of Legitimacy, Religious Orthodoxy and Social Deviance', in: A.B. Lloyd (ed.), *Studies in Pharaonic Religion and Society in Honour of J. Gwyn Griffiths*, London, 189–200 (The Egypt Exploration Society Occasional Publications 8).

Ritner, R.K. (1995a), 'The Religious, Social, and Legal Parameters of Traditional Egyptian Magic', in: M.W. Meyer/P.A. Mirecki (eds.), *Ancient Magic and Ritual Power*, Leiden, 43–60 (Religions in the Graeco-Roman World 129).

Ritner, R.K. (1995b), 'Egyptian Magical Practice under the Roman Empire: The Demotic Spells and their Religious Context', in: W. Haase/H. Temporini (eds.), *Aufstieg und Niedergang der Römischen Welt* 2.18.5, Berlin/New York, 3333–3379.

Sarischouli, P. (2019), 'Key Episodes of the Osirian Myth in Plutarch's *De Iside et Osiride* and in Greek and Demotic Magical Papyri: How do the Sources Complement Each Other?', in: S. Torallas Tovar/A. Nodar (eds.), *Proceedings of the 28th International Congress of Papyrology, Barcelona 2016*, Barcelona, 310–324 (Scripta Orientalia 3).

Sarischouli, P. (2022), '*GEMF* 15 (= *PGM*/*PDM* XII): Production and Use of a Bilingual Magical Formulary', in: C.A. Faraone/S. Torallas Tovar (eds.), *The Greco-Egyptian Magical Formularies: Libraries, Books and Individual Recipes*, Ann Arbor, 248–281 (New Texts from Ancient Cultures).

Schlesier, R. (1991/1992), 'Olympian versus Chthonian Religion', in: *Scripta Classica Israelica* 11, 38–51.

Scibilia, A. (2002), 'Supernatural Assistance in the Greek Magical Papyri: The Figure of the Parhedros', in: J.N. Bremmer/J.R. Veenstra (eds.), *The Metamorphosis of Magic from Late Antiquity to the Early Modern Period*, Leuven/Paris, 71–86.

Scullion, S. (1994), 'Olympian and Chthonian', in: *Classical Antiquity* 13, 75–119.

Sourvinou-Inwood, C. (2003), 'Festival and Mysteries: Aspects of the Eleusinian Cult', in: M.B. Cosmopoulos (ed.), *Greek Mysteries. The Archaeology and Ritual of Ancient Greek Secret Cults*, London/New York, 25–49.

Suárez de la Torre, E. (2012), 'The Library of the Magician', in: M. Piranomonte/F. Marco Simón (eds.), *Contesti Magici / Contextos Mágicos*, Rome, 299–306.

Suárez de la Torre, E. (2014), 'Pseudepigraphy and Magic', in: J. Martínez (ed.), *Fakes and Forgers of Classical Literature. Ergo decipiatur!*, Leiden/Boston, 243–262 (Metaforms 2).

Tait, W.J. (1995), 'Theban Magic', in: S.P. Vleeming (ed.), *Hundred-gated Thebes: Acts of a Colloquium on Thebes and the Theban Area in the Graeco-Roman Period*, Leiden, 169–182 (P.L. Bat. 27).

Tobin, V.A. (1991), 'Isis and Demeter: Symbols of Divine Motherhood', in: *Journal of the American Research Center in Egypt* 28, 187–200.

Van den Broek, R. (1972), *The Myth of the Phoenix, According to Classical and Early Christian Traditions*, Leiden (Études préliminaires aux religions orientales dans l'Empire romain 24).

Watts, J.W. (2009), 'Ritual Rhetoric in Ancient Near Eastern Texts', in: C.S. Lipson/R.A. Binkley (eds.), *Ancient Non-Greek Rhetorics*, West Lafayette, IN, 39–66.

Zuntz, G. (1971), *Persephone: Three Essays on Religion and Thought in Magna Graecia*, Oxford.

Part III: **Religion and Rhetorical Performance**

Maik Patzelt
Trends in the Rhetoric of Prayer: The *Actio* of Prayer and the *Eloquentia Popularis*

Abstract: In shifting the focus from a logological approach to the rhetoric of public prayer and the moment of its performance, this contribution reconsiders Roman public prayers as expressions of the rhetorical capacities of the praying agent and not as entirely formalised, de-individualised scripts. This study, therefore, shifts the focus from prayer texts to prayer bodies – bodies of male aristocrats, bodies that perform physically and vocally. As will be argued, the capacity and range of physical and vocal expressions allowed for a trend in prayer rhetoric that displays the same characteristics as the regularly denounced *eloquentia popularis* in public speech. This is *precatio popularis*. This chapter focuses on the examination of clear voice (*clara vox*), the movements and the "double speech" (due to prompting, *praeire*).

1 Introduction

The relationship between rhetoric and religion, and between rhetoric and prayer in particular, has received a great deal of attention in recent years. This attention has manifested itself in particular in studies of public prayer in Greek religion.[1] Inspired by the approach taken by Kenneth Burke in his book *The Rhetoric of Religion*, these studies tend to be based on a notion of prayer rhetoric as a "technique, an art... in persuasive communication".[2] This persuasion operates on at least two levels: religious speech needs to persuade a deity to assist or intervene

---

1 Most influential has been Pernot 2006. Further pioneering approaches are those of Goeken 2010; Spina 2008; Dowden 2007; Deremetz 1994. A first attempt to unveil the aspect of embodiment in prayer rhetoric can be found in Patzelt 2018a. Speaking of rhetoric, I would like to thank Paul Scade who again did a wonderful job in transferring what was supposed to be English into actual English. I would also like to thank Eric Orlin, who provided me with valuable comments on the initial version of this paper, presented at a workshop on "Problems in Defining Prayer" in Amsterdam, April 2019. Finally, I would like to thank Daniel Falk and Rod Werline for having me there.
2 Spina 2008, 216; Dowden 2007, 320; Burke 1970, v.

https://doi.org/10.1515/9783110699623-007

in a particular situation, just as it needs to persuade the attentive human audience that the deity has been successfully persuaded.[3] To this end, prayer, probably more than any other rhetorical endeavour, requires a carefully chosen vocabulary;[4] for gods can express their dissatisfaction with inappropriate requests by bringing about catastrophic events or devastating military defeats. The vocabulary of prayer is thus arranged in a specific structure that is particularly concerned with persuasion and argumentation.[5] This structure involves an invocation, the request itself, and a clearly reasoned argument in favour of the request.[6] The "*actio* of prayer"[7] supports this persuasive purpose by accentuating what is said with gestures of reverence and clarity,[8] for instance by touching the object that is to be dedicated.[9]

Following Burke further, this need to persuade through arguments and structure locates religion and prayers in the realm of *discourse*.[10] Laurent Pernot, for instance, regards prayer as a "discourse *sui generis*", characterised by its structures, arguments, stylistic forms and *actio*.[11] This discourse, its arguments and forms, are embedded in higher discourses, discourses *about* the gods, *to* the gods or *of* the gods.[12] William FitzGerald, a distinguished expert in rhetorical studies on prayer, who likewise follows Kenneth Burke, widens the discourse that informs the performance. Prayer, on his definition, is "situated and situating discourse that speaks both from and to the conditions that give rise to its occasions and utterances".[13]

These conditions are not only formed by mere discourses on or about gods. They are also informed by personal experiences, attitudes and commitments, all of which were themselves shaped in earlier situations and cultural contexts, just

---

[3] Deremetz 1994, 160–165.
[4] Dowden 2007, 320; Pernot 2006, 238; Goeken 2010, 4.
[5] Pernot 2006, 240.
[6] Ausfeld 1903.
[7] Pernot 2006, 241
[8] FitzGerald 2012, 97–99.
[9] This could turn out to be a problem in itself, on which see North 2008. A full list of Roman prayer gestures is provided by Appel 1909, 184–214.
[10] On this topic see, at length, FitzGerald 2012. On Burke see Henderson 1989.
[11] Pernot 2006, 241–242. This focus on the phenomenology of prayer forms, genres and the archetypal gestures used in prayer goes back to Georg Appel (1909). For prayer in general, Marcel Mauss (2003 [1909]) has developed a similar archetypal model, on which see Deremetz 1994, 142–150.
[12] Pernot 2006, 235.
[13] FitzGerald 2012, 12.

as they in turn shape the contexts and situations in which they are applied.¹⁴ The *actio* of prayer is, strictly speaking, informed *by* and embedded *in* both the culture – or in the social reality, to put it another way – and, above all, the very situation in which it occurs. The advantage of such a rhetoric-based approach to prayer is that it allows for a bottom-up exploration of the topic that regards prayers not as mere expressions of formalistic typologies but as "discursive events… as singular occurrences rich in particularity".¹⁵

Yet, just like studies of rhetoric proper,¹⁶ studies of rhetoric and religion are also restricted to formal categories of form and content. All of these approaches take their starting point from Kenneth Burke, adopting his logological approach to rhetoric while also extending it to gestures. Language and discourse are, on this kind of account, primarily symbolic systems, i.e. systems of significations and meanings. However, a literary history of vocal performances such as speech, prayer or song has its limits,¹⁷ as even a cursory consideration of the sources reveals. If we turn our attention to ancient treatises on rhetoric, we find views that differ significantly from those that underlie modern approaches to the subject. With a few exceptions, such as Menander's 3rd-century elaborations on epideictic speeches in religious and political contexts,¹⁸ these ancient works on rhetoric are typically rather obsessed with intonation, the sounds of the words as they should be spoken.¹⁹

This interest fits well with the somewhat surprising preoccupation with voice in the Roman discourse on prayer. As the sources tell us, a cheerful public prayer, a *precatio* or *preces*,²⁰ needs to be performed with a clear voice, *vox clara*,²¹ whereas those prayers that are considered unbearable, indeed distressing, follow

---

14 FitzGerald 2012, 106–114. This strongly resembles a pragmatist approach to the study of religion.
15 FitzGerald 2012, 11.
16 For this criticism of rhetoric proper see Steel 2017, 17.
17 A strong argument unveiling these limits can be found in Habinek 2005, 2–3; cf. Habinek 1998.
18 The 3rd-cent. rhetorician Menander composed a manual for giving public speeches, which groups religious speech and political speech together without considering the significant differences between them. Religious speech, as construed by Menander, involves hymns to the gods (Men. Rhet. 1.1–10).
19 Above all, book 3 of Cicero's *De oratore* is preoccupied with proper vocal performances. In general, see Schulz 2014.
20 Prayer here also includes types such as *votum*, *dedicatio* or *consecratio*.
21 E.g. Liv. 10.19.17; 10.36.11; Suet. *Ner.* 37. Similar references are to be found in Greek sources, e.g. Dem. 18.259–260. For details see Aubriot-Sévin 1992, 146–171.

vocal patterns that are associated with hoarse and erratic sounds.[22] According to the structuralist and functionalist perspectives through which most scholars approach Roman religion, a clear voice makes the prayer audible, allowing persuasive communication as well as ensuring faultless pronunciation.[23] A hoarse and erratic voice would, on this view, put the correct pronunciation at risk and, therefore, threaten the validity of this legal operation.

Vox, however, is not the same as *oratio*, although ancient literature does sometimes tend to equate the two. That some grammarians reduce *vox* to its purpose of articulating words should not be surprising given their profession.[24] Other ancient scholars, such as Plutarch, elaborate on voice (φωνή) as sound.[25] Plutarch clearly distinguishes the effects of *parole* and the effects of *sonority*, emphasising that a voice like "harmonious music affects with delight".[26] This observation invites us to shift the focus from the *orality* of prayer to its *vocality*.[27] Seen in this way, prayer is no mere carrier of language. It is a carrier of sound, an acoustic phenomenon.[28]

Vocality is not a clear analytical tool. It serves as a means to enable us to focus on aspects other than form, content and meaning. It helps to highlight the "expressive aspect" of prayer performance – a performance that might not only be persuasive in content but also in sound. Whereas the prevailing scholarly approach to rhetorical acts foregrounds the agent's capacity to negotiate between the rhetorical tools available and the situation in which they are applied,[29] the approach I follow in this chapter suggests that the same negotiation process applies to the various sounds produced by the prayer. This contribution, in other words, seeks to show that legal speech and religious speech do not merely resemble one another in structure. They are two sides of one coin, aiming to excite the audience by means of voice and bodily expression.

---

22 On the sound that is commonly labelled as "magical" or "prophetic" see Crippa 2015b.
23 Versnel 1981, 26–37; Guittard 1989, 26–27; Scheer 2001, 39–42.
24 E.g. Varro, *Ling.* 6.56; cf. Crippa 2015a, 32–37.
25 Ps. Plut. *Plac.* 4.19 (*Mor.* 902c–f).
26 Ps. Plut. *Plac.* 4.20 (*Mor.* 903a).
27 Butler 2015, 17.
28 A strong argument for the study of voice rather than text is advanced by Butler 2015; Crippa 2015, esp. 23–32; Schulz 2014. On a more theoretical level see Krämer 2002. On voice in Greek prayer see Aubriot-Sévin 1992, 146–171.
29 FitzGerald 2012, 14–16. This recalls Lévi-Strauss' notion of *bricolage* (Lévi-Strauss 1966).

2 *Clara vox*: Public prayer and public rhetoric

References to *clara vox* normally reveal little about why such a voice is appropriate in a given situation. Occasionally, the formulation appears in contexts, religious and non-religious, in which the speaker aims to address a large crowd of people.[30] The same logic seems to apply to prayer on the battlefield.[31] The consul M. Atilius, for instance, makes a vow with *clara vox* in order to be heard by his troops (*ita ut exaudiretur*).[32] It seems that a "clear voice" serves a purely logological purpose. It seeks to make the spoken words audible by means of a loud voice.[33] But as ancient explanations of archaic prayer texts, such as those of the Salii, demonstrate, a clear voice is not only equated with loudness. It is also characterised by the accurate pronunciation of prayer words, the antiquity and consequent incomprehensibility of which makes them easy to mispronounce.[34] In both cases, audibility is no mere means of avoiding the suspicion that the speaker is making inappropriate requests to the gods, as the ancient and modern discourse on silent prayers would have us believe.[35]

Plutarch shows that such audibility serves purposes beyond the logological when he advises his readers to "pray to the gods with the mouth straight and aright" rather than "distorting and sullying one's own tongue with strange names and barbarous phrases". Apart from the right mind to which the rightly configured mouth alludes, and apart from the correct pronunciation of a formalised text, his advice highlights the audibility of a prayer as a matter of sound. He explains his advice with a reference to the *citharōdoi*, who are supposed to follow the same advice in order to "preserve the good old forms of music".[36] With this comparison, Plutarch introduces the right words for prayer as being inseparably

---

30 Liv. 7.9.8; Hor. *Epist*. 1.16.59–62; Pers. 2.8; Stat. *Theb*. 11.503.
31 Liv. 7.15.2; 7.31.12; 10.36.11.
32 Liv. 10.36.11.
33 Cf., for Athens, Dem. 18.259–260.
34 Quint. *Inst*. 1.6.39–40.
35 The most influential contributions to this discourse are: Freyburger 2001; van der Horst 1994; Versnel 1981, 21–26; Wagenvoort 1980 (which is an English translation of an article that originally appeared in Latin in 1964); McCartney 1948; Balogh 1925; Sudhaus 1906. Cf. Freyburger 2000, 11–12; Valette-Cagnac 1997, 42–45.
36 Plut. *De superst*. 3e = *Mor*. 168a–b: δικαίῳ τῷ στόματι τοὺς κιθαρῳδοὺς ἐκέλευον ᾄδειν οἱ τὴν νόμιμον μουσικὴν σῴζειν δοκοῦντες· ἡμεῖς δὲ τοῖς θεοῖς ἀξιοῦμεν ὀρθῷ τῷ στόματι καὶ δικαίῳ προσεύχεσθαι, καὶ μὴ τὴν ἐπὶ τῶν σπλάγχνων μὲν γλῶτταν εἰ καθαρὰ καὶ ὀρθὴ σκοπεῖν, τὴν δ' ἑαυτῶν διαστρέφοντας καὶ μολύνοντας ἀτόποις ὀνόμασι καὶ ῥήμασι βαρβαρικοῖς καταισχύνειν καὶ παρανομεῖν εἰς τὸ θεῖον καὶ πάτριον ἀξίωμα τῆς εὐσεβείας.

tied to the beautiful art over which the Muses preside. Plutarch moves the act of prayer closer to being a musical act, which certainly requires much more from the performer than just the raising of his voice. Prayer is, on this view, not merely a matter of using the right words. It also requires that one uses, indeed sings, these words aright – that is to say, that one utters the words in question in a rhythmical manner.

Recent studies in Roman rhetoric support this impression. Thomas Habinek, for instance, argues that performing public speeches audibly involved the use of devices that were also used for songs.[37] As the recent findings of a research group at the Fraunhofer Institute reveal, only professionally trained vocality enables the successful transmission of its orality. Such professional skills were acquired through the elite's rhetorical and poetic training.[38] Just as in the case of modern opera singers, what empowers these aristocrats to permeate the space with their voices is the ritualised and thus rhythmical speech that we tend to consider as song or poetry. It is not surprising, then, that "poetry shifts from a mere craft into a defining performance of elite Roman manhood".[39] Quintilian, too, extracts instructive advice for rhetoricians from poetry and music.[40] Just as public speeches require that these rhetorical skills should enable one's words to resound through public spaces, so praying in public with a *clara vox* might also require the very same skills if one actually wishes to reach one's audience. There are linguistic observations that support this hypothesis.

Public prayers follow the same stylistic patterns as do public, and especially legal, speeches. They share the same aspects of form, of style, of words, and of syntax, as Jacqueline Dangel has shown.[41] Elizabeth A. Meyer refers to this pattern in both public (legal) speech and public prayer as "*carmen*-style" or the "legal etiquette" of rhetoric. According to her, "this style is characterized by repetition; accumulated pleonastic synonyms (either nouns or verbs), often in asyndeton; detailed and precise identification of what is wanted or required; and the use of assonance and alliteration to create something that would sound rhythmical and impressive".[42] Meyer supports this argument with a long list of public prayers and *carmina*, including the famous *devotio Decii*.

---

[37] Habinek 2005, 65–66.
[38] My thanks to Christian Fron, who allowed me to profit from the knowledge he gained through his participation in this project. Cf. Habinek 1998.
[39] Habinek 2005, 82.
[40] He does so, however, with a certain caution: Quint. *Inst.* 10.1.27–28; cf. 1.8.14. See further Dozier 2012.
[41] Dangel 1996.
[42] Meyer 2004, 45.

The point made here is not that religious and legal speech share the same logological patterns or operate in accordance with the same logic of legally binding reciprocity.⁴³ Rather, it is the *carmen*-style's rhythmical sound that is of interest, for it allows the projection of Habinek's findings concerning poetic vocality in public speech onto the vocality of public prayer.⁴⁴ That is to say, public prayers deploy the same vocal skills that public speeches use to reach their audience. It is, thus, not unlikely that the praying agent has a similar goal. However, the permeation of a space with rhythmic sound is not the only effect of these rhetorical, indeed poetic, skills that are deployed in a public prayer. Cicero writes:⁴⁵

> For as art started from nature, it would certainly be deemed to have failed if it had not a natural power of affecting us and giving us pleasure; but nothing is so akin to our own minds as rhythms and words – these arouse us up to excitement, and smooth and calm us down, and often lead us to mirth and to sorrow. Though their extremely powerful influence is more suited to poetry and song, nor was it overlooked by that very learned monarch, King Numa, and by our ancestors, as is shown by the use of the lyre and the pipes at ceremonial banquets (*epulae sollemnes*), and by the verses of the Salii. (Cic. *De or.* 3.197; tr. Rackham 1942)

Cicero highlights the emotional quality of the poetically skilled utterance – that is, its rhythmic vocality – which is deployed in both public speech and public prayer. He even deploys the prayers of the Salii and – as the reference to the mythical king Numa and the *epulae sollemnes* clearly indicates – all forms of public religious speech, thus all forms of public prayers, as *exempla* of arousing voices and sounds. It is, as Quintilian and the author of the *Rhetorica ad Herennium* call it, the *suavitas* of the voice that arouses the audiences of speeches and prayers.⁴⁶ Modulation of the voice and the use of rhythms, alliterations, and archaisms all come together to elicit a soundscape that has an emotional impact on the audience. If the *carmen*-style and its impact is not sufficient for its task, so Cicero tells

---

43 On this reciprocity see Champeaux 2001; Versnel 1981, 56–58. On reciprocity as an essential mechanism in Roman religion see King 2003, 292–307.
44 Aubriot-Sévin 1992, 217–218 argues in favour of rhythm rather than legal precision with respect to Greek prayers.
45 *Ars enim cum a natura profecta sit, nisi naturam moveat ac delectet nihil sane egisse videatur. Nihil est autem tam cognatum mentibus nostris quam numeri atque voces, quibus et excitamur et incendimur et lenimur et languescimus et ad hilaritatem et ad tristitiam saepe deducimur; quorum illa summa vis carminibus est aptior et cantibus, non neglecta, ut mihi videtur, a Numa rege doctissimo maioribusque nostris, ut epularum solemnium fides ac tibiae Saliorumque versus indicant.*
46 *Rhet. Her.* 3.19–27; Quint. *Inst.* 11.3.150–156.

us, the audience boos the orator.⁴⁷ Persuasion in rhetoric, it seems, also operates on the vocal level.

Another shared detail of public prayer and public speech is the presence of the flute. According to Pliny the Elder, the "piper plays so that nothing but the prayer is heard".⁴⁸ That this effect is not guaranteed by the mere volume of the instrument is affirmed by simple logic, for otherwise the prayer would not be heard at all. We can also note that the commanding of silence, which is common in these contexts (*favere linguis*) to ensure that no other voices and sounds might interfere with the prayer, would be pointless if nothing but the flute could, in any case, be heard.⁴⁹ In addition to the role it is reported to play, the sound of the flute might have had another purpose, serving to help the orator maintain the pace of his speech. This use is reported in the case of ritual songs, such as the *carmen Saliare*.⁵⁰ Gaius Gracchus famously had a flutist at his side while giving a speech, helping him to modulate his voice most effectively.⁵¹ This special case already alludes to the close interrelation between effective religious and non-religious speech.

"Nothing but the prayer" cannot, then, refer to the orality of the speech alone. It must also refer to its vocality. The rhythm of the flute supports the rhythm of the prayer, indeed intensifies that rhythm and thus the whole soundscape, supporting the sound as it permeates the space. Given the widely reported emotional impact on the audience of flute tunes during ritual occasions and other public events,⁵² it is reasonable to assume that the combination of prayer and flute seeks to create a similar emotional effect. Another reason to think that this is so, is the way in which speech is always aligned with the sound of music. The affective quality of the voice is always referred to and explained by the affective quality of musical instruments.⁵³

---

47 Cic. *De or.* 3.196. Cf. Cic. *Brut.* 186.
48 Plin. *HN* 28.11: ... *tibicinem canere, ne quid aliud exaudiatur.*
49 Plin. *HN* 28.11; Sen. *De vit. beat.* 26.7; cf. *Ep.* 115.4; Ov. *Met.* 15.670–680; *Fast.* 2.649–655; Tib. 2.2.2–10. On this "holy silence" in Roman and Greek rituals see Gödde 2011, 13; Montiglio 2000, 13–17; Mensching 1926.
50 Dion. Hal. *Ant. Rom.* 2.70.
51 Cic. *De or.* 3.225–227.
52 Cens. 12.
53 Cic. *De or.* 3.216.

All of these observations derive from a rather traditional, comparative approach to the schemata of public speech. A final argument in support of my findings can be drawn from studies on the aesthetics of religion.[54] These studies generally regard every voice and every tone as an aesthetic device that manipulates the sensory-nervous system of the recipient. Just as does Cicero, an aesthetic approach highlights the fact that voices and sounds that a given culture deems beautiful have an immediate impact on the emotional state of the recipient, in our case, the audience to the prayer. Unfortunately, there are no sources from Late Republican and Early Imperial Rome that explicitly attest to such emotional impacts. As a result, a comparison with the vocal patterns of a *clara vox* in rhetoric offers the most fruitful strategy by which to shed light on these effects. It may, however, be worth noting that Huguette Fugier once made an argument that points in this direction,[55] inferring an *ecstatic* state of mind from the *sollemnia verba*,[56] which are essential elements of the above-mentioned *carmen*-style of prayer.

Taking these points together, we can see that praying in public is not just about raising one's voice in order to transmit the content of prayer properly. Praying in public also involves rhythms and melodies – voice and sound coming together to create an emotional impact on the attentive audience in an effort to persuade them. Praying in a way that is audible to other persons thus requires rhetorical, indeed poetic, training. In addition to certain religious specialists,[57] it was members of the Roman elite who reproduced and enhanced these special skills, bringing them to perfection. This fact is important, because it tells us that no "common man" could ever perform such a vocal masterpiece, given the years of training required.[58] Public prayer is, strictly speaking, a product of the most sophisticated rhetoric. The *discourse*, to use the term that is currently fashionable in scholarship, is that of a class-specific, elite vocality as it is conceived in works on rhetoric.

---

54 A wonderful overview is provided by Grieser/Johnston 2017. A cognitively oriented overview can be found in Kundtová Klocová/Geertz 2019.
55 Fugier 1963, 318–321.
56 List of references in Appel 1909, 207.
57 Juvenal provides an impressive, yet derogatory, list: Juv. 6.542–612.
58 On the strategies and styles of the "common man" see Versnel 1981.

3 Trends in ancient rhetoric – trends in prayer: A *precatio popularis*?

In Roman treatises about rhetoric, we detect an increasing concern with the *ostentatio* of voice, facial expressions, styles of walk and clothing, all of which are markers of performance.[59] This concern is not to be misinterpreted as an awareness of order, tradition or the appropriateness of public behaviour. Bearing in mind the competitive culture of the Roman elite,[60] we should rather see these concerns as reflecting the constant struggle for public favour. It seems unsurprising, then, that critics tended to recognise those who performed their speeches in an overtly ostentatious manner as *populares*.[61] Cicero and others accordingly frame this style of speech as *eloquentia popularis* or *oratio popularis*.[62]

For a *popularis*, anything that appeals to a crowd is appropriate. P. Servilius Rullus provides us with a telling example. According to Cicero, as soon as Rullus was elected as tribune, he changed his demeanour to a style that sought to move the *populus* to do whatever pleased him: "he practised putting on a different expression, a different tone of voice, and a different gait; his clothes were in rags, his person was terribly neglected, more hair about him now and more beard, so that eyes and aspect seemed to protest to the world the tribunician power".[63] Whilst, according to Cicero and Quintilian, a good orator should perform his speech in a moderate and calm manner,[64] the *orator popularis* apparently opts for a rather wild demeanour. Against their advice, this sort of orator – and Rullus was one such – exaggerates the common gestures of public speech, for he considers a moderate performance to be lukewarm and weak (*trepidus et infirmus*).[65]

The *orator popularis* prefers to move about the stage in an ungraceful, indeed effeminate manner, while stamping and almost wildly dancing (*saltatio*).[66] The

---

59 Cic. *Fin.* 2.77.
60 This feature of political life in Rome does not, of course, require extensive proof. Nevertheless, an excellent place to start is the treatment in Hartmann 2016.
61 An extensive discussion of this style of speech is provided by David 1980.
62 E.g. Cic. *Or.* 13; 151; *De or.* 1.81; *Brut.* 136; 164–165; cf. Cic. *Comment. pet.* 5.
63 Cic. *Leg. Agr.* 2.13: *Iam designatus alio vultu, alio vocis sono, alio incessu esse meditabatur, vestitu obsoletiore, corpore inculto et horrido, capillatior quam ante barbaque maiore, ut oculis et adspectu denuntiare omnibus vim tribuniciam ...*
64 Quint. *Inst.* 2.12.10; Cic. *De or.* 2.34–35; 3.224–227; *Rhet. Her.* 1.2.3.
65 Quint. *Inst.* 2.12.11.
66 Cic. *Brut.* 224–225; 141; *Fin.* 3.24; Quint. *Inst.* 11.3.89. On the long and thus flitting toga see also *Cluent.* 111.

toga is loosened, the right arm sways. In fact, those who stamp their feet, strike their chest and clap a lot are said to be well-appreciated, indeed cheered by their audiences.[67] The "different tone of voice" refers to a voice that might be hasty or enthusiastic.[68] Just as does moderation in movement, moderation, indeed sweetness, of voice fades. Pure rage and aggression, as reflected in Rullus' unusual form of expression, are the characteristics associated with *eloquentia popularis*.[69] *Furor, turbulentus* or *audacia* are just some of the words that mould the semantic field in this regard.[70] Other than the mocking remarks in Cicero's *Brutus*, it is probably Pliny the Younger who draws the best image of such a popular orator:[71]

> Indeed, it was beginning to go to the bad in other ways when Afer thought that it had already gone to the bad, but it is now practically ruined and destroyed, root and branch. I am ashamed to tell you what an affected delivery (*fracta pronuntiatione*) these people have and with what unnatural cheering their speeches are greeted. Their sing-song style (*canticis*) only wants clapping of hands, or rather cymbals and drums, to make them like the priests of Cybele, for as for howlings (*ululatus*) – there is no other word to express the unseemly applause in the theatres – they have enough and to spare. (Plin. *Ep.* 2.14.12–13; tr. Firth 1990)

Pliny here makes the very same argument that I have set out to develop in the present chapter. He identifies the parallel between religious and non-religious speech. His references do not, however, represent an ideal public prayer. In fact, references to the Galli or to an "oriental cult" point in the opposite direction.[72] However, as recent research has shown, these performances can be identified as reflecting religious trends or innovations that do not necessarily contradict the pre-existing modes for the performance of prayers.[73] They rather exaggerate and accelerate them, i.e. perform them in an ostentatious and hasty manner,[74] just as the popular orators do. Interestingly enough, circling like a *saltator* repeatedly

---

67 Quint. *Inst.* 2.12.10.
68 David 1980, 184.
69 Cic. *Brut.* 164. Further instances are cited in David 1980, 181.
70 David 1980, 182; Quint. *Inst.* 2.12.10–11.
71 *Quod alioqui perire incipiebat cum perisse Afro videretur, nunc vero prope funditus exstinctum et eversum est. Pudet referre quae quam fracta pronuntiatione dicantur, quibus quam teneris clamoribus excipiantur. Plausus tantum ac potius sola cymbala et tympana illis canticis desunt: ululatus quidem (neque enim alio vocabulo potest exprimi theatris quoque indecora laudatio) large supersunt.*
72 On the problem of the term "oriental cult" see Witschel 2012. On the gender discourse imposed on the Galli see Šterbenc Erker 2013, 245–256.
73 Auffarth 2007.
74 Patzelt 2018b, 179–194.

appears in descriptions of public prayers that sought to impress their audience.[75] The preferences of the people, which is supposed to be the benchmark of *eloquentia popularis*, apparently translate into both realms of public vocal performance: public speech, debased as *oratio popularis*, and public prayer, which we can probably call *precatio popularis* by this point.

Eloquentia popularis in both realms is, thus, a purely expressive phenomenon – a matter of vocality, of ostentatious expression of voice and body. As the examples quoted above clearly indicate, this popular rhetoric and its popular vocality in particular is what William FitzGerald defines as "situated and situating discourse". Orality, vocality, gestures, postures and even facial expressions are products of that situated and situating discourse, of the conditions that make this prayer appropriate. Apparently, one of the most essential conditions for this type of speech is the presence of a public audience that does not accord with Cicero's exquisite taste in rhetoric. The audience simply wants to be cheered up.

For Roman politicians, it was, of course, an open secret that those who blame others for their behaviour tend to behave in the same manner when it suits their own interests. In fact, what the one author praises as exemplary eloquence is easily denigrated by another as the pursuit of populist measures. Quintilian makes unmistakably clear that these ostentatious orators are not isolated maniacs. On the contrary, they are educated by teachers (*praeceptores*) and thus by Quintilian's competitors in the discourse about proper oratory.[76] One might thus agree with Jean-Michel David that the sense of "ostentation" lies in the eye of the beholder and is sometimes used as invective against certain types of people, *homines novi* in particular.

One does not, however, need to follow the argument that an elite ideology imposes on the practices of others and in doing so produces these stereotypes. Yet a certain gender ideology cannot be denied. Just as in any other case in Roman politics, the demeanour of an orator could easily fall victim to accusations of unmanly or homosexual attitudes. A failure to perform a speech or a prayer in accordance with Cicero's guidelines was in itself enough to give Cicero grounds on and material with which to accuse his opponents of effeminate behaviour, indeed effeminate dance movements.[77] Aulus Gabinius is probably a good a exam-

---

75 The use of dancing in circles as a common gesture in prayer is documented by Plin. *HN* 28.25; Plut. *Quaest. Rom.* 14; Plut. *Marc.* 6.5–6. For a concrete example see Suet. *Vit.* 2.5.
76 Quint. *Inst.* 2.12.11.
77 Craig 2004; Corbeill 2004, 120–124.

ple in this respect. His public appearances are depicted not merely as the performances of a *saltator*, which would be abhorrent enough, but of a *saltatrix*.⁷⁸ Another example would be that of Cicero's nemesis Publius Clodius Pulcher. Clodius' public prayers are described by Cicero in terms of *eloquentia popularis*. Cicero, who seeks to invalidate the dedicatory prayer that Clodius performed on September 29th, 57 BC, portrays a furious man who performs a furious prayer. According to Cicero, Clodius' voice was rushing and enthusiastic and, just like a popular orating *saltator*, he is described as rushing over the stage with his prayer performance. Clodius breaks with Cicero's ideal, as expressed with reference to Crassus: "no violent movements of the body, no sudden variation of voice, no walking up and down, no frequent stamping of the foot".⁷⁹ Instead, Clodius does exactly what Quintilian complains about. He accelerates and suddenly varies his voice, he walks hastily up and down, and he stamps and jumps around.⁸⁰ In accordance with the goal of amplifying such a description by adding sexist overtones, the Clodius is introduced as a woman praying among men,⁸¹ indeed a *saltatrix* among men, if we apply Cicero's general accusation here.

Despite the overtones Cicero seeks to impose on this performance, Clodius seems to have translated the popular style of speech into his prayer performance, wild dancing included. Or rather, he is *accused* of having a popular style and of translating this into his prayer performance. Again, public prayer and public speech appear to be two sides of one coin: public performances that are inspired by rhetoric tend towards enthusiastic vocality with the goal of emotional persuasion. That Clodius is also accused of being a popular priest, a *sacerdos popularis*,⁸² might support this observation.

4 The "double speech": The act of *praeire*

The act of prompting, *praeire*, is perhaps the most peculiar feature of public Roman prayer. As a journey through the sources on public prayer performances reveals, whether the performances are referred to as *precatio*,⁸³ *nuncupatio*,⁸⁴ or

---

78 Cic. *Pis*. 18.
79 Cic. *Brut*. 158.
80 Cic. *Dom*. 139–141. On this see Patzelt 2019.
81 Cic. *Dom*. 139.
82 Cic. *Sest*. 66.
83 Plin. *HN* 28.11; Val. Max. 4.1.10; Suet. *Claud*. 22; Liv. 8.9.4; 9.46.6; 10.28.14; 41.21.11; 42.28.9.
84 Liv. 36.2.3–5; 31.9.9; Sen. *Clem*. 1.19.7.

consecratio/dedicatio,⁸⁵ an official almost always relies, when praying, on the prompting of a pontiff.⁸⁶ The most renowned and most quoted description of this prompting is found in Pliny the Elder:⁸⁷

> We see also that our chief magistrates have adopted fixed formulas for their prayers; that to prevent a word's being omitted or out of place a reader dictates beforehand the prayer from a script; that another attendant is appointed as a guard to keep watch, and yet another is put in charge to maintain a strict silence; that a piper plays so that nothing but the prayer is heard. (Plin. *HN* 28.11; tr. Jones 1963)

About 120 years later,⁸⁸ the church father Tertullian took up this peculiarity to make a distinction between Christian and non-Christian prayer:⁸⁹

> Looking up to heaven, the Christians – with hands outspread, because innocent, with head bare because we do not blush, yes! and without one to give the form of words (*monitor*), for we pray from the heart – we are ever making intercession for all the Emperors. (Tertull. *Apol.* 30.4; tr. Stevenson 1957)

The noun *monitor* implies a system of double-reminders: text *and* priest.⁹⁰ Tertullian's use of this term fosters a notion of *praeire* as a logological and, therefore, purely functional phenomenon. Consideration of juridical contexts seems to support this function. As Emmanuelle Valette-Cagnac and Elizabeth Meyer have pointed out, monitoring or prompting emanate from the very heart of Roman rhetoric – public speeches.⁹¹ In a telling passage in his speech in defense of L. Murena, Cicero exhaustively ridicules the lack of professionalism and the lack of sense-making in these contexts. As he informs his listener, the *praetor* adheres closely to legal formulae, the *carmina composita,* no matter how ridiculous they

---

85 Valette-Cagnac 1997, 271–280.
86 An exhaustive list is provided by Appel 1909, 207.
87 *Videmusque certis precationibus obsecrasse summos magistratus et, ne quod verborum praetereatur aut praeposterum dicatur, de scripto praeire aliquem rursusque alium custodem dari qui adtendat, alium vero praeponi qui favere linguis iubeat, tibicinem canere, ne quid aliud exaudiatur.*
88 The *Natural History* was probably published around AD 77. Tertullian's apology was published in or about AD 197.
89 *Illuc suspicientes Christiani manibus expansis, quia innocuis, capite nudo, quia non erubescimus, denique sine monitore, quia de pectore oramus, precantes sumus semper pro omnibus imperatoribus.*
90 Cf. Valette-Cagnac 1997, 251–252.
91 Meyer 2004, 75–77; Valette-Cagnac 1997, 295.

might be.⁹² It is precisely these kinds of composed *carmina* that we know as *verba certa* or *verba sollemnia* in contexts of prayer.⁹³

However, as Valette-Cagnac has made clear,⁹⁴ if *praeire* was merely a matter of prompting, then the Romans could have just expressed this with *dictare* throughout.⁹⁵ With this in mind, we might consider the following question: if the prayer scroll already bears the correct text, what is it that makes it necessary for a person to read the text to the individual performing the text? When priestly groups, such as the Arvals, performed their prayers, they were capable of doing so while holding the text themselves.⁹⁶ The word *praeire*, on the other hand, implies a subsequent performance. On this interpretation, it implies two diligent performances of that prayer,⁹⁷ which might again imply that there is an acoustic purpose to this double speech.

With this concern in mind, it is reasonable to consider the double speech in terms of double sound. On this account, two members of the elite, probably reasonably enculturated in rhetoric, do not merely duplicate the words – the orality – of the prayer. Rather, they duplicate the prayer's vocality, and it may be that in doing so they team up to perform an impressive vocal masterpiece that seeks to persuade, and thereby win over, the audience. In the case of Clodius' failed prayer, his prompting priest L. Pinarius Natta delivers the same hasty and rushing performance as does Clodius.⁹⁸ As the priests are responsible for an appropriate vocalisation of the prayer formula, it is worth recalling that it is the audience which determines what is appropriate or not. At least, that is the accusation against *eloquentia popularis* that we can identify in the public prayers of Clodius and others. As these accusations make clear, the appropriateness of what is said is judged according to the acoustic and visual delight it evokes.

---

92 Cic. *Mur.* 26–29. Cf. Meyer 2004, 80–85; Varro *Ling.* 5.14.80; 5.16.87.
93 Valette-Cagnac 1997, 295–296; cf. Meyer 2004, 62–63; Champeaux 2010.
94 Valette-Cagnac 1997, 249.
95 *Dictare verba*: Juv. 6.391. *Dictare vota*: Val. Flacc. *Arg.* 1.685.
96 *ILS* 5039 = *CIL* VI 2104a = *CFA* 100a, 31–38.
97 Valette-Cagnac 1997, 285–286.
98 In fact, Cicero criticises the absence of such a pontiff during Clodius' prayer. However, he also makes clear that this absence was moral rather than actual, for Clodius' brother-in-law, L. Pinarius Natta, was present. Instead of doing what Cicero regards as appropriate, Natta instead did what Clodius seems to have regarded as such, joining in the *eloquentia popularis* of his relative (Cic. *Dom.* 139 compared to 134–135). Livy provides an abundance of scenes in which the pontiff intervenes in a prayer (e.g. Liv. 31.9.6–10; 41.16.1–2; see also Val. Max. 1.1.8). These interventions, however, are primarily concerned with the appropriateness of a specific gift or measure.

The repeated signifier of such double performance of prayer texts is *sollemnis*.[99] This word has a complicated history, but one that perfectly supports these observations. As Huguette Fugier has pointed out, *sollemnis* is no mere indicator of fixed ritual dates. It is also to be taken literally, as indicating something festive and cheering. More precisely, it connotes an experience of something exalted and ecstatic.[100] The descriptions of *sollemnis* experiences perfectly match those of ecstatic experiences that took place during wild prayer performances. These performances, commonly referred to as "mystical" or "oriental", are reflected in the ululating response of *eloquentia popularis*. *Praefari*, a word closely related to *praeire*, frequently appears in prophetic and oracular contexts, in which it implies a prophetic voice.[101]

This observation corresponds with the close analyses undertaken by Alex Hardie of *carmina*, legal and religious, as poetic masterpieces. His close reading of numerous instances of the word *carmen* reveals that a *carmen* is semantically connected in each case with aroused – or, again, *ecstatic* – states of mind on the part of the performer and the audience.[102] Since public prayers are frequently referred to as *carmina*, and since public rhetoric has intrinsically poetic and musical qualities, this ecstatic effect was most likely also experienced by audiences exposed to the vocality of a public prayer.

5 Conclusions

Putting the pieces together, we can see that public prayer was a persuasive performance that responded to the very context in which it was deployed. The measures taken to meet the requirements of this context are less oral than they are vocal. Given the variety of contexts and the variety of possible public audiences, with their desire to be entertained during these occasions, this vocality, together with the expressive accompaniment of physical gestures, established trends in prayer that go beyond the commonly acknowledged style formalised in

---

99 For such *verba certa* or *verba sollemnia* see Valette-Cagnac 1997, 295–296; cf. Meyer 2004, 62–63; Champeaux 2010.
100 Fugier 1963, 306–321, esp. 318–321.
101 Valette-Cagnac 1997, 267–268; e.g. Liv. 5.41.3.
102 Hardie 2005.

the entirely modest *actio*. Instead, the performers of public prayer avail themselves of those rhetorical trends otherwise known as *eloquentia popularis* – a rather ostentatious manner of vocally and physically performing public speeches.

Bibliography

Aubriot-Sévin, D. (1992), *Prière et conceptions religieuses en Grèce ancienne jusqu'à la fin du Ve siècle av. J.-C.*, Lyon.

Auffarth, C. (2007), '*Religio migrans*: Die "orientalischen Religionen" im Kontext antiker Religion. Ein theoretisches Modell', in: *Mediterranea* 4, 333–363.

Ausfeld, K. (1903), *De Graecorum precationibus quaestiones*, Leipzig (Jahrbücher für klassische Philolologie Suppl. 28).

Balogh, J. (1925), 'Lautes und leises Beten', in: *Archiv für Religionswisschenschaft* 23, 345–348.

Burke, K. [1961] (1970), *The Rhetoric of Religion: Studies in Logology*, Berkeley.

Butler, S. (2015), *The Ancient Phonograph*, New York.

Champeaux, J. (2001), 'La prière du Romain', in: *Ktèma* 26, 267–283.

Champeaux, J. (2010), 'Certis precationibus: Une prière ritualisée', in: S. Roesch (ed.), *Prier dans la Rome antique: études lexicales*, Paris, 13–34.

Corbeill, A. (2004), *Nature Embodied: Gesture in Ancient Rome*, Princeton.

Craig, C. (2004). 'Audience Expectations, Invective and Proof', in: J. Powell/J. Paterson (eds.), *Cicero the Advocate*, Oxford, 187–214.

Crippa, S. (2015a), *La voce: sonorità e pensiero alle origini della cultura europea*, Milan.

Crippa, S. (2015b), 'Les savoirs des voix magiques: réflexion sur la catégorie du rite', in: M. de Haro Sanchez (ed.), *Écrire la magie dans l'antiquité: actes du colloque international (Liège, 13 – 15 octobre 2011)*, Liège.

Dangel, J. (1997), 'Le carmen latin: rhétorique, poétique et poésie', in: *Euphrosyne* 25, 113–131.

David, J.-M. (1980), '*Eloquentia popularis* et conduites symboliques des orateurs à la fin de la République: problèmes d'efficacité', in: *Quaderni Storici* 12, 171–211.

Deremetz, A. (1994), 'La prière en représentation à Rome: de Mauss à la pragmatique contemporaine', in: *Revue de l'Histoire des Religions* 211.2, 141–165.

Dowden, K. (2007), 'Rhetoric and Religion', in: I. Worthington (ed.), *A Companion to Greek Rhetoric*, Malden, 320–335.

Dozier, C. (2010), 'Poetry, Politics, and Pleasure in Quintilian', in: I. Sluiter/R.M. Rosen (eds.), *Aesthetic Value in Classical Antiquity*, Leiden, 345–364.

Firth, J.B. (tr.) (1900), *The Letters of the Younger Pliny*, London.

FitzGerald, W. (2012), *Spiritual Modalities: Prayer as Rhetoric and Performance*, University Park, PA.

Fless, F. (1995), *Opferdiener und Kultmusiker auf stadtrömischen historischen Reliefs: Untersuchungen zur Ikonographie, Funktion und Benennung*, Mainz.

Freyburger, G. (2001), 'Prière silencieuse et prière murmurée dans la religion Romaine', in: *Revue des Études Latines* 79, 26–36.

Fugier, H. (1963), *Recherches sur l'expression du sacré dans la langue latine*, Paris.

Gödde, S. (2011), *Euphêmia: Die gute Rede in Kult und Literatur der griechischen Antike*, Heidelberg.

Goeken, J. (2010), 'Avant-propos: pour une rhétorique de la prière Grecque', in: J. Goeken (ed.), *La rhétorique de la prière dans l'Antiquité Grecque*, Turnhout, 3–16.

Grieser, A.K./Johnston, J. (2017), 'What is an Aesthetics of Religion? From the Senses to Meaning—and Back Again', in: A.K. Grieser/J. Johnston (eds.), *Aesthetics of Religion: A Connective Concept*, Berlin, 1–49.

Guittard, C. (1989), 'Ritualisme et sentiment religieux dans la prière à Rome et en Ombrie', in: A. Caquot/P. Canivet (eds.), *Ritualisme et vie intérieure: religion et culture*, Paris, 17–33.

Habinek, T. (1998), 'Singing, Speaking, Making, Writing: Classical Alternatives to Literature and Literary Studies', in: *Stanford Humanities Review* 6, 65–75.

Habinek, T. (2005), *The World of Roman Song: From Ritualized Speech to Social Order*, Baltimore.

Hardie, A. (2005), 'The Ancient Etymology of Carmen', in: *Papers of the Langford Latin Seminar* 12, 71–94.

Hartmann, E. (2016), *Ordnung in Unordnung: Kommunikation, Konsum und Konkurrenz in der stadtrömischen Gesellschaft der frühen Kaiserzeit*, Stuttgart.

Henderson, G. (1989), 'Logology and Theology: Kenneth Burke and the Rhetoric of Religion', in: *Method & Theory in the Study of Religion* 1, 20–39.

King, C. (2003), 'The Organization of Roman Religious Beliefs', in: *Classical Antiquity* 22, 275–312.

Krämer, S. (2002), 'Sprache – Stimme – Schrift: Sieben Gedanken über Performativität als Medialität', in: U. Wirth (ed.), *Performanz: Zwischen Sprachphilosophie und Kulturwissenschaften*, Frankfurt, 323–346.

Kundtová Klocová, E./Geertz, A.W. (2019), 'Ritual and Embodied Cognition', in: R. Uro/J.J. Day/R. Roitto/R.E. DeMaris (eds.), *The Oxford Handbook of Early Christian Ritual*, Oxford, 74–94.

Lévi-Strauss, C. (1966), *The Savage Mind*, Chicago.

Mauss, M. [1909] (2003), *On Prayer*, New York.

McCartney, E.S. (1948), 'Notes on Reading and Praying Audibly', in: *Classical Philology* 43, 184–187.

Meister, J.B. (2012), *Der Körper des Princeps: Zur Problematik eines monarchischen Körpers ohne Monarchie*, Stuttgart.

Mensching, G. (1926), *Das heilige Schweigen: Eine religionsgeschichtliche Untersuchung*, Gießen (RGVV 20.2).

Meyer, E.A. (2004), *Legitimacy and Law in the Roman World: Tabulae in Roman Belief and Practice*, Cambridge.

Montiglio, S. (2000), *Silence in the Land of Logos*, Princeton.

North, J.A. (2008), 'Action and Ritual in Roman Historians: Or How Horatius Held the Door-Post', in: A. Holm Rasmussen/S.W. Rasmussen (eds.), *Religion and Society: Rituals, Resources and Identity in the Ancient Graeco-Roman World*, Rome, 23–36.

Patzelt, M. (2018a), 'The Rhetoric of Roman Prayer: A Proposal for a Lived Religion Approach', in: *Religion in the Roman Empire* 4, 162–186.

Patzelt, M. (2018b), *Über das Beten der Römer: Gebete im spätrepublikanischen und frühkaiserzeitlichen Rom als Ausdruck gelebter Religion*, Berlin (RGVV 73).

Patzelt, M. (2019), 'Praying as a 'Woman among Men': Reconsidering Clodius' Failed Prayer in Cicero's Speech On his House', in: *Religion in the Roman Empire* 5, 271–291.

Pernot, L. (2006), 'The Rhetoric of Religion', in: *Rhetorica: A Journal of the History of Rhetoric* 24, 235–254.
Scheer, T.S. (2001), 'Die Götter anrufen: Die Kontaktaufnahme zwischen Mensch und Gott in der griechischen Antike', in: K. Brodersen (ed.), *Gebet und Fluch: Zeichen und Traum: Aspekte religiöser Kommunikation in der Antike*, Münster, 31–56.
Schulz, V. (2014), *Die Stimme in der antiken Rhetorik*, Göttingen.
Spina, L. (2008), 'Fall and Rise of Religion and Rhetoric', in: *Rhetorica: A Journal of the History of Rhetoric* 26, 209–220.
Steel, C. (2017), 'Defining Public Speech in the Roman Republic: Occasion, Audience and Purpose', in: C. Rosillo-López (ed.), *Political Communication in the Roman World*, Leiden, 15–33.
Šterbenc Erker, D. (2013), *Religiöse Rollen römischer Frauen in "griechischen" Ritualen*, Stuttgart.
Sudhaus, S. (1906), 'Lautes und leises Beten', in: *Archiv für Religionswissenschaft* 9, 185–200.
Valette-Cagnac, E. (1997), *La lecture à Rome: rites et pratiques*, Paris.
van der Horst, P.W. (1994), 'Silent Prayer in Antiquity', in: *Numen* 41, 1–25.
Versnel, H.S. (1981), 'Religious Mentality in Ancient Prayer', in: H.S. Versnel (ed.), *Faith, Hope, and Worship: Aspects of Religious Mentality in the Ancient World*, Leiden, 1–64.
Wagenvoort, H. [1964] (1980), 'Orare, precari', in: H. Wagenvoort (ed.), *Pietas: Selected Studies in Roman Religion*, Leiden, 197–209.
Witschel, C. (2012), '"Orientalische Kulte" im römischen Reich – Neue Perspektiven der altertumswissenschaftlichen Forschung', in: M. Blömer/E. Winter (eds.), *Iuppiter Dolichenus: Vom Lokalkult zur Reichsreligion*, Tübingen, 13–38.

Christopher Degelmann
Between Compassion and Aggression: The Rhetoric of Mourning in Republican and Early Imperial Rome

Abstract: The contribution focuses on the frequently appearing connection between rhetoric and mourning in ancient Rome, as well as its development from the Republic to the early Imperial time. Furthermore, it examines the creative appropriation of burial rites and funeral rhetoric for political purposes. The chapter shows how the Romans integrated a wide-ranging repertoire of signs for expressing grief into their political rhetoric not linked to deaths in the narrower sense, benefiting from the moving emotions connected with the traditional *laudatio funebris*. However, this was only thinkable because of the deep religiosity of the Romans. According to Polybius, religion played little, if any, role in Roman grief practices. In contrast, mourning was rather a social phenomenon, with the funeral speech referring only indirectly to beliefs about the afterlife.

When a Roman aristocrat died, his relatives organised an elaborately staged *pompa funebris* through the streets of Rome, an extraordinary event that required approval from the aediles.[1] The Greek historian Polybius provides a detailed description of what took place during these funeral processions:

> Whenever any illustrious man dies, he is carried at his funeral into the forum to the so-called *rostra*, sometimes conspicuous in an upright posture and more rarely reclined. Here, with all the people standing round, a grown-up son if he has left one who happens to be present, or if not some other relative, mounts the rostra and discourses on the virtues and successful achievements of the dead man during his lifetime. As a consequence, the multitude, and not only those who had a part in these achievements but those also who had none, when the facts are recalled to their minds and brought before their eyes, are moved to such sympathy that the loss seems to be not confined to the mourners, but a public one affecting the whole people. Next, after the interment and the performance of the usual ceremonies, they place the image of the departed in the most conspicuous position in the house, enclosed in a wooden shrine. This image is a mask reproducing him with remarkable

---

Many thanks to my colleagues and friends Niklas Engel (Berlin/Potsdam) and Maik Patzelt (Osnabrück) as well as to the two editors of the volume, who read the contribution carefully and saved me from mistakes. Finally yet importantly, I owe a debt of gratitude to Paul Scade.

1 Dion. Hal. *Ant.* 9.54.5; see Blösel 2003, 54–55.

https://doi.org/10.1515/9783110699623-008

fidelity both in its modelling and in the complexion of the deceased. On the occasion of public sacrifices, they display these images, and decorate them with much care; when any distinguished member of the family dies, they take the images to the funeral, putting them on men who seem to them to bear the closest resemblance to the original in stature and carriage. These representatives wear togas, with a purple border if the deceased was a consul or praetor, whole purple if he was a censor, and embroidered with gold if he had celebrated a triumph or achieved anything similar. They all ride in chariots preceded by the fasces, axes, and other insignia by which the different magistrates are wont to be accompanied according to the respective dignity of the honours held by each during his life; and when they arrive at the rostra they all seat themselves in a row on ivory chairs. There could not easily be a more ennobling spectacle for a young man who aspires to fame and virtue. For who would not be inspired by the sight of the images of men renowned for their excellence, all together and as if alive and breathing? What spectacle could be more glorious than this? Besides, he who makes the oration over the man about to be buried, when he has finished speaking of him recounts the successes and exploits of the rest whose images are present, beginning from the most ancient. By this means, by this constant renewal of the good report of brave men, the celebrity of those who performed noble deeds is rendered immortal, while at the same time the fame of those who did good service to their country becomes known to the people and a heritage for future generations. But the most important result is that young men are thus inspired to endure every suffering for the public welfare in the hope of winning the glory that attends on brave men. (Polyb. 6.53.1–54.3; tr. Paton 2011, modified)[2]

Obviously, the funeral speech and funeral procession were closely intertwined.[3] Polybius had seen several such processions during his time as a hostage in Rome between 168 and 150, and had heard many funeral speeches at the forum. In the house of the Scipiones, the scholarship assumes, Polybius must also have witnessed the extensive preparations that were made prior to the funeral of M. Cornelius Scipio Maluginensis (praet. 176).[4] His statements were, therefore, based on personal experience. In the morning, the ceremony began in the house of the deceased with the opening of the wooden shrines in the *atrium*, in which the ancestral wax masks (*imagines maiorum*)[5] were stored. Participants received the *imagines* and put on their official dress prior to the funeral procession, and then set

---

[2] See Flaig 1995; 2003a; Hölkeskamp 1996, 320–323; 2017, *passim*; 2020, 72–85 (with the latest literature); Flower 1996; Blösel 2003; Walter 2003, 260–268; 2004, 89–108.
[3] For the entanglement of procession and speech see Moretti 2015; Kierdorf 1980 and Flower 1996 are fundamental; also Ramage 2006; Covino 2011 and now Beck 2018.
[4] *MRR* I, 400.
[5] The shape and form of the *imagines maiorum* have been controversial for a long time. In addition to Polybius, other sources include Plin. *Nat.* 35.4–14, esp. 6, and Tac. *Ann.* 2.73.1; 3.5; 3.76; 4.9.2, but it is still unclear whether the *imagines* were made directly from an impression of the

out, following the route to the political heart of the city, the forum. Once there, the *laudatio funebris* was held by the *rostra*.⁶

The funeral eulogy recorded in this source is the earliest and most authentically Roman evidence for the use of the art of oratory in Roman (political) culture.⁷ According to Polybius, the speech involved the recitation of the individual achievements of the deceased (*honores*) and of his deeds on behalf of the Republic (*res gestae*), to which the speaker added the *honores* and *res gestae* of all the members of the clan who were symbolically present at the funeral through the display of the *imagines*.⁸ The *laudatio funebris* stimulated the audience to condole with the deceased and his family. Yet, at the same time, the oration could also stir up feelings of anger and rage – even hate – against a person or a group who could be blamed for a premature death, as when Marc Antony used his famous *laudatio* for Caesar to attack the dictator's murderers.

Against this background, I will argue in this chapter that funeral speeches that appealed to the emotions of the audience were sometimes so successful in stirring listeners to action that members of the noble *gentes* began to use elements of the funeral oration in other contexts in seeking to achieve their political ends. Indeed, it is unsurprising that public beliefs about the merits of a family and their legacy (*commendatio maiorum*) could be leveraged for certain ends. Jurors, for instance, are known to have discharged members of noble families on occasion after they had brought their *imagines* to the court or verbally described them in

---

individual's face (using wax or clay) or were copied (in clay) from a sculpture. Kierdorf 1998 provides a good overview of the main research problems; cf. Blome 2001. The most comprehensive analysis of the problem is provided by Flower 1996, 32–59, who assumes lifelike wax masks.

6 The earliest evidence is Plin. *Nat.* 7.139 (= *ORF*⁴ No. 6, frg. 2) from the year 221; see also Polyb. 6.53.1–54.3; Dion. Hal. *Ant.* 5.17.2–6; cf. Kierdorf 1980, 10–21; Hölkeskamp 1995, 11–17; 1996, 320–321; Flower 1996, 136–141; Flaig 1995, 129–131; 2003; see also the fake funeral speech for M. Claudius Marcellus (cos. I 222) in Beck 2005, 325–326. This was followed by another *pompa* to the family grave outside the city, where the body was finally buried (not specifically mentioned by Polybius). In the evening, the *imago* of the deceased was placed together with the other portraits in the wooden shrine of the *atrium*, which ended the day of mourning. There were *tituli* on the shrines themselves; see Flower 1996, 40–41; Blösel 2003, 59.

7 Some see Enn. *Ann.* frg. 304–308 Manuwald on M. Cornelius Cethegus (cos. 204) as a first reminiscence of a *laudatio funebris*, but from Cic. *Brut.* 57–60 it seems that Ennius merely wrote about his rhetorical style after the death of Cethegus; the poet may have used a *laudatio* for his verses since he was offering ample biographical details of the former consul.

8 The much cited *ius imaginum* (Cic. *Ver.* 5.14.36; cf. Cic. *Rab. Post.* 16–17) is more likely to be a learned construction of research than a rigid reality: see Drerup 1980, 108; Flower 1996, 53–59, who suggests "that the *imagines* had traditionally been subject to decisions made within the family" (ibid. 58).

order to draw attention to their illustrious family history. Similarly, the *populus* typically cast their votes in favour of *nobiles* magistrates rather than upstart newcomers (*homines novi*). I seek to show that Roman politicians began to deploy both verbal and non-verbal parts of the traditional *laudatio funebris* in legal and political frames in order to transmit the emotions stirred up by mourning. In order to establish an atmosphere of grief, they made use of signs and behaviours associated with a funeral ceremony – such as clothing, dishevelled beards and tears – in the courts, in the forum and in the Senate. This oratorical borrowing was not grounded on arguments based on evidence but on attempts to persuade through emotional appeals.

In the first part of the chapter, I reconstruct the funeral eulogies of the Roman elite from the Republic to the Early Empire in order to pinpoint what it was that made these speeches so important. In doing so, I highlight the main structural elements of the funeral speech and the developments it underwent during this time. I then go on to offer some methodological remarks concerning the study of the emotions from a historical perspective. Finally, I draw attention to the intersections of the verbal and non-verbal elements of the speeches with social and political contexts that, at first sight, have nothing to do with death or burial. In these instances, political agents exploited the emotional ambivalence of grief to draw responses from their audiences that alternated between compassion and aggression.

1 The structure of the republican funeral eulogy and a very brief history

The *laudatio funebris*, or often just *laudatio*, was a eulogy for the deceased that was held in connection with the funeral (*funus*).[9] Upper-class burials probably took place at Rome from the end of the 4th century BC. From a *rostrum*, the eulogy was given by a son or other close relative, as young as possible,[10] who, in addition to speaking of the deceased, also highlighted the actions and virtues of his ancestors (*maiores*). Inexperienced speakers, and not only youths, spoke from manuscripts that had been prepared in advance by professional rhetoricians.[11] From

---

9 Quint. *Inst.* 3.7.2; Gell. 13.20.17; only *laudatio*: Cic. *Mil.* 33; Liv. 27.27.13; Tac. *Ann.* 13.3.1.
10 Tac. *Ann.* 3.76.2: *laudatio pro rostris*; only *pro rostris*: Sen. *Dial.* 6.15.3; Tac. *Ann.* 3.5.1; for the youth: Polyb. 6.53.1.
11 Cic. *De or.* 2.341; Cic. *Ad Q. fr.* 3.6.5; see also Cic. *De or.* 2.341; *Sch.* Bob. 118 Stangl.

about 100 BC, this ceremonial form of *laudatio funebris* was extended to women of the senatorial class.¹²

In addition to the *laudatio pro rostris*, there was probably also a simpler form of the *laudatio funebris* which was held at the pyre or at the grave,¹³ as the so-called *Laudatio Murdiae* illustrates.¹⁴ This latter type of speech, given to a private audience, would have been prepared at home by family members, while those given in public were sometimes prepared by professionals; in all cases the speech would be written down and archived by the family in their *domus*.¹⁵ Some *laudationes* were published¹⁶ and were available to ancient scholars, who used them for various purposes, such as for the compilation of genealogies or, in the case of Graeco-Roman historians,¹⁷ as sources for events. The publication of a speech in stone as an inscription, as in the case of Murdia, was rare.¹⁸

Over time, the form of the *laudatio funebris* changed significantly, as Wilhelm Kierdorf notes in his seminal study.¹⁹ Kierdorf identifies three phases of development, the last of which took place during the high Imperial era and Late Antiquity and, as such, need not concern us here. The first phase spanned the period from the beginning of the tradition through to the middle of the 2nd century BC. During this time, the speakers were still completely unaffected by the rhetorical theory of the Hellenistic world, as can be seen from the composition and language of the *laudationes*.²⁰ As Polybius emphasised, praise of familial ancestors was simply

---

12 Initially Q. Lutatius Catulus for his mother Popilia: Cic. *De or.* 2.44; then especially Caesar for both his aunt and his young wife; Plu. *Caes.* 5.2–5; see in general Pepe 2015.
13 Durry 1950, LXXIX; Flower 1996, 131.
14 *CIL* VI 10230 = *ILS* 8394 is dated to the Late Republic or the Early Imperial period; see Lindsay 2004.
15 Cic. *Brut.* 62; Plin. *Nat.* 7.139-140 also suggests that this was the case.
16 See the *laudatio* by P. Fabius Maximus Allobrogicus (cos. 121) as a young man and by C. Laelius (cos. 140) to P. Cornelius Scipio Africanus minor: Cic. *De or.* 2.341; see Cic. *Mur.* 36; *Sch.* Bob. 118 Stangl with Badian 1971.
17 Liv. 27.27.13 (speech for M. Claudius Marcellus (cos. 196) for his father of the same name (cos. 222, 216, 214, 210 and 208); Cic. *Cato* 12 (speech of Q. Fabius Maximus Verrucosus (cos. 233, 228, 215, 214, 209) for his son of the same name (cos. 213); Plin. *Nat.* 7.139-140 (speech of Q. Caecilius Metellus, cos. 206) for his father Lucius (cos. 251). A list of the attested funeral speeches can be found in Kierdorf 1980, 137–149; see also Gell. 13.20; cf. Cic. *Brut.* 62.
18 See *Laudatio Turiae*: *CIL* VI 1527 (Osgood 2014) and also for the high Imperial period *CIL* XIV 3579 (Hadrian for his mother in law Matidia) with Jones 2004.
19 Kierdorf 1980; Durry 1950, XXXV-XLIII argues for more continuity.
20 Already Durry 1942.

added to the praise for the dead man.[21] Just as did prayers and magical incantations, these *laudationes* deployed a variety of formulaic elements, such as assonance, repetitions of words and the use of rhythmical structures. There were no consolatory elements in the speeches of this first phase, as their inclusion would have been at odds with the speaker's goal of making the audience aware of the magnitude of the loss that had been suffered.[22]

In the second phase, lasting from the second half of the 2nd century BC through to the 3rd century AD, the *laudatio funebris* was still characterised by a combination of praise and complaint unaccompanied by any elements of consolation.[23] However, innovations were made in other areas, with the funeral speech becoming increasingly influenced by principles of rhetorical design (*ornatus* and *decorum*). This development involved the adaptation of rhetorical rules for the composition of the eulogy as well as the progressive inclusion in the *laudatio* of new features, such as references to the education or lifestyle of the deceased. According to Dio Cassius, as well as giving details of the descent and deeds of C. Julius Caesar, Marc Antony also spoke of the upbringing and the character of the murdered dictator.[24] Above all, people began to integrate panegyric elements into the quasi-biographical scheme of the *encomium*. The *maiores* were no longer relegated to the part of the speech that followed the description of the actions of the deceased but were moved to the beginning, and their actions were now directly connected to the offices they had held. For example, in the funeral speech for Emperor Claudius prepared by Seneca for the new *princeps*, the philosopher has Nero speak of the "family, the consulates and the triumphs of his ancestors" before mentioning the deceased's own *providentia* and *sapientia*, which, of course, provoked considerable amusement among the audience.[25]

---

21 Polyb. 6.54.1 f. (tr. Paton 2011): "[...] when he has finished speaking of him recounts the successes and exploits of the rest whose images are present, beginning from the most ancient", ἐπὰν διέλθῃ τὸν περὶ τούτου λόγον, ἄρχεται τῶν ἄλλων ἀπὸ τοῦ προγενεστάτου τῶν παρόντων, καὶ λέγει τὰς ἐπιτυχίας ἑκάστου καὶ τὰς πράξεις.
22 Kierdorf 1980, 83–85; for the "carmen style" in magic formulas and prayers see Meyer 2004, 45 and the contribution of Maik Patzelt in this volume.
23 The more personal tone of the *Laudationes Turiae Murdiaeque*, on the other hand, may have something to do with the fact that they were not *pro rostris*.
24 Cass. Dio 44.36.1 (tr. Cary 1916): "[...] but after making a few remarks about his family, his education, and his character, and perhaps mentioning his services to the state [...]", ἀλλ' ὀλίγα ἂν περί τε τοῦ γένους καὶ περὶ τῆς παιδείας τῶν τε τρόπων αὐτοῦ εἰπών, καί πῃ καὶ τῶν ἐς τὸ κοινὸν αὐτῷ πεπολιτευμένων μνησθείς [...]. See Pepe 2011. Prokoph 2010 even tries to show that the origins of biographical writing lie in the *laudatio funebris*.
25 See Tac. *Ann.* 13.3.1 (tr. Jackson 1937): "on the day of the obsequies, the prince opened his panegyric of Claudius. So long as he rehearsed the antiquity of his family, the consulates and

The fundamental goal of the Republican and Early Imperial *laudatio funebris* was, as Polybius reports, to involve the audience in the process of remembrance and lamentation by praising the dead man and his family.²⁶ This collective feeling of grief and loss was particularly intensified by the presence of the *imagines* of those ancestors who were mentioned. Indeed, according to Polybius it was primarily due to the many ancestors of the deceased person that those present in the forum were deeply moved by the ceremony they witnessed. The "presence" of the ancestors was in itself impressive and was further heightened by the funeral speech, which set out and praised their deeds and virtues, effectively enumerating and elaborating on the symbolic capital of a family. This capital encompassed the family's entire reputation, present and past: the heroic deeds and honours of the *nobilis* at the centre of the ceremony as well as the services that the ancestors had performed for the *res publica* in previous generations.²⁷ The accumulation of achievements and recognition across generations resulted in the social prestige of a noble family acquiring an almost countable value, and it was this that was presented to the people in the *laudatio*. As a result, the length of the speech was, itself, a notable indicator of the social prestige of the deceased and his family.²⁸

At the same time, the eulogy also helped to define the inner hierarchies of the Roman aristocracy; the reputation of consulars and censors naturally ranked above that of praetors, and the prestige of a praetor in turn took precedence over that of former aediles. In the speech and *pompa*, the classification criteria of *nobilitas* are reflected and further tightened.²⁹ The main purpose of the speech – as an institution, not as an *oratio* – was to make transparent the social hierarchies of the Republic and thereby gain the acceptance and approval of the population.

---

the triumphs of his ancestors, he was taken seriously by himself and by others. Allusions, also, to his literary attainments and to the freedom of his reign from reverses abroad had a favourable hearing. But when the orator addressed himself to his foresight and sagacity, no one could repress a smile [...]". *Die funeris laudationem eius princeps exorsus est, dum antiquitatem generis, consulatus ac triumphos maiorum enumerabat, intentus ipse et ceteri; liberalium quoque artium commemoratio et nihil regente eo triste rei publicae ab externis accidisse pronis animis audita: postquam ad providentiam sapientiamque flexit, nemo risui temperare [...]*.
26 Polyb. 6.53.3 ff.
27 On the Bourdieuian category in classics see Hölkeskamp 2010, 107–124.
28 Since the route of the *pompa* was not predetermined, it is very likely that the procession headed for the most important monuments in the city that were related to the deceased or his ancestors (statues in honour of individuals, equestrian or otherwise, as well as consecrated temples or monumental arches). Perhaps the *pompa* even stopped at special monuments, which were then shown reverence; see Walter 2004, 90–91.
29 Flaig 1995, 197–203; Beck 2005, 89.

2 Reactions to the funeral speech

It is inherent in the power of speech that it intends to do what it says; according to Judith Butler, a performative action is one that evokes or stages what it names, thus underlining the constitutive or productive power of performative speech.[30] The so-called "speech-act theory" of John L. Austin and John R. Searle underlines the rhetorical and performative dynamics of language.[31] In consequence, whoever says "mourning" means that there should be "mourning".

The *populus Romanus* provided the social framework within which an aristocratic burial took place. The urban population actively participated, both when the body was shown on the *pompa* and in the *laudatio*.[32] Nevertheless, the reactions of the listeners were as diverse as the audience itself. The audience for a funeral speech consisted of several distinct "interpretive communities".[33] A large number of ordinary Roman citizens were present at all stages of the funeral ritual. In the morning, the clients of the family would have been present during the *salutatio* at the opening of the shrines; *gentes* like the Fabii Maximi or the Caecilii Metelli might have had hundreds of visitors. The funeral procession was then observed by many spectators at the roadside, who often followed the *pompa* to the forum. There, the funeral speech is said to have taken place in the presence of "the whole people" (παντὸς τοῦ δήμου), as Polybius writes, which implies at least several thousand listeners. According to Polybius, this part of the ceremony was so moving that the loss seemed to hurt not only the relatives, but the whole people (κοινὸν τοῦ δήμου).

Not everyone had to feel moved, but people usually expected there to be lament of some kind, whether collective or individual, although we should not interpret this as an immediate expression of emotional mood. From an emotional science perspective, on one view the emotions should be understood as universal, crossing both temporal and cultural boundaries,[34] while on another the feelings are analysed largely as socially and culturally constituted.[35] This latter perspective assumes that emotions are subject to historical changes and that, as a result, speaking of mourning or grief today does not necessarily convey the same

---

[30] Butler 1995, 9–11.
[31] Austin 1962; Searle 1969; see also Fischer-Lichte 2015 for another approach and a new application of the theory.
[32] On the "co-presence" of the audience, Jehne 2001, 89; Hölkeskamp 2017, 200–201.
[33] See Fish 1980, 147–174 with Serafim 2017, 5–6.
[34] This is a tradition usually drawing on the works of Paul Ekman, e.g. Ekman 2003.
[35] See e.g. Harré 1986; Stearns 1986; Reddy 1997.

meaning as it did in Rome. In addition, there is a second, historical, debate about the extent to which feelings were rationalised in certain epochs. At the centre of this discussion is the question of the degree of affect control. An older position from the early 20th century and its epigones postulated a tendency, from the late Middle Ages onward, to rationalise and thus control the emotions. However, most scholars now reject the idea of a strict epochal separation and assume that emotions could be controlled in premodern epochs as well. The notion of asserting control over one's feelings should not be misunderstood: emotions were not necessarily instrumentalised; they were only stimulated by creating significant situations.[36] It is, thus, reasonable to assume a high degree of staging in Roman oratory and the use of emotions for persuasive purposes.

It is methodologically important that emotional responses are reported in the sources, although these are only perceptible in the form of gestural expressions; one cannot gain access to the internal states of historical actors, but their physical expressions are made visible in our sources. Robert Kaster addresses the problem by analysing emotional forms of expression and their display.[37] Emotions are staged through gestures. Ritualised acts, such as those that are subsumed under the term *planctus*, were expected to signal mourning and the omission of such signals of grief was all the more meaningful. The Romans used various gestures and signs during the funeral ceremony to draw attention to their grief or to signal loss of all kinds. Specific accessories made of dark colours were used for clothing, for instance. People went without jewellery and signs of rank, and loosened and tussled their hair to take on a dishevelled look, with the head left uncovered to convey a departure from social norms. Romans cried, wailed, tore their clothes and slapped their chests. The mourning gestures also included beating other parts of the body, such as the cheeks, eyes, temples and arms.[38] In ancient times, the scratching of one's cheeks had been part of mourning behaviour but this was prohibited in Rome by the *Twelve Tables*. However, men allowed their beards to grow[39] and sons covered their heads with their robe. These ostentatious, auto-aggressive examples of *planctus* – a word which was derived from the striking of the chest (*pectus plangere*) – included all forms of violence used in the context of mourning against oneself.[40] In contrast, *maeror* described the self-contained,

---

36 Hagen 2017, 14–66, from a classicist's perspective, and Plamper 2015, in general.
37 Kaster 2005; on the problem of the interior view of historical individuals, Groebner 2013.
38 Ps.-Ov. *Cons. ad Liv.* 318; Prop. 2.9.10; Stat. *Theb.* 8.644–645; 12.110; Verg. *Aen.* 7.503; Ov. *Met.* 4.138; Sen. *Tro.* 120; Quint. *Decl. mai.* 10.3; Apul. *Met.* 8.9.2.
39 Sen. *Dial.* 11.17.5; Suet. *Cal.* 24.2; Frontin. *Strat.* 4.5.6, Late Republican coins show mourning beards of Antony, Octavian, Sex. Pompey and Brutus; see Biedermann 2013.
40 *ThLL* Bd. X, 1. fasc. XV (2005), 2305–2308 s.v. *planctus*; see Degelmann 2018, 136–137.

quiet sadness of the mourner, while *maestitia* expressed a permanent depression. *Tristia* and *tristitia* were another facet of mourning, a certain melancholy that also included a degree of severity.⁴¹ All of these forms of expression appealed to the audience's compassion.

The translation of historical terms for emotions is another methodological problem because feelings were experienced differently in different historical settings; most of the time, the emotional constructs that appear in the Roman literary tradition cannot be assumed to be identical with the phenomena and expressions of the range of emotions experienced today. While the experience of grief is a constant, since loss remains an inescapable feature of the human condition, the way in which grief is experienced has changed over time.⁴² We should, therefore, assume *mixed emotions* that add numerous other, sometimes strange, facets to our expectations of the emotions we know today.⁴³

In the senatorial families, the *laudatio funebris* combined efforts to emphasise the political importance and the leadership claim of the *gens*, or even to increase it through exaggeration. According to Cicero and Livy, individual *gentes* integrated invented consulates and triumphal processions from the early history of Rome into their eulogy without this being verifiable.⁴⁴ Occasionally, the *laudatio* is apologetic in character, as in the case of M. Claudius Marcellus,⁴⁵ or it serves as a weapon in political business, as the speech for Caesar by M. Antony illustrates particularly well.⁴⁶

Dio Cassius vividly describes the change of heart among the audience during Antony's speech.⁴⁷ First, the *plebs* became excited, then embittered, and finally enraged. The crowd spontaneously wanted to cremate the body in the building where Caesar had been murdered. Marauding mobs made their way to the houses of the conspirators. In doing so, one group seized C. Helvius Cinna, whom they

---

41 *ThLL* Bd. VIII (1936/61), 41-43 s.v. *maeror*; 44-45 s.v. *maestitia*; on *tristitia* Graßl 1975; Wacke 1979.
42 Liebsch/Rüsen 2001, 7-10.
43 Konstan 2003; on the concept of *mixed emotions*, Sanders 2014, 114.
44 Cic. *Brut*. 62; Liv. 8.40.4-5; see Ridley 1983; Lehmann 2017.
45 Liv. 27.27.13-14 mentions that the folly of exploring the area as a consul and without protection led to his death and needed justification.
46 Kierdorf 1980, 151-153; Sumi 2005, 100-112; Hall 2014, 134-140.
47 On Antony's *laudatio* see App. *Civ*. 2.600-614; Plu. *Ant*. 14.7-8; Quint. *Inst*. 6.1.30-31; Cass. Dio 44.36.1-52.3 and Suet. *Iul*. 84.2-3, who believed that Antony had read the will and said only a few words; see Flower 1996, 125-126; Matijevic 2006, 101-104 argues against an express staging and conscious acceptance of unrest by Antony. The reactions of the audience in Matijević 2006, 101 n. 168, Gotter 1996, 267.

mistook for the conspirator L. Cornelius Cinna, and tore him into pieces – a form of killing common in the context of mourning.⁴⁸ Suetonius also claims that the mob brought flammable material to enlarge the pyre because the size of the *rogus* was an indication of the status of the deceased. The pyre's exclusivity was underscored by the addition of precious gifts: veterans gave their weapons, housewives their jewellery and their children's clothes to the fire. Showmen tore up their robes and funeral chants (*lamentatio*) typical of various groups of people were heard. The staging, on the other hand, was designed to present Caesar in as unadorned a way as possible, which made the *rogus* appear all the larger. Only once the body had been cremated were the houses of Caesar's assassins, Brutus and Cassius, assailed.⁴⁹

The sources undoubtedly intend to show how easy it was to inflame the crowd. Exaggerations can, therefore, be expected. On the one hand, the veneration of Caesar by the people is demonstrated, while, on the other hand, the unfair means by which he and his followers tried to seize the favour of the "fickle" plebs is revealed. The authors succeed in their goal, but this does not detract from the reality that grief was, in fact, choreographed using rhetorical means.⁵⁰ In view of the power and impact of the staging of an event such as Caesar's cremation, especially when combined with speeches and the behaviour associated with mourning, it should come as no surprise that the historical actors sought to make use of particular aspects of the ritual and attempted to apply them outside of their original setting.

3 Appropriating the rhetoric of mourning

The ability of the *laudatio* to generate pity, to win sympathy and sometimes to stir up aggression was so great that individual members of the upper class began to use it in a targeted manner. Since it was common to mourn in cases of death, a

---

48 The mistake is well documented: Val. Max. 9.1.1; Suet. *Iul.* 85.1; Plu. *Caes.* 68.3–6; *Brut.* 20.8–11; App. *Civ.* 2.613; Cass. Dio 44.50.4; see also Morgan 1990.
49 Suet. *Iul.* 85.1–2; App. *Civ.* 2.147–148 added incorrectly that Caesar had been burned in the Theatre of Pompey; a short report with similar features in Plu. *Caes.* 68.1–7; *Brut.* 20.2–7; *Ant.* 14.2–4.
50 Matijevic 2006, 103; Bodel 1999, 274. App. *Civ.* 2.147 emphasised that the funeral of Caesar was a tragic performance by mentioning a mechanical device that turned round the corpse in all directions (τὸ δὲ ἀνδρείκελον ἐκ μηχανῆς ἐπεστρέφετο πάντῃ) usually used in the theatre; indeed, tragedy is all about generating emotion in the audience.

specific practice evolved in which signs of mourning, such as beards and specific forms of clothing, were appropriated and displayed in completely different situations that were unrelated to the prior death of a family member. In these new contexts, the signs took on additional symbolic meanings that could assist in the settling or sharpening of conflicts.[51] This custom was often combined with the use of signs and gestures which originally had nothing to do with mourning or burial practices. The appropriation of signs and gestures in a way that partly inverts their original meaning is a device that also appears in the literary tradition, with a number of authors using it to embroider scenes of mourning.[52] After the Second Punic War, this practice of symbolic mourning continued to expand before declining rapidly during the early Imperial era. There exist almost one hundred historical records of this kind of practice, including examples in historiography, biography, speeches, letters, papyri, and portraits on coins, busts and gems. Early research has referred to this custom as *squalor* since it involved the wearing of dirty clothes and the neglect of one's scalp and facial hair.[53] At times, mourning acts are presented in our sources as referring directly to the funeral speech or *pompa*, with the authors using the same terminology or making an explicit comparison between *squalor* and *laudatio*. Sometimes the practice itself or its consequences also suggest a comparison.[54]

Cicero's speech to the Senate after his return from exile in 57 BC emphatically illustrates how the funeral oration could be appropriated. He tells how the *gens Metella* collectively campaigned for the return of Q. Caecilius Metellus Numidicus, who had been in exile since 100 BC:[55]

> *Pro me non [...] ut pro Q. Metello, summo et clarissimo viro, spectata iam adulescentia filius, non L. et C. Metelli, consulares, non eorum liberi, non Q. Metellus Nepos, qui tum consulatum petebat, non Luculli, Servilii, Scipiones, Metellarum filii flentes ac sordidati populo Romano supplicaverunt.* (Cic. *Red. Sen.* 37)

> I had not, to plead for me, [...] as had that great and famous gentleman Q. Metellus, a son whose qualities had won him respect in spite of his youth; not for me did the ex-consuls L. and C. Metellus, nor their children, nor Q. Metellus Nepos, who was at that time a candidate

---

51 For the social setting and environment of mourning and burial see Hope/Huskinson 2011; Hope 2009; Schrumpf 2006; Hinard 1995; Toynbee 1971.
52 Degelmann 2018; Dighton 2017; Flaig 2003, 99–110.
53 Becker 1849, 157; Mommsen 1899, 390–391 n. 2. Hall 2014, 18 suggests that *squalor* was first used in a broad range of social contexts and was then later exploited particularly in the courts – a view that is not confirmed by the sources; both aspects seem to arise simultaneously.
54 Cic. *Quir.* 6; *Red. Sen.* 37; Sen. *Contr.* 10.1 ff.; Tac. *Hist.* 3.67.2.
55 On the background of Metellus' exile see Degelmann 2018, 77–78.

for the consulship, nor the Luculli, the Servii, the Scipiones, whose mothers were of the family of Metellus, intercede before the Roman people in tears and dishevelled garb. (tr. Watts 1923, modified)

Numerous relatives, we are given to understand, appeared publicly to advocate the return of Numidicus. As in a *pompa funebris*, they were dressed in mourning (*sordidati*) and relied on the visualised symbolic capital of their family, although the consular had not died. Cicero used the example to emphasise his own position as a *homo novus* in the face of impending exile. Unlike Metellus, he had no prestigious family support he could rely on to protest against Clodius' legislation. On the contrary, we know that he was chased away from the forum performing his *squalor*, and that his brother Quintus' requests as *sordidatus* gained no traction.[56]

The speech adapts the *laudatio* by identifying those who had been involved in the action of the *Metelli*. One encounters in some detail L. Caecilius Metellus (cos. 117) and his younger brother Gaius (cos. 113), who was a censor with Numidicus. The sisters of the pair were married to C. Servilius Vatia (cos. 79) and P. Cornelius Scipio Nasica (cos. 111). The first connection came from the son Publius called Isauricus (cos. 79), the second marriage from the son of the same name (praet. 93). The *Luculli* join via Numidicus' sister, the mother of the famous general L. Licinius Lucullus (cos. 74). These three outstanding personalities are only alluded to indirectly, perhaps because some of them were still alive when Cicero gave the speech, and drawing excessive attention to them would have left open room for them to contradict him. He completely renounced the Claudian sons of the *Metellae* and the *Crassi* because, in view of his hostility to Clodius and his ambivalent relationship with Crassus, they might not appear to be suitable examples. The further omission of the prominent brothers Cn. and L. Domitius Ahenobarbus (cos. 96 and 94), whose support was secured by a letter from Metellus from exile, served him well because Cicero wanted to give the impression of a gallery of ancestors while the *Domitii* were neither paternally nor maternally related to the family.[57] There were other highly decorated *Metelli* who would have been available in 99 BC but who are also omitted by Cicero, such as M. Metellus (cos. 115) and perhaps also Metellus Balearicus (cos. 123), censor of the year 120 – if

---

56 Plu. *Cic.* 30–31; on the context of Cicero's banishment see Degelmann 2018, 77–83.
57 For the offices see *MRR*. The evidence for the *Ahenobarbi* can be found in Gell. 15.13.7; 17.2.7; see *FRM* 47–48. Kelly 2006, 86–87 explains their absence unsatisfactorily: Cicero suggests that this is just the tip of the iceberg, probably based on his access to the letter of Numidicus; see *FRM*, 44–46. On the *Caecilii Metelli*, now Hölkeskamp 2017, 273–309.

still alive. In consequence, the wearing of the ancestral masks of these two deceased family members is also a conceivable way of expanding the symbolic capital. At least we know that *imagines* were shown in court and were considered a convincing argument in that context.[58] Finally, Cicero explicitly mentions the son of Numidicus, who was to be given the honorary name Pius (cos. 80), and the son of Balearicus, Nepos, who was currently running for the consulship (cos. 98).

Cicero lists the relatives of Numidicus in the style of a *laudatio*. He begins with the oldest cousin and his younger brother, continues with the generation of the sons, and finally gives a brief mention to the less important matrilineal relatives. In each case a memorable story would have been available for the orator or the audience to call up if necessary: L. Metellus was given the nickname Diadematus since he used to cover a wound he had sustained in battle with a diadem;[59] C. Metellus celebrated a triumph (*pompa triumphalis*) on the same day as his brother Marcus; Servilius Vatia celebrated two triumphs alone and received his epithet from a victory over the Isaurians, whose defeat meant the establishment of the province of Cilicia; the less successful Scipio Nasica is not only important because of his place in the family network, but also because he was responsible for entrusting a son to the childless Metellus Pius for adoption (cos. 52).[60] Pius is also an exception in Cicero's list: while he starts by naming Pius, he suddenly switches his attention to the older *Metelli*. The reason for this was that Pius' special commitment as the son of an exile meant that he obviously supported the actions of his father, Numidicus, who had earned his honorary name as victor over Numidia. Pius thus somehow appears as the speaker of a eulogy for his father. The reference to the underage children of certain defendants in court or of otherwise overtly threatened individuals, such as Sulpicius Galba (149 BC) or Tiberius Gracchus (133 BC), probably points towards and evokes the fact that the *laudatio funebris* was given by the youngest possible member of the mourning *gens*.[61] In Cicero's own time, the younger Metellus had already turned into an *exemplum pietatis* – also contributing to his own prestige by having coins with relevant symbols minted in his consulship. Nepos' epithet indicates affectionate

---

58 Flower 1996, 151; Brooke 2011, 96–97; Pernot 2005, 90.
59 Plu. *Coriol.* 11.3.; cf. *MRR* I, 528 and 531.
60 Vatia in Amm. 14.8.4; Eutr. 6.3; *MRR* II, 90–91; the younger Pius in Ascon. 66 Clark; *MRR* II, 234–235.
61 Liv. *Per.* 49; Cato *FRH* 7.1 (= Cic. *Brut.* 89–90); 7.2 (= Front. *Ep.* 3. 21.4) and App. *Civ.* 1.62, respectively.

closeness to his grandfather, and he acts here as *sordidatus* instead of *candidatus*; the deeds carried out on behalf of the community were thus extended into the past, in the sense reported by Polybius,[62] and remembered in the present.

But what made Cicero's strategy so haunting was that it inverted a crucial aspect of the normal funeral speech. Usually, the deceased ancestors whose deeds were being praised appeared in their former official robes, while the relatives who mourned the deceased appeared in mourning. In Cicero's speech, it appears that the figures to be honoured are shrouded in mourning. From Cicero's point of view as a *homo novus* speaking 40 years later, the individuals mentioned were to be seen as *maiores*, and not just of one family but of the entire *res publica*. Portraying them as mourning participants in a funeral instead of those being honoured was a rhetorical trick designed to elicit sympathy from the listener. The passage thus testifies to the appropriation of the funeral ceremonial by the *Metelli* as well as to the rhetorical appropriation and reinterpretation of the event by Cicero.

4 Conclusion

On the one hand, this chapter has sought to draw attention to the specific connection between rhetoric and mourning, as well as to its development in the Roman Republic and the early Imperial period. On the other hand, the creative appropriation of funeral rhetoric for political purposes has also been demonstrated. It turns out that the Romans had available to them a wide-ranging set of signs for expressing grief, and that they also used these on other occasions, taking advantage of the haunting effect of the *laudatio funebris* on the emotional state of their listeners in circumstances that were not linked to deaths in the narrower sense. However, this was only possible because the deep religiosity of the Romans, also described by Polybius,[63] played little, if any, part in their mourning. Grief was rather a social phenomenon, with the funeral ritual referring to beliefs in the afterlife only indirectly, if at all. Ultimately, in the eyes of a Roman, individuals continued to live for as long as posterity – whether in the form of family, government or the masses – remembered the deceased; the funeral speech also commanded this commemoration. However, this tie between mourning and *memoria* did not require a specific connection between grief and the afterlife.

---

[62] Polyb. 6.54.3.
[63] Polyb. 6.56.6–15.

Bibliography

Austin, J.L. (1962), *How to Do Things with Words*, Cambridge, MA.
Badian, E. (1971), 'Three Fragments', in: D.M. Kriel (ed.), *Pro Munere Grates. Studies Presented to H.L. Gonin*, Pretoria, 1–6.
Beck, H. (2005), 'Züge in die Ewigkeit. Prozessionen durch das republikanische Rom', in: *Göttinger Forum für Altertumswissenschaft* 8, 73–104.
Beck, H. (2018), 'Of Fragments and Feelings. Roman Funeral Oratory Revisited', in: Ch. Grey et al. (eds.), *Reading Republican Oratory. Reconstructions, Contexts, Receptions*, Oxford, 263–280.
Becker, W.A. (1849), *Gallus: oder Römische Scenen aus der Zeit Augusts. Zur genaueren Kenntnis des römischen Privatlebens*: 1. Teil. 2. verm. u. ber. Ausg. v. W. Rein, Leipzig.
Biedermann, D. (2013), 'Zur Bärtigkeit römischer Porträts spätrepublikanischer Zeit', in: *Bonner Jahrbücher* 213, 27–50.
Blome, P. (2001), 'Die *imagines maiorum*: ein Problemfall römischer und neuzeitlicher Ästhetik', in: G. Boehm (ed.), *Homo Pictor*, München/Leipzig, 305–322.
Blösel, W. (2003), 'Die *memoria* der *gentes* als Rückgrat der kollektiven Erinnerung im republikanischen Rom', in: U. Eigler et al. (eds.), *Formen römischer Geschichtsschreibung von den Anfängen bis Livius*, Darmstadt, 53–72.
Bodel, J. (1999), 'Death on Display. Looking at Roman Funerals', in: B. Bergmann/C. Kondoleon (eds.), *The Art of Ancient Spectacle*, Washington, 259–282.
Brooke, E. (2011), '*Causa ante mortua est quam tu natus es*: Aspects of the Funeral in Cicero's Pro Rabirio Perduellionis Reo', in: V. Hope/J. Huskinson (eds.), *Memory and Mourning. Studies on Roman Death*, Oxford/Oakville, 93–112.
Butler, J. (1995), *Körper von Gewicht. Die diskursiven Grenzen des Geschlechts*, Berlin (engl. 1993).
Cary, E. (tr.) (1916), *Dio Cassius, Roman History. Vol. 4: Books 41-45*, Cambridge, MA/London.
Covino, R. (2011), 'The *Laudatio Funebris* as a Vehicle for Praise and Admonition', in: Chr. J. Smith/R. Covino (eds.), *Praise and Blame in Roman Republican Rhetoric*, Swansea, 69–81.
Degelmann, Chr. (2018), *Squalor. Symbolisches Trauern in der Politischen Kommunikation der Römischen Republik und Frühen Kaiserzeit*, Stuttgart.
Dighton, A. (2017), '*Mutatio Vestis*: Clothing and Political Protest in the Late Roman Republic', in: *Phoenix* 71, 345–369.
Drerup, H. (1980), 'Totenmaske und Ahnenbild bei den Römern', in: *Mitteilungen des Deutschen Archäologischen Insituts (Röm. Abt.)* 87, 81–129.
Durry, M. (1942), 'Laudatio funebris et rhétorique', in: *Revue de Philologie, de Littérature et d'Histoire Anciennes*, 105–114.
Durry, M. (1950), *Éloge funèbre d'une matrone Romaine*, Paris.
Ekman, P. (2003), *Emotions Revealed: Recognizing Faces and Feelings to Improve Communication and Emotional Life*, New York.
Fischer-Lichte, E. (2015), *Performativität. Eine Einführung*, Bielefeld.
Fish, St. (1980), *Is There a Text in This Class? The Authority of Interpretive Communities*, Cambridge, MA.
Flaig, E. (1995), 'Die *pompa funebris*. Adlige Konkurrenz und annalistische Erinnerung in der Römischen Republik', in: O.G. Oexle (ed.), *Memoria als Kultur*, Göttingen, 115–148.
Flaig, E. (2003), *Ritualisierte Politik. Zeichen Gesten und Herrschaft im Alten Rom*, Göttingen.

Flower, H.I. (1996), *Ancestor Masks and Aristocratic Power in Roman Culture*, Oxford.
Gotter, U. (1996), *Der Diktator ist tot! Politik in Rom zwischen den Iden des März und der Begründung des Zweiten Triumvirats*, Stuttgart.
Graßl, H. (1975), 'Tristitia als Herausforderung des Prinzipats', in: *Grazer Beiträge* 4, 89–96.
Groebner, V. (2013), 'Ein Staubsauger namens Emotion. Geschichte und Gefühl als akademischer Komplex', in: *Zeitschrift für Ideengeschichte* 7, 109–116.
Hagen, J. (2017), *Die Tränen der Mächtigen und die Macht der Tränen. Eine emotionsgeschichtliche Untersuchung des Weinens in der kaiserzeitlichen Historiographie*, Stuttgart.
Hall, J. (2014), *Cicero's Use of Judicial Theater*, Ann Arbor.
Harré, R. (ed.) (1986), *The Social Construction of Emotion*, Oxford.
Hinard, F. (ed.) (1995), *La Mort au Quotidien dans le Monde Romain*, Paris.
Hölkeskamp, K.-J. (1995), 'Oratoris Maxima Scaena. Reden vor dem Volk in der politischen Kultur der Republik', in: M. Jehne (ed.), *Demokratie in Rom? Die Rolle des Volkes in der Politik der römischen Republik*, Stuttgart, 11–49.
Hölkeskamp, K.-J. (1996), '*Exempla* und *mos maiorum*. Überlegungen zum kollektiven Gedächtnis der Nobilität', in: H.-J. Gehrke/A. Möller (eds.), *Vergangenheit und Lebenswelt. Soziale Kommunikation, Traditionsbildung und historisches Bewußtsein*, Tübingen, 301–338.
Hölkeskamp, K.-J. (2010), *Reconstructing the Roman Republic. An Ancient Political Culture and Modern Research*. Revised, updated, and augmented by the author, Princeton et al.
Hölkeskamp, K.-J. (2017), *Libera Res Publica. Die politische Kultur des antiken Rom – Positionen und Perspektiven*, Stuttgart.
Hölkeskamp, K.-J. (2020), *Roman Republican Reflections. Studies in Politics, Power, and Pageantry*, Stuttgart.
Hope, V. (2009), *Roman Death. The Dying and the Dead in Ancient Rome*, London/New York.
Hope, V./Huskinson, J. (eds.) (2011), *Memory and Mourning. Studies on Roman Death*, Oxford/Oakville.
Jackson, J. (tr.) (1937), *Tacitus, Annals. Vol. 5: Books 13–16*, Cambridge, MA.
Jehne, M. (2001), 'Integrationsrituale in der römischen Republik. Zur einbindenden Wirkung der Volksversammlungen', in: G. Urso (ed.), *Integrazione, mescolanza, rifiuto. Incontri di popoli, lingue e culture in Europa dall' Antichità all' Umanesimo*, Rome, 89–113.
Jones, Ch. (2004), 'A Speech of the Emperor Hadrian', in: *Classical Quarterly* 54, 266–273.
Kaster, R. (2005), *Emotion, Restraint, and Community in Ancient Rome*, Oxford.
Kelly, G.P. (2006), *A History of Exile in the Roman Republic*, Cambridge.
Kierdorf, W. (1980), *Laudatio funebris. Interpretationen und Untersuchungen zur Entwicklung der römischen Leichenrede*, Meisenheim am Glan.
Kierdorf, W. (1998), 'Art. *imagines maiorum*', in: *Der Neue Pauly* 5, 947.
Konstan, D. (2003), 'Translating Ancient Emotions', in: *Acta Classica* 46, 5–19.
Lehmann, A. (2017), 'Le témoignage de Cicéron sur la *laudatio funebris*: forme inchoative d'historiographie ou art de la déformation historique', in: W. Kofler/A. Novokhatko (eds.), *Pontes 7. Verleugnete Rezeption: Fälschungen antiker Texte*, Freiburg i.Br., 77–94.
Liebsch, B./Rüsen, J. (2001), 'Vorwort', in: B. Liebsch/J. Rüsen (eds.), *Trauer und Geschichte*, Köln, 7–11.
Lindsay, H. (2004), 'The *Laudatio Murdiae*. Its Content and Significance', in: *Latomus* 63, 88–97.
Matijevic, K. (2006), *Marcus Antonius. Consul – Proconsul – Staatsfeind. Die Politik der Jahre 44 und 43 v. Chr.*, Rahden.

Meyer, E.A. (2004), *Legitimacy and Law in the Roman World. Tabulae in Roman Belief and Practice*, Cambridge.

Mommsen, T. (1899), *Römisches Strafrecht*, Repr. Darmstadt 1955.

Moretti, G. (2015), 'Il funus, le imagines, la laudatio: alle origini dell'impiego di "visual tools" a supporto dell'oratoria nella tradizione romana', in: C. Pepe/G. Moretti (eds.), *Le parole dopo la morte: forme e funzioni della retorica funeraria nella tradizione greca e romana*, Trento, 113–146.

Morgan, J.D. (1990), 'The Death of Cinna the Poet', in: *Classical Quarterly* 40, 558–559.

Osgood, J. (2014), *Turia: A Roman Woman's Civil War*, Oxford.

Paton, W.R. (tr.) (2011), *Polybius, The Histories. Vol.3: Books 5-8*. Tr. By W.R. Paton; rev. by F.W. Walbank, C. Habicht, Cambridge, MA.

Pepe, C. (2011), 'Tra *laudatio funebris* romana ed ἐπιτάφιος greco: l'esempio degli elogi in morte di Cesare', in: *I Quaderni del Ramo d'Oro On-Line* 4, 137–151.

Pepe, C. (2015), 'La fama dopo il silenzio: celebrazione della donna e ritratti esemplari di bonae feminae nella laudatio funebris romana', in: C. Pepe/G. Moretti (eds.), *Le parole dopo la morte: forme e funzioni della retorica funeraria nella tradizione greca e romana*, Trento, 179–221.

Pernot, L. (2005), *Rhetoric in Antiquity*, Washington.

Plamper, J. (2015), *The History of Emotions. An Introduction*, Oxford.

Prokoph, F. (2010), '*Vitam narrare* à la romaine: l'intérêt biographique et son passage de l'oral républicain à l'écrit imperial', in: Y. Perrin/M. de Souza (eds.), *Neronia VIII: Bibliothèques, livres et culture écrite dans l'empire romain de César à Hadrien*, Bruxelles, 273–289.

Ramage, E. (2006), 'Funeral eulogy and propaganda in the Roman Republic', in: *Athenaeum* 94, 39–64.

Reddy, W.M. (1997), 'Against Constructionism. The Historical Ethnography of Emotions', in: *Current Anthropology* 38, 327–351.

Ridley, R.T. (1983), '*Falsi triumphi, plures consulatus*', in: *Latomus* 42, 372–382.

Sanders, E. (2014), *Envy and Jealousy in Classical Athens. A Socio-Psychological Approach*, Oxford.

Schrumpf, S. (2006), *Bestattung und Bestattungswesen im Römischen Reich. Ablauf, soziale Dimension und ökonomische Bedeutung der Totenfürsorge im lateinischen Westen*, Göttingen.

Searle, J.R. (1969), *Speech Acts. An Essay in the Philosophy of Language*, Cambridge.

Serafim, A. (2017), *Attic Oratory and Performance*, London/New York.

Stearns, P.N./Stearns, C.Z. (1985), 'Emotionology. Clarifying the History of Emotions and Emotional Standards', in: *The American Historical Review* 904, 813–830.

Sumi, G.S. (2005), *Ceremony and Power. Performing Politics in Rome Between Republic and Empire*, Ann Arbor.

Wacke, A. (1979), '*Tristitia* als Ehrenkränkung und Ausdruck politischer Opposition', in: *Labeo* 25, 293–294.

Walter, U. (2003), 'Ahn Macht Sinn. Familientradition und Familienprofil im republikanischen Rom', in: K.-J. Hölkeskamp et al. (eds.), *Sinn (in) der Antike. Orientierungssysteme, Leitbilder und Wertkonzepte im Altertum*, Mainz, 255–278.

Walter, U. (2004), *Memoria und res publica. Zur Geschichtskultur im republikanischen Rom*, Frankfurt a.M.

Watts, N.H. (tr.) (1923), *Cicero. Pro Archia. Post Reditum in Senatu. Post Reditum ad Quirites. De Domo Sua. De Haruspicum Responsis. Pro Plancio*, Cambridge, MA.

Glenn Holland
Argument and Performance in the Creation of a Rhetorical Matrix in Paul's Congregations and Beyond

Abstract: This chapter examines the means by which writings of Paul of Tarsus, initially written to address situations in specific congregations at specific times, became authoritative for all early Christian communities. Holland considers Paul's use of rhetorical methods to persuade the audiences of his letters to adopt particular beliefs and patterns of behaviour, and elements of the rhetorical matrix Paul employed. Holland then discusses the secondary performance of Paul's letters beyond their original audiences and the further dissemination of Paul's ideas through letters attributed to him but written by others. Holland concludes that the rhetorical matrix of Paul's own letters determined both how his congregations thought and what they thought about, but the spread of his ideas beyond his original audiences was primarily the result of re-performance of his own letters and later letters attributed to him, letters that emphasised the universal applicability of Paul's ideas while providing their own interpretive frameworks.

1 Introduction

Paul of Tarsus is, for good or ill, the most influential figure in the history of the Christian movement after Jesus of Nazareth himself. Although Christians have always looked to Jesus not only as their primary teacher and example but also as their Lord and Saviour, it is Paul whose work and letters have largely shaped what Christians believe about Jesus and how they live out those beliefs in community. Paul's missionary outreach to several of the Hellenistic cities of the Aegean and the eastern Mediterranean led first to the establishment of congregations of Jesus' followers and later to the propagation of Paul's understanding of the gospel message he proclaimed beyond those congregations, out into the larger Mediterranean world.

Although himself a Jew and in his youth an adherent to the teachings of the Pharisees,[1] it was Paul who pioneered and justified the inclusion of Gentiles

---

[1] Paul several times refers explicitly to his Jewish heritage and beliefs in his surviving letters, notably in Romans 11.1, 13–14, Galatians 1.13–14, Philippians 3.4b–6.

https://doi.org/10.1515/9783110699623-009

among the Jesus congregations he founded without requiring them to obey all the stipulations of Torah. Most notably he did not require the males among them to be circumcised and developed a theological argument for foregoing the ritual (cf. Romans 1.16–2.29, 4.1–25; cp. Galatians 3.6–29, 4.21–5.1). When Paul's practice led to opposition from at least some of the other Jewish leaders of the Jesus movement, Paul's arguments for including uncircumcised Gentiles contributed to a more general re-evaluation of the role of Torah observance among Gentile members of Jesus congregations (Galatians 2.1–10; cp. Acts 15.1–21).

Beyond his immediate influence upon those congregations he founded and others that were sympathetic to his understanding of Jesus and the Jesus movement, Paul also left a legacy that has shaped all later Christian thinkers down to the present day. The letters Paul wrote to his congregations form the earliest stratum of the later New Testament and inspired many of the later authors – both followers and opponents of Paul – whose work has also been included among its writings.[2]

However, as we know, at least some of Paul's letters – those that survive – have had a life extending far beyond their first reading to their original recipients. That is, they continued to be read even after the occasion prompting their composition was presumably resolved. Not only were Paul's letters apparently preserved by at least some of the congregations to which they were addressed, they were in time circulated to other congregations recognising Paul's authority, and eventually gathered into a collection preserved and augmented in the New Testament. But before that, after their initial reading to their original recipients, Paul's letters were circulated, read and re-read before new audiences in other congregations around the Mediterranean basin. As a result, Paul's ideas, expressed in his terms and supported by his arguments, became authoritative for an ever-larger group of followers of Jesus.

---

[2] Followers include the authors of those letters pseudonymously attributed to Paul and the author of Luke/Acts, who makes Paul the hero of Acts 13–28. Opponents arguably include the authors of the gospel of Matthew (cf. Matthew 5.17–20), the letter of James (cf. James 2.14–26) and Revelation (cf. Revelation 2.19–20; cp. 1 Corinthians 10.25–11.1).

2 Paul's use of the techniques of rhetoric in his letters

Paul makes it clear in his letters that he considers them something of an emergency measure, a means of communicating with his congregations in times of need when it was impossible for him to address them face-to-face or through a close trusted associate (cf. 1 Corinthians 4.14–21, 2 Corinthians 1.23–2.1, Philippians 2.19–30, 1 Thessalonians 2.17–3.10). But the exigencies of communicating through letters led Paul to shape them into something more than just a collection of greetings and instructions. They were instead works intended to persuade their audiences by various means to recognise Paul's authority as an apostle and to adopt his way of thinking. Despite his status as the founder of many of the congregations he addressed, Paul's authority was not universally accepted by all the members of those congregations.[3] Therefore, he employed the persuasive art of rhetoric in many aspects of his letters, including various rhetorical tropes and, often it seems, the structure of the letters as well.

It is generally agreed among scholars that Paul received, in addition to a religious education in the traditions of his fathers, some sort of Hellenistic education, which would have included at least some study of the art of rhetoric.[4] His letters include rhetorical devices and techniques, including notably the extensive use of irony, especially in 2 Corinthians 10–13.[5] At the same time, there is disagreement over the extent and nature of Paul's use of rhetoric in his letters and how modern exegetes might best use rhetorical analysis as a means of understanding Paul's letters.[6] But as Christopher Forbes has written,

> Paul was... a highly experienced speaker, and, from what we can tell, in his own time and place a persuasive one. He may or may not have had formal rhetorical training, but he knew from observation and experience what styles of argument would, and would not, hold the attention of his target audience. Arguments that his letters ought to be expected to conform more to epistolary than to rhetorical conventions have this weakness: Paul was not writing

---

[3] The most prominent example of members of a congregation rejecting Paul's authority may be found in Paul's letters to Corinth, which reflect a situation that went from bad to worse before its ultimate resolution in a general acknowledgement of Paul's authority; cf. 1 Corinthians 1.10–17, 5.1–6.20, 11.17–22; 2 Corinthians 10.1–13.10; 2 Corinthians 1.16–2.13, 7.5–16.
[4] For Paul's education and knowledge of the art of rhetoric see Pitts 2016, Kremmydas 2016, Hughes 2016, all in Porter/Dyer 2016.
[5] For an extended discussion of Paul's use of irony see Holland 2000, 119–156.
[6] Lampe 2010 provides an overview of some of the issues; see also the discussion in Classen 2016.

letters to individuals, to be read at their leisure. He was writing letters to Christian assemblies, where his letter would be read aloud, often in polemical situations.[7]

This fact provides a key to understanding the composition of Paul's letters: the letters would be read aloud to the members of the congregation addressed by a lector, that is, by someone other than Paul himself. This was in part because literacy was uncommon (and generally unnecessary) in the early Roman Empire,[8] and in part because most reading, even if a person was reading to himself/herself, was most often a matter of speaking the words of the text out loud rather than scanning them silently.[9] But of course the primary reason Paul's letters were read aloud was because they were addressed to a congregation, a gathering of Jesus followers. The only way of sharing a letter's contents with all the members of a group simultaneously was to read it aloud.[10] But reading a text aloud produces a performance.

By "performance" I mean what ancient rhetoricians called *hypocrisis*, "delivery" – which I have elsewhere defined as "the complete impression the orator makes on the audience by means of the entire physical apparatus he employs to perform the speech" – augmented by factors external to the speaker, such as place, occasion and audience, that also determine how the orator's words are received by the listeners both as a group and as individuals.[11] As I have written elsewhere:

> ... each reading aloud constitutes a unique performance, shaped not only by the choices and skills of the reader/performer in the specific circumstances of an individual reading, but also by the audience involved in that specific reading at a given time in a given space. Audiences are "involved" in a performance in two distinct senses of the word. An audience

---

[7] Forbes 2016, 214.
[8] There are various estimates of literacy in the early Roman Empire, but even if there are disagreements about specific percentages and variations among peoples and regions, it is safe to say most Roman subjects were not literate or only marginally literate. But imperial society and culture in general did not require literacy for full participation. See Poirier 2016, 68–74; for a fuller treatment see Johnson/Parker 2009.
[9] The tendency to read everything aloud was to some extent the result of the nature of ancient writings, which were written in *scripto continuo* and lacked the many reading aids familiar in modern European languages, including paragraphs and sentences, word separation, capitalisation and punctuation. Reading was therefore always to some extent a work of deciphering, and speaking aloud the words read made the task easier. At the same time, silent reading to oneself was not so uncommon in antiquity as some scholars have maintained; see Burnyeat 1997.
[10] Holland 2016b, 241–46.
[11] Holland 2016a, 120, 123–25.

is involved as a necessary component of a performance but also involved in the performance insofar as its members are *emotionally invested* in what they experience – aurally, visually and otherwise – while the performance takes place. Further, as [Marvin] Carlson notes, "All reception is deeply involved with memory, because it is memory that supplies the codes and strategies that shape reception, and, as cultural and social memories change, so do the parameters within which the reception operates… The expectations an audience brings to a new reception experience are the residue of memory of previous such experiences". In other words, past performances define the parameters for further performances and each performance is "haunted" by similar performances members of its audience have experienced in the past.[12]

Every performance of a written text is an in-the-moment experience for both reader and audience that is unique and irreducible.

A number of consequences follow from a letter being read aloud to a group rather than being read silently by an individual.[13] Notably, the person reading aloud essentially speaks "as Paul", that is, as if the Apostle was himself speaking to the congregation. The letter itself essentially disappears as the words Paul dictated in its composition are read aloud, again giving voice to the words that had been rendered mute by being reduced to marks on a page.[14] In each of his letters Paul speaks "directly" to his audience, through the voice and person of the lector.

Therefore, although someone else read his words aloud, Paul could insist he was somehow "present in spirit" when his letters were read (cf. 1 Corinthians 5.3).[15] This "presence" allowed Paul to act authoritatively within a congregation even when absent (cf. 1 Corinthians 5.4–5). Paul, apparently like some of his opponents, was also able to contrast his weak "bodily presence" with the boldness and confidence of his written words (2 Corinthians 10.1, 9–10). But the boldness and confidence were something his audiences experienced first-hand whenever his letters were read aloud, that is, when they were communicated through a skilled lector's performance. The contrast between Paul's letters in performance and Paul's own voice and bodily demeanour when present among the members of a congregation was apparently a source of considerable disappointment, to the point that it undermined his apostolic authority in the minds of some members of his congregations (2 Corinthians 10.9).[16]

---

12 Holland 2016b, 245–246, quoting Carlson 2002, 5.
13 Holland 2016a, 123–140.
14 Holland 2016a, 130.
15 Holland 2016a, 130–134.
16 Holland 2016a, 128–130.

3 Paul's central metaphors and themes

As noted earlier, the letters written by Paul provided the rhetorical matrix in which his ideas about Jesus and the faith based on belief in Jesus as Lord were received and understood by the members of the Jesus congregations Paul founded. Different letters reflect distinct situations and have particular points of emphasis, but each of Paul's undisputed letters reveal different aspects of a single, even if evolving, complex of theological ideas. By "undisputed letters" I mean those letters attributed to Paul in the New Testament that virtually all scholars agree are in fact essentially the work of Paul.[17] These undisputed letters are (in canonical order) Romans, 1 and 2 Corinthians, Galatians, Philippians, 1 Thessalonians and Philemon. These letters were directed to congregations – that is, groups of believers[18] – and were always read aloud – performed – for those to whom they were addressed. Ephesians, Colossians and 2 Thessalonians were probably similarly performed for their audiences, although the purpose and origin of those letters called "the Pastorals" – 1 and 2 Timothy and Titus – makes the circumstances of their transmission and their intended audience difficult to identify.[19]

Because his words were heard rather than seen, Paul's arguments had to be rhetorically effective and fully persuasive when spoken aloud the first time, like the arguments in an oration. Similarly, Paul's metaphors and the ideas they conveyed had to be arresting and memorable, designed both to make a point effectively in the moment and to linger in the audience's memory after they had been heard. In other words, the argument in a letter had to stimulate the short-term memory in members of its audience so they could follow and accept the argument

---

[17] "Essentially the work of Paul" recognises both that Paul dictated his letters to a scribe and that the nature of authorship in the early Roman Empire was different from authorship in the modern world. For Paul's method of composition and some of the consequences for how his letters are to be understood see Holland 2016a, 125–128.

[18] Philemon, despite its assigned title, is addressed "to Philemon our beloved friend and co-worker, to Aphia our sister, to Archippus our fellow soldier, *and to the congregation in your house*", Philemon 1a–2 (my translation; emphasis added).

[19] Ephesians, Colossians and 2 Thessalonians are often identified as "deutero-Pauline", that is, the work of an unknown author presenting himself/herself as Paul in the last third of the 1st century AD. The Pastorals, letters supposedly written to Paul's younger associates Timothy and Titus, are substantially different from Paul's own letters and probably date from the first third of the 2nd century AD. For some of the issues involved in distinguishing Paul's own letters from the deutero-Pauline and Pastoral letters see Collins 1988, esp. 75–86, and the various commentaries in Krodel 1993.

as they heard it unfold, and also gain a foothold in their long-term memories so they would later recall and more fully assimilate the argument into their own way of thinking. Arguments had to be persuasive both when they were first presented and heard and when they were later recalled.

This is why slogans and catchphrases that epitomise a particular argument or point of view are rhetorically effective. For example, one of the pillars of Paul's argument that Gentiles should be included within Jesus communities without requiring the men among them to be circumcised is summarised in the slogan, "For God shows no partiality" (οὐ γάρ ἐστιν προσωπολημψία παρὰ τῷ θεῷ; Romans 2.11).[20] Paul expresses the same idea in different words and with different implications in Galatians 2.6b (πρόσωπον θεὸς ἀνθρώπου οὐ λαμβάνει). The saying appears with more general application in the deutero-Pauline letters Colossians (3.25b: καὶ οὐκ ἔστιν προσωπολημψία) and Ephesians (6.9c: καὶ προσωπολημψία οὐκ ἔστιν παρ' αὐτῷ). Finally, we find the saying used in its original sense but in the mouth of Peter rather than Paul in Acts 10.34 (οὐκ ἔστιν προσωπολήμπτης ὁ θεός). Despite the change in specific wording, the idea is shared by Paul and his later followers, who apply the same general principle in different ways.

Most of Paul's central metaphors were drawn from institutions familiar to virtually every person living in the Mediterranean basin and under the sway of the early Roman Empire. First there is the arena, the venue of athletic competition. From the arena Paul takes the metaphor of the foot race (1 Corinthians 9.24–27, Philippians 2.16; cp. Galatians 2.2, 5.7), boxing (1 Corinthians 9.26), self-discipline and the victor's wreath (1 Corinthians 9.25). The arena presents the believer's life as a contest (against whom and what sort of contest varies from one use to another), a life-long struggle that requires discipline, single-mindedness and self-command (σωφροσύνη), a primary virtue in Greek and Hellenistic philosophy.

Second, the slave market provides the metaphor of enslavement itself (for example, to the spirit or to the flesh, Romans 6.16–22, 7.14, 7.25, 8.15; or to the "elemental spirits", Galatians 4.1–9; or to the law, Galatians 4.22–31), but also the idea of salvation as "redemption" (ἀπολύτρωσις; cf. Romans 3.24, 8.23, 1 Corinthians 1.30), paying the price required to free an enslaved person (ἐξαγοράζω, Galatians 3.13, 4.5; cp. 1 Corinthians 7.23, Galatians 5.1, 5.13). The metaphor includes the idea of absolute obedience towards one's "master" and suffering as a necessary part of a believer's life of obedience.[21] This is especially true of apostles,

---

[20] Unless otherwise noted, translations of biblical passages are those of the New Revised Standard Version.
[21] Martin 1990, 51.

each one "a slave of Christ Jesus" (δοῦλος Χριστοῦ Ἰησοῦ; cf. Romans 1.1, 2 Corinthians 4.5, Galatians 1.10, Philippians 1.1; for suffering, cf. 2 Corinthians 6.3–9, 11.21b–29).[22] As Dale Martin has put it, "popular myths about slavery in the ancient world provided a plausibility structure for portraying both abasement and exaltation, humiliation and the possibilities of honor. In sum, precisely because the social institution of slavery carried different connotations in different contexts, reference to slavery could represent self-abasement as well as upward mobility and access to high status".[23]

Third, the law-court is a particularly influential source of metaphors in Paul's letters, notably in Paul's use of the idea of δικαιοσύνη, "righteousness" or "justification", and its cognates (cf. Romans 3.24–28, 5.17–19, Galatians 2.19, 3.6–14, Philippians 3.9). The idea derives from a verdict in a court proceeding, as one person in a legal action is declared "in the right" (δίκαιος) while the other is not. Those who put their trust in the crucified Christ as Lord receive the ruling "in the right" from God as judge (cp. Zechariah 3). The metaphor of the law-court also provides a contrast between two means of vindication: the law (νόμος), in Paul meaning preeminently the stipulations of Torah, on the one hand, and the grace of God that arises from a believer's faith in Jesus as Lord on the other (cf. Romans 3.21–26).[24]

A fourth metaphorical complex relates to the body. It may represent the situation of those who have not yet become followers of Jesus when the body or "flesh" (σάρξ) is set in contrast to the "spirit" (πνεῦμα; cf. Romans 6.6, 7.4, 8.10–13, 1 Corinthians 15.42–44; cp. 2 Corinthians 12.2–3). But it functions notably to express the cohesiveness of Jesus communities despite the many different sorts of people (each with distinct abilities and strengths) such voluntary associations bring together. Paul presents the Jesus community as an organic whole in which every "member" has a specific and necessary function for the good of the whole congregation, understood as a body (cf. Romans 12.5, 1 Corinthians 10.17, 12.12–28; cp. Ephesians 4.11–16).

Paul's central metaphors shaped not only *how* those in his congregations thought and talked about matters in relation to their faith, but *what* they thought

---

22 Paul also refers repeatedly to the situation of enslaved persons who are members of Jesus congregations; cf. 1 Corinthians 7.21–22, 12.13, Galatians 3.28; cp. Colossians 3.11, Philemon 1.16; cp. the instructions to the enslaved to be faithful servants of their masters in Ephesians 6.5–8, Colossians 3.22–25, 1 Timothy 6.1, Titus 2.9.
23 Martin 1990, 132.
24 Although the Roman law-court is the immediate source for the metaphor, the concept of δικαιοσύνη is an extraordinarily complex one with, as indicated, strong connections with the Hebrew Bible and later Jewish tradition. See Sanders 1977, 474–508, and Brauch 1977.

and talked about. To discuss reconciliation with God in terms of δικαιοσύνη, for example, means not to talk in terms of participation in ritual observances, purification through ascetic practice or animal sacrifice, or a saving body of esoteric knowledge (γνῶσις) available only to an elite. Similarly, the topics addressed in Paul's letters and the specific ways in which he addressed them determined what would become the primary tenets of the beliefs and practices of Paul's congregations and other Jesus communities that looked to Paul as their guiding authority.

But Paul's influence was not merely a direct influence on the congregations he addressed in his letters, nor even the larger number of congregations he founded; rather, his ideas proved a lasting influence on all aspects of the later Christian movement. How did the letters of a single missionary apostle – no matter how profound his ideas or persuasive his arguments – become so important and so authoritative for so many?

4 Paul's letters beyond their initial performance

The initial performance of one of Paul's letters to the congregation he addressed was the purpose for which the letter was written. But each of his surviving letters also had a life that far surpassed its initial performance. This was presumably not Paul's intention, since he expected, at least initially, the return of Jesus before his own death (1 Thessalonians 4.15–17). Paul preferred to interact with his congregations in person and to deal with any problems that might have arisen in the community face-to-face, although such interactions did not always have the results he desired. When he was unable to visit a congregation where problems had arisen, or perhaps felt that circumstances made a personal visit inadvisable, his first choice was to send a surrogate, one of his close associates such as Timothy, Titus or Epaphroditus, perhaps carrying a letter, to deal with the situation and report back to Paul.[25] If one of his close associates was unable to visit a congregation when the need arose, Paul would send a letter, presumably by means of an emissary. But letters, of course, are only able to address a situation as it had been described to Paul, either by a person or by another letter (as in 1 Corinthians 1.11,

---

25 Paul does this at least once during the series of conflicts that arise in Corinth. Paul experienced a "painful visit" to Corinth; subsequently he decides to avoid another and so sends Titus in his stead with a letter, which makes up a portion of the canonical 2 Corinthians (see following note). Paul in another case writes to the congregation in Philippi that he wishes to send Timothy to visit them and himself to follow soon after, but in the meantime sends Epaphroditus as an emissary, presumably with the surviving Philippian letter(s); Philippians 2.19–30.

7.1a), and reflect Paul's response at the time a letter was written, while the situation in the congregation may have continued to evolve.

The Corinthian correspondence – 1 Corinthians and the various letters that make up 2 Corinthians[26] – reveals an evolving situation in the congregation Paul struggled to address both in person and through letters. There was an exchange of letters between Paul and the Corinthians. In part of 1 Corinthians Paul explicitly addresses a letter he had received from members of what appears to be a faction within the congregation, providing rebuttals to points questioning some of Paul's teachings and the limits of his authority (1 Corinthians 7.1–40). He quotes sections of the letter he had received and modifies them, essentially saying, "yes, but ..." (cf. 1 Corinthians 7.1b–3, 8.1–3; cp. 6.12–14). The letter begins with Paul reacting to what he has learned from "Chloe's people", a delegation sent by the woman who was presumably patroness of the congregation, and again quotes and responds to slogans reflecting the varying opinions of different groups among the members of the Corinthian congregation (1 Corinthians 1.10–13).

2 Corinthians demonstrates the same sort of interactions between Paul and his congregations even more vividly. In two different letters (2 Corinthians 2.14–6.13, 7.2–16 and 2 Corinthians 10.1–13.13), Paul attempts to explain his previous behaviour and reassert his authority over the congregation, despite open rebellion against him among some of its members abetted by those he calls "superlative apostles" (2 Corinthians 11.5). These letters apparently succeed in winning over the congregation, and Paul writes again to celebrate his reconciliation with the congregation (2 Corinthians 1.1–2.13, 7.5–16). Later he writes two letters concerning a collection of funds for the congregations in Judea, one addressed specifically to the Corinthian congregation (2 Corinthians 8) and the other addressed to congregations throughout the region of Achaia (2 Corinthians 9).

In short, the Corinthian correspondence reflects an extended continuing conversation between Paul and the members of the congregation in Corinth about various aspects of correct belief and practice among followers of Jesus. It represents not only Paul's own thoughts, but his reactions to written and spoken communication from members of the congregation, the related reports of emissaries,

---

26 Theories that 2 Corinthians is made up of two or more letters were prompted by the abrupt transitions and apparent dislocations within the letter in its canonical form. The clearest division is between 2 Corinthians 1–9 and 10–13, but there are also dislocations between 2 Corinthians 1.1–2.13 and 7.5–16; and 2.14–6.13 and 7.2–16. Further, 2 Corinthians 6.14–7.1 appears to be a non-Pauline interpolation, and 2 Corinthians 8 and 9 each present essentially the same material from different perspectives for what appear to be two different audiences. For a history and critical appraisal of the various partition theories see Betz 1985, 3–36.

reinterpretation of the message of earlier letters and a sustained meditation in 2 Corinthians 10–13 on the ironic nature of an apostle's calling.[27]

Galatians addresses Jesus followers within a region rather than a congregation within a city, as indicated by the address, "To the congregations (ταῖς ἐκκλησίαις) of Galatia" (1.2b, my translation). This suggests, first, congregations within a given region shared theological ideas and personal and ritual practices to a greater or lesser extent, and so could be addressed as a group by a commonly-recognised authority.[28] Second, there appears to have been intercommunication between such congregations, so that Paul could send a letter to a single destination and assume all those in the congregations addressed would hear it. Despite the fact that several congregations are addressed, Paul responds to a single distressing situation among them with a single letter directed to all the Jesus congregations in Galatia, with specific application to each of them.

The letter to Rome – essentially a letter of introduction for Paul and the basics of his theological thinking – demonstrates that the Apostle's reputation (and so also his influence) extended beyond the congregations he had founded, all the way to the imperial capital. As with the letter to the Galatians, the address of the letter to the Romans ("to all those in Rome who are God's beloved, called to be holy people [ἁγίοις]", Romans 1.7, my translation) does not focus on a single congregation. This suggests the letter was written with a number of congregations in mind, since the capital was apparently home to many communities of Jesus' followers, primarily composed of Gentile believers.

This evidence from Romans, Galatians and the Corinthian correspondence indicates Paul's letters were not necessarily performed only once for a single audience. Rather they might be performed for several audiences in separate congregations in a single city or region, or re-performed for a single addressed congregation as the need arose. After the performance of a letter for its intended audience in Rome or Corinth or Galatia or Philippi or Thessalonica, a letter might be circulated and performed later among other congregations Paul had founded, or among other congregations that recognised Paul's authority as an apostle. Although Paul's original intention in writing a letter may no longer have been operative in its re-performance for other audiences, its content was passed on as of more general interest and applicability for members of all Jesus congregations,

---

27 See Holland 2000, 126–149, esp. 137–149.
28 Of course, the primary point in contention among the congregations in Galatia is whether or not they *will* recognise Paul's authority (cf. Galatians 1.6–2.14) and the authority of his version of the gospel message (cf. Galatians 2.15–3.29). For the situation in Galatia see the discussion in Betz 1979, 1–9.

even as the original context that prompted Paul's words was lost.[29] The ultimate outcome of the circulation of Paul's letters, of course, was the inclusion of at least some of them in the canon of the New Testament.

5 Paul's continued influence and authority after his death

We find further clear evidence that Paul's letters were re-performed for new audiences beyond their original addressees in both the existence and the content of the so-called deutero-Pauline letters 2 Thessalonians, Colossians and Ephesians.[30] All three of the deutero-Pauline letters refer to the idea of Paul's letters being circulated beyond, and read to audiences other than, the congregations Paul originally addressed. The author of 2 Thessalonians, for example, warns his audience "not to be quickly shaken in mind or alarmed, either by spirit or by word or *by letter, as though from us*, to the effect that the day of the Lord is already here" (2 Thessalonians 2.2; emphasis added). The letter also includes a note of authentication, "I, Paul, write this greeting with my own hand. This is the mark in every letter of mine; it is the way I write" (2 Thessalonians 3.17).[31] 2 Thessalonians assumes or asserts that forgeries of Paul's letters are being circulated among Jesus congregations, forgeries that are promulgating misunderstandings (at best) and corruptions (at worst) of Paul's ideas. But this means Paul's genuine letters were themselves already being circulated among his and other congregations by the time 2 Thessalonians was written, since any forgeries would be written to be accepted as one of Paul's own letters in circulation. The "authenticating" signature, ironically enough, seems to suggest none of the authentic letters of Paul known

---

29 The author of 2 Peter, usually believed to be the latest of the writings preserved in the New Testament and dating to the mid-2nd century AD, wrote of Paul's letters, "there are some things in them hard to understand, which the ignorant and unstable twist to their own destruction, as they do the other scriptures" (2 Peter 3.16b). He confirms both that Paul's writings were authoritative for his community and on a par with the Septuagint, and that their original meaning and intentions were obscure some eighty years after their composition.
30 See note 19, above.
31 The fact that Paul did *not* write a greeting in his own hand "in every letter of mine", and that when Paul does write in his own hand it is to affirm what is being said (cf. Galatians 6.11–16, Philemon 19a), are among the reasons many scholars designate 2 Thessalonians as deutero-Pauline. See Holland 1988, 57–58, 89–90; compare the "handwritten" greeting in Colossians 4.18a, which serves no such affirming purpose.

to the author were autographs, to the extent that term has any meaning in the 1st century. Rather, Paul's letters were already being copied and circulated before 2 Thessalonians was written.

Colossians presents a somewhat different situation. Unlike 2 Thessalonians, Colossians is "addressed" to a congregation Paul himself did not establish and where he was not known (Colossians 1.7–8). Unlike the situation that led to the composition of Romans, "Paul" does not express any intention to visit Colossae, although he sends an emissary with the letter (Colossians 4.7–9). The letter is general in its content, offering exhortation and instruction without any specific reference to the congregation's situation. The letter is in fact so general that the author asserts its contents will apply equally well to another congregation: "and when this letter has been read to you, have it read also in the congregation of the Laodiceans; and see that you also hear read the letter from Laodicea" (Colossians 4.16; my translation). It is hard to imagine why such a general letter would need to be seconded by another letter with (presumably) equally general content – since it is apparently just as applicable to the Colossians as to the Laodiceans – directed to another (non-Pauline) congregation. Colossians is predicated on the idea not only that Paul wrote "circular" letters of general content relevant to all Pauline congregations, but that he wrote such letters to congregations he had not founded.

Ephesians is addressed to a congregation Paul visited, but did not establish. According to the account in Acts of the Apostles 19.1–7, there were already followers of Jesus in the city when Paul arrived, although their beliefs and practices were not entirely in line with Paul's own. In the letter, the author is apparently not known directly by his audience, nor they to him; he writes, "I have heard of your faith in the Lord Jesus and your love toward all the saints" (1.15; cp. Colossians 1.4). Moreover, the content of Ephesians is general; in fact, it closely resembles Colossians. Many early manuscripts of Ephesians lack the reference to Ephesus in Ephesians 1.1 (reading "to the holy people who are also faithful in Christ Jesus", τοῖς ἁγίοις καὶ πιστοῖς ἐν Χριστῷ Ἰησοῦ) and so do not refer to a specific congregation. The shorter address, as well as the letter's general exhortation and instruction – so similar to that found in Colossians – indicates Ephesians too is a deutero-Pauline work presented and intended as a circular letter.

In short, all three deutero-Pauline letters are based on an underlying fiction that each is a letter originally written by Paul to a specific congregation now "re-performed" for new audiences – audiences that are not in Thessalonica, Colossae or Ephesus. In this sense, each letter also builds on and advances the assumption that anything the apostle wrote for any audience in any situation at any time is relevant and important for all Jesus communities in all places, all situations and all times. This is the primary reason the authors write in Paul's name, both to claim his authority and influence and to reinforce them for the Jesus followers of their own generation. Once Paul is increasingly considered an apostle for all Jesus congregations, those who consider themselves Paul's theological heirs work to ensure his legacy will be understood in the "proper" way.

Each of the deutero-Pauline letters builds on Paul's use of specific terminology and rhetorical structure – sometimes by outright imitation of another letter, as in 2 Thessalonians – to expand and develop Paul's ideas to address the needs of a new, later audience and the goals of its actual author. Ephesians includes many parallels to Paul's genuine letters, acting as something of a synthesis of Paul's thought re-presented for a later generation, although the letter also exhibits a style and vocabulary at odds with Paul's own.[32] Ephesians and Colossians bear a marked similarity to each other in style and content, suggesting literary dependence of one on the other.[33] 2 Thessalonians, on the other hand, slavishly follows the model of 1 Thessalonians, except notably when presenting its unique apocalyptic scenario.[34]

The performance and re-performance of the deutero-Pauline letters served in part to promulgate further Paul's terminology, rhetorical strategies and theological ideas among the Jesus congregations of the eastern Mediterranean. But the apostle's terminology, strategies and ideas were now presented within the context of their interpretation and development by each of the deutero-Pauline authors. Both Colossians and Ephesians, for example, include guidelines for proper behaviour based on a person's role within a household. These guidelines go beyond Paul's express desire that his congregations should "aspire to live quietly" (1 Thessalonians 4.11a; cp. 5.13b) and submit to the authority of earthly rulers (Romans 13.1–7), instructing members of the household to "be subject to one another out of reverence for Christ" (Ephesians 5.21). But this encouragement towards obedience is worked out entirely in terms of early imperial cultural ideas of power and submission. Wives are to be subject to husbands (Ephesians 5.22–24, Colossians 3.18), while husbands are told only to love their wives (Ephesians

---

[32] For an example of vocabulary, the author of Ephesians uses ἐπουράνιοι as a noun ("the heavenlies") in 1.3, 2.6, 3.10, 6.12; in Paul's undisputed letters it appears only as an adjective, 1 Corinthians 15.40, 48, 49; Philippians 2.10. In regard to style, the opening thanksgiving, Ephesians 1.3–14, is in Greek a single sentence, one far longer than anything found in Paul's undisputed letters. An English translation retaining this structure may be found in the Revised Version (1903).
[33] Apart from the list of household rules in each letter in Ephesians 5.21–6.9, Colossians 3.18–4.1 (see below), compare the commendation of Tychicus in Ephesians 6.21–22, Colossians 4.7-9.
[34] The parallels between 1 and 2 Thessalonians are discussed at length in Holland 1988, 59–90.

3.25–33, Colossians 3.19); children are to obey their parents (Ephesians 6.1–3, Colossians 3.20), while fathers are told only not to provoke their children (Ephesians 6.4, Colossians 3.21); and the enslaved are told to be obedient and diligent, "as to the Lord" (Ephesians 6.5–8, Colossians 3.22–25) while masters are to treat their enslaved servants well because they also have a Master in heaven "and there is no partiality" (Ephesians 6.9c, Colossians 3.25–4.1). In short, Ephesians and Colossians suggest that a faithful life means complete acceptance of the social and cultural structures of the early Roman Empire, and this call for conformity to the *status quo* colours their re-presentation and promulgation of Paul's own standards for behaviour within a Jesus congregation.

Similarly, the author of 2 Thessalonians presents an elaborate apocalyptic scenario that stands in tension with Paul's portrayal of his own expectations for the future of the faithful in 1 Thessalonians.[35] At the same time, 2 Thessalonians claims to offer this scenario as a corrective to false apocalyptic narratives including, possibly, Paul's own narrative in 1 Thessalonians. At the very least, 2 Thessalonians is intended to be the lens through which 1 Thessalonians is understood by a new generation of audiences.

The deutero-Paulines show a consistent tendency to universalise ideas that Paul first expresses in letters addressing specific situations in specific congregations, in the process making Paul an authoritative apostle for all Jesus congregations. Ephesians 2.11–16 notably promotes the idea of a "new humanity" that is neither Jew nor Gentile: "he has abolished the law with its commandments and ordinances, that he might create in himself one new humanity in place of the two, thus making peace, and might reconcile both groups to God in one body through the cross, thus putting to death that hostility through it" (Ephesians 2.15–16). This is a concept that would have been both alien and illogical to a Jew like Paul, but one that would resonate with an increasingly Gentile Jesus movement.[36] The idea of a new humanity is also a "fleshly" literalisation of Paul's statement of spiritual unity across cultural distinctions "in Christ Jesus" in Galatians 3.28, although the

---

35 For an extended examination of the apocalyptic scenario of 2 Thessalonians in contrast to Paul's expectations for the future in 1 Thessalonians and other letters see Holland 1988, 91–127.
36 For Jews in the 1st century, anyone who was not a Jew was a Gentile, and (although it was never expressed in these terms), a non-Gentile was a Jew. One could not be both [not a Jew] and *not* [not a Jew]. Gentile believers in the late 1st century, on the other hand, were already thinking of themselves as inheritors of the promises made to Israel, not alongside the Jews, as in Romans 11, but in place of the Jews, since the vast majority of Jews did not accept Jesus as messiah. One example of this way of thinking may be found in the Letter of Barnabas, 1–17, where the author asserts the writings of the Hebrew Bible may be understood properly only by followers of Jesus.

distinction between male and female clearly remained in place (cf. Colossians 3.11).

Colossians sometimes, like Ephesians, also extends Paul's ideas by proposing some sort of reality in place of what Paul offers as a metaphor. For example, as we have seen, Paul uses the extended metaphor of the human body to argue that all members of a congregation have an important part to play in the proper functioning of the whole community (1 Corinthians 12.12–27). The author of Colossians, on the other hand, makes Paul's metaphor into a cosmic reality, based on the idea of Jesus as "the image of the invisible God, the firstborn of all creation; ... He himself is before all things, and in him all things hold together. He is the head of the body, the church; he is the beginning, the firstborn from the dead... in him all the fullness of God was pleased to dwell" (Colossians 1.15–19). In Colossians 1.24b, "Paul" writes, "I am completing what is lacking in Christ's afflictions for the sake of his body, that is, the church" (ἡ ἐκκλησία, here referring to the entire membership of the Jesus movement, not a single congregation, as Paul uses the term). Colossians 2.18–19 exhorts its audience to beware of false forms of worship "and not holding fast to the head, from whom the whole body, nourished and held together by its ligaments and sinews, grows with a growth that comes from God" (Colossians 2.19). The metaphorical "body" of Paul's letters has been made literal, a cosmic reality.

The result of the performance and re-performance of deutero-Pauline letters is a wide-spread acceptance of a particular understanding of the content of Paul's letters, an understanding arising in the generation after the apostle's death. The deutero-Pauline letters promote a normative understanding of the language, metaphors and theological arguments in Paul's own letters, an understanding they believed was intended not just for Pauline congregations, but for all Jesus congregations that recognised Paul's authority. The deutero-Pauline letters' intended audience was the majority of Gentile congregations that wished to identify themselves as the proper inheritors of the promises to Israel (cf. Acts 7) without the obligation to follow the covenantal stipulations – notably the practice of circumcision – that were the hallmarks of Jewish covenantal identity.

6 Conclusion

Re-performance of Paul's letters and the creation of deutero-Pauline letters that imitate his words and views while also adapting them to new situations, ultimately led to Paul's ideas becoming "canonical", a normative standard for the entire Jesus movement. But Paul's influence in the 2nd century Jesus movement

– the emerging Christian church – is a product not so much of the original performance of Paul's letters by lectors in the specific congregation each letter addresses, but of the letters' later repeated re-performance by a variety of readers before innumerable congregations over a period of decades. But Paul's influence was also spread and enhanced by later letters attributed to him that suited the particular needs of an increasingly Gentile Jesus movement concerned with the cosmic identity of Jesus as Christ, his relationship with the Father, and his role in a future apocalypse, as well as gaining the approval of their neighbours by conforming to the expected societal norms of the early Roman Empire.[37] The rhetorical matrix of Paul's letters in time became the dominant rhetorical matrix of the early Christian movement, even as later Christians adapted and modified Paul's theological ideas to suit their own circumstances and imperatives. Those letters attributed to Paul but written by his later followers determined how Paul's own letters would be understood and, in time, subsumed into the various theologies arising in the early centuries of the Christian movement.

Despite modern biblical scholarship's concern with the original situations that gave rise to Paul's letters and the specific rhetorical and theological strategies he used to promote his particular understanding of what it meant to be a follower of Jesus living in community with others, Paul's influence in the Jesus movement was not primarily the product of his own missionary work or the initial performance of the letters that were a part of it. Rather, it was through re-performance of Paul's letters before audiences beyond their original recipients and of other, later letters attributed to him that Paul's understanding of the Jesus faith in time became normative for all believers. Paul's incalculable influence on the Jesus movement and later Christianity is therefore best understood as the result of repeated *re*-performance of his letters and the concurrent re-performance of letters attributed to him by later writers.

---

[37] This process was continued by the author(s) of the Pastoral letters (1 and 2 Timothy, Titus), presented as "private" letters from "Paul" supposedly addressed to his two associates. These letters focus on how followers of Jesus are to live faithful lives within an evolving institutional church with distinct offices (cf. 1 Timothy 3), where women and enslaved persons know their proper place (cf. 1 Timothy 2.8–15, 5.3–16, Titus 2.3–5; 1 Timothy 6.1–2, Titus 2.9–10).

Bibliography

Betz, H.D. (1979), *Galatians: A Commentary on Paul's Letter to the Churches in Galatia,* Philadelphia.

Betz, H.D. (1985), *2 Corinthians 8 and 9: A Commentary on Two Administrative Letters of the Apostle Paul,* Philadelphia.

Brauch, M.T. (1977), 'Perspectives on "God's Righteousness" in Recent German Discussion', in: E.P. Sanders (ed.), *Paul and Palestinian Judaism: A Comparison of Patterns of Religion,* London/New York, 523–542.

Burnyeat, M.F. (1997), 'Techniques of Reading in Classical Antiquity', in: *Classical Quarterly* 47, 56–73.

Carlson, M. (2002), *The Haunted Stage,* Ann Arbor.

Classen, C.J. (2016), 'Can the Theory of Rhetoric Help Us to Understand the New Testament, and in Particular the Letters of Paul?', in: S.E. Porter/B.R. Dyer (eds.), *Paul and Ancient Rhetoric: Theory and Practice in the Hellenistic Context,* New York, 13–39.

Collins, R.F. (1988), *Letters That Paul Did Not Write: The Epistle to the Hebrews and The Pauline Pseudepigrapha,* Wilmington.

Forbes, C. (2016), 'Paul and Rhetorical Composition', in: J.P. Sampley (ed.), *Paul in the Greco-Roman World,* Volume I, London, 196–229.

Holland, G.S. (1988), *The Tradition that You Received from Us: 2 Thessalonians in the Pauline Tradition,* Tübingen.

Holland, G.S. (2000), *Divine Irony,* Selinsgrove.

Holland, G.S. (2016a), '"Delivery, Delivery, Delivery": Accounting for Performance in the Rhetoric of Paul's Letters', in: S.E. Porter/B.R. Dyer (eds.), *Paul and Ancient Rhetoric: Theory and Practice in the Hellenistic Context,* New York, 119–140.

Holland, G.S. (2016b), 'Paul and Performance', in: J.P. Sampley (ed.), *Paul in the Greco-Roman World,* Volume II, London, 230–269.

Hughes, F.W. (2016), 'Paul and Traditions of Greco-Roman Rhetoric', in: S.E. Porter/B.R. Dyer (eds.), *Paul and Ancient Rhetoric: Theory and Practice in the Hellenistic Context,* New York, 86–95.

Johnson, W.A./Parker, H.N. (eds.) (2009), *Ancient Literacies: The Culture of Reading in Greece and Rome,* New York.

Kremmydas, C. (2016), 'Hellenistic Rhetorical Education and Paul's Letters', in: S.E. Porter/B.R. Dyer (eds.), *Paul and Ancient Rhetoric: Theory and Practice in the Hellenistic Context,* New York, 68–85.

Krodel, G. (ed.) (1993), *The Deutero-Pauline Letters: Ephesians, Colossians, 2 Thessalonians, 1-2 Timothy, Titus,* Minneapolis.

Lampe, P. (2010), 'Rhetorical Analysis of Pauline Texts – Quo Vadit? Methodological Reflections', in: J.P. Sampley/P. Lampe (eds.), *Paul and Rhetoric,* London/New York, 3–21.

Martin, D. (1990), *Slavery as Salvation: The Metaphor of Slavery in Pauline Christianity,* New Haven.

Pitts, A.W. (2016), 'Paul in Tarsus: Historical Factors in Assessing Paul's Early Education', in: S.E. Porter/B.R. Dyer (eds.), *Paul and Ancient Rhetoric: Theory and Practice in the Hellenistic Context,* New York, 43–67.

Poirier, J.C. (2016), 'Paul and Literacy', in: J.P. Sampley (ed.), *Paul in the Greco-Roman World,* London, 68–88.

Porter, S.E. (2016), 'Ancient Literate Culture and Popular Rhetorical Knowledge: Implications for Studying Pauline Rhetoric', in: S.E. Porter/B.R. Dyer (eds.), *Paul and Ancient Rhetoric: Theory and Practice in the Hellenistic Context*, New York, 96–115.

Sanders. E.P. (1977), *Paul and Palestinian Judaism: A Comparison of Patterns of Religion*, London.

Part IV: **The Rulers' Religion**

Vasileios Liotsakis
Beloved of the Gods, Son of the Gods, Rival of the Gods: Alexander and the Rhetoric of Religion in Plutarch, Arrian and Curtius Rufus

Abstract: This chapter examines the ways in which three authors of Alexander the Great (Plutarch, Arrian and Curtius Rufus) incorporate in their accounts the following aspects of Alexander's rhetoric of religion: (a) his claims that he was descended from Ammon Zeus; (b) stories and anecdotes which promoted the idea that the king enjoyed divine favour; and (c) Alexander's rivalry with gods and demi-gods, such as Dionysus and Heracles. The present comparative analysis focuses on the narrative means by which each of these writers leads the reader to specific verdicts about the aforementioned three aspects of Alexander's relationship with religion, and endeavours to shed light on the levels on which each author differentiated himself from the others in this respect.

1 Introduction

One of the most popular subjects in modern scholarship on Alexander III of Macedon is how he used religious propaganda as a means of imposing specific communicative and political principles in his relationship both with the Greeks and the Anatolians. Alexander, indeed, playing in many respects with the religious beliefs of the masses, occasionally offered rhetoric of religion a cardinal place in his official agenda of self-fashioning. In many of his enterprises – be it a siege of a city, a battle or an expedition to an unexplored area – he endeavoured to boost the morale of his army and elicit their hopes for a successful outcome by invoking the divine favour he claimed he enjoyed. Furthermore, already before conquering Egypt but especially after his visit to the oracle of Ammon in the oasis of Siwah, he promoted the idea that he was the son of Ammon Zeus, an idea which may occasionally have proved to be compatible with the philosophy of the Egyptian or even the Persian royal protocol, but which was negatively received by the Macedonians and the rest of the Greeks.¹ What is more, he contented himself neither with the image of the "beloved of the gods" nor with that of the "son of Zeus"; for he also wished to fashion himself as a "competitor of the gods", superior to them in terms of exploits, a worthy pretender to the glory of mythical heroes, semi-gods and deities, such as Achilles, Castor and Pollux, Heracles and Dionysus.² In his effort to prove that he possessed each of these qualities, Alexander was assisted by a miscellaneous group of people, such as soothsayers, priests and writers who followed him in Asia and glorified his image with their flattering accounts or even gave him a place among the gods.³

Alexander's relationship with religion had already attracted much attention among those we today describe as his first historians, either those who followed him in Asia or those who wrote their histories in the first decades after his death.⁴ Although these first accounts are today lost, due to the vast number of citations of them by later authors we are in a position to know that these first historians shaped and handed down to the next generations of writers the main agenda of *topoi* in the ancient literary tradition of Alexander.⁵ However, as is the case with sundry other motifs of this kind, we can only detect the presence of Alexander's abuse of religion in these first accounts, but not the way this topic was incorporated into their overall narrative arrangement. Still, even this fragmentary

---

1 The literature on these issues is vast. See, selectively, the precious discussions of Hogarth 1887; Balsdon 1950; Edmunds 1971; Dreyer 2009; most recently Antela-Bernárdez 2016 and 235 n. 1 with further bibliography.
2 On Alexander and Achilles see Liotsakis 2019, 11-13 and 12 nn. 32-35 with sources and bibliography, 78-79, 97 n. 46, 163-168, 166 n. 13, 167 n. 17, 173-179, 173 n. 31, 184-185, 184 n. 62, 197-198, 200-204, 214-225, 229. On Alexander's rivalry with Heracles see Hogarth 1887, 320, 326; *HCA* II, 180ff; Balsdon 1950, 377; Edmunds 1971, 372 ff.; Worthington 2014, 241-243; Liotsakis 2019, 18-19, 28, 30-32, 38, 40-43, 45-47, 114-118, 134, 170, 173, 223 n. 132, 234. For Alexander's use of Dionysus as a policy of controlling his men and the Anatolians see Mederer 1936, 97-107; Goukowsky 1978; Seibert 1985, 204-206; Bosworth 1996a, 121-126 and 1996b; Dreyer 2009, 219-221; Worthington 2014, 238-239.
3 Callisthenes' (*FGrH* 124) account was oriented towards a laudatory promotion of Alexander's image as a ruler who enjoyed the favour of the gods (see Pearson's (1960) and Pédech's (1984) respective sections on Callisthenes and Prandi 1985 *passim*).
4 *FGrH* 124 F14a-b, F31 and 36; *FGrH* 125 F8; *FGrH* 126 F5; *FGrH* 129 F1; *FGrH* 134 F39; *FGrH* 136 F4; *FGrH* 137 F9 and F17; *FGrH* 138 F8-9 and F16; *FGrH* 139 F7a-b, F13-15, F30, F47, F49b, F54-56, F58; *FGrH* 142 F3.
5 The fragments of the Alexander historians were first collected by Jacoby. See also Auberger's (2001) collection and Gilhaus' (2017) excellent edition with updated bibliography and discussion. See also the seminal studies of Pearson 1960, Pédech 1984, Prandi (1985 on Callisthenes and 1996 on Cleitarchus), and Strasburger 1934 and Kornemann 1935 on Ptolemy.

knowledge is profitable enough for us because to know that this theme was from the outset included in the primordial literary tradition of Alexander helps us apprehend in a clearer way the procedures of reception and transformation of this *topos* by later writers, whose works have been fully preserved, such as Plutarch, Arrian and Curtius Rufus.

In contrast to Diodorus' general indifference in the matter,[6] Plutarch, Arrian and Curtius demonstrate a keen interest in Alexander's rhetoric of religion and each of them adopts a different approach of it. Still, there is no comparative study of the ways they differentiate themselves from each other.[7] In this chapter I focus on the narrative techniques through which these three writers unearth the interconnections between rhetoric and religion in Alexander's self-fashioning mainly, but not exclusively, on three different levels: (a) divine favour; (b) divine origins; and (c) the king's competitiveness towards Heracles and Dionysus. Although, in the process of my analysis, I discuss many points of coincidence between the three authors, my main goal is to tip the scale towards the ways they differentiated themselves in terms of both narrative style as well as their attitude towards each of the aforementioned levels of Alexander's religious propaganda.

Allow me, at this point, to clarify the notion of *rhetoric of religion*, and the similar of *religious rhetoric*, which are both used throughout this chapter. These are two overarching terms that refer to the ways in which literary sources, especially those of the three authors that are under investigation in this chapter, i.e. Plutarch, Arrian and Curtius Rufus, offer stories in which Alexander is presented

---

[6] The cases in which Diodorus allows some space for the element of Alexander's religious' propaganda to enter his narrative are the following: At the proem of Book 17, where he admits that Alexander's glory is equal to that of heroes and semi-gods (17.1.4); at Troy Alexander claims that he conquered Asia with the aid of the gods (17.17.2); the king believes that the gods offered him the opportunity to defeat Darius at Issus (17.33.1); Diodorus explains that the Egyptians welcomed Alexander because the Persians had not respected Egyptian religion (17.49.2); he also mentions the assistance Alexander was believed to have been offered by the gods in his crossing of the desert towards the oasis of Siwah (17.49.2–6), as well as the oracles offered to the king that he was the son of Zeus (17.51.1–4), but, contrary to what Plutarch, Arrian and Curtius do (see below), he never expresses his opinion on whether these events did actually indicate that Alexander was helped by the gods or that he descended from Zeus; 17.85.1–2 on Aornus and Heracles, but once again in an indifferent way.

[7] To my knowledge, the sole study of this kind is McKechnie's (2009) comparison of Diodorus, Plutarch and Arrian in terms of the way each of them incorporates the omens of Alexander's death in their accounts; still, this study does not explore the presence of Alexander's religious rhetoric in the aforementioned accounts but only the tradition on the signs which were taken to have foreshadowed his death.

as using religion as a means of self-fashioning, persuasion or mass manipulation – thus, political/military propaganda. Rhetoric is seen, therefore, as an all-encompassing term that refers to the use of codified language that conveys ideas, beliefs and attitudes of people towards religion, and points to its use as a means of winning over, or manipulating, the audience. This rhetoric works at two levels: first, I use these terms in order to describe Alexander's use of religion as an attempt to convince his men or the Anatolians that he enjoys the favour of the gods, descends from them or surpasses them in terms of military exploits. All three authors under examination – Plutarch, Arrian and Curtius – offer stories in which Alexander is presented as using religion as a means of persuasion and self-fashioning. In some cases, they mention those incidents in an indifferent or even a pejorative fashion. However, they also at times use these stories as a means to delineate a favourable picture of Alexander, and this is the second level of religious rhetoric to which I refer in this chapter: namely the narrative techniques and the literary schemes through which the narrators themselves use religion in order to underline to their readers Alexander's special relationship with the divine.

2 Plutarch

Plutarch is quite indifferent regarding Alexander's competitiveness towards Heracles and Dionysus.[8] Instead, he repeatedly takes advantage of Alexander's claims that he was the son of Zeus and that he enjoyed the favour of the gods. To begin with the issue of Alexander's descent from Zeus, the biographer employs an abundance of aspects of Alexander's propaganda about his alleged divine origins as a means by which to stimulate readerly interest on the matter. The main technique through which Plutarch endeavours to elicit our curiosity lies in that he retains our uncertainty with regard to the question of whether or not Alexander descended from Ammon Zeus. In what follows, we analyse the passages in

---

[8] In his *Alexander* he never discusses or even mentions Alexander's rivalry with Heracles and Dionysus; neither does he record the rumours on their alleged presence in the areas visited by the Macedonians. Heracles is merely mentioned as Alexander's ancestor from his father's side (*Alex.* 2.1) and as the king's helper in the Tyrian episode (*Alex.* 24.5). Dionysus is only mentioned twice in a ritualistic context (*Alex.* 2.7 and 67.6) and as the god whose nemesis caused Alexander's murdering Clitus and the Macedonians' unwillingness to follow their king beyond the Hyphases (*Alex.* 13.4–5).

which the biographer elaborates on this issue. These passages are (a) the introductory chapters of the *Life*, which are dedicated to the circumstances under which Alexander was conceived (*Alex.* 2–3.4); and (b) the account on Alexander's visit to the oracle of Ammon at the oasis of Siwah (*Alex.* 26.10–27).

To begin with the narrative of Alexander's conception, it is worth noting that the opening chapters of Plutarch's *Lives* have a programmatic role, as they offer – if not impose – those filters through which the author invites his readership to perceive and assess the life of the individual in question.[9] In a similar vein, in *Alexander*, it should be taken as no coincidence that Plutarch chooses to touch upon the issue of Alexander's descent from Zeus in the very introduction of the work and not only later on, i.e. at the chapters on the king's visit to the god's oracle in Egypt. The biographer thereby turns this issue into one from among the focal points of speculation for the reader. Now, the fact that the account of Alexander's conception is rich, as we will see, in predictions of supernatural elements, such as oracles, omens and dreams, comes as no surprise for us, given that Plutarch is very keen on using such elements in his *Lives* as overtures to pivotal events, including one's birth.[10]

So, Plutarch dedicates the first chapters of his *Life* to narrate those stories of the literary tradition of Alexander which implied that the king was a son of Ammon. According to Plutarch, a night before her wedding to Philip, Olympias felt that a thunderbolt struck her belly and that the fire which emerged from the collision spread from her body towards all directions and was extinguished (*Alex.* 2.3). Far from offering a decisive answer with regard to Alexander's origins, this short story raises more questions for the reader, as Plutarch does not relate what truly happened but only Olympias' impression (ἔδοξε) about what happened. What is more, he never explains to the reader whether or not he believes that what Olympias felt really took place. He merely presents this story, as well as the ensuing ones, as rumours (introducing all these stories with the phrase: λέγεται δέ), which are opposed to the safe information (*Alex.* 2.1: τῶν πάνυ πεπιστευμένων ἐστί) about the family tree of Alexander.

Equally obscure is the next anecdote. After the wedding Philip had a dream, in which he sealed his wife's belly. Aristander, the soothsayer, judged that the

---

9 Duff 2014; Chrysanthou 2017, 129–133. For bibliography on Plutarch's prologues see Chrysanthou 2017, 128 n. 2.
10 On dreams in Plutarch's *Lives* see Brenk 1975 and 1977; Pelling 2010; Fournel 2016 also elaborates on how Plutarch uses dream narratives already existing in other sources and incorporates them into the logic of his own accounts. On dreams in *Alexander* see King 2013. See, also, Bosman's (2011) analysis of the ways Plutarch structures his narrative on the basis of supernatural signs (oracles, portents, omens and dreams).

dream was a sign that Olympias was pregnant, given that, Aristander argued, nothing empty can be sealed (*Alex.* 2.4–5). Here too, the reader is left oscillating between two scenarios: the dream could either have no meaning at all or Aristander was right and the woman was indeed pregnant at the time when Philip saw the dream. In the minds of a superstitious readership of Plutarch's era, Aristander's credibility in both the *Life* and the literary tradition of Alexander could serve as a potential indication of the contingency that Olympias was carrying a baby.[11] But still, all readers cannot but wonder if the child Aristander talks about was the son of Philip or of Zeus, given that the preceding story, the one on the lightning strike, does not clarify whether or not the thunderbolt – namely, for many readers, Ammon – impregnated Olympias.[12]

Equally vague is the account of the oracle Philip was offered by Apollo. According to this story, whose content is cautiously offered not as a fact but merely as a rumour (λέγουσιν), after seeing a big snake lying next to her on their bed, Philip hesitated to sleep with his wife, either because he feared that she would exercise magic upon him or because he did not wish to defile a woman who seemed to be the lover of a god (*Alex.* 2.6). Philip's suspiciousness indicates that he either treated the snake he had seen with his wife as a manifestation of magic or as a deity in disguise. However, once again Plutarch avoids expressing his own view on the matter and thereby entraps us in the dilemma of which of these two explanations we, as readers, should take as the most possible for the king's erotic alienation from his queen. Plutarch initially conveys the impression that the snake could merely have been an accessory typical of those women who, just like Olympias, were initiated in religious rituals (*Alex.* 2.7–9). However, he eventually provides us with an alternative explanation (connecting it with the preceding one by means of the antithetical phrase οὐ μὴν ἀλλά in *Alex.* 3.1), i.e. that the snake was indeed a god.[13] For he writes that Philip sent Chaeron of Megalopolis to the oracle of Delphi to ask Apollo about the meaning of all these and the god answered that (a) Philip would lose one of his eyes, the one with which he saw his wife joining the god on their bed and (b) that he must from now on honour Ammon (*Alex.* 3.1–2). One could take the oracle of Apollo as a reliable testimony to the fact that Alexander was a son of Ammon, but Plutarch, as demonstrated

---

11 On Aristander as a respectful figure in Arrian, Plutarch, Curtius and Artemidorus see Nice 2005. On Arrian's favourable treatment of Aristander see Berve 1926 I, 90–92 and Liotsakis 2019, 31–32 and 62–63.
12 Cf. Hamilton 2002, 4.
13 Cf. Lucian *Alex.* 7 and Justin 11.11.3–6, who connect this snake with Alexander's divine descent. For these as well as other sources on the matter see Hamilton 2002, 4–5.

above, has from the very outset of the anecdote defused the strength of the story by presenting it as a mere rumour (*Alex.* 3.1: λέγουσι). However, once again he neither confirms nor belies this rumour.

This is also the case with the very last information we are offered about Alexander's descent. According to Eratosthenes, Olympias, when she said goodbye to her son, who was marching to Asia, revealed only to him some secret details about his conception and advised him to think of himself in a manner worthy of his origins (*Alex.* 3.3). It is worth keeping in mind the phrasing used by Plutarch for the secret information Alexander received from his mother (φράσασα μόνῳ τὸ περὶ τὴν τέκνωσιν ἀπόρρητον) because, as is demonstrated in what follows, these words have a decisive role in the way Plutarch, on a level of macrostructure, invites us to assess the possibility that Alexander was the son of Ammon Zeus. For now, it suffices to note that the impression the reader is invited to infer from these preparatory chapters about Alexander's alleged divine origins is that this issue was, both in Alexander's time as well as in the narrator's mind, an indecipherable secret between mother and son. The sole reliable witness on the matter, Olympias, refuses to reveal the truth to anyone else but Alexander.

So, in these first chapters of the *Life*, Plutarch wants to have his cake and eat it too. On the one hand, he very carefully retains the profile of an author who is not carried away by stories of supernatural content and records them in a distanced fashion by stressing the very fact that they are rumours.[14] On the other hand, however, this distancing by no means entails, on the narrator's part, a clear-cut refutation of these rumours; this is a small but important detail of the *modus narrandi* in these chapters, a detail which, at the same time, allows Plutarch to succeed in delineating an atmosphere of mystery around this issue and thus in eliciting and retaining readerly interest unabated. In this way, the religious rhetoric of a 4th-century BC Macedonian king, who struggles to elicit his people's admiration and obedience, transcends the boundaries of Hellenistic politics and enters the realm of the Second Sophistic literature, in that it is transformed by the biographer from a sophism of political potency into a narrative means of stimulation of his readership's attentiveness.

This technique is also discernible in the second passage in which Plutarch discusses the issue of Alexander's divine origins, i.e. the account of the king's visit to the oracle of Ammon Zeus in the oasis of Siwah. The chapters of the *Live*

---

14 Cf. Bosman 2011. Generally, on this interpretation of anonymous source citations in Plutarch's *Lives* see Cook 2002, 329 n. 1 with exhaustive bibliography. Cook (2002) brilliantly proves that Plutarch also used phrases such as λέγεται and λέγουσι(ν) for purposes which transcend the narrow limits of doubt and suspicion.

dedicated to the Macedonians' stay in Egypt can be organised into four parts: (a) the foundation of Alexandria (*Alex.* 26.3–11); (b) the crossing of the desert which leads to the oasis of Siwah (*Alex.* 26.11–27.4); (c) Alexander's discussion with the priest of the oracle of Ammon (*Alex.* 27.5–9); and (d) a group of anecdotes which reflect Alexander's attitude towards the issue of his divine descent (*Alex.* 27.10–28.6).

Already in the account of Alexandria's foundation, Alexander is presented as enjoying supernatural aid. Homer visits him in his dream and indicates to him where to build the city (*Alex.* 26.5), while during the designing process a favourable omen foretells the illustrious future of the city (*Alex.* 26.9–10). Taken as a whole, these two incidents serve as a prelude to the divine help the king will be offered during his journey through the desert. Plutarch follows the tradition of stories on this affair and informs us that during that march Alexander and his army were assisted by the gods in two different ways: first, an extraordinarily large amount of rain fell so that the Greeks escaped the danger of water scarcity (*Alex.* 27.1–2); second, when strong winds disturbed the sand and made the signs of the route disappear, two ravens appeared and showed the travellers the way to the oasis of Siwah (*Alex.* 27.3–4). Plutarch explicitly states that the first incident was a gift from Zeus (*Alex.* 27.2: ἐκ Διὸς ὕδωρ πολὺ καὶ διαρκεῖς ὑετοὶ γενόμενοι), thus predisposing the reader in favour of the possibility that Alexander was offered help from Ammon Zeus and, subsequently, that this god might be the king's father. Plutarch also comments that it was these two occurrences of divine help (*Alex.* 27.1: τὰ συντυχόντα ταῖς ἀπορίαις παρὰ τοῦ θεοῦ βοηθήματα) that convinced people at that time about the validity of the ensuing oracle offered by the priest to Alexander that he was indeed Ammon's offspring (*Alex.* 27.1). Once again, already before revealing to us the oracle (cf. the oracle of Apollo above), he forces us speculate about the contingency that this oracle is valid. Not only he does not deny it, but instead he uses the two παρὰ τοῦ θεοῦ βοηθήματα as proofs in Alexander's contemporaries' minds that the priest of Ammon spoke the truth. Other sources too mention the rain and the ravens, and some of them recognise that they might have been manifestations of divine favour,[15] but only Plutarch presents them as facts which could be taken – and, according to him, they *were taken* – as evidence that Ammon was Alexander's genitor.

---

15 Apart from Plutarch, only Arrian (*An.* 3.3.3–6) takes both incidents as manifestations of divine favour. Curtius (4.7.13) attributes the rain either to the gods or to fortune, while he records a flock of ravens, which seemed to act as guides, but does not clarify whether or not he treats this event as a sign from the gods (4.7.15). Diodorus (17.49.2–6), although recognising that these events were taken as help from the gods, does not express his view on the matter.

Now, as far as the oracles themselves are concerned, Plutarch offers us a detailed account of Alexander's conversation with Ammon's priest.[16] The priest claims to transfer to Alexander Ammon's greeting as if the god was Alexander's father (*Alex.* 27.5). Furthermore, as soon as Alexander asks to know whether or not he has punished all the assassins of his father (referring to Philip), the priest admonishes him for blaspheming, explaining to him that his father cannot be harmed by humans (*Alex.* 27.5–6). Only when Alexander restates his question in compliance with the priest's admonition, the latter answers that he had punished all the assassins of Philip. Last, the king asks if he will conquer the world and receives an affirmative response (*Alex.* 27.6–7).

At this point, Plutarch points out that all these are what he found written in his sources and that Alexander never confirmed this information (*Alex.* 27.8). As his mother, the sole witness of Alexander's conception, did not reveal to anyone but her son whether or not he was the son of a god, Alexander too, the sole witness of his tête-à-tête with the representative of Ammon, wishes to reveal exclusively to his mother, through a letter, the secret oracles he received from the priest. The only individuals who can have contacted Ammon Zeus keep their secret only for themselves, and the reader is forced, through this rhetorical narrative technique, to receive no answer to the question about Alexander's possible descent from Ammon. That this is the purpose of Plutarch is suggested by the characteristically deliberate cross-referencing between Olympias' revelation of the secret to Alexander (*Alex.* 3.3: φράσασα μόνῳ τὸ περὶ τὴν τέκνωσιν ἀπόρρητον) and Alexander's to Olympias (*Alex.* 27.8: πρὸς τὴν μητέρα... μαντείας ἀπορρήτους... ἅς... φράσει πρὸς μόνην ἐκείνην), which transforms Olympias' and Alexander's rhetoric towards the Macedonians into Plutarch's narrative rhetoric of manipulation of his readers.

Plutarch ends his account on this affair with the admission that Alexander did indeed use those oracles as part of his rhetorical strategy towards the Persians and, less frequently, towards the Greeks (*Alex.* 28.1). After gathering some short anecdotes reflecting Alexander's restraint in this respect (*Alex.* 28.1–6), Plutarch concludes this section of the *Live* with the words "it is clear that Alexander himself was not foolishly affected or puffed up by the belief in his divinity, but used it for the subjugation of others" (*Alex.* 28.6). For Plutarch, Alexander was never carried away by the view that he was the son of Zeus; this was for him merely a means of propaganda in his effort to control both his army and the subdued foes. However, Plutarch never clarifies whether or not Alexander believed that he was

---

[16] Cf. D.S. 17.51.1–4; 4.7.25–32; Str. 7.43 p. 813–814. See, *contra*, Arrian's (*An.* 3.4.5) indifferent short comment.

the son of a god, even if he was not affected by such a view. Only later on does Plutarch admit that Callisthenes, by preventing the imposition of Alexander's *proskynēsis* by the Greeks, protected them and the king from disgrace (*Alex.* 54.3). Such a view can hardly be expressed by someone who believes that Alexander was the son of Zeus. However, as just mentioned, this comment comes very late; up to this point, Plutarch has carefully avoided refuting the rumours about Alexander's divine origins, very possibly in order to use this theme as a means by which to irritate readerly interest. After all, as mentioned at the opening remarks of this section, he could have hardly resisted the lure of playing with the issue of Alexander's relationship with Ammon, given that the stories on this issue which he found in his sources were rich in supernatural *topoi* (oracles, dreams, omens, etc.) which he vastly used throughout his biographical oeuvre.

Apart from the issue of divine origins, Plutarch also embraces Alexander's occasional invocation of divine favour. This choice of Plutarch is exemplified in the most characteristic way by the account of Tyre (*Alex.* 24.4–25.3). The siege of the city was indeed one of the most challenging tasks for the Macedonian army during the expedition in Asia. Tyre was built at a highly inaccessible spot and the Macedonians were very sceptical as to the possibility of a successful outcome in that enterprise.[17] For this reason, Alexander, in order to give a boost to the morale of his men, employed a means of religious rhetoric different than that of his divine origins: he claimed that he and his army enjoyed divine favour in their effort to occupy the city.[18] Our sources inform us that Alexander said that Heracles, who was identified with Melqart, the local god of Tyre, visited him in his dreams (see, also, Sections 2 and 3). Aristander and other soothsayers, instigating the king's rhetoric of raising his troops' spirit, interpreted the dreams as signs sent from the god that he would help Alexander conquer the spot. What is more, as we will see in Section 3, Curtius comments that those claims were deliberate on Alexander's part. However, Plutarch introduces the account with such anecdotes on Alexander's dream of Heracles and Apollo's signs that he would help the Macedonians (*Alex.* 24.5–9), but he never explains to the reader that the dreams Alexander claimed to have seen were merely his fabrications. What is more, the biographer ends his Tyrian account by saying that the occupation of the city fulfilled one of

---

[17] Cf. Scyl. (pseudo-) 104; D.S. 17.40.5 ff.; Curt. 4.2.7–15; Str. 16.2.23, p. 756C.35–757C.33; Plin. *NH.* 5.76. On the Tyrian territory as an obstacle to the Macedonians' efforts to conquer the city see Eißfeldt *RE* VII A, 1, cols. 1877–1879; Green 1974, 248; *HCA* I, 239–240; Stewart 1987, 97–99; Romane 1987; Grainger 1991, 35–40; Hammond 1997, 92–94; *AAA* I, 445; Heckel 2008, 67–69; Worthington 2014, 174.

[18] *HCA* I, 239; O'Brien 1991, 83; Bloedow 1994, 68 n. 12; Amitay 2008.

Aristander's prophecies (*Alex*. 25.1–3). By means of this ring composition that emphasises the reference to the divine favour towards Alexander and the Macedonian troops, Plutarch invites the reader to consider the possibility that the city was taken by them with the aid of the gods.

3 Arrian

Similarly to Plutarch, in his *Anabasis of Alexander* Arrian also transforms Alexander's rhetoric of religion into a narrative means by which to disseminate to the reader favourable messages with regard to Alexander's portrait. The main purpose of Arrian in these cases is to lead the reader to the conclusion that Alexander enjoyed divine favour in varied manifestations of his expansionistic enterprise, such as the occupation or the destruction of a city and his victory in a battle. The king is also presented as fulfilling the will of the gods even in those cases in which he perpetrates moral misdeeds in his personal life, the most striking example being the murder of Clitus.

One of the passages most representative of this technique is the account on the utter destruction of Thebes (*An*. 1.7–9), in which Arrian's main goal is admittedly to mitigate the cruelty with which Alexander treated the Thebans. The Macedonian king is presented as repeatedly offering the Thebans the opportunity to surrender before he strikes the decisive blow to their homeland (*An*. 1.7.7; 1.7.9; 1.7.11). His clemency is also discernible in the information that, after defeating them, it was not him but the rest of the Greek allies who decided that the city be razed to the ground (*An*. 1.9.9–10). Modern scholarship has treated all this information as a reflection of the pro-Macedonian accounts of the first historians of Alexander, with the main suspect being Ptolemy, who, along with Aristobulus, has been one of Arrian's main sources.[19]

Arrian defends Alexander not only by delineating for him the portrait of the clement conqueror but also by almost flatly propagating the idea that Alexander, by destroying Thebes, fulfilled the gods' will, in that he contributed to the punishment of the Thebans for the crimes they had perpetrated in the past at the expense of the Greeks. For he ends his account with an extensive flashback, in which he gathers these misdeeds of the Thebans, namely their medism in the Persian Wars, their central role in the destruction of Plataea in the Peloponnesian

---

19 See, most recently, Liotsakis 2019, 24–29 with analysis and exhaustive bibliography. On Arrian's stance towards the issue of Alexander and violence see Gilhaus 2021 (forthcoming).

War and, at the end of it, their insistence upon the utter destruction of Athens (*An.* 1.9.6–8). Through an authorial comment, Arrian supports that, given the Thebans' contemptible prehistory, their misfortunes "were quite naturally set down to divine wrath" (*An.* 1.9.6). Although not admitting that this assumption of the Greeks did indeed correspond to the truth, Arrian, by means of this religious rhetoric, essentially allows the reader to feel comfortable in speculating that Alexander, in punishing the Thebans, might have served as the hand of the gods. Arrian must have found this claim in his sources, since we find similar information in Diodorus too (17.10).[20] In any case, through the aforementioned flashback and the authorial comment, one of the cruellest moments in Alexander's career at the expense of a Greek city is transformed into a manifestation of divine punishment.

Pro-Macedonian propaganda is also reproduced in the chapters on Alexander's visit to Gordium and his untying of the Gordian knot (*An.* 2.3). Arrian opens his account by relating the very myth of Gordius' waggon and his son Midas (*An.* 2.3.2–6) and completes his narration with the famous prophesy included in this myth that "anyone who untied the knot of the yoke would rule Asia" (*An.* 2.3.6). Arrian seems, at least up to a certain point, to adopt a rational attitude towards both the prophecy and Alexander's thoughts about it. The historian does not express his view about the validity of the prophecy and reveals to the reader that Alexander used his untying of the knot as a means of boosting his men's morale with regard to the question of whether or not he will succeed in conquering Persia. In particular, we read that "Alexander was unable to find how to untie the knot but unwilling to leave it tied, in case this caused a disturbance among the masses" (*An.* 2.3.7). However, at the end of his account, Arrian renders his narration, as in the Theban account, an extension of Alexander's rhetoric. For the story ends with thunder and lightning appearing in the sky, elements which Arrian readily takes as "sign from heaven" (ἐξ οὐρανοῦ ἐπεσήμαναν; cf. τοῖς φήνασι θεοῖς τά τε σημεῖα) that the prophecy was fulfilled and that Alexander will rule Asia.[21] What was succeeded in the Theban narrative by means of an authorial comment here is realised by the confirmative divine epiphany at the end of the account.

---

20 Cf. *HCA* I, 89; *AAA* I, 331–332. See, *contra*, Ael. *VH* 12.57 (with *HCA* I, 89), who records that the portents were taken as signs for the Macedonians' fall.
21 For this omen and others as well, which convey the message that the occupation of the Persian Empire was predestined by the gods see Liotsakis 2019, 44 n. 74, 93–94 and 236. On Alexander's policy and the Gordian knot see *AAA* I, 399; Munn 2008.

The conquest of the Persian Empire, apart from being presented as the fulfilment of the Gordian prophecy and thus as predestined since centuries ago, also emerges as the manifestation of the divine, cosmic principle that dynasties inevitably succeed one another. In the account on the battle of Issus, we read that Darius commits a crucial strategic mistake: although he had camped with his army at Sochi, where the battlefield was wide enough for him to take advantage of his vast forces and especially of his cavalry, he transferred his army to the narrow spot close to the city of Issus (*An.* 2.6.1–6). Arrian considers Darius' changing of the battlefield an error of decisive gravity for the eventual outcome of the battle because, in his opinion, this error deprived the Persian king of the luxury of using as many as possible branches of his troops. More importantly, Arrian supports that "some divine power led Darius (καί τι καὶ δαιμόνιον τυχὸν ἦγεν αὐτόν) into the very position where his cavalry did not much help him [...]. In fact it was destined that the Persians should forfeit the sovereignty of Asia to Macedonians, just as Medes had lost it to Persians, and Assyrians even earlier to Medes" (*An.* 2.6.6–7).

As demonstrated above, authorial comments have a central role in the religious colouring of the narration. This colouring is here reinforced by the words of the protagonists in the ensuing narrative. Arrian's comment is transformed into the king's rhetoric in his effort to raise the morale of his companions in his exhortation speech at the dawn of the battle. The king urges his men to believe that they have divine favour on their side, as it was the gods who led Darius to the mistake of changing the battlefield (*An.* 2.7.3). In the ensuing chapters, Darius sends his first letter of reconciliation to Alexander, in which he admits that his defeat at Issus reflected the gods' will (2.14.3: τὴν μὲν δὴ μάχην ὡς θεῶν τῳ ἔδοξεν οὕτω κριθῆναι). In his answer to him (*An.* 2.14.4–9), Alexander, although refuting every single point of Darius' argumentation, agrees only with Darius' view that his victory at Issus was sent by the gods (*An.* 2.14.7: ἐπεὶ δὲ μάχῃ νενίκηκα... νῦν δὲ σὲ... καὶ τὴν χώραν ἔχω τῶν θεῶν μοι δόντων). In neither of these two statements do we find an explicit reference to Darius' mistake. However, if we read them close to *An.* 2.6.6–7 and *An.* 2.7.3, we are led to the conclusion that the two men refer to this error. This net of cross-references is aimed to serve as a persuasive tripartite scheme, in which both narrator and his protagonists (victor and defeated) testify to the same view: Alexander was predestined by the gods to defeat the Persians at Issus and conquer their empire.

The account of Tyre (*An.* 2.15.6–24) resembles at many points that of Plutarch. Arrian too conceals Alexander's intention to use Heracles as a rhetorical tool of encouragement for his men. Furthermore, as Plutarch does, Arrian shapes his narrative in such a way that he leaves room for the thought that the semi-god indeed helped the Macedonians in their effort to occupy the city. The account begins with Alexander asking the Tyrians to allow him enter their city and offer sacrifice to Melqart, whom Alexander identifies with Heracles (*An.* 2.15.6–7 and 16.7–8). In a short digression, Arrian exhibits to the reader his knowledge about the exact identity of this local god, by explaining that this Heracles is not to be confused with the Greek Heracles but is that of the Phoenicians (*An.* 2.16.1–6). However, although this clarification instantly indicates in the reader's mind that Arrian will treat Alexander's claims about his dreams with Heracles in a more sober way than Plutarch does, he too arranges his material in a way that allows the possibility that Heracles assisted Alexander and his men. Arrian mentions that Alexander saw a dream, in which Heracles revealed to him that he would help him, an interpretation which is confirmed by Aristander (*An.* 2.18.1–2). However, in contrast to what we read in Curtius, Arrian does not present Alexander as using the dream as a means of persuasion for his disheartened soldiers but as being sincerely motivated by the dream in his decision to besiege Tyre. In this way, the dream of Heracles is artfully turned from a rhetorical tool of persuasion into an omen which the devout king believes in. The latter's expediency is thus replaced by the element of piety. Strikingly, the account ends, as that of Plutarch does, in a ring composition, as the last information we receive about this affair is that Alexander, after conquering the city, ordered that the priests and the suppliants who had sought refuge in the temple of Heracles/Melqart be spared, while he also dedicated to the god the besieging machine which struck the decisive blow to the wall of the city, as well as an epigram (*An.* 2.24.5–6).

As transpires from our analysis of the *Life of Alexander* and the *Anabasis*, both Plutarch and Arrian embraced Alexander's religious propaganda in order to convey to their readers' minds messages similar to those Alexander tried to convince his troops for: that throughout his military career he enjoyed divine favour, when he aspired to conquer a city or win a battle, or even when he envisioned that he would conquer the Persian Empire. However, differently than Plutarch, Arrian seems to know where to stop nurturing Alexander's abuse of religion. In contrast with Plutarch's *Life*, Arrian never encourages his readers to speculate that Alexander might have been the son of Zeus. For Arrian, Alexander can claim that he is the favourite of the gods, but not their son or not even someone who can be compared with them in terms of exploits. In the chapters on the king's visit to the oracle of Ammon, the narrative unfolds in a ring composition, but, conversely to the accounts of the Gordian knot and Tyre, this scheme serves diametrically opposite goals. Arrian may argue that the ravens at the desert towards the oasis of Siwah was certainly divine help (*An.* 3.3.5–6). However, both at the beginning and at the end of his account, he derides Alexander in a cold fashion for wishing to tell his men that he received from the priest of Ammon the responses he wished for. Arrian opens his account with the words "in any case he set out for Ammon with this idea, hoping to secure more exact knowledge of his affairs, or at least to say he had secured it" (*An.* 3.3.2). He similarly notes at the end of the story that "he [i.e. Alexander] received the answer his heart desired, as he said, and turned back to Egypt" (3.4.5). In this way, the historian reveals to his readers that Alexander's alleged descent from Zeus was not only a sophism of political propaganda, but also that it was promoted by the king himself.[22]

Arrian also castigates Alexander's competitive attitude towards Heracles and Dionysus. The literary tradition on the Macedonian king is full of stories in which his flatterers or he himself boasts that his achievements surpassed those of the two aforementioned deities. In the episodes of Clitus and Callisthenes, in which we read that both men were killed by Alexander because they opposed his arrogant, in their opinion, competitiveness towards Heracles and Dionysus and his wish to impose on the Greeks his *proskynēsis*, Arrian criticises both men for the insolent manner in which they expressed their indignation on the matter (*An.* 4.8.5 and 4.9.1 on Clitus; *An.* 4.10.1–2 and 4.12.6–7 on Callisthenes), but he also recognises that Alexander treated the gods in an arrogant and blasphemous way (*An.* 4.12.6).[23]

On a narrative level, this cold attitude of Arrian towards Alexander' expression of his rivalry with Dionysus and Heracles emerges in the last three books of the *Anabasis* by a gradual route, which escalates from neutrality towards irony and, eventually, towards a more intense criticism through dramatisation. This critical stance of Arrian stands in sharp contrast with his unremitting eagerness of the first books to use Alexander's rhetorical abuse of religion as part of his favourable portraiture of Alexander. However, this antithesis is due to the fact that in each part of his work Arrian was invited to handle different aspects of the Macedonian religious rhetoric. Up to the account of Tyre, Arrian was faced with Alexander's claims that he was favoured by the gods, and, as already demonstrated, has no qualms about presenting the king as such. Nevertheless, Arrian never accepts in his work Alexander's greed, which made him not be content with divine favour and wish instead to share with the gods the very essence of their nature. In Arrian's ethical world, this attitude is unacceptable.

The tripartite escalation of Arrian's criticism is realised in the episodes of Aornus (4.28.1–30.4) and Nysa (*An.* 5.1–3) as well as in the narrative about the army's

---

22 Cf. Liotsakis 2021 (forthcoming).
23 Cf. Liotsakis 2021 (forthcoming).

unwillingness to follow Alexander beyond the Hyphasis (*An*. 4.25–29).[24] To begin with the first one, Aornus was a city which, according to the natives, not even Heracles succeeded in conquering (*An*. 5.28.1). Arrian overtly doubts that Heracles ever visited the place (*An*. 4.28.2), and at the end of his account, when Alexander has already occupied the spot, comments "and Alexander was now in possession of the rock Heracles could not take" (4.30.4). Read under the prism of his preceding explicit refutation of the rumours about Heracles' presence in this area, Arrian's comment carries an inherent ironic meaning. Moreover, in contrast to what he does in the Tyrian, here he is clearly unwilling to confirm what he presents as being the king's allegations.[25]

Alexander arrives at Nysa, which was claimed by its inhabitants to have been founded by Dionysus. The god, after conquering some areas of India, decided to leave the area and built a city, which was inhabited by those from among his soldiers who were unable to serve. Alexander is told this story by the governor of the city, who uses this myth as an argument in order to convince the king to spare his homeland out of respect to Dionysus (*An*. 5.1.3–6). Arrian comments that Alexander, on his part, was happy to hear that Nysa was Dionysus' city because such rumours could help him convince his men to follow him in India by arguing that they would thereby increase their glory by conquering places where not even Dionysus had visited (*An*. 5.2.1). Furthermore, in contrast with what he does in the accounts of Thebes, the Gordian knot and Tyre, Arrian expresses here his scepticism about whether or not Dionysus ever reached so far as this place. As in the account of Heracles and Aornus, in this story too, Arrian stresses the fact that Dionysus was also used by Alexander as a means of propaganda. Most importantly, one further contrast with the Tyrian narrative lies in that nowhere in these chapters can we discern Arrian's intention to lead the reader through his narrative to the conclusion that Alexander occupied the city with the aid of a god, i.e. of Dionysus. On the contrary, the historian begins to highlight Alexander's competitive attitude towards the god, an issue already introduced in the episodes of Clitus and Callisthenes in the pivotal digression of ch. 4.8–14.

Arrian's hostility towards Alexander's abuse of Dionysus and Heracles reaches its culmination in the narrative of Hyphasis. Here we read that the Macedonians refuse to follow Alexander beyond the river (*An*. 5.25.2 and 27–29). Alexander delivers a speech, in which he struggles to persuade his men to continue the expedition (*An*. 5.25.3–26.8), and one of the lures he offers to them is the glory they will earn by visiting places which not even Heracles and Dionysus had ever

---

24 For a detailed analysis of this issue see Liotsakis 2019, 40–47 and 67–74.
25 Liotsakis 2019, 43–47.

seen. In this context, the king reminds the army of the illustrious occupations of Nysa and Aornus (*An.* 5.26.5). The dramatisation of the situation exposes the inefficiency of Alexander's rhetoric, as we watch the troops remaining untouched by their king's invocation of *fama posthuma* (*An.* 5.27.1: πολὺν μὲν χρόνον σιωπὴ ἦν οὔτε ἀντιλέγειν τολμώντων πρὸς τὸν βασιλέα ἐκ τοῦ εὐθέος οὔτε ξυγχωρεῖν ἐθελόντων, "for a long time there was silence; no one either dared to oppose the king on the spur of the moment, or was yet willing to agree"). The Macedonians adopt an equally disparaging attitude towards Alexander's claims that he is the son of Ammon, when, in the mutiny of Opis, they decide to abandon him by mockingly saying to him that he can now fight the world with the aid of Ammon (*An.* 7.8.3).

4 Curtius Rufus

An edifying way for someone to introduce the comparison of Curtius Rufus with the rest of our sources in terms of how he incorporates elements of religious rhetoric in his account is to proceed with the following general observation which pertains to his entire work: no other writer on Alexander is more interested than Curtius in the psychology of the masses, both of the Greeks as well as of the subdued nations, and no other writer on Alexander penetrates more than Curtius does into the degree to which and the ways in which the mentality and behaviour of the masses affected the historical development during the Macedonian expedition in Asia. Although this distinctive feature of Curtius' account has repeatedly been noticed by modern scholarship,[26] little has been written on how this aspect of Curtius' historical perspective differentiates him from other sources in the way he invites the reader to grasp the effects of Alexander's religious propaganda upon his relationship both with his troops and the Anatolians. We may beforehand answer this question by offering the following three observations, which are the main points of argument in this last section: (a) some celebrated moments of the expedition are approached only by Curtius from the perspective of religious propaganda and of its impact on the psychology of the masses; (b) in Curtius, Alexander's rhetoric of religion often manifests itself with regard to themes which transcend the narrow limits of divine favour and divine origins; (c) finally yet importantly, Curtius brings to the foreground, more than any other writer does, the subdued nations' reactions to this rhetoric of religion.

---

[26] McQueen 1967, 29; Diadori 1981; Morrison 2001; Bichler 2016; Liotsakis 2020, 261–270.

To begin with the Greeks, the episode on the cure offered to Alexander by Philip of Acarnania in Tarsus (3.5.1–6.20) exemplifies in a striking way Curtius' method. This story is popular in the literary tradition of Alexander and is typically used as a reflection of Alexander's well-known faith in friendship.[27] Alexander, the story goes, got sick in Tarsus, either because he swam in the cold waters of the Cydnus or for some other reason. While no physician dared or could offer a cure to the king, the physician Philip of Acarnania, who was also an intimate friend of Alexander, urged him to trust him and accept a treatment he made especially for this occasion. In the meantime, Parmenio sent a letter to Alexander, warning him to beware of Philip, who is said to have been bribed by Darius to assassinate Alexander. Alexander reads the letter and gives it to Philip. The story ends with a highly suspenseful scene, in which Alexander is drinking the medicine while Philip is reading the letter, in order to show to the physician how much he trusts their friendship.

Whereas the rest of the surviving sources focus on the interaction exclusively between the king and the physician,[28] Curtius also frames the anecdote with the troops' reactions. At the beginning of the account, the soldiers are presented as mourning for their king, full of fear for his life, and as worrying about how they will return home without his guidance (3.5.4–9). At the end of the narrative, they congratulate Philip as if he was a god (3.6.17). At this point, Curtius offers us a unique scene in the literature of Alexander, which relates to the divine favour Alexander claimed to enjoy. We learn that the Macedonians themselves believed that their king, given that he had managed so much in such a young age, certainly had the gods on his side in whatever enterprise he wished to undertake. And Curtius concludes by saying that such a king was justly loved so much by his men (3.6.17–20). In essence, Curtius does what Plutarch and Arrian do, i.e. he transforms Alexander's rhetoric about the divine favour he allegedly enjoyed into his own narrative rhetoric, in his effort to delineate his own laudatory image of the king. However, only Curtius approaches this issue from the Macedonians' perspective. In other sources we merely read that Alexander promoted such an idea and we are encouraged to accept this view. Curtius, on the contrary, uniquely adds that this view was also the assumption of the Macedonians and one of the main reasons why they loved their king.

Curtius is also the only author to highlight Alexander's manipulation of his troops' superstitions at the dawn of the battle at Gaugamela. Once again, the focal point of interest in this account is the effect of religious rhetoric on the masses'

---

[27] D.S. 17.31.4–6; Plu. *Alex.* 19; Arr. *An.* 2.4.7–11.
[28] Except Plutarch's (*Alex.* 19.10) short mention of the troops' anxiety at the end of his account.

psychology. A few days before the battle, a moon eclipse took place and disheartened Alexander's army (4.10.1–2). This information is also offered by Arrian (*An.* 3.7.6) and Plutarch (*Alex.* 31.8) in a fleeting way and with no reference to the effect of the eclipse on the troops' morale.[29] By contrast, Curtius composes a vivid episode, in which the tension created in the army is presented to have nearly turned to a mutiny against the king (4.10.2–3). Alexander used the Egyptian soothsayers and disseminated the message that the sun represented the Greeks, the moon the Persians, and that a moon eclipse always portended that the Persians would fight without divine favour (4.10.4–7). The troops are presented to be tranquilised and Curtius ends his account with the comment that "nothing sways the common herd more effectively than superstition; generally uncontrolled, savage, fickle, when they are victims of vain superstition, they obey the soothsayers better than they do their leaders" (4.10.7).

We also find a unique case of rhetoric of religious nature in the account of Alexander's effort to face his men's desire to return home after the battle of Gaugamela and Darius' murder by Bessus (6.2.15–4.1). This is a scene we find in other sources as well, but only Curtius presents Alexander as exercising rhetoric with religious connotations.[30] Alexander, worried by the turbulence in his army, gathers his generals and complains to them that his very soldiers will deprive him of the glory of conquering India and the rest of the Orient. In this context, he argues that it is not his men's cowardice that stands in his way but "the envy of the gods" (6.2.19). Later on, after his generals have quieted the troops, Alexander delivers a speech to the whole army, in which he tries to persuade them by means of certain arguments of strategic and geopolitical content (6.3.1–18). However, he also argues that if they continue the enterprise and go after Bessus, the Persians will welcome them as the punishers of an impious traitor and thus as the conductors of a pious war (6.3.17–18). Other sources too offer an idealised picture of Alexander as the one who wishes to punish Bessus motivated by his sincere sense of justice.[31] Curtius, apart from this element, also pinpoints the element of respect of the divine. In both speeches of Alexander, the one addressed to his generals and the other to the entire army, the rhetorical invocation of the divine is presented as an organic part of an effective argumentation, especially if we consider the positive reactions of the audience (6.2.20 on the general's reaction and 6.4.1

---

29 Cf. Pliny *NH* 2.180; Ptol. 1.4.2; Cic. *De div.* 1.121.
30 D.S. 17.74.3; Justin 12.3.
31 On this issue see Liotsakis 2019, 81–121 with special emphasis on Arrian and 118–120 on Diodorus and Plutarch too.

on the troops' enthusiastic response to Alexander's speech). Furthermore, the element of *pietas* is highlighted as a piece of argument aiming not only at the Macedonians but also at the Persians.

It is exactly Curtius' intense interest in the psychology of the masses, combined with his general scepticism towards omens and the validity of their interpretations, which distinguish his account on the siege of Tyre from those of Plutarch and Arrian, in terms of how he treats the traditional anecdotes about the supernatural aid Alexander was said to have enjoyed. Curtius too mentions what we also read in other sources, namely Alexander's wish to offer a sacrifice to the Tyrian Heracles and the Tyrians' rejection of his demand (4.2.2–5). He has also included in his narrative the Tyrians' tying of Apollo's statue and added to this the information that some other Tyrians had also suggested that they sacrifice a freeborn boy to Saturn in order to secure divine favour in their efforts to defend their city (4.3.21–23). Last, Curtius also touches upon Alexander's claim that he saw Heracles in his dream assuring him that he would help him conquer Tyre.

However, the way Curtius uses this material is far from reminiscent of the spirit in which Plutarch and Arrian used the same stories. For we have already demonstrated that both of them shaped their Tyrian accounts in a ring composition in order to allow for speculations that in his siege of Tyre Alexander was assisted by the gods. On the contrary, Curtius relates supernatural stories of this kind in an ironical way and with great emphasis on the impact of such rumours upon the troops' morale. His own ring composition is aimed at criticising the naivety with which, in his opinion, both sides, the Macedonians and the Tyrians, were swayed by their superstitions during the siege of the city. This ring composition begins at the opening paragraphs of the account, in which we read that the two armies were simultaneously interpreting a couple of omens as a favourable sign. In particular, we read of the Tyrians' construction of defensive weaponry and that "when the iron which it was necessary to forge had been placed in the furnaces, [...] streams of blood are said to have flowed out in the very midst of the flames, and this the Tyrians interpreted as portending the destruction of the Macedonians" (4.2.13). During the same period, Curtius says, the Macedonians noticed drops of blood coming out of their breads, a portent which was interpreted by Aristander as a sign that the Tyrians were doomed (4.2.14). The contrast between the hopes of each side leads us to doubt the validity of those interpretations. We find a similar story shortly before the Tyrians' fall. A sea monster appears at the sea and both sides take it as a favourable omen. The Tyrians also celebrated as they believed that Neptune was expressing to them his favour, and Curtius sarcastically comments that "so over-hasty were they to perceive, not only an omen of victory, but even an occasion for celebrating one" (4.4.5).

It is in this atmosphere of irony towards the futility of the masses' interpretations of omens[32] that Curtius narrates Alexander's claims that he saw Heracles in his dream. In ch. 4.2.16–18 we read that the Macedonians feared that not even the gods could help them build a causeway between the shore and Tyre. At this point, Curtius explains to the reader that Alexander, "who was by no means inexperienced in working upon the minds of soldiers, announced that an apparition of Heracles had appeared to him in his sleep, offering him his right hand; with that god leading him and opening the way he dreamed that he entered the city". What Plutarch and Arrian used as a narrative seed to be artfully presented as being fulfilled, is here presented as mere means of rhetoric on the king's part in his effort to raise his men's morale.

The religious propaganda also transcends the limits of its sender, Alexander, and is related to its reception by others with regard to Alexander's descent from Ammon. We saw that Plutarch and Arrian, too, address this issue, but Curtius differs from them in that he relates this issue with all three crucial moments of turbulence in the relationship of Alexander with his men, i.e. Philotas' alleged treason (6.7.1–7.2.38), the murder of Clitus (8.1.19–2.12) and the conspiracy of the pages (8.6.1–8.23). Plutarch presents only Clitus as mocking Alexander for this matter and as accusing him of denying Philip as his father (*Alex.* 50.11), while he does not mention Philotas' and the pages' dissatisfaction on this issue. Arrian, on his part, vaguely writes that Clitus long before his death had opposed Alexander's robust competitiveness towards Heracles and Dionysus (*An.* 4.8.4) but not his claims that he was the son of Zeus. Neither does Arrian refer to any reason of Philotas' hostility, while he presents only Hermolaus as accusing Alexander not of his propaganda concerning Ammon but of his wish to impose his *proskynēsis* (*An.* 4.14.2). Curtius, on the other hand, touches upon all three individuals' resentment towards the issue of Alexander's origins from Ammon. Philotas, according to Alexander, had expressed an ironic comment on the matter to Alexander himself (6.9.19) and in his trial he shares his regret for having believed that he could advise Alexander as a friend without the motives of his advice being misunderstood (6.10.26–29). Also, as in Plutarch, Clitus, "mocking the oracle of Jupiter, whom Alexander claimed as his father, said that he himself had spoken to the king more truly that his 'father' had done" (8.1.42). Last, Hermolaus explains that one of the main reasons why he and his comrades decided to kill Alexander was his claim that he was descended from Zeus (8.7.13–14).

---

32 Cf. Curtius' irony towards Alexander's superstition in times of crisis in ch. 7.7.6–8 and ch. 7.7.20–29.

Now the episode on the conspiracy of the pages is indeed one of the most illuminating passages of the work also in terms of the degree to which Curtius is interested in the effects of Alexander's propaganda about his divine origins upon the morale of his foes. Curtius repeatedly castigates Alexander's claims about his origins from the gods and his superiority over them (3.12.18–20; 4.7.29–32). Also, as Arrian does, Curtius too takes Alexander's boasts as a sign for the deterioration of his character due to his success. Both Arrian and Curtius delineate a dynamic portrait for Alexander, by sketching him as being gradually corrupted by the glory of his own feats; and in both Arrian and Curtius, Alexander's rivalry towards the gods and his wish to be treated as one of them are the two main elements which mark this character deterioration.[33] However, as transpires from the following analysis, differently than Arrian, Curtius also recognises the effective impact of this rhetoric upon the Anatolians' morale. This message is conveyed through the confirmation of Alexander's response to Hermolaus by certain events described in Books 8 and 9.

Let us begin with Alexander's words. As soon as Hermolaus completes his speech, Alexander delivers his own as a response to the boy's arguments (8.8.1–19). And one of the issues he addresses in his response to the conspirator is the latter's accusations against the king's claims that he descends from Ammon. Alexander develops the following points of argument: first, he invokes the validity of the oracle of Ammon's priest and explains that he has no power to doubt what the gods choose to reveal to men. Since the god offered him the title of his son, he could not but accept it (8.8.14). Second, to accept the title of the son of Ammon benefits the plans in which he and his men are engaged. In particular, Alexander says:

> *Utinam Indi quoque deum esse me credant. Fama enim bella constant, et saepe etiam, quod falso creditum est, veri vicem obtinuit. An me luxuriae indulgentem putatis arma vestra auro argentoque adornasse? Adsuetis nihil vilius hac videre materia volui ostendere, Macedonas invictos ceteris ne auro quidem vinci. Oculos ergo primum eorum sordida omnia et humilia despectantium capiam et docebo nos non auri aut argenti cupidos, sed orbem terrarum subacturos venire.*
>
> (8.8.15–17)

> Would that the people of India may believe me to be a god. For wars depend upon reputation, and often even what has been falsely believed has gained the place of truth. Do you think it was to gratify my luxury that I adorned your arms with gold and silver? I wished to

---

[33] On Curtius' and Arrian's dynamic portraits of Alexander see respectively Baynham 1998 and Liotsakis 2019.

show to those who are accustomed to nothing cheaper than those metals that the Macedonians, who are invincible in other things, cannot be outdone even in gold. Therefore I will first of all captivate the eyes of those who despise everything that is usual and humble and will show them that we are coming, not because we are desirous of gold and silver, but to subdue the whole world. (tr. Rolfe 1946)

This is the sole passage in the surviving sources in which Alexander is presented as explaining the benefits of his claims that he is the son of Zeus for the future of the expedition. Other writers recognise that Alexander used this issue as a weapon of foreign policy, although without having Alexander confirm their judgment by means of a speech. Only here do we see Alexander *himself* supporting such a view. Furthermore, only here are we invited by the following account to assess the soundness of Alexander's political reasoning, given that, in the ensuing chapters, Curtius weaves a narrative thread of four instances which confirm Alexander's view that it will be easier for him and his men to conquer India if its inhabitants take him for a god.

The first incident occurs when Alexander enters India (8.10.1). Some trivial kings of the area surrender to him by saying that he, after Heracles and Dionysus, is the third son of Zeus who visits their district and that, although they know of the first two gods only from myths, they are lucky enough to meet at least the third offspring of Zeus. This incident does not, of course, necessarily prove that those kings did believe that Alexander was the son of Zeus (however, see below); it rather reflects something which Alexander must have faced many times in his career in Asia, namely the flattering fireworks of the frightened governors of the areas he subdued in their efforts to save themselves and their cities. As we saw in Section 2, Arrian too records a similar scene with the governor of Nysa blandishing Alexander with the argument that he had reached an area which was a remnant of Dionysus' glory. However, never again in his account on Alexander's activities in India does Arrian return to the Indians' reception and flattering abuse of Alexander's religious propaganda. By contrast, in Curtius this event, which reveals how Alexander's religious propaganda affected his diplomatic intercourse with the Asians, paves the way to three further events which foreground this issue on anthropological and military levels as well.

The second confirmation of Alexander's argumentation comes in ch. 8.10.27– 36. The Macedonians besiege a city in the land of the Indian nation Mazagae, which is strongly fortified with imposing mural constructions but also by the geomorphology of its position. While inspecting the walls of the city, Alexander gets injured in the calf, but, absorbed by his desire to complete his reconnoitre, rides a horse and keeps checking the wall. However, as the pain caused by his wound grew, he said to his soldiers "that he was indeed called the son of Jupiter, but that he felt the effects of an ailing body". Later on, when the Macedonians had already covered the caverns which were around the wall with mound and transferred the siege-engines close to the wall, the inhabitants of the city, seeing for the first time this kind of military technology, surrendered their city to Alexander, as they "believed that such massive structures, aided by no visible power, were moved by the will of the gods; the mural pikes also, and the heavy spears hurled by the engines, they said were not compatible with mortal power". Similarly, in ch. 9.1.18 we read that some other Indians, after being defeated by the Macedonians, fled and terrified the inhabitants of the neighbouring towns by saying that "an invincible army, surely made up of gods, had come".

The last example is found in ch. 9.8.4–8. The Macedonian fleet sails down the waters of the Indus river and reaches the land of the Sambagrae, a nation which had 60,000 infantry, 6,000 cavalry and five hundred chariots. By offering these details on this army and by describing this nation as "a strong race of India", Curtius elicits readerly expectation that these brave Indians will resist the Macedonians in a battle. However, the episode ends up being a near miss, as eventually the Sambagrae surrender. The villagers of the riparian territory were amazed by the Macedonian fleet which had covered a great part of the river, and by the shining armour of countless, in their eyes, soldiers, so that they believed that "an army of gods was coming and another Father Liber, a name celebrated among those nations". They ran to their soldiers "crying that they were mad and were about to do battle with gods".

All the aforementioned examples reveal an abundance of factors which made Alexander's foes treat him and his army as gods. These factors, which transcend the usual myths of Dionysus' and Heracles' presence in India, are the military technology of the Macedonians, their courage and virtue in battle, as well as their imposing interaction with the local landscape, all of which are presented to be in the natives' minds so extraordinary and unprecedented that the latter believed that they were being attacked by the gods. This assumption of the Indians made them, as we saw, repeatedly flee, a behaviour which confirms Alexander's view that the idea that he is a god will certainly demoralise his enemies.

5 Conclusion

By the time Plutarch, Curtius and Arrian wrote their stories, Alexander and his army had long ago entered the last realm they would ever visit, the underworld. And if there is indeed any kind of the underworld, we can imagine the king and his men, all together – and from then on as equals – laying in the eternal fields of Hades and laughing with the king's foxy rhetorical manoeuvres of religious content, by means of which he had at times been enraging them by his hubristic stance or, at some other times, had been coaxing them into following him to the remotest parts of the world. In the meantime, however, in the world of the living there may be none of these soldiers to be allured by their king's rhetorical propaganda, but instead there were now readers to be excited by the supernatural flavour of the stories on Alexander and his men. These readers, distant heirs of Alexander's and his Macedonians' feat, lived in a world of globalisation, whose boundaries, they knew, were first opened and established by Alexander and his men. For the people of the Imperial Era, the king who initiated this great world cannot have been anything but great; hence, in a sense, Alexander "the Great". And for many readers, as is evident in the sources of that era, it made sense that the greatness of this sovereign may also have emerged from the favour of the gods. This is a view which, as we saw, is rhetorically promoted by all three authors under examination.

However, somewhere at this point romanticism ends. The other two elements of Alexander's rhetoric of religion, i.e. divine origins and rivalry towards the gods, were not welcomed by Plutarch, Arrian and Curtius. As for the issue of Alexander's descent from Ammon Zeus, Arrian and Curtius do not tolerate the king's claims and do not deign to elicit readerly interest in this issue. On the other hand, Plutarch is in narrative terms the boldest of all three authors, in that he, although not believing in Alexander's divine nature, occasionally plays with Olympias' and Alexander's alleged secret, does not belie it and thereby leaves the reader to speculate on the matter. Finally, as for Alexander's rivalry with Heracles and Dionysus, while Plutarch is quite indifferent in this issue, Arrian and Curtius adopt an intense critical stance towards Alexander's boastfulness and render it as one of the strong pieces of evidence for the view that the Macedonian conqueror was eventually conquered, on a moral level, by his own success. Still, while Arrian approaches this issue with an exclusively critical eye, Curtius, with his distinctive interest in the psychology of the masses, is not swayed by his negativism on the matter and recognises that, although Alexander's claims that he was the son of gods and a worthy rival for their glory are hubristic, this communicative policy occasionally helped him control the morale of his foes.

Bibliography

AAA: Sisti, F./Zambrini, A. (2001–2004), *Arriano. Anabasi di Alessandro*, vols. I-II, Milan.
Amitay, O. (2008), 'Why Did Alexander the Great Besiege Tyre', in: *Athenaeum* 96, 91–102.
Antela-Bernárdez, B. (2016), 'Like Gods among Men. The Use of Religion and Mythical Issues during Alexander's Campaign', in: K. Ulanowski (ed.), *The Religious Aspects of War in the Ancient Near East, Greece, and Rome. Ancient Warfare, vol. I*, Leiden/Boston, 235–255.
Auberger, J. (2001), *Historiens d'Alexandre. Textes traduits et annotés*, Paris.
Balsdon, J.P.V.D. (1950), 'The Divinity of Alexander', in: *Historia* 1, 363–388.
Baynham, E. (1998), *Alexander the Great: A Unique History of Quintus Curtius*, Ann Arbor.
Berve, H. (1926), *Das Alexanderreich auf Prosopographischer grundlage*, vols. I-II, Munich.
Bichler, R. (2016), 'Die Bewährung der Soldaten in den Unbilden der Natur: ein Beitrag zu Curtius' Erzählkunst', in: H. Wulfram (ed.), *Der römische Alexanderhistoriker Curtius Rufus*, Vienna, 239–261.
Bloedow, E.F. (1994), 'Alexander's Speech on the Eve of the Siege of Tyre', in: *L'Antiquité Classique* 63, 65–76.
Bosman, P.R. (2011), 'Signs and Narrative Design in Plutarch's *Alexander*', in: *Akroterion* 56, 91–106.
Bosworth, A.B. (1996a), *Alexander and the East. The Tragedy of Triumph*, Oxford.
Bosworth, A.B. (1996b), 'Alexander, Euripides, and Dionysos. The Motivation for Apotheosis', in: R.W. Wallace/E.M. Harris (eds.), *Transitions to Empire. Essays in Greco-Roman History, 360-146 B.C., in Honor of E. Badian*, Norman, OK/London, 140–166.
Brenk, F.E. (1975), 'The Dreams of Plutarch's *Lives*', in: *Latomus* 34, 336–349.
Brenk, F.E. (1977), *In Mist Apparelled. Religious Themes in Plutarch's Moralia and Lives*, Leiden.
Chrysanthou, C. (2017), 'The Proems of Plutarch's *Lives* and Historiography', in: *Histos* 11, 128–153.
Cook, B.L. (2002), 'Plutarch's Use of λέγεται: Narrative Design and Source in *Alexander*', in: *Greek, Roman and Byzantine Studies* 42, 329–360.
Diadori, P. (1981), 'La rappresentazione della massa nell'opera di Q. Curzio Rufo', in: *Maia* 33, 225–231.
Dreyer, B. (2009), 'Heroes, Cults, and Divinity', in: W. Heckel/L.A. Tritle (eds.), *Alexander the Great. A New History*, Malden, MA, 218–234.
Duff, T.E. (2014), 'The Prologues', in: M. Beck (ed.), *A Companion to Plutarch*, Malden, MA/Oxford/Chichester, 333–349.
Edmunds, L. (1971), 'The Religiosity of Alexander', in: *Greek, Roman and Byzantine Studies* 12, 363–391.
Fournel, E. (2016), 'Dream Narratives in Plutarch's *Lives*: The Place of Fiction in Biography', in: V. Liotsakis/S. Farrington (eds.), *The Art of History. Literary Perspectives in Greek and Roman Historiography*, Berlin/Boston, 199–216.
Gilhaus, L. (2017), *Fragmente der Historiker. Die Alexanderhistoriker (FGrH 117-153)*, Stuttgart.
Gilhaus, L. (2021 forthcoming), 'Arrian's Praise and Criticism of Violence in the *Anabasis*', in: J. Degen/R. Rollinger (eds.), *The World of Alexander in Perspective: Contextualizing Arrian*, Wiesbaden.
Goukowsky, P. (1978), *Essai sur les origines du mythe d'Alexandre (336-270 av. J.-C.). I. Les origines politiques*, Nancy.

Grainger, J.D. (1991), *Hellenistic Phoenicia*, Oxford.
Green, P. (1974), *Alexander of Macedon, 356-323 B.C. A Historical Biography*, Berkeley/Los Angeles.
Hamilton, J.R. (2002), *Plutarch. Alexander*, Second edition, Oxford.
Hammond, N.G.L. (1993), 'Alexander's Letter Concerning Samos in Plut. *Alex.* 28.2', in: *Historia* 42, 379–382.
Hammond, N.L.G. (1997), *The Genius of Alexander the Great*, London.
HCA: Bosworth, A.B. (1980–1995), *A Historical Commentary on Arrian's History of Alexander*, vols. I-II, Oxford.
Heckel, W. (2008), *The Conquests of Alexander the Great*, Cambridge/New York.
Hogarth, D.G. (1887), 'The Deification of Alexander the Great', in: *The English Historical Review* 2, 317–329.
Jacoby, F. (1923-), *Die Fragmente der griechischen Historiker*, Berlin/Leiden.
King, C.J. (2013), 'Plutarch, Alexander, and Dream Divination', in: *Illinois Classical Studies* 38, 81–111.
Kornemann, E. (1935), *Die Alexandergeschichte des Königs Ptolemaios I. von Aegypten. Versuch einer Rekonstruktion*, Leipzig/Berlin.
Liotsakis, V. (2019), *Alexander the Great in Arrian's Anabasis. A Literary Portrait*, Berlin/Boston.
Liotsakis, V. (2020), 'Disunity and the Macedonians in the Literature of Alexander: Plutarch, Arrian and Curtius Rufus', in: A.N. Michalopoulos/A. Serafim/F. Beneventano della Corte/A. Vatri (eds.), *The Rhetoric of Unity and Division in Ancient Literature*, Berlin/Boston, 245–274.
Liotsakis, V. (2021 forthcoming), 'How to Satisfy Everyone: Diverse Readerly Expectations and Multiple Authorial *Personae* in Arrian's *Anabasis*', in: M. Baumann/V. Liotsakis (eds.), *Reading History in the Roman Empire*, Berlin/Boston.
McKechnie, P. (2009), 'Omens of the Death of Alexander the Great', in: P.V. Wheatley/R. Hannah (eds.), *Alexander and His Successors: Essays from the Antipodes*, Claremont, CA, 206–226.
McQueen, E.I. (1967), 'Quintus Curtius Rufus', in: T.A. Dorey (ed.), *Latin* Biography, London, 17–43.
Mederer, E. (1936), *Die Alexanderlegenden bei den ältesten Alexanderhistorikern*, Stuttgart.
Morrison, G. (2001), 'Alexander, Combat Psychology, and Persepolis', in: *Antichthon* 35, 30–44.
Munn, M. (2008), 'Alexander, the Gordian Knot, and the Kingship of Midas', in: T. Howe/J. Reames (eds.), *Macedonian Legacies. Studies in Ancient Macedonian History and Culture in Honor of Eugene N. Borza*, Claremont, CA, 107–143.
Nice, A. (2005), 'The Reputation of the 'Mantis' Aristander', in: *Acta Classica* 48, 87–102.
O'Brien, J.M. (1991), *Alexander the Great. The Invisible Enemy. A Biography*, London/New York.
Pearson, L.I.C. (1960), *The Lost Histories of Alexander the Great*, New York.
Pédech, P. (1984), *Historiens, compagnons d'Alexandre. Callisthène – Onésicrite – Néarque – Ptolémée – Aristobule*, Paris.
Pelling, C.B.R. (2010), '"With Thousands Such Enchanting Dreams": The Dreams of the *Lives* Revisited', in: L. van der Stockt/F.B. Titchener/H.-G. Ingenkamp/A. Pérez Jiménez (eds.), *Gods, Daimones, Rituals, Myths and History of Religions in Plutarch's Works: Studies Devoted to Professor Frederick E. Brenk by the International Plutarch Society*, Logan, UT, 315–332.

Prandi, L. (1985), *Callistene. Uno storico tra Aristotele e i re macedoni*, Milan.
Prandi, L. (1996), *Fortuna e realtà dell'opera di Clitarco*, Stuttgart.
Rolfe, J.C. (tr.) (1946), *Quintus Curtius. History of Alexander, Volume I: Books 1-5; Volume II: Books 6-10*, Cambridge, MA.
Romane, J.P. (1987), 'Alexander's Siege of Tyre', in: *Ancient World* 16, 79–90.
Seibert, J. (1985), *Die Eroberung des Perserreiches durch Alexander d. Gr. Auf kartographischer Grundlage*, Wiesbaden.
Serafim, A. (2020), *Religious Discourse in Attic Oratory and Politics*, London/New York.
Stewart, A.F. (1987), 'Diodorus, Curtius, and Arrian on Alexander's Mole at Tyre', in: *Berytus* 35, 97–99.
Strasburger, H. (1934), *Ptolemaios und Alexander*, Leipzig.
Worthington, I. (2014), *By the Spear. Philip II, Alexander the Great, and the Rise and Fall of the Macedonian Empire*, Oxford.

Kelly E. Shannon-Henderson
What Makes a *Divus*? The Prospective Rhetoric of Deification in Pliny's *Panegyricus*

Abstract: This paper offers an interpretation of references to the deification of emperors in Pliny's *Panegyricus* as a meditation on Trajan's future deification after his death, and argues that Pliny's *Panegyricus* is an example of pseudo-deification. Although the speech also emphasises Trajan's *civilitas*, humility and respect for the law, Pliny prepares his audience for the fact that Trajan will ultimately become a god. Pliny describes Trajan's earthly powers as approaching or even exceeding those of the gods, and compares Trajan favourably with both *mali principes* and previously deified emperors, suggesting that he, even more than previous *divi*, will earn a place in heaven upon his death. Far from being in conflict, these two notions reinforce each other and are crucial to understanding Pliny's celebration of Trajan's reign.

1 Introduction

Pliny's much maligned *Panegyricus*, for all its turgid bulk and off-putting adulatory tone, is the only piece of Latin oratory to survive complete from the period between 43 BC and AD 289.[1] It is also full of religion: references to the divine run through the speech "da cima a fondo",[2] bracketed by prayers to Jupiter at beginning (*Pan.* 1) and end (*Pan.* 94). Scholars assessing how religious concerns shape Pliny's depiction of Trajan in the speech have tended to fall into one of two camps based on which of two contradictory ideas about Trajan's relationship to the divine they believe to be predominant. Some emphasise the distinction between Domitian's alleged encouragement of the worship of himself as a god during his

---

I am grateful to David Levene for his suggestions for improvement of this paper, and to my colleagues Matthew Feminella, Jessica Goethals, Alessandra Montalbano and Gina Stamm for their comments on presentation and organisation. Thanks also to the editors of this volume for their helpful suggestions. All translations of ancient texts throughout are mine. All errors remain my own.

1 For criticisms see, e.g., Radice 1968, 169–170; Seelentag 2004, 214. For its significance see, e.g., Roche 2011, 4–5.
2 Soverini 1989, 550.

own lifetime and the more moderate outlook Pliny sees (or hopes to see) in Trajan. Whereas Domitian famously referred to himself as *dominus et deus* (Suet. *Dom.* 13.2, Dio 67.5.7), Trajan condemns any such adulation, and Pliny refuses to offer it; "let us nowhere offer flatteries as to a god or divinity" (*Pan.* 2.3: *nusquam ut deo, nusquam ut numini blandiamur*), he enjoins his audience. This and other similar passages suggest that Pliny rejects the possibility that Trajan is divine, for to claim otherwise would be to put him too close to the theocratic tendencies of the hated Domitian when Pliny's goal is to emphasise the gulf between them; while Trajan may be aided or protected by the gods, he is not and cannot be one himself.³ Other scholars highlight the opposite idea, for throughout the speech Pliny also emphasises Trajan's similarity to or backing by the divine,⁴ twice calling Trajan a "*princeps* most similar to the gods" (*dis simillimus princeps*, *Pan.* 1.3; cf. *Pan.* 7.5).

Yet these alternatives are not mutually exclusive, and the best scholarly treatments of the *Panegyricus* recognise the contrast between its rejection of theocratic tendencies and its nudging of Trajan toward the divine, and find that meaning is made in the paradoxical overlap of humanity and divinity in the person of Trajan. David Levene's analysis, for example, starts from the point of view that references to the emperor's divinity "are in some sense intended literally" when they are delivered in a world in which ruler cult exists, and cannot be dismissed as mere metaphor or hyperbole.⁵ Others since Levene have taken similar views.⁶ Levene's work is undergirded by the foundational research of Simon Price, who emphasised the multifaceted and often ambiguous nature of the emperor's place in the man-god hierarchy: because "no clear relationship was established between the categories of *deus* and *divus*, the institution of the imperial cult produced a system whose relationship to both gods and men was ambiguous".⁷

Levene views the speech's ambiguities as placing it precisely at the interface between belief and scepticism: compared with Greek culture's longer tradition of ruler-cult, Latin panegyric, he argues, while it maintained a discomfort with religious language that "points to a greater fragility in Roman religious belief itself",

---

3 For Schowalter 1993, 71, 73–74, one of the speech's goals is to teach Trajan that he is not a god and should not behave like Domitian. Cf. Brunt 1979, 172; Sordi 2003, 269; Kersten/Syré 2013, 420–422.
4 E.g. Fears 1977, rightly critiqued by Brunt 1979 and Schowalter 1993, 13–27.
5 Levene 1997, 69 n. 20, 82–83.
6 E.g. Rees 2001, 164–165; Seelentag 2004, 229; Hoffer 2006, 87; Ronning 2007, 112–115. For similar observations before Levene see Fell 1992, 24; Cid López 1993, 51.
7 Price 1984, 220. For Levene's indebtedness to Price see, e.g., Levene 1997, 72.

nevertheless continued to use "religious motifs to describe the ruler".[8] Yet I believe there is further still we can go. This chapter seeks to build on Levene's analysis by examining the ambiguities about Trajan's divine status that abound in the *Panegyricus* through the lens of further developments in research on emperor cult since the work of Price. Manfred Clauss, for example, emphasises the wide variety of types of treatment afforded to "Gottheiten". It was possible for such figures to move up through a variety of "Zwischenstufen" of increasingly official, public and widespread worship, the pinnacle of which was to be declared a *divus* by the Senate, an honour which not every emperor or member of the imperial family attained.[9] Another crucial advance in the understanding of emperor cult has been made by Gradel, who uses the terms "absolute" and "relative divinity" to describe the problem. Roman religion, he argues, had no prescriptive ideas about what made someone a god in an ontological or "absolute" sense; emperors and traditional gods alike were worshipped "for the sake of their enormous power over the worshippers, not because divine nature gave them any claim a priori to such honours" – that is, because of their divinity "relative" to those performing their rituals.[10] Levene has rightly critiqued this model, observing that while it works reasonably well to explain the *practice* of emperor cult, it works less well for understanding descriptions of divinity in *literature*, especially poetry, where there is compelling evidence for a conception of gods and humans as two different "species".[11] This is particularly so, he argues, in panegyric, because the question of "absolute truth or falsehood" is essential to the genre.[12] Yet I think that even with Levene's caveats, Gradel's concept of relative divinity still has something to offer for interpreting the *Panegyricus*: the speech does certainly imply Trajan's divinity quite unambiguously in places (as we shall see), but there is also enough hedging and claims to the contrary in this long and unusually structured praise oration that a more flexible interpretive framework is appropriate.

Both of these models can give us a new and enhanced understanding of emperor cult in Pliny's *Panegyricus*. In Clauss' terms, we could say that Pliny uses the *Panegyricus* to explore a variety of "Zwischenstufen" between humanity and divinity. In Gradel's terms, Pliny can disclaim "absolute" divinity within Trajan while also suggesting quite strongly that, relative to other human beings, Trajan is nearer to the gods than not – even if, as Levene would perhaps remind us, this

---

8 Levene 1997, 100–102.
9 Clauss 1999, 36–37, citing Germanicus as one example.
10 Gradel 2002, 25–32, 321–324.
11 Levene 2012.
12 Levene 2012, 76.

degree of uncertainty is somewhat problematic within the framework of the truth-claims demanded by the genre of panegyric. In what follows, I will examine several strategies Pliny uses in the speech to lay the groundwork for the Senate's official deification of Trajan that he assumes will follow upon Trajan's death. I term this Pliny's rhetoric of "prospective deification" – that is, the use of religious material to build a case for Trajan's divinity even as he simultaneously stresses Trajan's *civilitas*, humility and respect for the law. As Hutchinson, in his analysis of the literary concept of the sublime in the speech, succinctly puts it, "Pliny truly asserts Trajan's near-divinity, and implies his future divinity. It is through Pliny's language that Trajan sublimely reaches the border; but Trajan's own restraint attains a special kind of sublimity through denying sublimity".[13] As we shall see, this is true not only from a literary perspective, but also from a religious one: Pliny's *Panegyricus*, as it probes the contrasts between Trajan's divinity and his humanity, is an active and ongoing meditation on his status that performs important theological work before an audience of senators early in the reign of their *optimus princeps*.[14]

2 Good and bad *divi*

Trajan's is not the only divinity discussed in the *Panegyricus*. Pliny provides some clues as to what actions he thinks do (and do not) merit worship of an emperor through his discussions of Trajan's predecessors, especially Nerva and Domitian. It is not just Pliny who thinks this way: there is strong evidence that an emperor had to "earn" official deification by good (especially pro-senatorial) conduct in life. The idea of earned divinity was present in contemporary rhetorical theory: in his precepts for how to construct an epideictic speech in praise of a god, Quintilian states, "in some gods you must praise the fact that they were born immortal, in others the fact that they *achieved* immortality through excellence (*Inst.* 3.7.9: *laudandum in quibusdam quod geniti inmortales, quibusdam quod inmortalitatem virtute sint consecuti*). Similarly, one corollary of Gradel's concept of relative divinity is the idea that only some emperors and members of the imperial family really merit deification: "by voting state divinity to dead emperors, the Senate didactically displayed to the ruling emperor, and empress, the reward awaiting

---

[13] Hutchinson 2011, 131.
[14] On the occasion of the speech see Radice 1968. For *Pan.* as a senatorial speech see Durry 1938, 21–24; Seelentag 2004, 224–230; Gangloff 2019, 175.

them if they ruled and behaved according to the senatorial ideal", whereas *divi* and *divae* who were not felt to be particularly relevant or powerful tended to fade into obscurity when their dynasties ended.[15] Even Levene's critique is still compatible with the idea that some gods are more powerful than others: "it is true that individual gods' powers, like the powers of individual humans, varied".[16] In other words, all *divi* and *divae* were equal, but some were more equal than others.

Early in the speech, Pliny asserts categorically that the newly-deified Nerva deserves his status:[17]

> Quem tu lacrimis primum, ita ut filium decuit, mox templis honestasti, non imitatus illos qui hoc idem sed alia mente fecerunt. Dicavit caelo <u>Tiberius Augustum, sed ut maiestatis crimen induceret</u>; <u>Claudium Nero, sed ut irrideret</u>; <u>Vespasianum Titus, Domitianus Titum, sed ille ut dei filius, hic ut frater videretur</u>. Tu sideribus patrem intulisti <u>non ad metum civium, non in contumeliam numinum, non in honorem tuum</u>, sed quia deum credis. Minus hoc est, cum fit ab iis qui et sese deos putant.
>
> Pan. 11.1–3

> You honoured him first with tears, as befitted a son, and then with temples – but not in imitation of those who did the same thing but with a different mindset. Tiberius consecrated Augustus to heaven, but only so that he could introduce the accusation of *maiestas*; Nero did the same for Claudius, but only to mock him; Titus did the same for Vespasian and Domitian for Titus, but only so that they would be seen as the son and brother, respectively, of a god. But you brought your father among the stars not for citizens' fear, mockery of divinities, or for your own honour, but because you believed him a god. This is worth less when it is done by those who think that they themselves are also gods.

Pliny pairs two tricola that discuss deifications performed by Tiberius, Nero and the Flavians, and Trajan's rejection of the motivations for each, to drive home the point that Trajan is superior to the emperors of the previous two dynasties in his reasons for conferring divinity upon Nerva.[18] Trajan's tears and swift pivot from grief to temple-building are depicted as signs of genuine emotion and *pietas*,[19] and the statement that he actually *believed* his father to be a god is a relatively

---

15 Gradel 2002, 347, 345–349.
16 Levene 2012, 70.
17 Cf. Henderson 2011, 152: "this version [of deification] will not just tick the boxes... but grasp the logic".
18 For the tricolon, which *Rhet Her.* 4.26 refers to as "the most appropriate and complete" (*commodissima et absolutissima*) number of cola in which to arrange one's words, see Lausberg 1998, §§733, 933.
19 Fedeli 1989, 255; Barbu-Moravová 2000, 10–11.

unusual way of talking about emperor cult.[20] By suggesting the possibility of belief in a *divus*, Pliny shows that he is not critical of emperor cult in general, only of what he feels are cases of misapplication.[21] The idea that Augustus and Claudius, the first two *divi*, did not fully merit deification can be found in other texts as well. Pliny's contemporary Tacitus would write of grousing about Augustus' deification from his critics (*Ann*. 1.10.6), and the ways Tiberius allows alleged offenses against *divus Augustus* to become the subjects of *maiestas* trials – Pliny's exact criticism here – is a recurring theme in *Annals* 1–6.[22] Claudius' failure to merit real divinity is the joke that drives an entire Senecan text, the *Apocolocyntosis*: the gods refuse to admit the newly deceased *divus Claudius* to heaven, saying that no one will "believe" (*credet*) such an incompetent to be a god (*Apoc*. 11.3).[23] Pliny's criticism of the deifications of Vespasian and Titus perhaps suggests a real discomfort among the senators who were Pliny's audience for the *Panegyricus* with the deifications of the Flavian era,[24] here depicted as theocratic self-aggrandisement. It is important to note that Pliny is not suggesting that any of these *divi* should be removed from the pantheon; indeed, he later claims that Titus' actions against the *delatores* earned him his place among the stars (*Pan*. 35.4), and an inscription found near his hometown of Comum suggests he even served as *flamen divi Titi*.[25] But he claims Trajan's motives in requesting consecration for Nerva are the purest of any emperor who ever deified a predecessor, because his motivation is not self-aggrandising. Contrast the behaviour of Domitian, the obvious referent of *iis qui et sese deos putant*; Domitian's encouragement of the worship of himself cheapened the deification of Titus which he requested, but Trajan's continuous refusal of divine honours for himself lends legitimacy to his request of them for Nerva.

The distance Trajan constantly puts between himself and the divine, and how different this makes him from Domitian, is a theme that returns later in the speech. We are told that Trajan only allows a limited number of statues of himself, cast in a modest mortal's bronze, on the Capitoline, and insists that they stay

---

[20] Cf. Shannon-Henderson 2019, 341–344 on accusations that Thrasea Paetus did not believe Nero's wife Poppaea to be divine (Tac. *Ann*. 16.22.3: *Poppaeam divam non credere*).
[21] Schowalter 1993, 63–65.
[22] Cf. Durry 1938, 101. On *Ann*. 1.10.6 see Shannon-Henderson 2019, 30–35. On *maiestas* see ibid. 40–45, 50–56.
[23] On *Apoc*. and emperor cult see Gradel 2002, 325–330.
[24] Paladini 1962, 1201.
[25] *CIL* 5.5667; cf. Schowalter 1993, 34 n. 14.

outside in the vestibule of Jupiter's shrine like sentries;[26] that he never enters sanctuaries as anything other than a human worshipper (*Pan.* 52.2: *tu delubra non nisi adoraturus intras*; note the emphatic use of litotes that makes Trajan look superior to those emperors who, presumably, entered shrines to be worshipped themselves);[27] and that he refuses any worship of his own *genius*, preferring veneration be directed to Jupiter Optimus Maximus (*Pan.* 52.6). Domitian, on the other hand, had many statues in gold, silver and ivory of himself wearing a radiate crown installed all along the approach to the temple and throughout its courtyard (*Pan.* 52.3), to which he wanted victims be sacrificed (52.1: *augustioribusque aris et grandioribus victimis invocaretur*). He even diverted lines of sacrificial victims headed for the Capitoline and had them sacrificed before his own statue (*Pan.* 52.7), a sharp contrast with Trajan's modest attitude to statues of himself (*Pan.* 55).[28] Even before describing the sacrifices and statues Domitian demanded, Pliny primes us to see their inefficacy by reminding us that he could not protect himself from death. Referring obliquely to the fact that Domitian's assassination involved members of his household, Pliny says that although he tried to hide away in his palace, "he shut in with himself trickery, plotting, and a god who avenges crimes. Punishment moved aside and broke through the guards... Far away from him then was his divinity" (*Pan.* 49.1: *dolum secum et insidias et ultorem scelerum deum inclusit. Dimovit perfregitque custodias Poena... longe tunc illi divinitas sua*). Domitian is no match for the gods' punishment: "real divine agency... undoes Domitian's false sublimity".[29] In Clauss' terms, Domitian appropriated various "Zwischenstufen" but never climbed the ladder to true divinity; in Levene's (or Gradel's), because he failed to prove his (relative) divinity, he was destined to live and die among the emperors never worthy of godhead.

A secondary motive for Pliny's discussing Nerva's consecration seems to be to show that Trajan is also closer to being divine than Domitian ever was. For as Pliny outlines in the chapter preceding his discussion of Nerva's deification,

---

26 *Pan.* 52.2, with Moreno Soldevila 2010, 67 n. 394; *Pan.* 52.3; *Pan.* 55.6, with Kühn 1985, 192 and Moreno Soldevilla 2010, 72 n. 417.
27 Litotes, a rhetorical figure that "says less than it means" (Don. Ter. *Hec.* 775), "combin[es]... emphasis and irony" via "the filling-in of the intended meaning in stages"; Lausberg 1998, §586.
28 This is probably the equestrian statue of Domitian in the Forum mentioned by Statius *Silv.* 1; Durry 1938, 164; Malcovati 1949, 52. Cf. Suet. *Dom.* 15.2; Jones 1996, 125–126; Moreno Soldevila 2010, 68 n. 400. On Trajan and statues see Scott 1932, 163.
29 Hutchinson 2011, 129. Cf. *Pan.* 78.2 on the mortality of *principes* (i.e. Domitian) who believe themselves to be gods; Sordi 2003, 269; Moreno Soldevila 2010, 101 n. 535. On the idea of the revocation of divine protection from emperors who do not respect the Senate see Seelentag 2004, 237–238.

Nerva earned divinity by adopting Trajan.[30] Trajan had prayed to the gods to remain a private citizen (*privatus*) for as long as possible while Nerva reigned (*Pan.* 10.4), an important indicator of his modesty:[31]

> *Audita sunt tua vota, sed in quantum optimo illi et sanctissimo seni utile fuit, quem di ideo caelo vindicaverunt, ne quid post illud divinum et **immortale** factum **mortale** faceret: deberi quippe maximo operi hanc venerationem, ut novissimum esset, auctoremque eius statim consecrandum, ut quandoque inter posteros quaereretur, an illud iam deus fecisset.*
>
> Pan. 10.5

> Your prayers were heard, but only for as long as it was useful for that best and most holy old man, whom the gods claimed for heaven expressly so that he should do nothing mortal after that divine and immortal deed. For they thought that this greatest task deserved the honour of being Nerva's last, and that the deed's author had to be consecrated immediately so that someday future generations would ask whether he had already been a god when he performed it.

In *oratio obliqua* Pliny purports to give us the gods' own view[32] on why Nerva deserved deification: adopting Trajan was enough all by itself. Wordplay on *facere* emphasises that the adoption's status as *divinum... factum* is sufficient to prove its doer's divinity (*deus fecisset*), and Nerva's swiftly following death was designed to stop him from sullying this with any mortal action (a contrast emphasised by the rich combination of rhetorical figures in the phrase *post... immortale factum mortale faceret:* antithesis, anaphora and ABAB arrangement of elements).[33] Yet the effect of this assertion that Nerva earned his divinity through adoption paradoxically underscores his inferiority to the mortal person he adopted. Nerva's life had practically no purpose other than choosing a successor better than himself,[34] and Trajan has the power to make Nerva divine simply by being chosen. Even as Pliny shows Trajan performing that most mortal act of praying piously for long life for his father (10.3: *precarere*), what he actually achieves is "a blurring of status between Nerva as god-emperor (virtually already dead/deified) and Trajan as emperor-private citizen".[35] This is reinforced in the

---

[30] For speculation on the political realities behind the adoption see Fedeli 1989, 450; Cid López 1993, 58.
[31] See Rees 2001, 158 on the oxymoronic *privatus princeps* motif that pervades *Pan.*
[32] Cf. Durry 1938, 100.
[33] For antitheton of single words (here *immortale* and *mortale*) see Lausberg 1998, §§787–792. For anaphora not involving a noun (here with the verb *facio*), sometimes called *derivatio*, see Lausberg 1998, §648.
[34] Cf. Moreno Soldevila 2010, xlix–l.
[35] Hoffer 2006, 83.

following chapter when Pliny says, "in a *princeps* who yields to his fate after choosing a successor, the one surest proof of divinity is likewise a good successor" (*Pan.* 11.3: *in principe enim qui electo successore fato concessit, una itemque certissima divinitatis fides est bonus successor*). This sequence comes early in the speech, the place that in a panegyric should (according to the rhetoricians) be occupied by praise of the *laudandus*' ancestors: by focusing solely on Nerva's deification, Pliny "neatly assert[s] superhuman status right at the start".[36] From the first, then, and despite the repeated emphasis on Trajan's mortal modesty, Pliny makes clear that Nerva's divinity was deserved, while subtly suggesting that Trajan could one day join Nerva among the stars.

This point is made explicit later in the speech:

Ingenti quidem animo diuus Titus securitati nostrae ultionique prospexerat, ideoque numinibus aequatus est: sed quanto tu quandoque dignior caelo, qui tot res illis adiecisti, propter quas illum deum fecimus!... Quae singula quantum tibi gratiae dispensata adiecissent! At tu simul omnia profudisti, ut sol et dies non parte aliqua sed statim totus, nec uni aut alteri sed omnibus in commune profertur.

Pan. 35.4–5

Divine Titus had seen to our security and vengeance with magnanimous spirit, and for that reason was made equal to the divinities: but how much more worthy of heaven *you* will be one day, who have added so many things to the policies on account of which we made him into a god!... How much gratitude these measures would have brought you if they had been dispensed one by one! But you poured them all out at once, just as the sun and daylight is brought forth not just in one area but in its entirety at once, not to one man or another but to everyone in common.

Praise of a god for his or her "discoveries which brought something useful to mankind" is a *locus* recommended by Quintilian (*Inst.* 3.7.7: *inventa quae utile aliquid hominibus attulerint*); here we see Pliny applying this strategy not only to the god Titus but also to the mortal Trajan. It is significant that this statement comes in the context of the punishment of *delatores* who had victimised members of the senatorial class; Pliny notes with delight their banishment to the same desert islands to which their accusations had once exiled senators (*Pan.* 35.2). In attaching the earning of deification to Titus' and Nerva's actions in this arena, and in holding out promise of the same to Trajan for continuing to improve upon their policies, Pliny makes Trajan's eventual earning of divinity contingent specifically

---

[36] Braund 1998, 59. For the *genus* of the *laudandus* as an expected topic in epideictic praise speeches see Quint. *Inst.* 3.7.10–11 and Lausberg 1998, §245; cf. also Quint. *Inst.* 5.10.24.

upon his relationship with the Senate.³⁷ Yet any element of *quid pro quo* is left implicit. What *is* stated outright is that Trajan will one day deserve divinity even more than Titus did, and Pliny's closing simile suggests more subtly that he is already well on his way there. Likening Trajan's scattering of blessings to the sun's scattering of light over all mankind draws a parallel between the emperor and the sun-god, and suggests that even in life, Trajan's beneficence already puts him in a divine category.³⁸ Trajan is compared to a star (*sidus*) on two other occasions (*Pan.* 19.1; 80.3: *velocissimi sideris more omnia invisere omnia audire*).³⁹ These comparisons not only lend Trajan the generative powers and omniscience of the life-giving, all-seeing sun,⁴⁰ but they also evoke the practice of deification, which had carried with it the notion of placing an emperor-god among the stars (cf. *Pan.* 11.2: *tu sideribus patrem intulisti*) ever since the *sidus Iulium* sighted at the death of Julius Caesar was taken to prove he had become a god.

To deserve eventual deification, then, an emperor must: have eschewed (or at least not have encouraged) worship of himself during his lifetime; have ensured he would be followed by a successor at least as good as himself; and above all, have ruled beneficently, taking especial care to treat the Senate with respect. But in the course of establishing these principles, Pliny's secondary purpose is to make it clear that Trajan satisfies these conditions already, even surpassing his deified predecessors. Early in his reign, he has begun to make his divinity abundantly clear.

3 Hercules, heroes and the attainment of divinity

Another of Pliny's rhetorical strategies for Trajan's prospective deification is to compare him to gods of the traditional pantheon.⁴¹ The most important of these is, of course, Jupiter, whom I will consider below; less obvious but equally important *comparanda* are Hercules and other unnamed heroes of Greek mythology. The comparison to Hercules comes early in the speech when Pliny discusses

---

37 Scott 1932, 163; Schowalter 1993, 65–66; Backhuys et al. 2013, 487. Cf. Seelentag 2004, 226.
38 Bartsch 1994, 164; Backhuys et al. 2013, 487.
39 For the comparison as an assertion of Trajan's divinity, cf. Kersten/Syré 2013, 433–434.
40 See Moreno Soldevila 2010, 103 n. 546 and comparisons there cited for these ideas applied to the sun elsewhere in ancient literature.
41 For the use of *exemplum*, a type of *similitudo*, see Lausberg 1998, §§415–425.

Trajan's military career prior to becoming emperor, specifically the moment when he was summoned from Spain by Domitian to settle a mutiny in Germany:[42]

> Nec dubito quin ille... tantam admirationem tui non sine quodam timore conceperit, quantam ille genitus Iove post saevos labores duraque imperia regi suo indomitus semper indefessusque referebat, cum aliis super alias expeditionibus itinere illo dignus invenireris.
> Pan. 14.5

> I do not doubt that he... conceived (not without some fear) as great an admiration for you as the admiration that the man born of Jupiter, always undefeated and unfatigued after savage labours and harsh commands, brought home to his king, since because of that journey you were found worthy of campaign after campaign.

"The man born of Jupiter" tasked with many labours that took him on long journeys is clearly *antonomasia* for Hercules. This is one of only two references to Greek mythology in the *Panegyricus*,[43] but Hercules is not a surprising choice: as a symbol of a civilising force who could restore order to the furthest corners of the world by subduing monsters, Hercules had a long history of being compared to rulers.[44] But for Trajan, Hercules is particularly significant: according to myth, in the context of his Tenth Labour involving the cattle of Geryon, Hercules travelled eastward from Spain into Italy. There was an important sanctuary of Hercules at Gades, and Trajan, born in Spain, seems to have encouraged people to think of that connection by showing Hercules on his coins as early as AD 100.[45] Just as Hercules travelled from Spain to Rome to destroy the monster Cacus (e.g. Vergil, *Aen.* 8.201–204), Trajan was summoned from Spain to settle disorder. Furthermore, Pliny also refers to the king who assigned Hercules his labours: Eurystheus, here implicitly compared to Domitian. This increases sympathy for Trajan for successfully carrying out the orders of a tyrannical figure, denigrates Domitian for his harsh demands and suggests that "Domitian held Trajan in great admiration for his deeds, but also lived in fear of his competence, feeling the same mixed emotions towards him that Hercules inspired in Eurystheus".[46] But there is also a third important resonance to the comparison: Hercules, admitted to Olympus for his achievements, is the example *par excellence* of a human who

---

42 For the situation see Bennett 1997, 44.
43 Rees 2014, 113; the other is *Pan.* 82.7, discussed below.
44 Durry 1938, 108; Fedeli 1989, 486; Alvar 2003, 201.
45 Braund 1998, 67; Seelentag 2004, 286–287.
46 Bennett 1997, 44. See also Seelentag 2004, 285.

earned divinity through meritorious conduct and is therefore particularly significant for emperor cult.[47] Pliny's oscillation throughout the *Panegyricus* between emphasising Trajan's humanity and his divine qualities puts him in the same liminal mortal-immortal status.[48] Thus Pliny's comparison of Trajan with Hercules is another way for him to reinforce the idea of his eventual divinity: Hercules shed his humanity and earned his place in heaven[49] by executing difficult tasks, and so will Trajan.

Even Trajan's leisure activities move him toward the realm of the divine. In *Pan.* 81–82, Pliny praises Trajan for spending his free time on the wholesome and active pursuits of hunting and sailing, unlike his predecessors who wasted their idle hours "on dicing, sex and luxury" (*Pan.* 82.9: *in aleam, stupra, luxum*):

> ego... et laetum opere corpus et crescentia laboribus membra mirabor. video enim iam inde antiquitus maritos dearum ac deum liberos nec <parentum divinitate nec> dignitate nuptiarum magis quam his artibus inclaruisse.
>
> *Pan.* 82.6–7

> I... shall admire a body that exults in hard work and limbs that grow from labours.... For I see that ever since ancient times, the husbands of goddesses and children of gods have grown famous no more from the divinity of their parents or the impressiveness of their marriages than from these skills.

While Quintilian marks bodily *robur* as a praiseworthy quality in a *laudandus* that can be included in an epideictic speech of praise (*Inst.* 3.7.12), Pliny's admiration is not simply praise of Trajan's physically demanding pastimes for their own sake, but actually an important means of showing that Trajan is like the gods. Many mortal heroes married to goddesses (e.g. Peleus) and semi-divine offspring of such unions (e.g. Achilles) are known for hunting.[50] Pliny does not name any specific individuals, but we might be meant to think particularly of Hercules the "civilising hunter", six of whose twelve labours involved killing a wild animal or monster.[51] Pliny's reference to "labours" (*laboribus*), a repetition of the same word used of Hercules' tasks in *Pan.* 14.5 (*labores*), also suggests that Hercules is meant. This encourages the reader to think again of Trajan as Hercules, and can

---

47 For Hercules' deification and its similarities to emperor cult see Gradel 2002, 321. See also Levene 2012, 55, 59.
48 Moreno Soldevila 2010, lviii; cf. Fedeli 1989, 486.
49 Levene 2012, 55, 59.
50 For other examples see Malcovati 1949, 85; Kühn 1985, 195; Manolaraki 2012, 185.
51 Manolaraki 2012, 185.

be read as "a delicate hint that Trajan too will earn deification".[52] Greek demigods and heroes were famous not just because of their divine parents or wives, but because of their meritorious actions; Trajan, too, it is implied, by being the kind of emperor who hunts in his free time, can expect one day to become a god like Hercules.

4 Jupiter: Protector or equal?

Jupiter is without a doubt the god who plays the biggest role in the *Panegyricus*. Pliny opens the speech with a prayer to Jupiter, addressed as *optime* (*Pan.* 1.6), in thanks for his special role in selecting Trajan. Pliny suggests that Jupiter had a hand in Trajan's accession, putting the *optimus princeps* under the protection of the chief god of the Roman state religion:

> *Quod enim praestabilius est aut pulchrius munus deorum, quam castus et sanctus et dis simillimus princeps? ... Non enim <u>occulta</u> **potestate fatorum**, sed **ab Iove ipso** <u>coram ac palam</u> repertus electus est: quippe inter aras et altaria, eodemque loci quem deus ille tam manifestus ac praesens quam caelum ac sidera insedit.*
>
> *Pan.* 1.3, 5

> For what gift of the gods is more outstanding or more beautiful than a *princeps* who is pure, holy, and very similar to the gods? ... For he was found and chosen not by the fates' hidden power, but by Jupiter himself, openly and without intermediary, seeing that it happened among altars and altar-fittings, and in the same place which that god inhabits as clearly and with as much presence as he occupies the heaven and the stars.

The motif of Trajan as *dis simillimus* will recur later in the speech at *Pan.* 7.5, but there the phrase gives Nerva's rationale for choosing him. Here Trajan is explicitly referred to as the gods' gift rather than Nerva's choice, and his succession is touted as the example powerful enough to settle the long-held debate about whether the gods take an active role in human affairs or simply leaves things to chance (*Pan.* 1.4).[53] In Trajan's case it is clearly Jupiter and not the Fates who is in charge, as emphasised by Pliny's use of chiastic word order.[54] The proof of Jupiter's involvement, Pliny says, is the location of Trajan's adoption: not just in Ju-

---

52 Innes 2011, 82. Cf. Sordi 2003, 270.
53 Cf. Fears 1977, 15.
54 For chiastic arrangement of elements see Lausberg 1998, §723.

piter's sanctuary but at the altar and the *altaria* (a word designating either a receptacle for offerings or the offerings themselves), the parts of the sanctuary most directly connected to cult activity where centuries of annual sacrifices to Jupiter had been performed.[55] Similar themes are reprised in *Pan.* 8, where Pliny discusses the adoption, which occurred "not in a bedroom but in a temple, and not before a conjugal bed but before the couch of Jupiter Optimus Maximus" (*Pan.* 8.1: *non in cubiculo sed in templo, nec ante genialem torum sed ante pulvinar Iovis optimi maximi*): Trajan's adoption's legitimacy is undergirded by the fact that it takes place at a site of cult activity, here the god's *pulvinar*, and even while a ritual act is being performed. As Nerva was depositing into the lap of Jupiter's statue the victory laurel Trajan had brought back from his campaign in Pannonia,[56] he "suddenly appeared taller and more distinguished than usual, and called a council of humans and gods" to complete the adoption (*Pan.* 8.3: *repente solito maior augustiorque advocata contione hominum deorumque*). This vivid description makes it sound as though Jupiter's power somehow entered Nerva at the moment of Trajan's adoption.[57] While in *Pan.* 1 no direct mention was made of Nerva, here he is explicitly described as the agent of the gods, whose control is emphasised by the insistent anaphora of *horum*: "for the gods have claimed that glory for themselves; this was *their* task, *their* order. Nerva was only their servant, and in adopting you was following orders just as much as you were in being adopted" (*Pan.* 8.2: *sibi enim gloriam illam di vindicaverunt: horum opus, horum illud imperium. Nerva tantum minister fuit, utque adoptaret, tam paruit quam tu qui adoptabaris*). Trajan and Nerva, in their positions as initiator and object of the adoption (note the repetition *adoptaret… adoptabaris*),[58] both obey Jupiter as any good mortal should; Pliny's motif of Trajan's election by Jupiter thus has the twin effects of emphasising his divinely-ordained specialness while also keeping a separation between the emperor and the god. Indeed, one of the reasons for the prominence Pliny gives to Jupiter is probably a "desire to pull back from the way in which Domitian had too obviously assumed various aspects of Jupiter in his self-presentation".[59] This is reinforced midway through the speech, when in discussing the worship of Domitian's statues Pliny is sure to emphasise that Trajan does not allow himself to be thanked with prayers to his *genius*, instead wanting

---

55 *OLD*, s.v. *altaria* 1, 2; cf. Shannon-Henderson 2019, 346 on Tac. *Ann.* 16.33.1.
56 Malcovati 1949, 9; Kühn 1985, 186; Bennett 1997, 45–46; Moreno Soldevila 2010, 12 n. 74.
57 Henderson 2011, 150.
58 On *polyptoton* of words other than nouns see above, n. 34.
59 Gibson 2011, 114. Cf. Gangloff 2019, 147 on Domitian's self-aggrandising devotion to Jupiter Custos/Jupiter Conservator, who allegedly helped him survive the burning of the Capitoline unscathed in AD 70 (Tac. *Hist.* 3.74.1).

them to be directed to Jupiter Optimus Maximus (*Pan.* 52.6). Trajan is depicted as attempting to restore the proper emperor-Jupiter hierarchy that Domitian disrupted,[60] as being under Jupiter's special protection, but not on the same plane.[61]

Yet in three passages toward the end of the speech, Pliny suggests that Trajan is on a level with Jupiter, or even poised to replace some of his functions. The first comes in the context of Pliny's discussion of Trajan's third consulship and his hope that the emperor will take up a fourth:

> *Talia esse crediderim, quae ille mundi parens temperat nutu, si quando oculos demisit in terras, et fata mortalium inter divina opera numerare dignatus est; qua nunc parte liber solutusque tantum caelo vacat, postquam te dedit, qui erga omne hominum genus vice sua fungereris. Fungeris enim sufficisque mandanti.*
>
> *Pan.* 80.4–5

> I would believe that these are the sorts of things the parent of the universe controls with a nod, if he has ever cast down his eyes upon the earth and deigned to reckon mortals' fates among his divine tasks; but now in this quarter he is free and unconstrained, and has leisure to deal with heaven alone, after giving us you to act in his stead in respect to the whole human race. And you *are* filling his role, and are enough to meet the needs of the one giving the order.

Trajan's swift and decisive actions in the administration of justice, emphasised by comparison with an all-seeing star (*Pan.* 80.3), put him in the same category as Jupiter, the referent by antonomasia of *ille mundi parens*. Jupiter is frequently said to be able to control the entire cosmos with one powerful nod.[62] Here Trajan's actions as consul – subduing foreigners, mediating provincial disputes, stopping magistrates' unfair behaviour and nullifying unjust policies (*Pan.* 80.3) – are compared to this absolute divine power; for this *princeps dis simillimus*, discharging the duties of Rome's highest magistracy is as easy as nodding. This motif of divine nodding has been applied to Trajan twice in the speech already.[63] So has the notion that Jupiter intervenes benevolently in mortal affairs (*Pan.* 1.4), and that he has given Trajan to Rome as part of that stewardship.[64] Yet whereas before Pliny made sure to emphasise that Trajan was only a mortal put in place by the gods, here he sets Trajan apart from humanity: it seems Trajan himself is not included in the *omne hominum genus* for whom he acts on Jupiter's behalf.[65] Jupiter

---

60 Alvar 2003, 196; cf. Schowalter 1993, 74; Cid López 1993, 57.
61 Brunt 1979, 172; Fedeli 1989, 484–485; Montero 2000, 19–20.
62 E.g. Cic. *Rosc.* 131, Verg. *Aen.* 9.106, and (of Zeus) Homer *Il.* 1.528–30.
63 *Pan.* 4.4; *Pan.* 78.4, with Schowalter 1993, 55–56; Levene 1997, 81.
64 *Pan.* 1.3; 8.2; 52.6.
65 Hoffer 2006, 76–77.

has made such a good choice of viceroy that he is now out of a job in the earthly realm. As Levene puts it, "now the concern is not to show Trajan's common touch, but the fact that he administers the empire unaffected by human cupidity and injustice. Correspondingly he is now tied more closely still to the divine".[66]

The impression that Trajan serves as an earthly Jupiter is strengthened when he is offered the god's very name. Eight chapters later Pliny discusses the conferral of the title *Optimus* upon Trajan, perhaps in an attempt to convince a hesitant Trajan that it is permissible for him to accept it, something he would not officially do until AD 114.[67] Pliny notes that *Optimus* was "available and common, but nevertheless new" (*Pan.* 88.4: *paratum... et in medio positum, novum tamen*) and hence preferable to sobriquets like *Felix* and *Magnus* used by famous generals of the Republic, none of which is quite good enough to capture all Trajan's positive qualities (*Pan.* 88.5–6).[68] But any notion that this is an ordinary name is swiftly undercut:

> *Merito tibi ergo post ceteras adpellationes haec est addita ut maior. Minus est enim imperatorem et Caesarem et Augustum quam omnibus imperatoribus et Caesaribus et Augustis esse meliorem. Ideoque ille parens hominum deorumque Optimi prius nomine, deinde Maximi colitur. Quo praeclarior laus tua, quem non minus constat optimum esse quam maximum.*
>
> *Pan.* 88.7–8

> Therefore you deserve having this name added after other titles, because it is greater. For it is less to be "commander" and "Caesar" and "Augustus" than it is to be better than all commanders, Caesars and Augusti. It is for the same reason that parent of humans and gods is worshipped first under the name "Best", then under the name "Greatest". Praise of you will be all the more splendid, you who are agreed to be no less the Best than you are the Greatest.

Trajan's superiority to all previous emperors is explicitly compared (*ideoque*) to the claim of Jupiter, universal progenitor, to be called "Best" and "Greatest"; Trajan is as far above all other emperors as Jupiter is above all other beings, human and divine.[69] But in that final sentence, Pliny leaves an ambiguity: Trajan's praise is said to be "more splendid", but what is the point of comparison? Probably previous *imperatores*, *Caesares* and *Augusti*; but the intrusion of Jupiter in the intervening sentence leaves open the possibility that Pliny wishes to say that Trajan's praise is even greater than that of Jupiter. The language is just fuzzy enough to

---

66 Levene 1997, 82. Cf. Hutchinson 2011, 132; Kersten/Syré 2013, 433–434.
67 Schowalter 1993, 40–44; see also Rees 2001, 160.
68 On the important implications of this statement see Seelentag 2004, 243–244.
69 Cf. Seelentag 2004, 243.

offer plausible deniability while also allowing Pliny to make the comparison between Trajan and Jupiter implicit in the reader's mind. So despite all his disclaimers about the ordinariness of the word *Optimus*, Pliny knows what he is doing.[70]

In the prayer to Jupiter at the end of the speech, Pliny fuses together the sometimes antithetical claims and suggestions he has been making about Trajan's relationship to Jupiter. Strikingly, the god is addressed as "Capitoline Jupiter" (*Pan.* 94.1), not as Jupiter Optimus as he was at the start (*Pan.* 1.6); as Gibson notes, "[o]ne effect of the different cult titles used at the beginning and end of the speech is to suggest that the title Optimus is in fact being reassigned away from Jupiter to Trajan himself".[71] Pliny explicitly brings up the topic of name-changes later in the prayer as he recounts Jupiter's past benefactions to Trajan: "you sent clear signals of your judgment when you yielded your name and your honour to him when he was setting out to the army" (*Pan.* 94.4: *tu clara iudicii tui signa misisti, cum proficiscenti ad exercitum tuo nomine tuo honore cessisti*). The statement that Jupiter handed over his name to Trajan refers to an accidental omen prefiguring his adoption, when Trajan climbed the Capitoline Hill and the crowd's cry of "*Imperator*!" meant for Jupiter was interpreted as a prediction of Trajan's eventual ascension to the throne (*Pan.* 5.2–4).[72] So the Jovian name to which Pliny refers here in the closing prayer is probably *Imperator* and not *Optimus*; but because Pliny does not say so explicitly, the reader may be more apt to link the statement with the name-handover of *Optimus* discussed more recently. This closing prayer has an element of ring composition, since it recalls the opening prayer in *Pan.* 1, and the closure has elements of the same drive to show that Trajan stands firmly on the mortal plane and is not one of the gods.[73] Yet the quite different implications of *Pan.* 80 and 88 are still ringing in our ears, and an alert auditor cannot help but notice that the handing over of Jupiter's title *Optimus* is now being performed before our eyes.

---

[70] Cf. Gowing 2005, 124.
[71] Gibson 2010, 132; cf. Gibson 2011, 114.
[72] Montero 2000, 20–21. This possibly occurred as part of the ceremonies before his departure to one of the Germanies in AD 96–97; Durry 1938, 91; Montero 2000, 21; Moreno Soldevila 2010, 8 n. 45.
[73] Gibson 2010, 125–126.

5 Trajan in time and space: Surpassing divinity

One final strategy Pliny uses to nudge Trajan toward the divine is perhaps the most extreme: he sometimes suggests that Trajan not only is on a level with the gods or has earned the right to become a *divus* after his death, but even that he has abilities *superior* to those of the gods. Building on the images of the star or the power-nod that suggest Trajan's divine qualities, these passages grant Trajan powers over space, time and nature that are said to surpass those of the gods. Here both Clauss' "Zwischenstufen" and Gradel's "relative divinity" break down as useful models for understanding what Pliny is doing. These assertions suggest not that Trajan is midway up a ladder connecting human and divine, but that he has already ascended it and is heading for whatever the next level is after "god"; not that Trajan's superior abilities and benefactions make him divine relative to humans only, but even that he might be a super-god relative to other gods.

One such quality is Trajan's ability to collapse geographical distance in his quest to distribute sustenance to the Empire. This is first hinted at in Pliny's discussion of Trajan's distribution of the *congiarium* to all plebeians, even if they are prevented by sickness, business, distance or adverse weather from coming to Rome (*Pan.* 25.4): "it is magnificent, Caesar, and typical of you, to as it were bring the most separated lands into contact through your ingenuity for generosity, and to shrink immense distances with your magnanimity" (*Pan.* 25.5: *magnificum, Caesar, et tuum disiunctissimas terras munificentiae ingenio velut admovere, immensaque spatia liberalitate contrahere*). Pliny implies, but does not state outright, that Trajan has divine qualities[74] by attributing to him the superhuman ability to join land masses and shrink insurmountable distances. He deploys the literary device of adynaton, which the rhetoricians say can be detrimental to one's argument,[75] but softens the blow with *velut*. But any hedging disappears when Pliny reprises the motif a few chapters later (*Pan.* 30–32) in his discussion of Trajan's response to a disastrous failure of the annual Nile flood, and the potential crop failure in the Empire's breadbasket and famine in Egypt and Rome itself that could have ensued without Trajan's intervention.[76] "Egypt then prayed for clouds and looked to the sky in vain" (*Pan.* 30.3: *frustra tunc Aegyptus nubile optavit caelumque respexit*) before turning its entreaties in a different direction: "therefore the region deprived of its flood, that is of its fertility, invoked the help

---

74 Moreno Soldevila 2010, lvii; cf. Rees 2001, 153 n. 30; Hutchinson 2011, 130.
75 See Lausberg 1998, §515, especially Aristotle, *Poetics* 1460a26 there cited.
76 Pliny does not specify a date, but probably refers to events of AD 99; see Blouin 2004.

of Caesar as it usually invokes its own river" (*Pan.* 30.5: *igitur inundatione, id est ubertate, regio fraudata sic opem Caesaris invocavit, ut solet amnem suum*). Trajan's solution to the problem was to reverse the longstanding practice of Egypt's providing grain for Rome and send supplies from the capital to the province: "we have given the Nile back its own abundance: it receives the grain which it had sent, and conveys back upriver the harvests it had once brought down" (*Pan.* 31.3: *refudimus Nilo suas copias: recepit frumenta quae miserat, deportatasque messes revexit*). This impossible-seeming action redounds to Trajan's credit:

> Et caelo quidem numquam benignitas tanta, ut omnes simul terras uberet foveatque: hic omnibus pariter si non sterilitatem, at mala sterilitatis exturbat, hic si non fecunditatem, at bona fecunditatis importat, hic alternis commeatibus Orientem Occidentemque conectit.
>
> *Pan.* 32.2–3
>
> Heaven never had such great kindness as to enrich and nurture all lands at the same time; but this man removes, if not barrenness itself, at least the evils of barrenness, and brings in, if not fertility itself, at least the benefits of fertility, for everyone equally, and connects West and East in alternating journeys.

Pliny is probably exaggerating the nature of Trajan's response for dramatic effect. It is more likely that the Prefect of Egypt (with the emperor's permission) would simply have released to the Egyptian markets surplus grain stored in Alexandria; but by claiming the grain was imported all the way from Rome, Pliny is able to present as "miraculous" what was probably a perfectly prosaic solution to the possible famine.[77] The result is that this sequence pits Trajan against the river-god of the Nile, and the emperor comes out indubitably ahead. While it was not unusual for a good Egyptian harvest to be attributed to the gods' favour for a king or emperor,[78] Trajan here replaces the Nile and surpasses it in power. When prayers to the Nile go unanswered, the Egyptians invoke Trajan instead, and he delivers the desired result. We also see several geographical adynata like those in *Pan.* 25, and Trajan's interventions in moving supplies from one place to another is "describe[d]… in terms of superhuman powers".[79] His solution to the problem reverses the normal direction of grain ships travelling along the Nile, as though Trajan is forcing the river and its god to reverse their course, and the swift movement of grain from West to East collapses the edges of the empire into one another. More strikingly, Trajan is said to be even more beneficent than "heaven"

---

[77] Blouin 2004, 44–45.
[78] Montero 2000, 42–43; Gangloff 2019, 199.
[79] Braund 1998, 64.

(*caelo*);⁸⁰ while the primary referent of *caelo* may be the climate or weather, it also signifies the gods collectively or their dwelling-place,⁸¹ especially in light of the Egyptians' vain prayers for rain while watching the sky (*Pan.* 30.3: *caelum*). The divine powers of the Nile and the Egyptian earth are admonished not to test the emperor's generosity again, and to do their jobs in the future so that he will not have to intervene (*Pan.* 32.3); this reinforces the notion that Trajan's power is superior to theirs. While it is of course true that Pliny's diminishing of the Nile's divine and nourishing powers may be motivated at least in part by anti-Egyptian xenophobia,⁸² it also has the effect of raising Trajan to a plane above that of the river-god in his beneficent command of the entire known world.

Trajan has super-divine powers over not only space, but also time: he has the power to change not only the future,⁸³ but also the past, a capacity that is explicitly denied to the gods. Trajan is praised for not only cancelling the 5% inheritance tax (*vicesima*) but also applying the exemption retroactively:

> in praeteritum subvenire ne di quidem possunt: tu tamen subvenisti cavistique ut desineret quisque debere, quod <nemo> esset postea debiturus, idem effecisti ne malos principes habuissemus. Quo ingenio, si natura pateretur, quam libenter tot spoliatis tot trucidatis bona et sanguinem refudisses!
>
> Pan. 40.3–4

> Not even the gods can remedy the past; but nevertheless, you remedied it, and saw to it that everyone should cease to owe a tax that no one would have to pay again, and likewise brought it about that we might never have had evil *principes*. With what glad disposition, if nature allowed it, would you have restored their goods to all those who were robbed, and their blood to all those who were slaughtered!

The repetition of the infinitive *subvenire* in its perfect tense form *subvenisti*, followed by the similar recapitulation of the infinitive *debere* with a periphrastic future form *esset... debiturus*,⁸⁴ mimics on a verbal level the way Trajan's actions have fixed not only the future but the past as well. Trajan's ability to turn back time, as Pliny's hyperbolising⁸⁵ description of the retroactive tax remittance goes, "suggests that Trajan has outdone even the gods".⁸⁶ And it is not merely previous

---

80 Cf. Schowalter 1993, 78, Rees 2001, 163; Hoffer 2006, 84.
81 *OLD* s.v. *caelum* 6–7; 3. See Hoffer 2006, 84.
82 Molin 1989, 789; Fedeli 1989, 469–470.
83 Cf. the claim at *Pan.* 26.4 that Trajan "will merit immortality" (*immortalitatemque merituro*) because he provides for the future when he distributes the *congiarium* to poor children.
84 On repetition of verbs in different forms see above, n. 33.
85 So Aubrion 1975, 119.
86 Braund 1998, 64; cf. Rees 2001, 163.

taxation practices that Trajan is able to change: this is tantamount to erasing the *mali principes* of the past as if they had never existed. Trajan, of course, cannot fix all the evils of the past, in that he cannot bring people back from the dead; presumably the final sentence refers to those who lost both their property and their lives to the *delatores* under Domitian and other bad emperors. Even the gods are said to be incapable of such resurrections or of preventing mortals' deaths,[87] but the ability to rewrite history with one tax policy gives Trajan the power to change aspects of the past that even the gods could not.

6 Conclusions

I hope to have demonstrated that in the *Panegyricus*, Pliny uses a variety of strategies to suggest, imply or state outright that Trajan has divine qualities and abilities that will one day earn him deification. Various "Zwischenstufen" between humanity and divinity are tried out: likening Trajan to an all-seeing star or the powerfully nodding father of the gods, comparing him to semi-divine Hercules, and ultimately reassigning Jupiter's title *Optimus* to him. Pliny likewise emphasises Trajan's divinity relative to other Romans, previous emperors, and other gods and *divi* by praising his outsized benefactions to the entire Empire and attributing to him super-divine powers over nature, distance and time. This has to be done with subtlety, because another part of Trajan's merit is his rejection of the theocratic (especially Jovian) strategies of self-aggrandisement practiced by Domitian.

While this assertion of humility may seem at odds with the rhetoric of prospective deification, for Pliny they are inextricably interconnected. In describing Trajan's entry into Rome as emperor, Pliny notes that while other emperors were carried in litters, Trajan humbly goes on foot: "that soil, common to all of us and mingled with a *princeps*' footsteps, raises you to the stars" (*Pan.* 24.5: *te ad sidera tollit humus ista communis et confusa principis vestigia*). Some scholars have dismissed the idea of Trajan being raised to the stars as hyperbole, a rhetorical figure meant as a form of praise and not to be understood literally.[88] Yet the phrase *ad sidera tollere* directly recalls Trajan's actual deification of Nerva (*Pan.* 11.2: *tu sideribus patrem intulisti*), meaning that we must take this seriously as a potential

---

[87] The example from epic *par excellence* is Zeus's inability to save his son Sarpedon from death (*Il.* 16.431–461).
[88] Aubrion 1975, 119; Gamberini 1983, 414; Soverini 1989, 538; Barbu-Moravová 2000, 7.

reference to Trajan's apotheosis,[89] especially when combined with the other Trajan-as-star imagery found in the speech. The paradoxical idea that walking upon common ground with the rest of the populace is what raises Trajan up to the stars is a good summation of Pliny's attitude to what makes a *divus*. For someone writing (and an audience listening/reading) within a religious culture that placed no absolute boundaries between human emperor and god, and in a political context where Rome's elite were recovering from a previous regime that combined religious self-aggrandisement with hostility to the Senate, this paradox makes perfect sense, and is perhaps in fact the only way Pliny could have convincingly addressed these issues. Rather than emphasising one side of the paradox or the other, we should rather acknowledge that the contrast itself *is* the essential theological work done by the text, as it shines a light exactly into those dim corners where human meets divine.

Bibliography

Alvar, J. (2003), 'Trajano y las religiones del Imperio', in: J. Alvar/J.M. Blázquez (eds.), *Trajano*, Madrid, 189–212.
Aubrion, É. (1975), 'Pline le Jeune et la rhétorique de l'affirmation', in: *Latomus* 34, 90–130.
Backhuys, T./Leiendecker, T./Rödder, S. (2013), '*Pulchrum spectaculum – exsecrabile spectaculum*: Ein Beispiel für das Herrscherlob im *Panegyricus* des Plinius (33–36)', in: *Hermes* 141, 476–490.
Barbu-Moravová, M. (2000), 'Trajan as an Ideal Ruler in Pliny's Panegyric', in: *Graecolatina Pragensia* 18, 7–18.
Bartsch, S. (1994), *Actors in the Audience: Theatricality and Doublespeak from Nero to Hadrian*, Cambridge, MA.
Bennett, J. (1997), *Trajan, Optimus Princeps: A Life and Times*, London.
Blouin, K. (2004), 'L'Égypte, grenier de Rome? Pour une relecture des paragraphes 30 à 32 du Panégyrique de Trajan de Pline le Jeune', in: *Cahiers des Études Anciennes* 61, 28–51.
Braund, S.M. (1998), 'Praise and Protreptic in Early Imperial Panegyric: Cicero, Seneca, Pliny', in: M. Whitby (ed.), *The Propaganda of Power: the Role of Panegyric in Late Antiquity*, Leiden, 53–76.
Brunt, P.A. (1979), 'Divine Elements in the Imperial Office', in: *Journal of Roman Studies* 69, 168–175.
Cid López, R.M. (1993), 'El culto imperial en la época de Trajano', in: J. González Fernández (ed.), *Imp. Caes. Nerva Traianus Aug.*, Madrid, 49–75.
Clauss, M. (1999), *Kaiser und Gott: Herrscherkult im römischen Reich*, Stuttgart.
Durry, M. (1938), *Pline le Jeune, Panégyrique de Trajan*, Paris.
Fears, J.R. (1977), *Princeps a Diis Electus: The Divine Election of the Emperor*, Rome.

---

89 Schowalter 1993, 77–78; Hutchinson 2011, 133.

Fedeli, P. (1989), 'Il Panegirico di Plinio nella critica moderna', in: *Aufstieg und Niedergang der Römischen Welt* 2.33.1, 387–514.
Fell, M. (1992), *Optimus princeps? Anspruch und Wirklichkeit der imperialen Programmatik Kaiser Traians*, Munich.
Gamberini, F. (1983), *Stylistic Theory and Practice in the Younger Pliny*, Hildesheim.
Gangloff, A. (2019), *Pouvoir impérial et vertus philosophiques: l'évolution de la figure du bon prince sous le Haut-Empire*, Leiden.
Gibson, B. (2011), 'Contemporary Contexts', in: P.A. Roche (ed.), *Pliny's Praise: The Panegyricus in the Roman World*, Cambridge, 104–124.
Gibson, B. (2010), 'Unending Praise: Pliny and Ending Panegyric', in: D.H. Berry/A. Erskine, *Form and Function in Roman Oratory*, Cambridge, 122–136.
Gowing, A.M. (2005), *Empire and Memory: The Representation of the Roman Republic in Imperial Culture*, Cambridge.
Gradel, I. (2002), *Emperor Worship and Roman Religion*, Oxford.
Henderson, J. (2011), 'Down the Pan: Historical Exemplarity in the *Panegyricus*', in: P.A. Roche (ed.), *Pliny's Praise: The Panegyricus in the Roman World*, Cambridge, 142–174.
Hoffer, S.E. (2006), 'Divine Comedy? Accession Propaganda in Pliny, *Epistles* 10.1–2 and the *Panegyric*', in: *Journal of Roman Studies* 96, 73–87.
Hutchinson, G.O. (2011), 'Politics and the Sublime in the *Panegyricus*', in: P.A. Roche (ed.), *Pliny's Praise: The Panegyricus in the Roman World*, Cambridge, 125–141.
Innes, D.C. (2011), 'The *Panegyricus* and Rhetorical Theory', in: P.A. Roche (ed.), *Pliny's Praise: The Panegyricus in the Roman World*, Cambridge, 67–84.
Jones, B.W. (1996), *Suetonius: Domitian*, London.
Kersten, M./Syré, E. (2013), 'Trajan, sein Pferd, sein Triumph und ein verschlungener Weg zu den Göttern: zur Poetik der Apotheose im *Panegyricus* des jüngeren Plinius', in: *Göttinger Forum für Altertumswissenschaft* 16, 419–436.
Kühn, W. (1985), *Plinius der Jüngere, Panegyrikus: Lobrede auf den Kaiser Trajan*, Darmstadt.
Lausberg, H. (1998), *Handbook of Literary Rhetoric: A Foundation for Literary Study*, tr. D.E. Orton and R.D. Anderson, Leiden.
Levene, D.S. (1997), 'God and Man in the Classical Latin Panegyric', in: *Proceedings of the Cambridge Philological Society* 43, 66–103.
Levene, D.S. (2012), 'Defining the Divine in Rome: In Memoriam S.R.F. Price', in: *Transactions of the American Philological Association* 142, 41–81.
Malcovati, E. (1949), *Plinio il Giovane: Il Panegirico di Traiano*, Florence.
Manolaraki, E. (2012), 'Imperial and Rhetorical Hunting in Pliny's *Panegyricus*', in: *Illinois Classical Studies* 37, 175–198.
Molin, M. (1989), 'Le "Panégyrique de Trajan": éloquence d'apparat ou programme politique néo-stoïcien?', in: *Latomus* 48, 785–797.
Montero, S. (2000), *Trajano y la adivinación: prodigios, oráculos y apocalíptica en el Imperio Romano*, Madrid.
Moreno Soldevila, R. (2010), *Plinio el Joven, Panegírico de Trajano*, Madrid.
Paladini, M.L. (1962), 'Divinizzazione di Traiano padre', in: *Hommages à A. Grenier*, Brussels, 1194–1206.
Price, S.R.F. (1984), *Rituals and Power: The Roman Imperial Cult in Asia Minor*, Cambridge.
Radice, B. (1968), 'Pliny and the *Panegyricus*', in: *Greece & Rome* 15, 166–172.
Rees, R. (2001), 'To Be and Not to Be: Pliny's Paradoxical Trajan', in: *Bulletin of the Institute of Classical Studies* 45, 149–168.

Rees, R. (2014), 'Adopting the Emperor: Pliny's Praise-giving as Cultural Appropriation', in: J. Majbom Madsen/R. Rees, *Roman Rule in Greek and Latin Writing: Double Vision*, Leiden, 105–123.

Roche, P.A. (2011), 'Pliny's Thanksgiving: An Introduction to the *Panegyricus*', in: P.A. Roche (ed.), *Pliny's Praise: The Panegyricus in the Roman World*, Cambridge, 1–28.

Ronning, C. (2007), *Herrscherpanegyrik unter Trajan und Konstantin: Studien zur symbolischen Kommunikation in der römischen Kaiserzeit*, Tübingen.

Schowalter, D.N. (1993), *The Emperor and the Gods: Images from the Time of Trajan*, Minneapolis.

Scott, K. (1932), 'The Elder and Younger Pliny on Emperor Worship', in: *Transactions and Proceedings of the American Philological Association* 63, 156–165.

Seelentag, G. (2004), *Taten und Tugenden Traians: Herrschaftsdarstellung im Principat*, Stuttgart.

Shannon-Henderson, K.E. (2019), *Religion and Memory in Tacitus' Annals*, Oxford.

Sordi, M. (2003), 'Plinio, Traiano e i Cristiani', in: L. Castagna/E. Lefèvre (eds.), *Plinius der Jüngere und seine Zeit*, Munich, 267–277.

Soverini, P. (1989), 'Impero e imperatori nell'opera di Plinio il Giovane: Aspetti e problem del rapporto con Domiziano e Traiano', *Aufstieg und Niedergang der Römischen Welt* 2.33.1, 515–554.

Hans-Friedrich Mueller
Tua Divinitas: Religious Self-fashioning in Tiberian Rome

Abstract: Because Valerius Maximus explicitly describes his personal emotions and experiences (*Praef.*, 2.6.8, 4.4.11, 4.7.*ext*.1, 3.4.*ext*.1, 6.1.*init.*, 9.11.*ext*.4), we may observe his rhetorical strategies for religious self-representation. Valerius combines rhetorical figures (*exempla*, *ēthopoiia*, "sincerity", *enargeia*) with the traditional vocabulary of Roman religion (e.g. allusions to *auspicia*) and religious themes (especially traditional gods and ancestral rites). The emotionally charged subjectivity that emerges from this combination embraces not only traditional religion, but also a new imperial religion centered on the divine Caesars, including the living emperor Tiberius. Valerius represents his own heart as a temple (cf. Tacitus *Ann.* 4.38), and locates Rome's new imperial religious identity in a subjective reinterpretation of the historical *exempla* of Rome's republican past. By tracking Valerius' (re)presentation of his own religious experiences and feelings, we may observe, too, how such self-fashioning itself constitutes a paradigm for readers to emulate.

The *Facta et dicta memorabilia* of Valerius Maximus appeared circa AD 30. The identity of the author of this crucial collection of historical anecdotes (or *exempla*) arranged according to categories of virtue and vice remains obscure,[1] but his work addresses religious self-fashioning in two important ways: the author represents his own emotionally resonant piety, and he provides through his selection of moral paradigms the tools for others to fashion themselves, too, according to the religious values (at least as Valerius conceives them) of society in Tiberius' Rome.[2] We see this most clearly in Valerius' preface and (rare) anecdotes in which

---

[1] See Briscoe 2019, 1–4, for a good summary of possibilities for Valerius' identity as well as the date of his work.
[2] I explore the topic of Valerius' uses of traditional Roman religion for the purpose of moral instruction in Mueller 2002. This essay focuses in particular on Valerius' self-presentation through his peculiar rhetorical style as moral exemplar or *exemplum imitandum*. See Rüpke 2016 for a more recent assessment of Valerius' use of Rome's religious history as an aspect of "Tiberian memory culture". For the use of *exempla* in Valerius Maximus see Mueller 2002, 6–9, and, for a detailed study of Valerian *exempla* in the construction of a moral system more generally, Langlands 2018, as well as Langlands 2006, especially 123–191, for Valerius' exemplary construction of paradigmatic sexuality.

https://doi.org/10.1515/9783110699623-012

the author directly expresses or (from a rhetorical point-of-view) "represents" his personal experience and opinions. The author's representation of his own religious piety (or "self-presentation") vis-a-vis the emperor Tiberius can be placed in a more general literary context, but with a difference. Valerian religiosity imbues his work more generally and thoroughly, and one would be hard-pressed to find any evidence within his text to contradict the plain meaning of his words. A key feature of Valerius' rhetorical style is his "sincerity".[3] That is, the author vouches for the truthfulness of what he relates on the basis of his own heartfelt or emotionally represented belief, his piety. "Sincerity", thus represents more than mere "honesty". *Res* and *verba* indeed align, but the author's religious professions include pious representation of his own feelings as genuine and authentic. When a speaker uses such rhetorical devices to represent someone's character (whether his own or another's), we generally call it *ēthopoiia*.[4] Broader terms for authors' representations of themselves include "self-representation" and "self-fashioning".[5] Finally, what is particularly striking about Valerian self-fashioning

---

3 I argue this point *in extenso* in Mueller 2002, which represents an effort to apply the suggestion of Michels 1962, 441, who was disturbed by the view of Latte 1960 of Roman religion, which seemed to her static, and thus drained of human experience: "one wonders what results might be obtained if one worked on the perhaps naive assumption that most Latin authors (not all) in most of their works (not all) were saying quite sincerely just what they really thought". After sustained assessment, Mueller 2002 concludes that one cannot find evidence in Valerius' text that his piety was feigned, i.e., the text offers no clues to indicate that the author said one thing, but meant another. One may thus assume "sincerity" (whether actual or rhetorically constructed) as a fundamental element of Valerian rhetoric.

4 See Serafim 2020, 65, on religious *ēthopoiia*, who writes that "the messages of a pious man, whose words show that he is respectful to and reveres the gods, are more easily accepted by the audience, and the speaker renders himself more credible and persuasive, even when there is a lack of proofs". For a useful account of how *ēthopoiia* may be used to represent one's character through emotion, especially in the *Progymnasmata* of the rhetorical schools see Gibson 2018, especially 299–306, on the presentation of inner suffering for public education.

5 Some may object to this simplification. For a detailed exploration of "self-fashioning" and the ancient rhetorical tradition in light of post-modern theory see Miller 2015, who well asks (326): "how does a speaker present himself as a purveyor of truth? Does this not require a certain stylization of the speaker, the fashioning of a receivable ethos? On what level is this stylization a mere matter of ornament, of verbal manipulation, and on what level is it a reformation of the self: an ethical act that changes the very nature and possibility of the truth?" For a full-scale study of self-fashioning in Valerius' early imperial predecessor Horace whose *pietas* likewise figures prominently in his works see Buczek 2008. For self-fashioning and the emotions, compare Craig 2014 on Cicero's presentation of his inner dialogue in order to portray his compassionate nature despite his stern prosecution of Catilinarians. For Ciceronian self-fashioning more generally in his rhetorical works see the detailed study of Dugan 2008 with extensive bibliography.

is its use of traditional religious vocabulary (e.g. allusions to *auspicia*, fundamental, of course, to the constitutional operation of the old Republic) and themes (traditional gods and other ancestral rites) in order to portray his own emotionally religious subjectivity as it invokes new gods (the Caesars), and thus offer an exemplar for others to imitate. Valerius combines standard figures from the rhetorical arsenal with traditional religious vocabulary, traditional religious themes and the new Caesarean religion, and it is this combination in his self-presentation that we may call "Valerian rhetoric".

The seeming sincerity of Valerius' rhetoric, as we shall see, may well lie behind or represent a reason for the relative neglect that his text long suffered as a literary work in its own right, as opposed to a collection of historically useful fragments. Even today, despite intermittent efforts since the late twentieth century to treat Valerius Maximus as an author[6] rather than merely as a source for historical facts when more reliable sources fail,[7] it would be difficult to argue that the authorial voice of Valerius is widely recognised or acknowledged. Harsh aesthetic judgments abide. Nineteenth-century students cursed Valerius' work, attributing its survival to "malignant fortune".[8] In their history of Latin literature, Schanz-Hosius deemed Valerius "unendurably tasteless (*unerträglich geschmacklos*)".[9] Eduard Norden concurred: "Valerius Maximus opens that long series of Latin authors who, on account of their artificiality, are unendurable to the point of desperation.... I have no desire to investigate the disgusting elements of his style".[10] And Valerius has not fared much better in the English-speaking world. In a study of historical anecdotes in Latin literature, Haight writes that "it may seem strange that I have not included

---

6 See especially Sinclair 1980, Skidmore 1988, Bloomer 1992, Weileder 1998, Mueller 2002, Lawrence 2006 and 2018, Lucarelli 2007 and Welch 2013.
7 Valerius' sources include highly regarded authors, e.g., Livy, Cicero and Varro. The edition of Kempf 1854 provided a solid foundation for studies of Valerius' sources. Subsequent studies include Elschner 1864; Zschech 1865; Kempf 1866; Kranz 1876; Krieger 1888; Maire 1899; Thormeyer 1902; Bosch 1929; Ramelli 1936; Helm 1939 and 1940; Klotz 1942; Bliss 1952; Helm 1955; Maslakov 1978 and 1984; and Bloomer 1987. Bloomer 1992, 59–146, offers a concise overview. The edition of Briscoe 1998 updates Kempf's lists. Maslakov and Helm conclude that Valerius is generally accurate in reproducing the facts that he finds in his sources.
8 Zschech 1865, 1: *Factorum dictorumque memorabilium libri a Valerio Maximo scripti, qua multa per saecula dignitate florebant, non auctori debere mihi videntur sed malignae fortunae, quae maximam literarum nobis romanarum partem eripuit parvamque compensationem scriptores secundi et tertii ordinis reliquit....*
9 Schanz 1935, 589.
10 Norden 1958 [1898], 303–304: Valerius Maximus eröffnet die lange Reihe der durch ihre Unnatur bis zur Verzweiflung unerträglichen Schriftsteller in lateinischer Sprache. ... Auf das Widerliche seines Stils... habe ich keine Lust einzugehen.

Valerius Maximus' collection of anecdotes in these essays. But his 'repertory for speakers' is a mere assemblage of useful anecdotes related in the plainest style and arranged under various classifications. It is not valuable for one who is interested in analysing the use of anecdotes as a form of art".[11] In the second edition of the *Oxford Classical Dictionary*, Whittick calls Valerius "shallow, sententious, and bombastic…".[12] The *Cambridge History of Classical Literature* effectively ignores Valerius by failing to include him in the appendices,[13] perhaps taking their cue from this long tradition of dismissal. One could go on, but this brief survey will suffice to document Valerius' stylistic and rhetorical reputation. One traditionally reads his work for what historical facts he preserves, not for his voice, his views or the elements of his rhetorical style. This is an error.

Valerius' preface will serve for many to illustrate not only the reason for the animus on display in such literary assessments, but also, for the purposes of this chapter, as the programmatic representation of Valerius' emotionally religious piety. Prefaces are, of course, crucial for understanding an author's purposes and thus deserve close attention.[14] Valerius begins by explaining his primary aim. He will gather "historical actions and utterances worth remembering" (*facta simul ac dicta memoratu digna*) to spare those in search of *documenta* (lessons, patterns, proof, examples) the effort of a long search (*praef.*). This statement will serve to illuminate Valerius' reputation as a "mere compiler". One might, however, compare Ovid's *Metamorphoses*. Although he drew on many sources, Ovid did not simply "compile" myths. The authorial voice remains consistently Ovidian.[15]

Valerius proceeds next to assert that he has no desire to include everything (*cuncta*) in a "limited number of rolls" (*modico voluminum numero*), i.e. a short work, and because he is sane (*compos mentis*), he cannot hope to record with "more painstaking care or more admirable eloquence the events of every age (*omnis aevi gesta*)", which are "lodged chronologically in domestic and foreign history (*praef.*)". How could such a modest statement of purpose have offended? This aim, so humbly and succinctly formulated, is followed by a prayer, and it is the prayer to which we shall devote greater attention:

---

11 Haight 1940, 178.
12 Whittick 1970, 1106.
13 Kenney/Clausen 1982.
14 See the classic study of Janson 1964.
15 To assert that an author indeed has his "own voice" or peculiar rhetorical style with a consistent point-of-view should not be construed as a value judgment on whether or not that voice is of high literary quality. One may, for example, recognise the consistent "voice" in a politician's speeches while detesting both the content and rhetorical style while others may simultaneously admire the effect or remain indifferent.

te igitur huic coepto, penes quem hominum deorumque consensus maris ac terrae regimen esse voluit, certissima salus patriae, Caesar, invoco, cuius caelesti providentia virtutes, de quibus dicturus sum, benignissime foventur, vitia severissime vindicantur: nam si prisci oratores ab Iove optimo maximo bene orsi sunt, si excellentissimi vates a numine aliquo principia traxerunt, mea parvitas eo iustius ad favorem tuum decucurrerit, quo cetera divinitas opinione colligitur, tua [i.e. divinitas] praesenti fide paterno avitoque sideri par videtur, quorum eximio fulgore multum caerimoniis nostris inclitae alacritatis accessit: reliquos enim deos accepimus, Caesares dedimus.

(*praef.*)

You, therefore, in support of this work just begun, (you,) in whose power the agreement of human beings and gods has desired command of sea and the land to abide, (you,) most secure safeguard of our fatherland, O Caesar, I summon, by whose heavenly foresight the virtues I am about to describe are most kindly nourished, but by whom the vices (that I am about to describe) are most strictly punished. For, if ancient orators could properly begin from Jupiter[16] [or, as I shall argue below: "with the authorization of Jupiter"] Best and Greatest, if the most distinguished prophets (and poets) could derive their sources[17] from some divine power, then so much the more rightly will my own insignificance have entrusted myself to your goodwill, especially as other godheads (*cetera divinitas*) are deduced on the basis of reputation, but your godhead (*tua [divinitas]*) appears through eyewitness proof equal to your father's and grandfather's star, by whose glorious illumination so much celebrated zeal (and enthusiasm) has accrued to our religious rites: indeed, although we inherited all the other gods, we ourselves have bestowed the Caesars. (tr. Mueller 2002, 13, modified)[18]

---

16 "Beginning from Zeus" had enjoyed a long tradition by the time Valerius echoes the phrase. We may compare Aratus *Phaenomena* 1–15, which begins Ἐκ Διὸς ἀρχώμεσθα. As Kidd 1997, 161, points out: "the main section is a hymn to Zeus, the divinity that pervades the whole cosmos and is the source of all forms of life. He is in this sense our father, and acts like a father in helping men to cope with the struggle for existence". One may compare Thom 2005, 8, on Cleanthes' *Hymn to Zeus*: "a perusal of the Hymn makes it clear that Zeus is not treated as some abstract, philosophical principle; on the contrary, he is presented in rather personalist and theistic terms as the king and ruler of the world; a divine father from whom all human beings have their origin and to whom they can turn for help; a god who can correct our mistakes; someone with whom we can communicate, and to whom we have an obligation". This moral aspect would certainly have appealed Valerius, who replaces Rome's Jupiter with Tiberius. Parallels cited by Kidd 1997, 163: "Cicero translates *ab Iove Musarum primordia* (*fr.* 1), Virgil imitates with *ab Iove principium* (*E.* 3.60), cleverly producing variation in each word, and there are later echoes of the phrase in Ov. *Met.* 10.148, *Fast.* 5.111, Calp. Sic. 4.82, V. Max. 1 *pr.* 17, Stat. *Sil.* 1. *pr.* 19".

17 *OLD* s.v. *principium* § 3: "that from which anything grows or develops, origin; *-ium ducere*, to originate, spring".

18 I have significantly modified the translation of Mueller 2002, 13, in an effort to render more clearly Valerius' religious rhetoric as well as to reflect a more nuanced view of what Valerius says. Unattributed translations, on the other hand, are my own, and were made for this chapter.

Valerius invokes the emperor Tiberius as a living god,[19] one for whom there is proof because he is visible (*praesenti fide*).[20]

Because this passage is formulated as a prayer, we may assess it according to the standard rhetorical or generic expectations of Roman prayer language.[21] Valerius begins by identifying precisely the god from whom he will make his request,[22] the guardian of the Roman state (*certissima salus patriae*), the one who rules over both land and sea. Jupiter Optimus Maximus was the supreme god of Republican Rome, and thus Rome's traditional *custos*; the divine *Caesares* have usurped this role, and Valerius could not be more explicit in making this clear by specifically mentioning the god upon whom he does *not* call, perhaps should the old god otherwise mistake himself as the one upon whom the author has called, but also (more below), and more importantly, to reveal a shift in the source of his authorisation to speak at all. Additional descriptive clauses (also standard in ancient prayer)[23] offer significant details. Through "godly foresight" (*caelesti provi-*

---

19 Williams 1978, 166, may serve to represent the traditional view, which contradicts the plain meaning of Valerius' words: "Valerius Maximus... stopped well short of viewing Tiberius as a god — as distinct from praising him as godlike — and he made the proper distinction between the traditional gods and the Caesars (the deification of the latter is honorific for qualities shown and services done)". This view no longer prevails.

20 Invoking Tiberius as a living god has likely cost Valerius readers. We may compare the praise of Baldur von Schirach for Adolf Hitler [as quoted by Reichelt 1990, 31]: *das ist an ihm das Größte: daß er nicht / nur unser Führer ist und vieler Held, / sondern er selbst: grade, fest und schlicht, / daß in ihm ruhen die Wurzeln unsrer Welt, und seine Seele an die Sterne strich / und er doch Mensch blieb, so wie du und ich* ("this is what is greatest about him, not just that he is our leader and the hero of so many, but his very person — upright, steadfast and sincere — that in him rest the roots of our world, and his soul touched the stars, and he nevertheless remained a human being, just like you and I"). The worship as divine of those who hold great power has neither ceased nor lost its power to disturb, but this is no reason, as scholars, to turn away from judicious assessment of such statements.

21 For an earlier and more detailed analysis, but with more general aims see Mueller 2002, 11–20. Both analyses rely on the work of Hickson 1993 whose study outlines the basic structure of Roman prayer language. For a study of Roman prayer as "religious experience", one may consult the study of Patzelt 2018 as well as Patzelt in this volume for a more general exploration of the rhetoric of prayer.

22 Hickson 1993, 33: "correct identification of the deity to be invoked was of the utmost importance; there would be absolutely no value in making a request of the wrong god".

23 Hickson 1993, 36–43. The pattern was ancient. Compare Chryses' careful identification of Apollo in Homer *Iliad* 1.37–39: κλῦθί μευ ἀργυρότοξ᾽, ὃς Χρύσην ἀμφιβέβηκας / Κίλλάν τε ζαθέην Τενέδοιό τε ἶφι ἀνάσσεις, / Σμινθεῦ ("hearken unto me, O Silver-Bow, you, who have protected Chrysa, and sacred Cilla, and with might rule over Tenedos, O Mouse-God!"). The priest left no room for confusion about precisely which Apollo he invoked.

dentia) Tiberius fosters morally correct conduct and punishes vice (*virtutes*... *benignissime foventur, vitia severissime vindicantur*). This clause thus attributes a deep concern with moral conduct to Valerius' preferred deity,[24] and because moral and immoral conduct represent the narrative point of Valerius' illustrative anecdotes, Tiberius emerges as an appropriate deity for an author who seeks divine assistance or authority. What does Valerius request from his god? He calls the god to the work he has begun (*te*... *huic coepto*... *invoco*). This is not unusual in works of epic poetry. Such an invocation is perhaps surprising, on the other hand, in a work of Latin prose that purports to offer historically true "actions" (*facta*) and actual "statements" (*dicta*). Do historians require divine authorisation? Valerius, however, although what he presents may factually be true, does not write history. This is a crucial generic distinction: Valerius, who collects historical anecdotes useful for orators, will seek an authorisation that is akin to, but not the same as, the authorisation that public speakers once sought from Jupiter Optimus Maximus. In Republican Rome, those who addressed the people in public speeches were generally magistrates.

Valerius justifies his choice of god overtly as well as his invocation of divinity more generally. In addition to the poets or prophets (*vates*)[25] who make use of a variety of deities (*numine aliquo*) as the source of their inspiration and "beginnings" (*principia*), Valerius cites ancient orators (*prisci oratores*). Orators, like Valerius, wrote in prose. Orators, at least those in the public or political sphere at Rome, had no right to speak, unless they did so at an authorised assembly.[26] An informal assembly, or *contio*, did not require the inauguration of a *templum* (and thus auspices[27]), as opposed to meetings of the *comitia*, which could take place only "after the auspices had been taken, on an inaugurated site".[28] The legal source for such auspices, that is, for permission to conduct public business, was, of course, during the Roman Republic, Jupiter Optimus Maximus.[29] Ancient orators, unlike ancient poets, did not necessarily ask for divine inspiration. *Roman*

---

24 Compare Alföldi 1978 [1970], 124–130, on the combined duties of a father and a god (*parens ac deus nostrae vitae*).
25 See Newman 1967 for the uses of the word *vates* in the Augustan period. Compare Buczek 2008, 25–26, on Horace as *pius vates* whose invocation of Jupiter will help ensure blessings from the gods.
26 See Mueller 2004, 82–84, for a discussion of authorised versus unauthorised assemblies with further references.
27 Treves and Lintott 2015.
28 Momigliano and Cornell 2016.
29 See Linderski 1986 for detailed discussion with relevant literature concerning Rome's augural law.

orators, at least those who held office, asked for permission to make an authorised beginning. Valerius thus places his work squarely in the public and political sphere as well as in the generic sphere of oratory (because he writes in prose), and will seek permission from the relevant deity, not auspicious Jupiter, but rather the god descended from Caesar and Augustus: Tiberius.

Once this god has been properly identified and summoned, does the petitioner recite works done by himself on behalf of this god? No. Does he vow anything that a traditional god might crave (e.g. sacrifices, an altar) in return for what he may request? No. Instead, Valerius contrasts his own insignificance (*mea parvitas*) with Tiberius' deity (*tua [divinitas]*). He asks for *favor*,[30] the benevolence or goodwill that will assist him in his pious task of describing the virtues and vices that the god himself promotes or punishes (*virtutes, de quibus dicturus sum,* [*et*] ... *vitia*). This task is, moreover, put forward on a legal basis analogous to that of authorised speakers in an assembly. Just as poets took their "beginnings" or "inspiration" (*principia*[31]) from a sympathetic deity (*numine aliquo*), orators properly began to speak in an assembly (*bene orsi sunt*) with the authority of (i.e. with *auspicia* received from) Jupiter Best and Greatest.[32] Valerius (*mea parvitas*) thus "more legally" (*iustius*[33]) seeks protective permission from the deity Tiberius (again, *tua [divinitas]*).

The prayer concludes with a precise description of the origin of the *Caesares* as a new race of gods. Valerius' comparison and contrast of traditional with new gods continues. Traditional gods are "gathered", that is, evidence for them is collected, and they are thus "deduced" to exist (*cetera divinitas... colligitur*[34]), on the basis of their "reputation" or what is "believed" (*opinione*). This statement recalls the signs collected, analysed and interpreted by religious specialists. There was ample proof for the power of the gods in earthquakes, plagues, omens of all sorts,

---

30 According to Hellegouarch 1963, 178–179, the word has its origins in religious ceremonies and theatrical spectacles.
31 Compare Otto 1962 [1890] s.v. *Iuppiter* § 1 on the association of Jupiter with the word *principium*; cf. Spoth 2009, 1312.3–37, on similar associations of *principium* with the divine mind of pagan deity more generally.
32 Linderski 1986, 2173 n. 94: magistrates rose between midnight and dawn to consult the will of Jupiter.
33 *OLD* 1968, s.v. *iustus* § 1: "recognised or sanctioned by law, lawful, legitimate".
34 *Colligo* is a technical term from traditional religion. Compare Linderski 1995 [1981], 525: "in the language of the augurs this term [i.e. *auspicia colligere*] denoted both the perception of a sign and its interpretation and classification according to the rules codified once and forever in the augural books".

and, of course, also in impetrative auspices, on the basis of which Rome's divinely authorised magistrates had conquered the Mediterranean. The new gods have become visible by signs both present and visible to all: the Caesarean star.[35] This scheme of traditional versus new gods is carried through to the end of the sentence when Valerius concludes that, although Rome inherited the other (traditional) gods — and this does not diminish their value — Rome has bestowed the Caesars (*reliquos... deos accepimus, Caesares dedimus*).[36]

We must, however, turn our attention to one troubled phrase that underscores a crucial aspect both of the new religion and of Valerius' rhetorical style more generally: emotion. The Caesars, by their superabundant splendour or glory (*eximio fulgore*) have added much popular enthusiasm (*multum... inclitae alacritatis*) to Rome's religious rites (*caerimoniis nostris*). *Alacritatis*, the reading of the best manuscripts, is oddly controversial, but was the choice of Kempf in the edition of 1854, who remarked that "although the vulgar reading was *claritatis*, I recalled that, not in a few manuscripts sometimes — as Torrenius asserts — but in almost all manuscripts, [the reading of] *alacritatis* has been confirmed; I do not understand why it has been rejected so unanimously by editors".[37] Nevertheless, Kempf adopted the reading *claritatis* without comment in his Teubner edition of 1888, and this is the reading one finds today in both Briscoe 1998 and Shackleton Bailey 2000. I will not repeat here my earlier arguments[38] in favour of the best manuscript reading, but I do wish to note that *claritatis*, "brightness" or "renown", is not only the less well-attested reading, it is both redundant and logically questionable: rather than add enthusiasm (*alacritas*), the bright Caesarean star's "splendour" (*fulgor*) would add additional "brightness" or more "renown" (*claritas*). This reading is out of step with Valerius' argument, which contrasts traditional Roman religion with Caesarean religion. Has worship of the Caesars rendered Roman religious rites more "renowned" among Romans (the people to whom Valerius speaks directly)? How does a people's own religion become more

---

35 For details about the role of *Caesaris astrum* in the religion of the new god see Weinstock 1971, 370–384.
36 On the misguided suggestion to emend *dedimus* to *videmus* see Wardle 1999. Valerius' sentiment conforms rather precisely with a similar statement by Valerius' contemporary Velleius Paterculus 2.126.1: *sacravit parentem suum [Tiberius] Caesar non imperio, sed religione, non appellavit eum, sed fecit deum*. Compare Woodman 1975, 18, on the subtleties of Velleius' contemporary observations.
37 Kempf 1854, 106: on the reading of *alacritatis*: *cum volgu legeretur claritatis, revocavi quod non paucis aliquot, ut narratur apud Torrenium, sed omnibus fere libris confirmatum, cur tanto consensu a grammaticis spretum sit non intellego.*
38 Mueller 2002, 17–20.

famous among them? *Alacritas*, on the other hand, contradicts long-held conceptions of Roman religion as distinct from Christianity in no small measure by an emphasis on practice as opposed to doctrinal belief and emotionally pious devotion. This emotional component, however, is a key feature of Valerius' rhetorical style (and we will soon turn to additional examples), as it is, of course, in rhetoric more generally,[39] and emotion is additionally a prominent feature in Valerius' presentation of himself as an exemplar of religious piety.

In Valerius 2.6.8, Valerius relates an event that he himself witnessed (*animadverti*) in the company of Sextus Pompeius on the island of Ceos.[40] This anecdote permits us to observe the combination of traditional religion with the author's representation of his own emotional response. An aged woman of the upper class requests the presence of the proconsul at her deathbed where she plans to drink poison. The woman is herself an exemplar of piety, and she expresses the wish that the gods of the living rather than the gods to whom she departs (*di magis quos relinquo quam quos peto*) remunerate Pompeius for his services (*gratias referant*), and in expressing this wish also demonstrates her gratitude for a prosperous life. She pours a libation to Mercury (*defusis Mercurio delibamentis*), whom she asks (*numine invocato*) to lead her to the dead. She drinks poison, and when she has died, her daughter performs the last rite of closing her eyes (*supremum opprimendorum oculorum officium*). How does this traditional scene of domestic religion affect the emotions of the Romans, including our author and self-described eye-witness, Valerius Maximus? The daughter sent the Romans away, who, as a group, were astonished (*obstupefacti*) and drenched in tears (*nostros... suffusos lacrimis dimisit*). As readers, we become witnesses to traditional religious rites, in a scene that is vivid (*enargeia*). While it is possible that such religious rites were merely perfunctory motions, a dying mother and exemplar of piety, together with a dutiful daughter, depict a scene of touching humanity designed to draw us in as viewers, so that we will participate vicariously in the emotions of the scene's participants. This conclusion is confirmed by the explicitly described tears of the Romans. As these Romans reacted, so should Valerius' readers. And to what did the Romans react? A dying mother and daughter, of course, but also Valerius' presentation of the rituals and prayers that frame the scene, and add to its evocative power. These religious elements are difficult, if not impossible, to separate from the scene's emotive power, to which power Valerius offers himself as eye-witness. Valerius once again fashions himself as

---

39 See Mueller 2002, 6–9, with references.
40 See Briscoe 1993 for the identification of Sextus Pompeius with the consul of AD 14 and proconsul in Asia in the 20s.

religiously pious, and religious elements themselves become emotional triggers, and it is in this sense, too, that religious elements may be described as part and parcel of Valerian rhetoric: they are crucial here in particular to *enargeia*, emotion, *ēthopoiia* as well as more generally to the construction of *exempla*.

Valerius opens his author's heart (or represents its emotions) to readers again when he compares those who, in his own day, lament their lack of wealth. Valerius tells us that he looks instead at the modest fortunes of Rome's ancient heroes (i.e. the Publicolae, Aemilii, Fabricii, Curii, Scipios, Scauri), and he exhorts his readers in the first person plural:

> *exsurgamus potius animis pecuniaeque aspectu debilitatos spiritus pristini temporis memoria recreemus: namque per Romuli casam perque veteris Capitolii humilia tecta et aeternos Vestae focos, fictilibus etiam nunc vasis contentos, iuro nullas divitias talium virorum paupertati posse praeferri.*
>
> 4.4.11
>
> Let us rather rise up in spirit, and, with the recollection of ancient times, let us restore minds crippled by the contemplation of wealth: for by Romulus' hut and by the ancient Capitol's humble temples and the everlasting flames of Vesta's hearth, even now content with clay vessels, I swear that no riches can be preferred to the poverty of such men.

An oath is, of course, a religious act, and Valerius deploys the fires of Vesta and the sacred landscape of Rome's Capitol to restore spirits. Valerius, in this insertion of personal experience and self-presentation, turns once again to religious elements in order to bolster his argument, to help assuage potentially aggrieved feelings, and to restore emotional equilibrium. Poverty is, moreover, when it appears in conjunction with other noble qualities, a virtue, and virtues are promoted and sustained by the gods of Valerian religion, including, of course, the new Caesarean gods.

A more positive as well as emotionally powerful virtue is friendship, the bonds of which are in Valerius 4.7.*ext*.1 expressly compared to religious obligations, so great are the "powers of friendship" (*vires amicitiae*). These powers "can implant contempt of death, extinguish pleasure in life, soften cruelty, change hatred into love, and repay punishment with a kindness" (*mortis contemptum ingenerare, vitae dulcedinem exstinguere, crudelitatem mansuefacere, odium in amorem convertere, poenam beneficio pensare potuerunt*).[41] Especially telling in

---

[41] A. Serafim (personal message) felicitously compares these *vires amicitiae* to the power of *logos* in Gorgias' *Encomium of Helen* 14: τὸν αὐτὸν δὲ λόγον ἔχει ἥ τε τοῦ λόγου δύναμις πρὸς τὴν τῆς ψυχῆς τάξιν ἥ τε τῶν φαρμάκων τάξις πρὸς τὴν τῶν σωμάτων φύσιν ("the power of speech

this emotive list are the terms *odium* and *amor*, two of the strongest of human feelings. And religion, according to Valerius, is even stronger than the *vires amicitiae*, for "to these (forces) almost as much ardent devotion is owed as to the religious ceremonies of the immortal gods (*quibus paene tantum venerationis quantum deorum immortalium caerimoniis debetur*). Valerius, in terms very similar to his programmatic preface, compares public safety, which depends on gods, with personal safety, which depends on the bonds of friendship, concluding that

> atque ut illarum aedes sacra domicilia, harum fida hominum pectora quasi quaedam sancto spiritu referta templa sunt.
>
> 4.7.ext.1

> just as shrines are the sacred homes of those (religious ceremonies), loyal human hearts serve as the temples (of these bonds of friendship), as if filled with a holy spirit.

Valerius uses simile to turn the emotional basis of friendship (*harum* [*virium amicitiae*]) into the ceremonies of traditional religion (*illarum* [*deorum immortalium caerimoniarum*]) while loyal human hearts (*fida hominum pectora*) become equivalent to the shrines (*aedes*), which serve as sacred dwelling-places (*sacra domicilia*) for public ceremonies. The comparison is clear, but Valerius pushes the comparison, explicitly and emphatically stating that these hearts serve *as if they were temples* (*quasi... templa*) filled with a spirit that is itself sacred (*sancto spiritu*). We observe once again that the external elements of traditional religion are conflated, as it were, with the author's interior emotional and spiritual life. Valerius' rhetorical style (i.e. the combination of standard rhetorical figures with religious vocabulary and imagery) thus does more than simply yoke traditional and Caesarean religion to the promotion of virtue (as promised in the preface): the author presents himself (or his own "loyal human heart") as an exemplar of emotional piety. Religion moves from public buildings and visible ceremonies to the individual human heart, and it is in this seat of human emotion that the religious elements of Valerius' rhetoric acquire additional emotive force.

How, though, can we be certain that this religious rhetoric is personal? Immediately after identifying the human heart as the temple for the powers of friendship, Valerius turns to his personal friend Sextus Pompeius, "in whose spirit as if in the heart of most loving parents my life's condition has thrived more happily" (*cuius in animo velut in parentum amantissimorum pectore laetior vitae*

---

has the same impact upon the state of the soul as the application of drugs to the state of the body").

meae status viguit). Valerius goes on to deploy terms that not only recall traditional religious concepts, but also echo the formulations of his programmatic preface: "and he has rendered my studies both brighter and more enthusiastic under his guidance and auspices" (*qui studia nostra ductu et auspiciis suis lucidiora et alacriora reddidit*). To Pompeius' "guidance (*ductu*)", "auspices (*auspiciis*)", "brighter light (*lucidiora*)" and "greater enthusiasm (*alacriora*)", we may compare Valerius' invocation of Tiberius himself, who, in the preface, "guides" by fostering virtue and punishing vice, "authorised" Valerius' beginnings (*principia*) analogously to the auspicious permission that Jupiter granted to ancient orators, and added "brilliance" (*fulgor*) as well as "enthusiasm" (*alacritas*) to Rome's religious rites. Such echoes (or repetitions) reinforce emotional patterns that we may attribute to the author's peculiar rhetoric: Valerius frequently turns at his most personal to traditional religious vocabulary.

It is in the context of these glimpses of our author's personal and emotional religiosity that we may place Valerius' rhetoric of personal piety more generally. Valerius' invocation of *pudicitia* may serve as an illustrative example:

> Unde te virorum pariter ac feminarum praecipuum firmamentum, Pudicitia, invocem? tu enim prisca religione consecratos Vestae focos incolis, tu Capitolinae Iunonis pulvinaribus incubas, tu Palatii columen augustos penates sanctissimumque Iuliae genialem torum adsidua statione celebras, tuo praesidio puerilis aetatis insignia munita sunt, tui numinis respectu sincerus iuventae flos permanet, te custode matronalis stola censetur: ades igitur et recognosce quae fieri ipsa voluisti.
>
> 6.1.*init.*[42]

From what source may I invoke you, O Chastity, principal mainstay of men just as of women? Inasmuch as you dwell upon Vesta's hearth consecrated by ancient religion, (inasmuch as) you haunt the couches of Capitoline Juno, (inasmuch as) you honour with ever-present vigilance the summit of the Palatine, the household gods of Augustus, the most holy marriage bed of Livia, (inasmuch as) by means of your fortification the tokens of childhood have been protected, (inasmuch as) the flower of youth persists uncut through reverence for your divine power, (inasmuch as) the matron's stole is valued with you as our protector: be therefore present and acknowledge what you yourself desired!

Valerius speaks in the first person. He links or conflates traditional religion (Vesta and Juno) with Caesarian religion and the *domus Augusta*[43] (the Palatine, *penates*,

---

[42] For a full discussion of *pudicitia* in Valerius see Mueller 2002, 21–43; cf. Langlands 2006, 123–191.

[43] Compare Wardle 2000 on Valerius and the *domus Augusta*.

and Livia⁴⁴), he links both old and new religious elements with the virtue of sexual continence (*pudicitia*), and he invokes the virtue itself (chaste conduct) as a deity in her own right (*Pudicitia*), that is, as a god with effective divine power (*tui numinis*) who resides, not only on Vesta's hearth, but also on Capitoline Juno's couch (*pulvinaribus*) and Livia's marriage bed (*genialem torum*),⁴⁵ thus linking Livia with both the goddess of chastity as well as the goddess of childbirth and marriage, i.e. the kind of *pudicitia* that promotes the production of legitimate children.⁴⁶ As Rüpke has well remarked, this "is not *the* religion of the Republic".⁴⁷ Valerius has rather "selectively memorialised"⁴⁸ the Republic's religious history to formulate a personal religion based on virtue, one "best exemplified by the living emperor, who is himself a god".⁴⁹

Rüpke's sound formulation, however, still omits the human heart, the temple, as it were, of this new Caesarean or imperial religion of virtue, i.e. personal conduct sanctioned on the basis of emotionally sustained religiosity. Indeed, Valerius informs us that the emotions are the source of human virtue. In Valerius

---

44 As Kempf 1854, 461, notes, after the death of Augustus, Livia became *Iulia Augusta*. For a useful discussion of the significance of the enhanced status that this posthumous adoption conferred see Bauman 1992, 131–137. Is it possible, however, that Valerius alludes here to Julia, daughter of Augustus, Tiberius' disgraced wife, who was exiled for *impudicitia* (Tacitus *Annals* 1.53)? Elschner 1864, 23; Thormeyer 1902, 11; Carter 1975, 32; and Bellemore 1989, 76, think so. The best argument for this position that I have found remains that of Oliverius [1491], *n. ad* Valerius Maximus 6.1.*init.*, who reasons that Julia's fecundity was proven and her children famously resembled her husband, and thus, on this superficial level at least, might serve as an imperial advertisement for *pudicitia*. One might add to the list of imperial Julias with unchaste marriage beds the elder Julia's daughter Julia (Suetonius *Augustus* 65; cf. Norwood 1963, 154–155) as well as Livia Julia, the wife of Tiberius' son Drusus (on whose *amissa pudicitia* with its Livian echoes of Lucretia, see Sinclair 1990, 240–242). Conscious allusion to any of these unchaste Julian beds would represent *aperta nimis adulatio* (Oliverius, *op. cit.*), malicious irony, shameless satire or tone-deaf stupidity. On the other hand, Helm 1955, 91–92, convincingly argues that Valerius can here refer logically only to Livia, an argument which should have been settled already by Pighius 1612 [c. 1567], 532 [*n. ad* Valerius Maximus 6.1.*init.*].
45 See van den Berg 2008, esp. 254–255, on the conflation of divine *pulvinar* with human *genialis torus*.
46 If one seeks an additional Julia beyond Livia for Valerius' invocation, one might mention the *lex Iulia de maritandis ordinibus* of 18 BC, which, together with the *lex Poppaea* of 9 BC, represented an effort to encourage and enforce the kind of *pudicitia*, i.e. sexual relations confined to the marriage bed in service of the production of legtimate children, that Valerius praises (cf. Baltrusch 1989, 162–189, and Treggiari 1991, 277–298).
47 Rüpke 2016, 107.
48 Rüpke 2016, 107.
49 Rüpke 2016, 107.

3.4.ext.1, we read that, according to the consensus of human beings (*hominum consensu*) as well as by the oracle of Apollo (*Apollinis oraculo*), Socrates was adjudicated the wisest of all human beings because, while other learned men engaged in pointless arguments about "measurements of the sun and the moon and the other stars" (*mensuras... solis ac lunae et ceterorum siderum*), Socrates investigated the human condition:

> *primus... animum suum intima condicionis humanae et in secessu pectoris repositos adfectus scrutari coegit, si virtus per se ipsa aestimetur, vitae magister optimus.*
>
> 3.4.ext.1
>
> He was the first to compel his spirit to examine the deepest matters of the human condition and the emotions arrayed in the recesses of the heart; if virtue itself is valued for its own sake, it is life's best instructor. (tr. Mueller 2002, 150)

The emotions (*adfectus*) reside in the human heart, and are life's best instructor, and thus represent, in Valerius' formulation, the ultimate source of virtues, which, we must continue to bear in mind, can be divinities in their own right and are, if we pursue Valerius' logic, supported and promoted by the gods, at whose head stand the new Caesars in general and Tiberius in particular. This view of the importance of emotions helps explain, too, their fundamental role in Valerius' virtuous self-fashioning.

We may note, in this context, that Tiberius' own "moderate" plea for temples, not of stone, but of human hearts that contemplate and recall Tiberian virtues seems perhaps a bit less moderate and rather more programmatic in this context:

> *Ego me, patres conscripti, mortalem esse et hominum officia fungi satisque habere si locum principem impleam et vos testor et meminisse posteros volo; qui satis superque memoriae meae tribuent, ut maioribus meis dignum, rerum vestrarum providum, constantem in periculis, offensionum pro utilitate publica non pavidum credant. haec mihi in animis vestris templa, hae pulcherrimae effigies et mansurae.*
>
> Tacitus *Ann.* 4.38
>
> I both bear witness before you, conscript fathers, that I am mortal, that I hold the offices of human beings, and that I consider it enough, if I occupy first place, and I want later generations to remember, who will grant enough and more than enough to my memory, should they believe that I was worthy of my ancestors, that I took care of your needs, that I was steadfast in danger, and that I was not fearful of unpopular obstructions for the sake of public welfare. Let these be my temples in your hearts, these my most beautiful and long-lasting effigies.

Tiberius was not satisfied with edificial forms. In his "modesty", he demands something even greater, living flesh, and Valerius sets an example for precisely the sort of loyal piety that Tacitus reports that Tiberius craved.

Just such a display of devotion toward Tiberius is on offer in Valerius 9.11.*ext.* 4. This anecdote also allows us to observe many of the elements of Valerius' rhetorical style — *ēthopoiia, enargeia,* religion, fevered emotions — in the context of an *exemplum* where the author weaves his own subjective emotional state into a narrative about the attack of Sejanus on Tiberius (that is, upon a living god, who promotes virtue and punishes vice).[50] When the author contemplates Sejanus' crime, Valerian emotion knows almost no bounds:

> *omni igitur impetu mentis, omnibus indignationis viribus ad id [scelus] lacerandum pio magis quam valido adfectu rapior.*
>
> 9.11.*ext.* 4
>
> I am seized therefore by every impulse of my mind, by all the powers of outrage, and by an emotion more devoted than effective to rip this crime to shreds.

This emotional storm, as it were, is moderated, to the extent that it is modulated at all, by devotion to Tiberius: Valerius' emotion, while not able to prevail by its own (ineffective) strength or on its own legal authority,[51] reflects rather his loyal devotion to Tiberius (and he is hence moved *pio magis quam valido adfectu*). Valerius then specifies Sejanus' vice: "the loyal bond of friendship had been extinguished" (*amicitiae fide extincta*), and, thus unfettered, Sejanus was capable of making his attempt:

> *tu... habenas Romani imperii, quas princeps parensque noster salutari dextera continet, capere potuisti?*
>
> 9.11.*ext.* 4
>
> Were you able to seize the reins of Roman command, which our ruler and father holds in his saving right hand?

The patterns of Valerius' rhetorical style are consistent. Tiberius, who holds the highest position in the state (and thus command), represents Rome's safety, and he is thus also father to all. (Modern readers will do well to remember, too, the fearful authority of *patria potestas*, which included originally the *ius occidendi*.[52])

---

50 See Hennig 1975, 146, on the validity of Valerius' contemporary testimony.
51 Cf. *OLD* 1968, s.v. *validus* §5d.
52 For examples of *patria potestas* and the *ius occidendi* in Valerius see Krause 2013; cf. Linderski 1995 [1990], 320–327.

Valerius asks Sejanus whether the world would have survived (*mundus in suo statu mansisset*), if Sejanus had succeeded in his raging madness (*te conpote furoris*), and then lists the disasters that would have paled in comparison to the loss of Tiberius: "Rome captured by Gauls and the river Cremera polluted with the massacre of three hundred men of a celebrated clan and the day of Allia and the overthrow of the Scipios in Spain and the Trasimene Lake and Cannae and the swords of civil wars dripping with blood".[53] What saved Rome? Tiberius' fellow gods were alert, and they assisted him, although ultimately Tiberius' own divine foresight saved the world from destruction:[54]

> sed vigilarunt oculi deorum, sidera suum vigorem obtinuerunt, arae, pulvinaria, templa praesenti numine vallata sunt, nihilque, quod pro capite augusto ac patria excubare debuit, torporem sibi permisit, et in primis auctor ac tutela nostrae incolumitatis ne excellentissima merita sua totius orbis ruina conlaberentur divino consilio providit.
>
> 9.11.*ext.* 4
>
> But the eyes of the gods remained alert; the stars preserved their strength; the altars, sacred couches, temples were defended by manifest divinity; and whatever was obligated to protect the August person and fatherland, allowed itself no slack, and first and foremost the author and safeguard of our security took care through his own divine planning to prevent through the destruction of the entire world the loss of his outstanding contributions (to our welfare).

Were all these divine forces necessary? Suetonius recounts the downfall of Sejanus as the result of Tiberius' own cunning and careful planning.[55] Valerius' rhetorical style, on the other hand, especially at its most personal and emotionally fever-pitched,[56] cannot refrain from bringing in the accoutrements of both tradi-

---

53 Translation from Mueller 2002, 180.
54 Compare Wardle 2002 on Valerius' "heroisation" of Tiberius.
55 Suetonius *Tiberius* 65.
56 The anonymous reviewer of this essay poses an interesting, indeed crucial, question: "do we presume similar sincere piety in the speech of Seneca composed for Nero giving thanks to the gods after the assassination of Agrippina?" No, absolutely not. And the reason for this will help illustrate the overarching argument of this essay. Seneca was, if not a politician, a political operative. His post required dissimulation. Politicians will in general represent their inner lives in a way that will earn them the good will of their audiences. We are especially fortunate in the case of Cicero, who, when he wrote philosophy for friends, was a sceptic, but, when he gave public speeches, touted Roman religiosity and his own piety. The study of Jocelyn 1966 offers an astute assessment of this phenomenon: "it is significant that Cicero never expresses the polite scepticism of the dialogues in speeches before his peers in the Senate house or in the law courts; rather

tional and Caesarean religion. The result is a well-ordered society: "peace prevails, laws bind, the conduct of private and public business is kept honest" (*stat pax, valent leges, sincerus privati ac publici officii tenor servatur*).[57] Sejanus, however, who — after breaking the bonds of friendship — attempted to overthrow this well-ordered society (*qui autem haec violatis amicitiae foederibus temptavit subvertere*), was crushed along with his entire family by the forces of the Roman people (*omni cum stirpe sua populi Romani viribus obtritus*), and also receives the punishments that he deserves in the underworld (*etiam apud inferos... quae meretur supplicia pendit*). And so the moral universe is complete. The strongest religious bonds, i.e. loyal devotion (*pietas*), prevail over the violation of the strongest human bonds, i.e. friendship (*amicitia*), and the god whom Valerius invokes in the strongest emotional terms in his programmatic preface proves capable of punishing vice, and promoting the virtues, which, as we have seen, reside in temples of flesh, the human heart.

In fleshing out the relationship of author and emperor as well as the dichotomy between old gods and new, we may observe not only the fundamental role that religious elements play in Valerius' rhetorical style, but also the repeated emphasis on emotional content that Valerius brings to the representation of his own religious subjectivity. These observations on Valerius' rhetorical style in turn provide insight into nothing less than the work's primary rhetorical purpose as a contribution to the (re)construction of Rome's religious identity under Tiberius. Valerius locates Rome's new religious identity in the exemplary fragments of

---

did he always assume that they believed in the existence and power of the gods and in the competence of the traditional ceremonies to placate them" (103–104), while, on the other hand, "[a]uthors with an interest in superstition, such as Valerius Maximus and Plutarch, were able to report plenty in both the beliefs and the behaviour of their Roman subjects" (103) (cf. Jocelyn 1976-1977). Again, as Mueller 2002 endeavours to demonstrate in detail, nothing in Valerius' text suggests anything other than a representation of sincere religiosity on the part of the author. Whether this representation of his sincerity was authentic or artificial is beside the point; Valerius' text was written to appeal to those who were inclined to feel emotions akin to those he describes as well as to encourage similar emotions. One may compare shopping for a greeting card that includes a pre-printed message that pithily captures one's feelings for the card's intended recipient. Whether or not the author of that card's message authentically felt what the purchaser perceives or feels is immaterial, so long as the message appears sincere. More to the point, *I can find no evidence in the text that Valerius did not mean what he plainly states.*

57 Serafim 2020, 32–62, in a chapter that surveys religious discourse in Attic oratory, offers a succinct introduction to common Greek and Roman beliefs about the interest of the gods in human political affairs and their interventions to protect the state.

Rome's republican past, and Valerian self-fashioning of a subjective religious experience emerges, in this wider view, as yet another paradigm for Valerius' audience to emulate.[58]

Bibliography

Alföldi, A. (1978) [1970], *Der Vater des Vaterlandes im römischen Denken*, Darmstadt.
Baltrusch, E. (1989), *Regimen morum: Die Reglementierung des Privatlebens der Senatoren und Ritter in der römischen Republik und frühen Kaiserzeit*, Munich.
Bauman, R. (1992), *Women and Politics in Ancient Rome*, London.
Bellemore, J. (1989), 'When did Valerius Maximus Write the *Dicta et Facta Memorabilia*?' in: *Antichthon* 23, 67–80.
Bliss, F.R. (1952), *Valerius Maximus and his Sources: A Stylistic Approach to the Problem*, Ph.D. Thesis, University of North Carolina at Chapel Hill.
Bloomer, W.M.S. (1987), *Valerius Maximus and the Idealized Republic: A Study in his Representation of Roman History*, Ph.D. Thesis, Yale University.
Bloomer, W.M.S. (1992), *Valerius Maximus and the Rhetoric of the New Nobility*, Chapel Hill.
Bosch, C. (1929), *Die Quellen des Valerius Maximus: Ein Beitrag zur Erforschung der Literatur der historischen Exempla*, Stuttgart.
Briscoe, J. (1993), 'Some Notes on Valerius Maximus', in: *Sileno* 19, 395–408.
Briscoe, J. (1998), *Valeri Maximi Facta et Dicta Memorabilia*, 2 vols., Stuttgart/Leipzig.
Briscoe, J. (2019), *Valerius Maximus, Facta et Dicta Memorabilia, Book 8: Text, Introduction, and Commentary*, Berlin.
Buczek, C.R. (2008), *Horatius Auctor: Ideological Self-Fashioning in the Augustan Age*, Ph.D. Thesis, University of New York at Buffalo.
Carter, C.J. (1975), 'Valerius Maximus', in: T.A. Dorey (ed.), *Empire and Aftermath: Silver Latin, II*, London/Boston, 26–56.
Craig, C.P. (2014), 'Rhetorical Expectations and Self-Fashioning in Cicero's Speech for P. Sulla, §§18–19', in: *Rhetorica: A Journal of the History of Rhetoric* 32, 211–221.
Dugan, J. (2005), *Making a New Man: Ciceronian Self-Fashioning in the Rhetorical Works*, Oxford.
Elschner, C. (1864), *Quaestiones Valerianae*, Berlin.
Gibson, C.A. (2018), 'Artist and Community in Rhetorical Education of the Imperial Period', in: *Journal of Late Antiquity* 11, 298–318.
Glare, P.W.G. (ed.) (1968), *Oxford Latin Dictionary*, Oxford.
Haight, E.H. (1940), *The Roman Use of Anecdotes in Cicero, Livy, and the Satirists*, New York.

---

[58] I thank Sophia Papaioannou and Andreas Serafim for their many helpful suggestions on earlier drafts of this chapter as well as the anonymous reviewer for corrections, questions and suggestions.

Hellegeuarc'h, J. (1963), *Le vocabulaire latin des relations et des partis politiques sous la République*, Paris.
Helm, R. (1939), 'Valerius Maximus, Seneca und die *Exempla* Sammlung', in: *Hermes* 74, 130–154.
Helm, R. (1940), 'Beiträge zur Quellenforschung bei Valerius Maximus', in: *Rheinisches Museum für Philologie* n.s. 89, 241–273.
Helm, R. (1955), 'Valerius Maximus', in: *Realencyclopädie* 8A, 90–116.
Hennig, D. (1975), *L. Aelius Seianus: Untersuchungen zur Regierung des Tiberius*, Munich.
Hickson, F.V. (1993), *Roman Prayer Language: Livy and the Aeneid of Vergil*, Stuttgart.
Janson, T. (1964), *Latin Prose Prefaces: Studies in Literary Convention*, Stockholm.
Jocelyn, H.D. (1966), 'The Roman Nobility and the Religion of the Republican State', in: *Journal of Religious History* 4, 89–104.
Jocelyn, H.D. (1976–1977), 'The Ruling Class of the Roman Republic and Greek Philosophers', in: *Bulletin of the John Rylands University Library of Manchester* 59, 323–366.
Kidd, D. (ed. & tr.) (1997), *Aratus: Phaenomena*, Cambridge.
Kempf, C.F. (ed.) (1854), *Valeri Maximi Factorum et dictorum memorabilium libri novem cum incerti auctoris fragmento De praenominibus*, Berlin.
Kempf, C.F. (1866), 'Novae quaestiones Valerianae', in: *Zu der öffentlichen Prüfung der Zöglinge des Berlinischen Gymnasiums zum grauen Kloster*, Berlin, 1–37.
Kempf, C.F. (ed.) (1888), *Valerii Maximi Factorum et dictorum memorabilium libri novem cum Iulii Paridis et Ianuarii Nepotiani Epitomis*, Leipzig.
Kenney, E.J./Clausen, W.V. (eds.) (1982), *The History of Classical Literature: Volume 2, Latin Literature*, Cambridge.
Klotz, A. (1942), *Studien zu Valerius Maximus und den Exempla*, Munich.
Kranz, M. (1876), *Beiträge zur Quellenkritik des Valerius Maximus*, Posen.
Krause, C. (2013), '*Patria Potestas* – Honour-Shame?: tote Töchter im Kapitel "De pudicitia" des Valerius Maximus', in: U.E. Eisen et al. (ed.), *Doing Gender – Doing Religion: Fallstudien zur Intersektionalität im frühen Judentum, Christentum und Islam*, Tübingen, 251–272.
Krieger, B. (1888), *Quibus fontibus Valerius Maximus usus sit in eis exemplis enarrandis, quae ad priora rerum Romanarum tempora pertinent*, Berlin.
Langlands, R. (2006), *Sexual Morality in Ancient Rome*, Cambridge.
Langlands, R. (2018), *Exemplary Ethics in Ancient Rome*, Oxford.
Latte, K. (1960), *Römische Religionsgeschichte*, Munich.
Lawrence, S.J. (2006), *Inside Out: The Depiction of Externality in Valerius Maximus*, Ph.D. Thesis, University of Sydney.
Lawrence, S.J. (2018), '*Vis* and *Seruitus*: The Dark Side of Republican Oratory in Valerius Maximus', in: C. Gray et al. (eds.), *Reading Republican Oratory: Reconstructions, Contexts, Receptions*, Oxford, 95–110.
Linderski, J. (1986), 'The Augural Law', in: *Aufstieg und Niedergang der Römischen Welt* 2.16.3: 2146–2312.
Linderski, J. (1995) [1981], '*Exta* and *Aves*: An Emmendation in Rufinus, *Origenis in Numeros Homilia* 17.2', in: *Roman Questions*, Stuttgart, 524–526.
Linderski, J. (1995) [1990], 'The Death of Pontia', in: *Roman Questions*, Stuttgart, 320–327.
Lucarelli, U. (2007), *Exemplarische Vergangenheit: Valerius Maximus und die Konstruktion des sozialen Raumes in der frühen Kaiserzeit*, Göttingen.
Maire, S. (1899), *De Diodoro Siculo Valeri Maximi Auctore*, Schoenberg.

Maslakov, G. (1978), *Tradition and Abridgement: A Study of the Exempla Tradition in Valerius Maximus and the Elder Pliny*. Ph.D. Thesis, Macquarie University.

Maslakov, G. (1984), 'Valerius Maximus and Roman Historiography: A Study of the *Exempla* Tradition', in: *Aufstieg und Niedergang der Römischen Welt* 2.32.1, 437–496.

Michels, A.K. (1962), 'Review of Kurt Latte, *Römische Religionsgeschichte*, Munich, C.H. Beck, 1960', in: *American Journal of Philology* 83, 434–444.

Miller, P.A. (2015), 'Placing the Self in the Field of Truth: Irony and Self-Fashioning in Ancient and Postmodern Rhetorical Theory', in: *Arethusa* 48, 313–337.

Momigliano, A./Cornell, T. (2016), Online, s.v. *comitia*, in: S. Hornblower et al. (eds.), *Oxford Classical Dictionary*, Oxford, https://doi.org/10.1093/acrefore/9780199381135.013.1747 [Last access: 17 August 2021].

Mueller, H.-F. (2002), *Roman Religion in Valerius Maximus*, London.

Mueller, H.-F. (2004), '*Nocturni Coetus* in 494 BC', in: C.F. Konrad (ed.), *Augusto augurio: Rerum humanarum et divinorum commentationes in honorem Jerzy Linderski*, Stuttgart, 77–88.

Newman, J.K. (1967), *The Concept of Vates in Augustan Poetry*, Brussels.

Norden, E. (1958) [1898], *Die Antike Kunstprosa*, 2 vols., Stuttgart.

Norwood, F. (1963), 'The Riddle of Ovid's "Relegatio"', in: *Classical Philology* 58, 150–163.

Oliverius Arzignanensis [1491], *Opus Valerii Maximi: cum noua ac praeclara Oliuerii Arzignanensi uiri p[rae]stantissimi examinata interpraetatione*, Venetiis [Venice]. https://mdz-nbn-resolving.de/urn:nbn:de:bvb:12-bsb00057339-8.

Otto, A. (1962) [1890], *Die Sprichwörter und sprichwörtlichen Redensarten der Römer*, Hildesheim.

Patzelt, M. (2018), *Über das Beten der Römer: Gebete im spätrepublikanischen und frühkaiserzeitlichen Rom als Ausdruck gelebter Religion*, Berlin/Boston.

Pighius, S. (1612 [c. 1567]), *Valerii Maximi Dictorum Factorumque Memorabilium Libri IX*, Lugdunum (Lyon).

Ramelli, A. (1936), 'Le fonti di Valerio Massimo', in: *Athenaeum* 14, 117–152.

Reichelt, W. (1990), *Das Braune Evangelium: Hitler und die NS-Liturgie*, Wuppertal.

Rüpke, J. (2016), 'Knowledge of Religion in Valerius Maximus' *Exempla*: Roman Historiography and Tiberian Memory Culture', in: K. Galinsky (ed.), *Memory in Ancient Rome and Early Christianity*, Oxford, 89–111.

Schanz, M. (1935), *Geschichte der römischen Literatur bis zum Gesetzgebung des Kaisers Justinian, zweiter Teil: Die römische Literatur in der Zeit der Monarchie bis auf Hadrian*, Munich.

Serafim, A. (2020), *Religious Discourse in Attic Oratory and Politics*, London/New York.

Shakleton Bailey, D.R. (ed.) (2000), *Valerius Maximus: Memorable Doings and Sayings*, 2 vols., Boston.

Sinclair, B.W. (1980), *Valerius Maximus and the Evolution of Silver Latin*, Ph.D. Thesis, University of Cincinnati.

Sinclair, P. (1990), 'Tacitus' Presentation of Livia Julia, Wife of Tiberius' Son Drusus', in: *American Journal of Philology* 111, 238–256.

Skidmore, C.J. (1988), *Teaching by Examples: Valerius Maximus and the Exempla Tradition*, Ph.D. Thesis, Exeter University.

Skidmore, C.J. (1996), *Practical Ethics for Roman Gentlemen: the Work of Valerius Maximus*, Exeter.

Spoth, F. (2009), 'Principium', in: *Thesaurus Linguae Latinae* 10.2.2: 1308–1320.

Thom, J.C., (2005), 'Doing Justice to Zeus: on Texts & Commentries', in: *Acta Classica* 48, 1–21.

Thormeyer, G. (1902), *De Valerio Maximo et Cicerone quaestiones criticae*, Göttingen.
Treggiari, S. (1991), *Roman Marriage: Iusti Coniuges from the Time of Cicero to the Time of Ulpian*, Oxford.
Treves, P./Lintott, A.W. (2015), Online, s.v. *contio*. in: S. Hornblower et al. (eds.), *Oxford Classical Dictionary*, Oxford, https://doi.org/10.1093/acrefore/9780199381135.013.1800 [Last access: 17 August 2021].
van den Berg, C. (2008), 'The *Pulvinar* in Roman Culture', in: *Transactions of the American Philological Association* 138, 239–273.
Wardle, D. (1999), 'The Preface to Valerius Maximus: A Note', in: *Athenaeum* 87, 523–525.
Wardle, D. (2000), 'Valerius Maximus on the *Domus Augusta*, Augustus, and Tiberius', in: *Classical Quarterly* 50, 479–493.
Wardle, D. (2002), 'The Heroism and Heroisation of Tiberius: Valerius Maximus and His Emperor', in: P. Defosse (ed.), *Hommages à Carl Deroux 2: Prose et Linguistique*, Brussels, 433–440.
Wardle, D. (2012), 'Suetonius on Augustus as God and Man', in: *Classical Quarterly* 62, 307–326.
Weileder, A. (1998), *Valerius Maximus: Spiegel kaiserlicher Selbstdarstellung*, Munich.
Weinstock, S. (1970), *Divus Julius*, Oxford.
Welch, T.S. (2013), 'Was Valerius Maximus a Hack?', in: *American Journal of Philology* 134, 67–82.
Whittick, G.C. (1970), 'Valerius (8, *PW* 239) Maximus', in: N.G.L. Hammond/H.H. Scullard (eds.), *Oxford Classical Dictionary*, 2nd rev. ed., Oxford.
Williams, G.C. (1978), *Change and Decline: Roman Literature in the Early Empire*, Berkeley/Los Angeles.
Woodman, A.J. (1975), 'Velleius Paterculus', in: T.A. Dorey (ed.), *Empire and Aftermath: Silver Latin, II*, London/Boston, 1–25.
Zschech, F. (1865), *De Cicerone et Livio Valerii Maximi Fontibus*, Berlin.

Part V: **Rhetoric and Religion in Verse Style**

Konstantinos Melidis
Biblical Epics: Intersection of Rhetoric and Religion in Greek and Latin Hexametric Paraphrases of Psalm 136 (137)

Abstract: In the fluid world of Late Antiquity, marked by the destruction of old traditions (paganism) and the strong quest for new religious foundations (Christianity), rhetoric provided a solid base of intellectual life. Over the past few decades, it has been acknowledged that late rhetorical theories exerted an important influence on the classicising Greek and Latin Christian poetry, the so-called *Biblical epic*. This chapter offers a comparative examination of the Ps.-Apollinaris' (Greek) and Paulinus Nolanus' (Latin) surviving paraphrases of *Psalm* 136 (137), with particular emphasis being placed on the rhetorical paraphrastic strategy of addition (*auxēsis, amplificatio*) adopted by their authors. Despite both poets' conscious effort to stick closely to the original, a good number of passages in their paraphrases present some peculiarities, concerning both simple explanatory and religious exegetical openings (*interpretatio*) of the text of the Psalm.

1 The Greek and Latin paraphrases of Psalm 136

Whereas numerous Biblical epic paraphrases have survived in Latin,[1] we possess only two such works in Greek: the 5th-century-AD *Metabolē Sancti Evangelii Ioannei* of Nonnus of Panopolis, and the supposedly 4th-century-AD *Metaphrasis psalmorum* (henceforward *Metaphrasis*), which is attributed to the corpus of

---

[1] Among other works: Juvencus (4th c.), *Evangelium Libri IV*; Sedulius (5th c.), *Carmen Paschale* (based on the four Gospels) and Avitus (5th/6th c.), *De spiritalis historiae gestis*. The term *Biblical epics* refers to what scholars used to call Christian epic poetry or Biblical paraphrases, namely poetic works in hexameters whose narrative depends on a Biblical sequence of events. These paraphrases are characterised by the imitation (*imitatio*) of ancient Greek and Latin epic poetry. For a brief but well-documented presentation of this literary genre see Navarro 2014, 69–73. For an overview of Christian epic poetry see Whitby/Roberts 2018, 225–227 (Greek) and 230–232 (Latin). See also Roberts 1985, 39–59, who proposes two categories of literary paraphrases: "rhetorical" and "grammatical". The Biblical paraphrases (investigated in this chapter) fall into the former category.

https://doi.org/10.1515/9783110699623-013

Apollinaris of Laodicea.² The *Metaphrasis* is an *intralingual translation*³ of the prose rendition of the Septuagint's *Book of Psalms* reconstructed in epic verse (namely, from the *koinē* to the Homeric idiom). It is an extensive work of 5300 hexametric verses which remains underexamined,⁴ and constitutes the sole surviving paraphrase of the Old Testament from Greek Late Antiquity. We are fortunate to have three paraphrased *Psalms* among the thirty-three poems which have been transmitted to us under the name of Paulinus, Bishop of Nola (4th c. AD):⁵ his seventh,⁶ eighth and ninth poems (ed. Hartel) correspond to *Psalms* 1, 2 and 136 respectively.⁷ These constitute the earliest surviving examples of paraphrased Old Testament work in Latin.⁸

Since Psalm 136 has been paraphrased by roughly contemporary authors and changed into the same literary form (Biblical epic), it offers a unique opportunity to examine and compare the paraphrastic procedure of both poets, Pseudo-Apollinaris and Paulinus of Nola, alongside what we know of late Greek and Latin

---

2 On the delicate subjects of dating and doubtful authorship see Ludwich 1912, v–xi; Golega 1960, 5–24; Agosti 2001, 87 and 92–93. Although the subject is beyond the scope of this chapter, it is worth mentioning that the authenticity of the work has recently been supported by Faulkner 2020, 1–31.
3 On this term, as opposed to "interlingual translation", see Faulkner 2014, 196 and Id. 2019, 212. It is worth mentioning that the ancient definition of "paraphrase" does not converge with its modern sense. In effect, the terms *paraphrasis* and *metaphrasis* (lit. "translation") were treated as synonymous by the ancient theoreticians: e.g. Theon, *Prog.* 15 (Patillon/Bolognesi 1997, 107): "*paraphrasis* consists of changing the form of expression while keeping the thoughts; it is also called *metaphrasis*" (tr. Kennedy 2003, 70). The same goes for the term *metabolē* (e.g. Nonnus' *Paraphrase of John's Gospel* bears the title *Metabolē tou kata Ioannēn evangeliou*). On the ancient terminology in general see Zucker 2011, §2.2–3.
4 Golega 1960 remains the only monograph dedicated to the *Metaphrasis*, and study of the work is hampered by the absence of an exhaustive commentary. Faulkner's recent critical edition (Faulkner 2020) replaces that of Ludwich 1912, and also provides an English translation; indeed Faulkner's is the first translation of this work in a modern language.
5 It is largely admitted that these three paraphrases were produced during his stay in Spain: Fabre 1948, 111–113. Lienhard 1977, 190 proposes the period 389–394 as the "Spanish" period. In any case, no poem was composed after the year 409: Walsh 1975, 3. On Paulinus' life and writings see Costanza/Ricci 2014, *s.v.* and White 2000, 57–58.
6 The seventh poem is composed in iambic *senarii*. For a comparative study on this paraphrase (Psalm 1) and its Ps-Apollinaris' equivalent see Ugenti 2008/2009.
7 Unlike Ps-Apollinaris' *Metaphrasis*, whose title reveals in a way its literary genre, Paulinus' Biblical poems have no particular titles. However, according to the ancient definitions of the term *paraphrasis*, they are commonly considered and studied as Biblical paraphrases. On these three poems see Walsh 1975, 16–20 and Green 2006, 146–148. The only article devoted to Paulinus' paraphrases is Nazzaro 1983, 93–119. Cf. n. 3 above on terminology.
8 Nazzaro 1983, 98; Ugenti 2008/2009, 351.

rhetorical theories. Although some brief information has been provided in a few articles, there is still no systematic work on the topic of comparative investigation of paraphrastic techniques employed by these two authors as well as how their work is influenced by rhetoric.[9] More specifically, by discussing the question of the synergy of rhetoric and religion in the work of the two authors, both of whom, as Nodes points out, lived in a period of religious syncretism and combination of classical poetic forms with Christian ideas,[10] I aim to examine the rhetorical paraphrastic technique of *auxēsis/adiectio* ("increase"), which both poets used to enhance the religious messages conveyed by their *Vorlage*.

This survey is set out in the form of a case-study, since the selection of representative passages allow space for a more thorough investigation of unexamined aspects of the rhetorical strategy of *auxēsis* employed in the two paraphrases. Accordingly, particular emphasis is placed on adjectival addition, a practice which both poets constantly apply in order to fulfil their respective aims. At the same time, an important aim of this chapter is to make some general comparative remarks regarding both authors' handling of direct and indirect statements. Finally, the chapter draws some general conclusions with respect, firstly, to the two authors' techniques in changing the original, and, secondly, to the impact of their stylistic, explanatory and theological insertions in the new poetic text. All the relevant texts are provided at the end of the chapter.

2 The rhetorical nature of paraphrase

Since the end of the nineteenth century, scholars have pointed out that the literary techniques used by the poets of Biblical paraphrases,[11] both Greek and Roman, are closely related to the traditional techniques of literary composition

---

[9] Such as Ugenti 2008/2009 and Faulkner 2014. In general, not much ink has been spilt in discussing the subject of comparative investigation of paraphrase in both Greek and Roman poets in general.
[10] Nodes 1993, 1–2.
[11] See Ludwich 1885, 483 and 599; Golega 1930, 92–98; Curtius 1953, 147–148. In his pivotal work dealing exclusively with Latin biblical epics, Roberts claims, on the basis of literary, rhetorical and papyrological evidence, that the literary genre of Biblical paraphrase originates from rhetorical training in paraphrastic techniques: Roberts 1985, 21–22: "the earliest Latin biblical paraphrases were inspired in part by the desire to produce a stylistically respectable version of the Biblical text, that is, a version in line with current literary values established in the schools of rhetoric".

taught in rhetorical schools, the so-called *progymnasmata* ("preliminary exercises"),[12] one of which was the exercise of *paraphrasis*: an important exercise for the young students, especially aiming at developing their intellectual text comprehension and composition skills.[13] According to Aelius Theon's (1st c. AD) fifteenth *progymnasma*,[14] the only surviving text on the art of paraphrasing that is viewed as a rhetorical preliminary exercise, *paraphrasis* is a form of *variatio* ("variation") which may be realised by four strategies: syntax (*transmutatio*/μετάθεσις), i.e. "the rearrangement of words and phrases";[15] addition (*adiectio*/αὔξησις); subtraction (*detractio*, ἔνδεια)[16] and substitution (*immutatio*/ἐναλλαγή), in addition to combinations of these four techniques.[17] Besides, Quintilian's *Institutio Oratoria*, the most important Latin source on paraphrasing (although it does not discuss *paraphrasis* as a separate *progymnasma*) places great emphasis on the embellishment of the original text (*ornatus*) and states that the main working tools of paraphrasers are the methods of *amplificatio*, *varietas*

---

12 The word *progymnasma*, bearing the meaning of "preparatory rhetorical exercise", is attested for the first time in the *Rhet. ad Alex.* 1435a25, albeit without any further information, and without any relation to paraphrase: Bonner 1977, 250. See also Suet. *Gramm.* 4.3. According to Clarke 1963, 166, the *progymnasmata* seem to have begun to be developed during the 2nd century BC, before flourishing in the age of empire: "our knowledge of the προγυμνάσματα comes from the writers of the Empire, but the system took shape earlier, perhaps in the 2nd c. BC". The surviving Greek treatises related to *progymnasmata* are: Theon (1st c. AD), Ps-Hermogenes (ca. 3rd c. AD), Aphthonius (4th c. AD), the ninety-six *progymnasmata* of Libanius (4th c. AD) and Nicolaus the Sophist (5th c. AD). The only Latin treatise on *progymnasmata* is Priscian's (6th c. AD) *Preexercitamina*. Heath 2002/3 provides an enlightening overview of the history of *progymnasmata*. Kennedy 2003 has collected and translated all the Greek surviving *progymnasmata* into English.
13 On *paraphrasis* in the school curriculum in general see Miguélez-Cavero 2008, 308–316. Cf. Zucker 2011, 5–8 and Whitby 2016, 217.
14 This part survives only in an Armenian translation (5th/6th c.). On the Armenian text see Patillon/Bolognesi 1997, cxxix–cxxx.
15 Neither the Greek nor the Roman poet applies *transpositio* in their paraphrases, i.e. the modification of order of the Biblical verses (change of order of the verses corresponds to change of the sequence of the facts). Transposition is, however, inevitable in a metrical paraphrase (within the metrical units): Golega 1960, 124.
16 The use of *omissio* is minimal in both paraphrases. Both authors occasionally omit insignificant prose-like words or phrases (such as the adverbs ἐκεῖ and *illic* of the first verse of the original respectively), but lengthy omissions are not attested – the omission of the articles, a standard practice in the *Metaphrasis*, is not taken into account.
17 Theon. *Prog.* 15 (Patillon/Bolognesi 1997, 107): "there are four main kinds: variation in syntax, by addition, by subtraction, and by substitution, plus combinations of these" (tr. Kennedy 2003, 70). This fourfold formula can be traced back to Aristotle and is related to all kinds of literary composition see Desbordes 1983, 23–30.

("variation") and *copia verborum* ("verbal abundance").¹⁸ The Roman rhetorician explains the main purpose of *paraphrasis*: "I do not want paraphrase to be a mere passive reproduction, but to rival and vie with the original in expressing the same thoughts" (*Inst.* 10.5.5, tr. Russell 2001, 359.)¹⁹

3 Amplification

3.1 *Auxēsis/adiectio* as a paraphrastic strategy

The most frequent strategy for reworking the original text applied by both poets discussed in this chapter is unquestionably the rhetorical principle of *auxēsis* (lit. "increase"). The term *auxēsis*, and its Latin equivalent *adiectio*, is used with varied meanings throughout Greek and Roman Antiquity and, especially with regard to paraphrase, it may, at least in part, be defined as "the deliberate expansion of a statement beyond what is necessary for its understanding".²⁰ As was already noted by ancient theoreticians, the rhetorical device of *auxēsis* can be understood thematically (conceptually) and formally (linguistically) and, therefore, may be designated as two-dimensional. More specifically, *auxēsis* involves expansion, which can refer both to an increase in the length of the discourse (horizontal expansion) and to text that serves to increase the reader's or audience's opinion of the importance or intensity of a subject (vertical expansion).²¹

According to Longinus:

κεῖται τὸ μὲν ὕψος ἐν διάρματι, ἡ δ'αὔξησις καὶ ἐν πλήθει. Διὸ κεῖνο μὲν κἂν νοήματι ἑνὶ πολλάκις, ἡ δὲ πάντως μετὰ ποσότητος καὶ περιουσίας τινὸς ὑφίσταται.

Long. *De Subl.* 12.1.5–7

---

18 Quint. *Inst.* 1.9.2 and 10.5.4–11. On *paraphrasis* in Quintilian see Roberts 1985, 13–20.
19 The concept of rivalry viewed as a motivation for reworking a speech is traced back to Isocrates, who argues that "one must not shun the subjects upon which others have spoken before, but must try to speak better than they" (Isocr. *Pan.* 8: οὐκέτι φευκτέον ταῦτ' ἐστὶ περὶ ὧν ἕτεροι πρότερον εἰρήκασιν, ἀλλ' ἄμεινον ἐκείνων εἰπεῖν πειρατέον). Tr. Norlin 1928, 125. Cf. supra, n.11, with Roberts' remark.
20 See Burke 1962, 593 and Montefusco 2004, 70–71, especially for the use of the term in Aristotle. On definitions of the term and its Latin equivalents *adiectio/amplificatio* see the authoritative works of Volkmann 1885 (repr. 1963), 266–271 and Lausberg 1998, 118–119 and 189–196. Martin 1974, s.v. provides a large number of *testimonia*.
21 Curtius 1953, 492.

> Stylistic elevation lies in intensity, *auxēsis* also (sc. in intensity and) in multitude. Consequently, elevation often exists in a single idea, *auxēsis* is an increment of all parts and topics inherent in a subject.

Cicero also refers to amplification in several passages; for him, the technique aims among other things to excite the emotions. Precisely, in Cicero this rhetorical device is used for the first time as a figure aiming not only at elaborating a subject, corresponding to the above-mentioned thematic subdivision, but also at stylistically embellishing the discourse (*ornatus*), namely, as equating to a figure of speech (σχῆμα τῆς λέξεως), which corresponds to the formal subdivision: *summa autem laus eloquentiae est amplificare rem ornando* ("but the highest distinction of eloquence consists in amplification by means of ornament").[22] This explicit statement on the stylistic function of amplifying is crucial for the theoreticians of rhetoric during the imperial centuries.

Quintilian, like Theon, as has been mentioned above, goes on to regard amplification and its opposite procedure (*brevitas*, "abbreviation") as essential techniques of paraphrasing:

> *tum paraphrasi audacius vertere, qua et breviare quaedam et exornare salvo modo poetae sensu permittitur.*
>
> Quint. Inst. 1.9.2
>
> Then make a bolder paraphrase, in which they are allowed to abbreviate and embellish some parts, so long as the poet's meaning is preserved. (tr. Russell 2001, 211)[23]

In the specific context of the amplificatory paraphrastic techniques of the poems investigated in this chapter, amplification refers to the quantitative development of the *Vorlage*, and, more precisely, as a figure of speech (*figura elocutionis*)[24] and not one of thought (*figurae sententiae*), since the latter are generally preserved unchanged from the original texts of the Psalms; the main purpose of both paraphrasers is clearly to change the linguistic form of their model while keeping its content identical.

---

[22] Cic. *De or.* 3.104. Tr. Rackham 1942, 83.
[23] Cf. *Inst.* 10.5.4–11 on paraphrase as a written rhetorical exercise.
[24] Most ancient theorists divide rhetorical figures into those of λέξις ("figures of speech", namely, modes of verbal expression; Lat. *figurae elocutionis*) and those of διάνοια ("figures of thought", the ideas, the content; Lat. *figurae sententiae* or *sensus* or *mentis*, inextricably tied to εὕρεσις/*inventio*). See for instance, Quint. *Inst.* 9.3.2–3. In addition to rhetorical schemes of *lexis* and *thought*, there is also the category of grammatical schemes: Lausberg 1998, 235–236 and 273–274. On *inventio* see Lausberg 1998, 119–120.

3.2 Adjectival addition

Summary of Psalm 136: the psalmist recounts the deplorable condition of the Israelites during their exile in Babylon. He focuses on how they cannot sing their songs as they remember their homeland, and then transitions from a pure lamentation into a prayer as they seek revenge for what they have suffered from their enemies.[25] This wish is expressed in the form of a cruel imprecation against the infidels, including merciless punitive measures.

This section of my chapter discusses the technique of adding single adjectives (in bold in the text at the end of the chapter), a stylistic preference of both poets, in order to accentuate and explain the ideas of the original text, and to create antithetical images, absent from their *Vorlage*. In other words, in contrast to the usual Homeric and Vergilian usage, the epithets in these scriptural paraphrases have a clear relevance to the context; they are not simply *epitheta ornantia*.

The cities mentioned in both the Greek paraphrase and the psalm itself are: Babylon and Zion (twice each) and Jerusalem (three times). While in the original text, only Babylon is followed by an adjective (ταλαίπωρος, "unfortunate"), in the *Metaphrasis*, all the cities are characterised:

Tab. 1: Adjectives describing the cities.

Cities	Psalm	Metaphrasis
Babylon	- (v. 1.1)	- (v. 1)
Zion	- (v. 1.3)	ἀριπρεπής (v. 2)
Zion	- (v. 3.3)	ἀγακλεής (v. 7)
Jerusalem	- (v. 5)	πολυήρατος (v. 9)
Jerusalem	- (v. 6.2)	- (v. 13)
Jerusalem	- (v. 7.1)	ἐρίτιμος (v. 15)
Babylon	ταλαίπωρος (v. 9.1)	περικάμμορος (v. 18)

The Homeric epithet ἀριπρεπής ("noble") is employed for the holy land of Zion,[26] which is also described as ἀγακλεής ("glorious"), an epithet usually employed in

---

25 Ross 2016, 787.
26 It appears ten times in the Homeric corpus, in order to characterise: the beauty (*Od.* 8.176), the twelve kings of the Phaeacians (*Od.* 8.390), a trunk (*Od.* 8.424), Hector's son (*Il.* 6.477), the stars (*Il.* 8.556), the people (*Il.* 9.441), aegis (*Il.* 15.309) and Idomeneus' horse (*Il.* 23.453). The

Homer for designating persons holding high positions, like the kings Priam and Menelaus.[27] Next, retaining the original psalmist's scheme of apostrophe, Jerusalem is characterised as πολυήρατος ("much loved").[28] The second adjective used for Jerusalem, ἐρίτιμος ("respectful"), is here used for the first time in Greek literature to describe a city. Finally, the *hapax legomenon* compound περικάμμορος ("deplorable")[29] occurs in the imprecation against Babylon, substituting for the *Vorlage's talaipōros* ("unfortunate"). By retaining once again the rhetorical figure of apostrophe, the elliptical nominal clause θυγάτηρ Βαβυλῶνος ἡ ταλαίπωρος in the text of the Psalm is converted into a verbal one: ὦ θύγατερ Βαβυλῶνος, ἀεὶ περικάμμορος εἴης ("daughter of Babylon, may you always be most wretched", tr. Faulkner 2020, 421).

As a result of these mild *amplificationes*, the poet creates a strong contrast between the land of the Hebrews and that of Assyria, i.e. between the captured and the captors. In other words, by virtue of slight additions, the metaphrast intensifies the emotionally "neutral" character of the original – which just mentions the cities – to give a more representative evocation of the position held by the Israelites exiled to Babylon; contrasting their memory of their beloved homeland with the misery of their present in Babylon as well as the moral rightness of Zion with the turpitude of the place in which they now find themselves. What is more, it is of great interest that the Greek poet chooses the adjective ἀγακλεής to characterise Zion in the frame of an order articulated by the enemy. The purpose is to underline the Babylonians' sarcastic and provocative stance against the captured Jews (*eirōneia*[30]).

Paulinus applies the literary device of antithesis through slight amplification in the last part of the same paraphrased Psalm by adding two single adjectives (*solidae*, v. 49, and *teneris*, v. 62) specific to his purpose, and without altering the original meaning of the model:

---

noun ἀλεωρή ("place of shelter") occurs also in Homer, but the two words never show up together in any of the extant Greek texts.
27 *Il.* 23.528 (Menelaus) and *Il.* 16.737 (Priam).
28 This adjective is only once used for a city, in the *Sib. Or.* 5.289 describing the city of Tralles.
29 In Hom. *Od.* 20.33, 11.216, the word is always separated into two parts (*tmēsis*).
30 On irony as a means of emphasis (by saying one thing while meaning another) see Swearingen 1991, 224–225.

Tab. 2: Adjectives inserted by Paulinus of Nola.

Ps. 2.9	Paulin. *Carm. IX*
	v. 48–49
Beatus qui tenebit, et allidet parvulos tuos ad petram.	Nec minus ille beatus erit, qui **parva** tenebit et simul elidet solidae tua **pignora** petrae.
Happy is the one who shall seize your infants and dash them against the rocks.	Equally happy will he be who seizes your *little cherished ones* and dashes them against the *unyielding* rock. (Tr. Walsh 1975, 56)
	v. 62
	[...] adhuc **teneris** vitiorum infantia membris.
	[...] while they are infants with limbs yet *soft*.

The original text's account of smashing babies on the rocks as an act of revenge is already cruel. By replacing *parvulos* with the poetic periphrasis *parva pignora* ("little cherished ones"), in a striking *hyberbaton*, and describing the "soft limbs" of the babies (*teneris membris*), Paulinus underlines the tender age of the children. It is also notable that *petra* is preceded by the adjective *solida*. Thus, by adding a couple of adjectives and contrasting the softness of the babies to the hardness of the rock, both notions absent from the *Vorlage*, Paulinus creates a contrasting image by means of emphasis, and thereby helps the reader get a better sense of the repulsive and unchristian action.[31]

The contrast between the captors and the captured, and the rock and the babies, can be seen as vehicles contributing to the better understanding of the text. We can, therefore, speak about simple *interpretatio* in its pure philological – not religious (*exēgēsis*) – sense. While both these contrasts add depth to the underlying concepts, Paulinus, nonetheless, also adds a theological exegesis of the Psalm, in order to change the unchristian image into a Christian one. Specifically, while the *Vorlage's* text is completed (at v. 49), Paulinus goes on beyond that point (and beyond the Greek metaphrast) to illustrate and interpret the symbolic function of the macabre benediction (*makarismos*) which closes the Biblical text.

---

31 The contrast is pointed out by Nazzaro 1983, 111. The account in Paulinus' *explicatio* draws heavily on his analysis. The rhetorical technique of oppositeness, the figure of *antitheton*, is one of the main stylistic means of Gorgias regarding both content (*dianoia*) and words (*lexis*). On *antitheton* see Lausberg, 349–358. See also Arist. *Rh.* 1404a26 and Dion. Halic. *Dem.* 4.4, 25.4.

Resorting to *New Testament* reminiscences, the stone is explained as Christ (v. 52),[32] Babylon is interpreted as confusion (v. 54)[33] and the daughter of Babylon symbolises the flesh, which is represented as the source of sin (personified in the babies, vv. 54–55: *filia cuius / est caro, peccatis mater*). It is these sins that are, therefore, smashed to pieces on the *solida petra*, Jesus Christ.[34] In addition, the Latin *retractatio* closes with an admonishment (*exhortatio / parainesis*) in a Christian apologetic tone, seeking to appease those readers who may have been terrified by the ghastly final image, especially in vv. 65–68.[35] More specifically, the didactic tone of the allegorical exegeses in the last verses, which are first addressed to the enemies of the Jews and then to the readers – yet another new element missing from the original Psalm – has a consoling character.[36]

Paulinus' elaboration (infants symbolising sin and the stone upon which they are hurled symbolising Jesus Christ) is clearly based on the allegorical readings of the Bible established a century previously by Origen. It should be noted, however, that Paulinus was not particularly familiar with the Greek language, as can be inferred from one of his letters addressed to Rufinus,[37] and therefore it is highly unlikely that he gets this idea directly from Origen's text. More likely, his primary source was Hilary of Poitiers, whose own commentary on the *Psalm* expresses identical ideas,[38] and who declares that sins have to be eliminated when they are still young. Indeed, Paulinus literally turns Hilary's exegesis into poetry, as can be inferred by the employment of some identical words:

---

32 *Cor.* 1.10.4.
33 *Gen.* 11.9.
34 See Nazzaro 1983, 108.
35 Walsh 1975, 18–20 argues convincingly for the historical allusions to contemporary Rome in all three paraphrases of Psalms of Paulinus. Cf. Nazzaro 1983, 108: "in Christian thought pagan Rome was identified to Babylon and, as such, was opposed to the New Jerusalem, *the civitas Dei*". Therefore, Paulinus opposes Jerusalem to the hardly-at the time-Christianised Rome and looks forward to the future triumph (v. 72: *triumphet*) of the New Jerusalem over Babylon (Rome).
36 *Interpretatio* through adjectival addition appears already from v.4, where Paulinus attempts to justify the fact of exile, by considering the misfortune of Israelites as a fair punishment, meted out by divine wrath (*meritum… exilium*).
37 *Ep.* 46.2. On this topic see Walsh 1975, 354 n. 54.
38 On Origen's influence on Hilary see Gillingham 2008, 36.

Tab. 3: Paulinus' direct and indirect influences.

Paulinus	Hilary[39]	Origen[40]
v. 52: petra Christus: in ipso	Et allidit ad petram. **Petra autem, secundum Apostolum, Christus est.**	Μακάριος, ὃς ἂν κρατήσας ἐδαφίσῃ πρὸς **τὴν πέτραν (τὸν Χριστὸν)** τὰ νήπια Βαβυλῶνος‹, πρὶν εἰς ἄνδρας προέλθωσιν. ἔτι δὲ μακαριώτερον ἐξολοθρεῦσαι **Βαβυλώνιον σπέρμα**, λογισμὸν δηλονότι **συγχυτικόν**.
v. 54: nam Babylon nomen Confusio	In quem beatus est, qui filiae **Babylonis parvulos**, id est, **tenera adhuc** corporis **vitia**, allidet et conteret.	
vv. 60–62: Difficili vinces luctamine: praeripe parvos, / dum rudis ex utero cordis per pectora capta / reptat adhuc teneris vitiorum infantia membris.		
You will have a hard struggle to conquer them. Govern these vices while they are small, while they are infants with limbs yet unformed, while they are unschooled and creep from the heart's womb through the breast which they occupy. (Tr. Walsh 1975, 57)		

Albeit more implicitly and on a much smaller scale, the Greek poet makes a similar attempt at interpretation, "Christianising" the original text. The Homeric adjective ὠλεσίκαρπος ("losing its fruit", v. 3) is introduced to characterise the poplar tree, on which the exiled Israelites, unable to sing in a foreign land, have hung their stringed instruments. This is the only time in extant Greek literature where ἰτέα takes the form ἰταίη, presumably for metrical reasons. This is one of the two cases in this psalm where the poet changes the grammatical number of nouns: the plural of the original (ἰτέαις) into singular – the other being the plural πυθμένας for the singular θεμέλιος (v. 17). In the entirety of extant Greek literature, starting with Homer (*Od.* 10.510), the adjective ὠλεσίκαρπος always goes

---

39 Hilarius Pictaviensis, *Tract. Ps.* 136.14 (*PL* 784). Hilary's influence is pointed out by Nazzaro 1983, 112.
40 Orig. *Fr. Jer.* (*in catenis*), 26.

together with the willow.⁴¹ At first sight, the adjective could be said to cover both metrical and stylistic needs (*ornatus*), which indeed it does. But why did the metaphrast choose this particular epithet?

Both the singular for the willow, as well as its designation as "infertile", strongly suggest that Pseudo-Apollinaris had been influenced by Cyril of Alexandria (4th/5th c.), who explains the verse as follows: ἄκαρπον γάρ, μᾶλλον δὲ ὠλεσίκαρπον ἡ ἰτέα φυτόν... Ἀνέκειτο τοίνυν εἰς ἀπραξίαν τε καὶ ἀκαρπίαν τὰ τῆς ᾠδῆς ὄργανα.⁴² Cyril insists on the sterile character of the willow's fruit, if consumed. Thus, the metaphrast, drawing his interpretation from the Homeric Greek use of the term, demonstrates in a literate manner that the musical instruments of the exiled people became "sterile" (εἰς ἀκαρπίαν), that is to say, "inactive" (εἰς ἀπραξίαν), silent, due to their captivity, thus recalling Pseudo-Origen's exegesis (2nd/3rd c.) which reads that those sitting in the shadow of the poplar tree are unaware and their speech is "fruitless": Ὅσαι ψυχαὶ κάθηνται ἐν σκιᾷ καὶ ἀγνωσίᾳ, ἰστέον ὅτι λόγον ἄκαρπον ἔχουσι, τὰ ὄργανα κρεμάσασαι τὰ συντελοῦντα εἰς τὴν πρακτικήν.⁴³ It should be noted, incidentally, that Paulinus mentions the "friendly" shadow of the willows in his paraphrase and creates a bucolic scene, thus contrasting the commonplace of the *locus amoenus* to the miserable state of the displaced people (vv. 5–6: "on that bank, planted with pliant willows and affording friendly shade to visiting throngs" etc., tr. Walsh 1975, 55).

4 Variation of expression: The handling of direct and indirect statements

Theon investigates how the same idea can be expressed in various modes (*tropoi*) of statement in paraphrased text;⁴⁴ for example, recasting a passage as a direct

---

41 There is, however, one exception: Greg. Naz. 888.5, where the epithet qualifies the noun χάρις ("grace").
42 Cyril. *De ador.*, PG 68, 209. Cf. Didymus the Blind (4th c.), *Comm. Eccl.* 11–12: αἱ ἰτέαι δὲ φυτόν ἐστιν ἀκάρπους κατασκευάζ<ο>ν τοὺς ἀνθρώπους.
43 Ps.-Orig. *Selecta in Psalmos*, PG 12, 1657. Cf. Methodius (2nd/3rd c.), *Symposium* 4.3, who refers to the willow as φυτὸν τῆς ἀγνείας ("plant of chastity") in a Christian context.
44 The most representative example of this type of paraphrase that depends on variation of expression, is the fragmentary work of Sopater (4th c. AD), *Metapoiēseis*. In this work, the author demonstrates his mastery of the handling of rhetorical tools by providing a large number of paraphrases of a single passage. Unfortunately, only seven variations on a Demosthenes' passage (*Cor.* 60) survive (from a total of seventy-four), as well as about fifty excerpts from a Homeric

statement, as a question, as an interrogation, as a wish, or in any other form of expression.⁴⁵ To Theon's pronouncements should be added a passage of Quintilian, in which the Roman rhetorician articulates that the value of paraphrasing lies in the *innumerabiles modi* it offers to express the same idea, although he does not provide any precise examples: "if there were only one way of saying a thing well, we might legitimately suppose that our predecessors blocked the road for us; but in fact there are countless ways, and many roads lead to the same destination".⁴⁶

This idea is evident in the famous fourth verse of *Psalm* 136 (πῶς ᾄσωμεν τὴν ᾠδὴν Κυρίου ἐπὶ γῆς ἀλλοτρίας; "How can we sing the song of the Lord in a foreign land?"), depicting the painful situation of the displaced people forced to sing of their homeland while in a foreign and hostile land, which receives very different treatment from the two poets: Pseudo-Apollinaris preserves the direct speech of the original text, while Paulinus incorporates the direct statement in the narrative discourse, as will be seen below, in an imaginative way.

The Greek literal paraphrase of the verse (*Met*. 136.8: Θεῖον ἐν ἀλλοδαπῇ πῶς κεν μέλος ἐστὶν ἀεῖσαι; "How is it possible to sing God's song in a foreign land?"),⁴⁷ switched to the impersonal expression "How is it possible to sing?", somehow decreases the affective tone of the original communal question of the exiled people (πῶς ᾄσωμεν; "How can we sing?"). In Paulinus, in the frame of a large twofold *elaboratio*, this single verse occupies the whole first part (vv.14–23). Animated by the collective question of the Biblical text (*Quomodo cantabimus canticum Domini in terra aliena?*), the poet forms four rhetorical questions embodied in the Israelites' answer to the enemy, preceded by a small discussion about singing holy songs in a foreign and unfaithful land (vv. 14–21):

> Shall we then sing God's praises, songs appropriate to virgin bands, in the midst of barbaric rites, polluted tombs, and altars kindled with funeral fires? Shall we sing them in our distress for men who take joy in our grief, and convert a holy liturgy to wicked wantonness by

---

passage (*Il*. 8.146–150, from a total of seventy-two). The only existing edition is that of Glöckner 1910, 504–514.

45 Theon, *Prog.* 62.16–19: Ἀλλὰ κατὰ πλείους (sc. τρόπους), καὶ ποτὲ μὲν ἀποφαινομένων ἡμῶν, ποτὲ δὲ ἐρωτώντων, ποτὲ δὲ πυνθανομένων, ποτὲ δὲ εὐχομένων, ποτὲ δὲ κατ' ἄλλον τινὰ τρόπον τὸ νοηθὲν ἐκφερόντων. Theon defends here the idea that the same thing can be said in numerous different ways, criticising thus Cic. *De or*. 1.154.
46 Quint. *Inst*. 10.5.7–8. Tr. Russell 2001, 359. Cf. ibid. 10.5.9: *pluribus modis tractare proderit... sententias quasdam easque versemus quam numerosissime*.
47 In the framework of *variatio*, in the entire *Metaphrasis*, nouns referring to God (especially Θεός and Κύριος) are regularly replaced by adjectives such as θεῖος, θεσπέσιος, θεοπρεπής, etc. In this particular verse, Θεῖον μέλος for ᾠδὴν Κυρίου is a case in point.

singing sacramental hymns for the diversion of the enemy? How shall we bear to sing sacred hymns in our present wretchedness? Or how can Babylon reasonably demand the hymns of Sion? (Tr. Walsh 1975, 55)

After changing the enemy's direct command from the original *Psalm* (*hymnum cantate nobis de canticis Sion*, "sing for us one of the songs of Zion") into an indirect statement (vv. 11–13: *quod solita… hostis*), and after quoting the four questions posed by the captured people, Paulinus presents the Israelites giving a collective answer to their captors – even though the question they are answering are their own. While in the original *Psalm* we have an inner expression of thoughts, an internal monologue – precisely, an apostrophe to Jerusalem – of the captive people, who prefer to lose both the skills of their body (hand paralysis) and their voice (tongues stuck to the larynx) rather than forget their homeland, in Paulinus, this information pertains to the answer given by the exiles to their abductors' request that they sing a song. More precisely, in the second part of this elaboration (vv. 24–38), the apostrophe encountered in the Psalm becomes the detained people's answer to their captors, and yet in the form of a song (vv. 31–38):

> Hear the Lord's hymn, Sion's song: 'If Jerusalem my love, I forget you, my city, may my right hand be ever forgetful of myself; may my tongue cleave with thirst to my mouth if I do not embrace you with abiding love, and if in the first period of my joy, on the threshold of the kingdom promised to me forever, I do not remember to prefer you before all lands'. (Tr. Walsh 1975, 56)

It is worth noting that this dialogue is not a structural element in the original text. In all probability, Paulinus introduces the dialogic form in order to dramatise the text, providing a liveliness akin to theatrical scenes. The readers are presented with a dramatic scene, a conversation where the answer seems to come from the leader of the chorus. Finally, it is of interest that the captors' request is repeated, incorporated this time in the speech of the coryphaeus (vv. 25–27: *et, si tantus amor, Sion pia noscere vobis*[48] / *cantica… Sion*); thus, through *repetitio*, uttered by the helpless mouth of the weaker party (captive), Paulinus provides an emotionally charged moment.

Paulinus' vivid description and visually arresting portrayal of the event serves to please and persuade the reader, and thus evokes the rhetorical practice of *ekphrasis*, an exercise (*progymnasma*) normally taught during basic rhetorical

---

48 Cf. Verg. *Aen.* 2.10: *sed si tantus amor casus cognoscere nostros*.

training.⁴⁹ This technique is here used to complement the *progymnasma* of *paraphrasis*, applying in general a relaxed style adorned with various figures in order to describe persons, objects, places, events etc. in a lively manner, and is closely related to vividness (*enargeia*), defined in ancient theory as "the description in words of an event that seems to pass before your eyes".⁵⁰

Nevertheless, the content of the song itself in Paulinus is taken faithfully from the Psalm, despite important formal modifications, such as the emphatic enjambment in two successive verses (vv. 33–34: *mea / dextra* and 34–35: *meis / faucibus*). By employing the enjambment twice, Paulinus obligates the reader to abandon the monotony of the dactylic sense autonomy, and to search for the fulfilment of the meaning in the next verse. Also, ignoring a few minor additions (πολυήρατε and φίλη / *mea moenia* and *mea cura*, for Jerusalem), it is worth mentioning that the chiastic structural scheme of the *Vorlage* is preserved unaltered by both poets:⁵¹

Tab. 4: Syntactic similarity between the *Vorlage* and the paraphrases.

Septuagint	Metaphrasis	Vulgate	Paulinus
A ἐὰν ἐπιλάθωμαί σου	A αἴ σεῖο λαθοίμην	A si oblitus fuero	A si fuero oblitus
B ἡ δεξιά μου	B δεξιτερὴ χείρ	B dextera mea	B mea dextra
B' ἡ γλῶσσά μου	B' ἐμὴ γλῶσσα	B' lingua mea	B' mea lingua
A' ἐὰν μή σου μνησθῶ	A' εἰ μὴ σευ μεμνημένος εἴην	A' si non meminero tui	A' nisi te complectar

---

49 Theon, *Prog.* 118.6–7 defines *ekphrasis* as "descriptive language, bringing what is portrayed clearly before the eyes". On *ekphrasis* see Webb 2009, 131, and 143–145; Serafim 2015, 97–98.
50 Zanker 1981, 297: with the stylistic effect of *enargeia* "circumstances are described in such a way that the listener will be turned into an eyewitness". Cf. Webb 2009, 105: *enargeia* refers to "a quality of language that derives from something beyond words: the capacity to visualise a scene". With regard to the practice of *ekphrasis*, ancient rhetorical treatises lay special emphasis on the importance of the vividness (*enargeia*) of the language employed in the description: for instance, Aphthonius (Rabe, 37–41) states that *ekphrasis* is a descriptive language bringing what is shown clearly (*enargōs*) before the eyes. See also *Rhet. ad Her.* 4.55.68: *Demonstratio* (= *enargeia*) *est, cum ita verbis res exprimitur, ut geri negotium et res ante oculos esse videatur*; Quint. *Inst.* 8.3.63–66. For the ancient theoretical background with regard to the *enargeia* in *ekphrasis* see further Zanker 1981, 301–302 and Goldhill 2007, 3–7.
51 For the structure of *Psalm* 136 (137) of the Hebrew text see Freedman 1971, 187–205.

5 Conclusion

This chapter has not presented a complete analysis of the rhetorical techniques applied by both Greek and Roman authors in their paraphrase of Psalm 136. Rather, it focuses primarily on those figures and rhetorical devices which can be regarded as a means of artistic literary expression, namely as a paraphrastic tool of a literary genre which needs special rhetorical training.

For the most part, both poets closely follow their *Vorlage* and avoid in general the technique of *omissio*. Particularly, Pseudo-Apollinaris takes only a few liberties with the Biblical text; each hexameter corresponds to each verse of the Psalm, without any long elaborations or significant interpretative expansions. On the contrary, while Paulinus' version is always based on the content of the original, he expands the sacred text both by stylistic embellishment (*ornatus*) and by inserting new structural elements (for example, enjambment, commonplace: e.g. description of scenery–*locus amoenus*, dialogue and song, theatricality and impressive visualisation). In contrast to his Greek counterpart, within the framework of a genuine Christian exegetical reworking, Paulinus does not consistently respect the original *parallelismus membrorum*.

In addition, as has been demonstrated, both poets are influenced by ancient commentaries and exegeses on the Psalms, and employ some of these readings in their paraphrases. Pseudo-Apollinaris seems to be aware of Origen's and Cyril's treatises, while Paulinus fulfils his need to explain the Biblical text by applying Hilary's *explicatio*. More specifically, the Greek metaphrast occasionally takes on the role of an interpreter of the text, whereas Paulinus consistently explains the text by creating more of an explanatory note. In this way, he offers a metrical commentary in poetic form rather than saying the same things by using different words.

Finally, both poets offer a text addressed to those with some experience of earlier pagan Greek and Latin literary production. They apply some identical techniques of paraphrasing, such as highlighting the *Vorlage's* meanings by the creation of antithesis through adjectival addition (*amplificatio*). Although the two authors appear to try to attain their objectives in a similar way (e.g. through contrast via addition), the poetic results differ radically. Pseudo-Apollinaris' interests seem to be purely literary, stylistic and illustrative (clarification of meaning), and hence more rhetorical. Paulinus, on the other hand, seems to be more audacious in his theological approach to the extent of adopting a defensive tone, as an apologist. Finally, Paulinus' closing *exhortatio* reveals the didactic goals of his composition, which are absent from the Greek version.

If we had to close with a general comparative remark, we could paraphrase (in the current meaning of the term) Green's statement comparing Sedulius with Juvencus, by replacing their names with those of our authors: "Paulinus is less of a paraphraser and more obviously an exegete than Pseudo-Apollinaris, and his presentation of Christ is moulded by a very clear theological agenda".[52]

6 Texts

Tab. 5: Greek: *Vorlage* and paraphrase.

Ps. 136 (ed. Rahlfs)	Met. 136 (ed. Faulkner)
Ἐπὶ τῶν ποταμῶν Βαβυλῶνος ἐκεῖ ἐκαθίσαμεν καὶ ἐκλαύσαμεν ἐν τῷ μνησθῆναι ἡμᾶς τῆς Σιών. ²ἐπὶ ταῖς ἰτέαις ἐν μέσῳ αὐτῆς ἐκρεμάσαμεν τὰ ὄργανα ἡμῶν· ³ὅτι ἐκεῖ ἐπηρώτησαν ἡμᾶς οἱ αἰχμαλωτεύσαντες ἡμᾶς λόγους ᾠδῶν καὶ οἱ ἀπαγόντες ἡμᾶς ὕμνον Ἄσατε ἡμῖν ἐκ τῶν ᾠδῶν Σιών. ⁴πῶς ᾄσωμεν τὴν ᾠδὴν Κυρίου ἐπὶ γῆς ἀλλοτρίας; ⁵ἐὰν ἐπιλάθωμαί σου, Ἱερουσαλήμ, ἐπιλησθείη ἡ δεξιά μου· ⁶κολληθείη ἡ γλῶσσά μου τῷ λάρυγγί μου, ἐὰν μή σου μνησθῶ, ἐὰν μὴ προανατάξωμαι τὴν Ἱερουσαλὴμ ἐν ἀρχῇ τῆς εὐφροσύνης μου. ⁷μνήσθητι, Κύριε, τῶν υἱῶν Ἐδὼμ τὴν ἡμέραν Ἱερουσαλὴμ τῶν λεγόντων Ἐκκενοῦτε, ἐκκενοῦτε, ἕως ὁ θεμέλιος ἐν αὐτῇ.	Κλαύσαμεν ἑζόμενοι ποταμῶν Βαβυλῶνος ὕπερθε, μνησάμενοι Σιῶνος ἀριπρεπέος τ' ἀλεωρῆς· ²μεσσόθι δ'αὖ ποταμῶν ὑπὲρ ὠλεσίκαρπον ἰταίην ἡμέτεραι φόρμιγγες ἀπηῴρηντο λίγειαι. ³Κεῖσ' ἀναειρόμενοι λῄστορες ἔννεπον ἄνδρες, 5 ἡμέας οἵ δέ τ' ἔπερσαν, ἀειδέμεναί σφισιν ὕμνον· 'ἐκ μελέων Σιῶνος ἀγακλέος εἴπατε μολπήν'. ⁴Θεῖον ἐν ἀλλοδαπῇ πῶς κεν μέλος ἐστὶν ἀεῖσαι; ⁵Αἴ, χ', Ἱερουσαλὴ πολυήρατε, σεῖο λαθοίμην, ἡμετέρη λελάθοιτο φίλη κατὰ δεξιτερὴ χείρ· 10 ⁶πηγνυμένη περὶ λαιμὸν ἐμὴ κάρφοιτο κε γλῶσσα, εἰ μὴ σευ κατὰ θυμὸν ἀεὶ μεμνημένος εἴην, ὡς Ἱερουσαλὴν καὶ ἐν εὐφροσύνῃ προβαλοίμην. ⁷Καὶ σύ, μάκαρ, τεκέων ἐπιλήθεο μή ποτ' Ἐδώμου,

---

52 Green 2006, xiii.
This chapter is a part of a larger project devoted to the Greek Biblical epics (University of Cyprus). The Project EXCELLENCE/1216/0400 is co-financed by the European Regional Development Fund and the Republic of Cyprus through the Research and Innovation Foundation. I am grateful to Associate Professor Maria Ypsilanti for reading a previous draft of this chapter and giving advice on it. Also, particular thanks go to the editors of this volume, Andreas Serafim and Sophia Papaioannou, for their invaluable comments.

Ps. 136 (ed. Rahlfs)	*Met.* 136 (ed. Faulkner)
⁸θυγάτηρ Βαβυλῶνος ἡ ταλαίπωρος, μακάριος ὃς ἀνταποδώσει σοι τὸ ἀνταπόδομά σου, ὃ ἀνταπέδωκας ἡμῖν· ⁹μακάριος ὃς κρατήσει καὶ ἐδαφιεῖ τὰ νήπιά σου πρὸς τὴν πέτραν.	ὄλβιον ἦμαρ ἔχειν Ἱερουσαλῆς ἐριτίμου, 15 τῶν ποτε βαζόντων· 'κενεή, κενεή τις ὄλοιτο, μηδέ τί οἱ φείδεσθε, ἕως ἔτι πυθμένας ἴσχει'. ⁸ὦ θύγατερ Βαβυλῶνος, ἀεὶ περικάμμορος εἴης· ὄλβιος, ὃς προτέρης σε βίης ἀποτίσεται ἀνήρ, ⁹ὃς πέτρης ὑπένερθε μολὼν σεο νήπια ῥήξει. 20

Tab. 6: Latin: *Vorlage* and paraphrase.

Ps. 136 (eds. Weber/Gryson)	Paulinus, *Carm.* IX (ed. Hartel)
¹Super flumina Babylonis, illic sedimus et flevimus, cum recordaremur Sion. ²In salicibus in medio eius suspendimus organa nostra: ³quia illic interrogaverunt nos, qui captivos duxerunt nos, verba cantionum, et, qui abduxerunt nos: Hymnum cantate nobis de canticis Sion. ⁴Quomodo cantabimus canticum Domini in terra aliena? ⁵Si oblitus fuero tui, Jerusalem, oblivioni detur dextera mea; ⁶adhaereat lingua mea faucibus meis, si non meminero tui, si non proposuero Ierusalem in principio laetitiae meae. ⁷Memor esto, Domine, filiorum Edom, in die Ierusalem; qui dicunt: Exinanite, exinanite usque ad fundamentum in ea. ⁸Filia Babylonis misera, beatus, qui retribuet tibi retributionem tuam, quam retribuisti nobis. ⁹Beatus, qui tenebit et allidet parvulos tuos ad petram.	Sedimus ignotos dirae Babylonis ad amnes captivi, Judaea manus, miserabile flentes. Cum patrium memori traheremus pectore Sion, et meritum justa suspiraremus ab ira exsilium: lentis qua consita ripa salictis, 5 hospitibus populis umbras praebebat amicas. Illic Assyriae mediis in moenibus urbis, obliti laetas per maesta silentia voces, de salicum ramis suspendimus organa nostra. Namque dabat nobis durum gravis ira dolorem, 10 quod solita in sancto depromi cantica templo haec ad delicias sibi nos cantare jubebat impius ille, domo qui nos abduxerat, hostis. Ergone divinas laudes et carmina castis apta choris, inter sacra barbara, foedaque busta. 15 Inter et accensas funestis ignibus aras, heu! male de nostro laetis moerore, canemus? Deque pio ritu luxum faciemus iniquum, mystica ad hostilem modulantes cantica ludum? Quo miseri nunc ore sacros cantabimus hymnos? 20 Quove loco Babylon poscit sibi cantica Sion? Sed Domini carmen tellus aliena mereri non capit, indignas sacra vox avertitur aures. Si tamen ut captis dominus violentior instas,

Ps. 136 (eds. Weber/Gryson)	Paulinus, *Carm.* IX (ed. Hartel)
	et, si tantus amor, Sion pia noscere vobis 25
	cantica, si pergis me cogere non tua fari,
	et divina tibi quaenam sint cantica Sion,
	accipe quid captae Deus ultor spondeat urbi.
	Ne longum speres isto gaudere triumpho
	impie; quo sacrum prodi tibi praecipis
	hymnum: 30
	Ecce quis est hymnus Domini, quae cantica Sion:
	Si fuero oblitus mea moenia, te mea cura,
	urbs Hierusalem, fiat mea non memor unquam
	dextra mei, mea lingua meis et adhaereat arens
	faucibus, aeterno nisi te complectar amore: 35
	et nisi principio promissi in secula regni,
	laetitiaeque meae primo reminiscar in anno,
	te cunctis Hierusalem praeponere terris.
	Esto memor tum prolis Edom, ut versa vice nostrum
	aspiciat confusa diem, quo plebs tua claram 40
	moenibus aeternis Hierusalem habitabit,
	cui nunc gens oblita tui, crudele minatur
	excidium, dicens: Invisam funditus urbem
	diruite et vacuate manu, vestigia donec
	nulla relinquantur, muris ad inane redactis. 45
	Infelix miserae Babylonis filia, felix
	qui tibi pro nobis in nos tua gesta rependet.
	Nec minus ille beatus erit, qui parva tenebit
	et simul elidet solidae tua pignora petrae.
	Si cupis exstincta Babylonis stirpe beari, 50
	in te ipso primis gliscentia crimina flammis
	frange fide, jam propter adest petra Christus: in ipso
	viperream sobolem validis elide lacertis.
	Nam Babylon nomen Confusio: filia cujus
	est caro, peccatis mater: quae turba saluti 55
	noxia, corporeis ducit mala semina fibris.
	Haec vincenda tibi, si vis evincere mortem:
	namque tuis tales inclusos ossibus hostes,
	si permittantur crescendo assumere vires,
	difficili vinces luctamine: praeripe parvos, 60
	dum rudis ex utero cordis per pectora capta

Ps. 136 (eds. Weber/Gryson)	Paulinus, *Carm*. IX (ed. Hartel)
	reptat adhuc teneris vitiorum infantia membris:
	quae nisi praecaveas, aucta virtute necabit concordem vitiis animam terrena propago. 65
	Ne parcas igitur talem mactare catervam.
	Non tibi crimen erit, nocituram perdere gentem,
	ultricemque malo perfundere sanguine petram:
	Gaudet enim justus, si concidat impia proles:
	nam magis atque magis pius ista caede piatur, 70
	si perimat peccata suis dominantia membris,
	et fracta in Christo vitiorum plebe triumphet.

Bibliography

Agosti, G. (2001), 'L'epica biblica nella tarda antichità greca. Autori e lettori nel IV e V secolo', in: F. Stella (ed.), *La scrittura infinita. Bibbia e poesia in età medievale e umanistica. Atti del Convegno Internazionale, Firenze, 26–28 giugno 1997*, Florence, 67–104.

Burke, K. (1962), *A Grammar of Motives and A Rhetoric of Motives*, Cleveland.

Clarke, M.L. (1963), *Rhetoric at Rome: A Historical Survey*, New York.

Costanza, S./Ricci, C. (2014), 'Paulinus of Nola', in: A. Di Berardino, Th.C. Oden, J.C. Elowsky and J. Hoover (eds.), *Encyclopedia of Ancient Christianity*, vol. 3, Downers Grove, 118–119.

Curtius, E.R. (1953), *European Literature and the Latin Middle Ages*, translation by W.R. Trask, New York.

Desbordes, Fr. (1983), 'Le schéma "addition, soustraction, mutation, métathèse", dans les textes anciens', in: *Histoire Epistémologie Language* 5/1, 23–30.

Fabre, P. (1948), *Essai sur la Chronologie de l'œuvre de Saint Paulin de Nole*, Paris.

Faulkner, A. (2014), 'Faith and Fidelity in Biblical Epic. The *Metaphrasis Psalmorum*, Nonnus and the Theory of Translation', in: K. Spanoudakis (ed.), *Nonnus of Panopolis in Context. Poetry and Cultural Milieu in Late Antiquity*, Berlin/New York, 195–210.

Faulkner, A. (2019), 'Paraphrase and Metaphrase', in: P.M. Blowers/P.W. Martens (eds.), *The Oxford Handbook of Early Christian Biblical Interpretation*, Oxford, 210–220.

Faulkner, A. (ed.) (2020), *Apollinaris of Laodicea: Metaphrasis Psalmorum*, Oxford.

Freedman, D.N. (1971), 'The Structure of Psalm 137', in: H. Goedicke (ed.), *Near Eastern Studies in Honor of W.F. Albright*, Baltimore/London, 187–205.

Gillingham, S. (2008), *Psalms through the Centuries: Volume One*, Malden, MA/Oxford.

Glöckner, S. (1910), 'Aus Sopatros Μεταποιήσεις', in: *Rheinisches Museum für Philologie* 65, 504–514.

Goldhill, S. (2007), 'What is *Ekphrasis* for?', in: *Classical Philology* 102, 1–19.

Golega, J. (1930), *Studien über die Evangeliendichtung des Nonnos von Panopoli*, Breslau.

Golega, J. (1960), *Der Homerische Psalter: Studien über die dem Apolinarios von Laodikeia zugeschriebene Psalmenparaphrase*, Ettal.
Green, R.P.H. (2006), *Latin Epics of the New Testament*, Oxford.
Hartel, G. (ed.) (1894), *Sancti Pontii Meropii Paulini Nolani Opera*, vol. 2 (*Carmina*), Vienna.
Kennedy, G.A. (2003), *Progymnasmata: Greek Textbooks of Prose Composition and Rhetoric*, Atlanta.
Lausberg, H. (1998), *Handbook of Literary Rhetoric*, Leiden.
Lienhard, J.T. (1977), *Paulinus of Nola and Early Western Monasticism*, Köln/Bonn.
Martin, J. (1974), *Antike Rhetorik: Technik und Methode*, Munich.
Miguélez-Cavero, L. (2008), *Poems in Context: Greek Poetry in the Egyptian Thebaid 200–600 A.D.*, Berlin/New York, 2008.
Montefusco, L. (2004), 'Stylistic and Argumentative Function of Rhetorical *Amplificatio*', in: *Hermes* 132, 69–81.
Navarro, A. (1983), 'La parafrasi salmica di Paolino di Nola', in: A. Stella (ed.), *Atti del Convegno. XXXI cinquantenario della morte di S. Paolino (431–1981)*, Rome, 93–119.
Navarro, A. (2014), 'Paraphrases, Biblical and Hagiographical', in: A. Di Berardino, Th.C. Oden, J.C. Elowsky and J. Hoover (eds.), *Encyclopedia of Ancient Christianity*, vol. 3, Downers Grove, 69–73.
Nodes, D.J. (1993), *Doctrine and Exegesis in Biblical Latin Poetry*, Leeds.
Patillon, M./Bolognesi, G. (eds.) (1997), *Aelius Théon, Progymnasmata*, Paris.
Roberts, M. (1985), *Biblical Epic and Rhetorical Paraphrase in Late Antiquity*, Liverpool.
Roberts, M./Whitby M. (2018), 'Epic Poetry', in: S. McGill/E.J. Watts (eds.), *A Companion to Late Antique Literature*, Medford, MA, 221–240.
Ross, A.P. (2016), *Commentary on the Psalms: Volume 3 (Ps. 90–150)*, Grand Rapids.
Russell A.D. (2001) (ed. and tr.), *Quintilian, The Orator's Education*, Cambridge, MA/London.
Serafim, A. (2015), 'Making the Audience: *Ekphrasis* and Rhetorical Strategy in Demosthenes 18 and 19', in: *Classical Quarterly* 65, 96–108.
Swearingen, J.C. (1991), *Rhetoric and Irony*, Oxford.
Ugenti, M. (2008/2009), 'La parafrasi del Salmo 1 nella *Metafrasi dei Salmi* attribuita ad Apollinare e nel *Carme* 7 di Paolino di Nola: due tecniche a confronto', in: *Rudiae* 20/21 (II), 340–356.
Volkmann, R. (1885, repr. 1963), *Die Rhetorik der Griechen und Römer, in systematischer Übersicht*, Munich.
Walsh, P.G. (1975), *The Poems of St. Paulinus of Nola*, London.
Webb, R. (2009), *Ekphrasis, Imagination and Persuasion in Ancient Rhetorical Practice*, Farnham/Burlington.
Zanker, G. (1981), 'Enargeia in the Ancient Criticism of Poetry', in: *Rheinisches Museum für Philologie* 124, 297–311.
White, C. (2000), *Early Christian Latin Poets*, London/New York.
Zucker, A. (2011), 'Qu'est-ce qu'une paraphrasis? L'enfance grecque de la paraphrase', in: *Rursus* 6 [online, https://doi.org/10.4000/rursus.476 (Last access: 17 August 2021)]

Notes on Editors and Contributors

Christopher Degelmann is Lecturer in Ancient History at Humboldt University Berlin.

Kyriakos Demetriou is Professor of Political Science at the University of Cyprus.

Jakub Filonik is Assistant Professor in Classics at the University of Silesia in Katowice.

William Furley is Emeritus Professor at the University of Heidelberg.

Edward M. Harris is Emeritus Professor of Ancient History at Durham University and Honorary Professorial Fellow at the University of Edinburgh.

Glenn Holland is the Bishop James Mills Thoburn Chair in Religious Studies at Allegheny College.

Despina Keramida is a Postdoctoral Fellow in Classics at the University of Cyprus.

Vasileios Liotsakis is Assistant Professor of Ancient Greek Literature at the University of the Peloponnese.

Konstantinos Melidis is a Postdoctoral Fellow in Classics at the University of Cyprus.

Hans-Friedrich Mueller is the Thomas Lamont Professor of Ancient & Modern Literature in the Department of Classics at Union College in Schenectady, New York.

Sophia Papaioannou is Professor of Latin at the National and Kapodistrian University of Athens.

Maik Patzelt is Lecturer in Ancient History at the University of Osnabrück.

Panagiota Sarischouli is Professor of Ancient Greek and Papyrology in the Department of Classics at the Aristotle University of Thessaloniki.

Andreas Serafim is a Research Fellow at the Research Centre for Greek and Latin Literature of the Academy of Athens.

Kelly E. Shannon-Henderson is Assistant Professor of Classics in the Department of Modern Languages and Classics at the University of Alabama.

General Index

Actio 9, 133–135
Adiectio 11, 271–273
Aelius Theon 272
Aggression 9, 143, 153, 155–157, 159, 161, 163, 165, 167
Alexander 10, 193–217
Amplificatio 11, 269, 272–274, 276, 284
Antigone 17, 21–23
Antiphon 53, 59–76
Apagōgē 39–40, 61
Appropriation 10, 153, 164, 167
Arrian 10, 193, 195, 196, 198, 200–201, 203–208
Asebeia 30, 39–40, 46, 53
Athens 3, 19–20, 26–29, 31, 33, 37–38, 40–56, 62, 68, 110, 119, 137, 204
Auspicia 11, 245, 247, 252
Authority 6, 10, 27, 44, 94, 172–173, 179–182, 184, 186, 251–252, 260
Auxēsis 11, 269, 271, 273–274

Biblical paraphrase 269, 271
Bilingual Theban Handbook 9, 101
Book of Psalms 270

Cicero 5, 90, 135, 139, 141–147, 162, 164–167, 246–247, 261, 274
Citharōdoi 137
Civilitas 11, 221, 224
Clara vox 9, 133, 137
Colossians 176–178, 182–186
Comedy 47, 73
Compassion 9, 153, 155–157, 159, 161–163, 165, 169
Creon 17, 21–23, 25
Cult/cultic 5, 8, 37–39, 41, 43, 45, 47, 49, 51, 53, 55, 102, 111–112, 124, 143, 222–223, 226, 232, 234, 237
Cultic regulations 8, 37, 39, 41, 43, 45, 47, 49, 51, 53, 55
Culture/cultural 7, 9, 26, 83, 106–109, 113, 121, 124, 134–135, 141–142, 155, 160, 174–175, 184–185
Curtius Rufus 193, 195, 209

Deianira 8, 83, 85–89, 91, 93–95
Deification 5, 10–11, 221, 223–231, 233, 235, 237, 239, 241, 250
Demosthenes 3–4, 8, 37–41, 48–49, 55–56, 69, 280
Denunciation 39, 42, 44, 47–54
Deutero-Pauline 10, 176, 182–186
Dihaeresis 67, 70
Dikē 37–41, 46, 72
Divinitas 11, 227, 245, 247, 249, 251–253, 255, 257, 259, 261, 263
Divus 10, 221–223, 225–227, 229, 231, 233, 235, 237–239, 241–242

Egypt/Egyptian 101–125
Eisangellein 37, 54
Eleusinian Mysteries 8, 37, 40–42, 111
Eleusis 40–42, 45, 47
Eloquentia popularis 133, 143–145, 147–149
Emotions 24, 76, 153, 155–156, 160–162, 231, 245–246, 254–255, 259–260, 274
Emperor cult 223, 226, 232
Empire 4–6, 31, 156, 174, 176, 185, 187, 204–206, 236, 238–239, 241, 272
Ephēgēsis 37–40, 53
Ephesians 176–177, 182–186
Epic 11, 251, 269
Eros 9, 108, 113–121, 123–124

Funeral Speech 153–160, 164, 167

Gods 1, 3, 5, 7–8, 10–11, 17, 19–25, 28, 193–197, 199–201, 203–207, 209, 211, 213–217, 221–228, 230, 233–241, 245, 247, 249, 250, 252–257, 261–262
Graeco-Egyptian formularies 109
Graphē 37, 40

Heka 101–102, 110
Heliaia 42, 44
Hexametric paraphrases 11, 269
Hierosylia 39

Homicide 24–25, 33, 53, 59–64, 71–72, 76
Hypocrisis 174

Impiety 37–38, 40–42, 45–46, 55–56, 65, 70–71

Kakourgoi 39,
Katharos 24
Kērygma 17, 21–22
Korē 9, 108–113, 124

Laudatio funebris 153, 155–159, 162, 167
Law 2, 6–8, 11, 17–29, 31, 33, 37–39, 42–48, 50–53, 55–56, 60–61, 63, 65, 68, 71–74, 76, 84, 89, 92, 103, 119, 177–178, 185, 221, 224, 251, 261–262
Logographos 59
Lycurgus 3, 24

Magic 1, 8–9, 81–97, 107–113, 115–117, 119, 121, 123–125, 158, 198
Graeco-Egyptian Magic 7, 9, 101, 103, 105, 107, 109–112, 115, 117, 119, 121, 123–125
Mēnyein 37, 48, 52
Metaphor 10, 103, 176–177, 186, 222
Metaphrasis 270
Miasma 61, 64, 66, 68–69, 76
Mourning 153, 156, 160–165, 167, 210

Narrative 5, 94, 96, 185, 193–197, 199, 201, 203–205, 207–208, 210, 212–213, 215, 251, 260, 269, 281
Nomos 22

Old Testament 270
Orality 136, 138, 140, 144, 147
Orpheus 8, 83, 89–92, 95
Ovid 8–9, 81–85, 87–89, 91, 93, 95, 97

Paulinus, Bishop of Nola 269–270, 277–285
Panegyric(us) 10, 158, 221–227, 229, 231–233, 235, 237, 239, 241
Paraphrase 269–275, 278, 280–281, 284–285

Performance 1, 7, 9–10, 81–83, 88–90, 95, 133–136, 142–145, 147–148, 153, 163, 171, 173–175, 177, 179, 181, 183, 185–187
Pharmakos 25
Phainein 42, 44–47, 51–52
Phasis 41–42, 46–47, 50–51
Phrazein 37, 41, 46–48, 50–51
Piety 66, 69, 89, 96, 245–246, 248, 254, 257, 260
Pisteis
Atechnoi 66–67, 70, 74
Entechnoi 60, 66, 73
Pliny the Elder 140, 146
Pliny the Younger 143
Polis-religion 1
Political culture 155
Politics 3–7, 33, 144, 199, 263
Pollution 5, 24–25, 33, 61–64
Praeire 9, 133, 145–148
Prayer 1, 3, 5, 8, 17, 86, 91, 96, 119, 121–124, 133–149, 158, 221, 228, 233, 237, 240, 250, 254, 275
Precatio popularis 133, 142, 144
Private associations 28, 33
Prosōpopoeia 82
Ps.-Apollinaris 269–270, 273, 280–281, 284–285
Psyche 9, 108, 110, 113–116, 124
Pygmalion 9, 83, 95–97

Rhabdophoroi 27
Religious argumentation 3
Religious discourse 2–3, 82, 262
Rites 8, 11, 23, 44–46, 48–49, 82, 111, 124, 153
Rituals 25–26, 28, 64, 82, 86, 93, 101–104, 107, 112, 115–116, 125, 223, 254
Private 101–105
Rome 4–5, 11, 82, 141, 153–154, 156, 161, 181, 235, 238–239, 242, 245, 247, 249–251, 253, 255, 257, 259, 261, 263, 278
Ruler 184, 194, 222–223, 260

Self-fashioning 10–11, 193, 195–196, 245–246, 249, 251, 253, 255, 257, 259, 261, 263

Sophocles 17, 20, 23, 25, 85
Statues 93, 95, 226–227, 234
Supplication 92, 96

Theban Magical Library 101, 103–104, 106, 108
Theodicy 59

Tragedy 64, 163
Trajan 221–242

Vocality 9, 136, 138–139, 141, 144, 148

Zētētai 54

Index Locorum

Aelius Theon
Progymnasmata 270–283 *passim*
Prog.
15 270 n.3; 272 n.17
62.16–19 281 n.45
118.6–7 283 n.49

Aeschines
3.18 45

Andocides
1.11 48
1.14 49; 54
1.16 54
1.17 48
1.20 55
1.27 48; 49; 54
1.27–28 53
1.31–32 64 n.27
1.45 53
1.66 55
1.111 53
1.112–132 46

Antiphon
1.3 61 n.8
1.8 64 n.27
1.17 48
1.21–31 65–66
1.28 64 n.27
2c3–8 (*Tetr. 2*) 69–70
3a2 (*Tetr. 3*) 62
3a3 (*Tetr. 3*) 63
3a4 (*Tetr. 3*) 64
5.11 64 n.23; 71
5.12 64 n.27; 71–72
5.29 72
5.46 54
5.48 53
5.62 63 n.18
5.81 67
5.88 66 n.30
6.2 61
6.3 66 n.30
6.4 63 n.18; 63 n.19
6.6 64 n.26
6.7 66 n.30
6.14 64 n.27
6.40 68

[Apollinaris]
Metaphrasis Psalmorum 280–283; 285–286

Appian
Civ.
2.147–148 164 nn.49, 50
2.600–614 162 n.47
2.613 163 n.48

Apuleius
Met.
4.28–6.24 114–115

Aristophanes
Ach.
819–820 47
823–826 47
911–914 47
917 47
Eq.
278–279 47
300–302 47
Neb.
844–846 47
Thesmo.
764 47

[Aristotle]
Ath. Pol.
57.1–2 53

Arrian
Anab. 203–209
1.7–9 203–204
2.3.1–7 204
2.6.1–7 205
2.7.3 205

2.14.3–9	205	3.196	140 n.47
2.15.6–24	205–206	3.197	139
3.3.2	207	3.216	140 n.53
3.3.5–6	206	3.224–227	142 n.64
3.4.5	207	3.225–227	140 n.51
3.7.6	211	*Dom.*	
4.8.4	213	139–141	145 n.80
4.8.5	207	139	147 n.98
4.9.1	207	*Fin.*	
4.10.1–2	207	2.77	142 n.59
4.12.6–7	207	3.24	142 n.66
4.14.2	213	*Leg. Agr.*	
4.28.1–30.4	207–208	2.13	142 n.63
5.1–3	207–208	*Or.*	
5.25.3–26.8	208–209	13	142 n.62
5.27.1	209	151	142 n.62
7.8.3	209	*Mil.*	
		33	156 n.9
Callimachus		*Mur.*	
Hymn.		26–29	147 n.92
2.110–112	109–110 n.42	36	157 n.16
		Pis.	
Cassius Dio		18	145 n.78
44.66.1–52.3	162 n.47	*Quir.*	
44.36.1	158 n.24	6	164 n.54
		Sest.	
Cicero		66	145 n.82
Ad Q.		*Rab. Post.*	
fr. 3.6.5	156 n.11	16–17	155 n.8
Brut.		*Red. Sen.*	
57–60	155 n.7	37	164–165
62	157 n.15; 162 n.44	*Ver.*	
136	142 n.62	5.14.36	155 n.8
158	145 n.79		
164	143 n.69	**CIL**	
164–165	142 n.62	VI 1527 (*Laudatio Turiae*)	157 n.18
186	140 n.47	VI 10230 = *ILS* 8394	157 n.14
224–225	142 n.66	XIV 3579 (*Laudatio Matidiae*)	157 n.18
Cato			
12	157 n.17	**Curtius Rufus**	
Comment. pet. 5	142 n.62	3.5.4–9	210
De or.		3.6.17–20	210
1.81	142 n.62	3.7.6	211
2.34–35	142 n.64	4.2.2–5	212
2.44	157 n.12	4.2.13–14	212
2.341	156 n.11; 157 n.16	4.2.16–18	213
3.104	274	4.3.21–23	212

4.4.5	212
4.10.1–7	211
6.2.1–4.1	211
6.3.1–18	211
6.7.1–7.2.38	213
6.9.19	213
6.10.26–29	213
8.1.19–2.12	213
8.1.42	213
8.6.1–8.23	213
8.7.13–14	213
8.8.1–19	214
8.8.15–17	214–215
8.10.27–36	215–216
9.1.18	216
9.8.4–8	216

Demosthenes

18.259–260	137 n.33
19.71	63 n.22
21.175	49
22.26–27	38–39
23.81	24
43.66	23–24

[Demosthenes]

59.46	54
59.66	49
59.116–117	45 n.33

Diodorus Siculus

1.22.6–7	118 n.79
17	195 n.6

Dionysius of Halicarnassus
Ant. Rom.

2.70	140 n.50
5.17.2–6	155 n.6

Ennius
Ann. frr. 304–308 Manuwald 155 n.7

GEMF 8 = PGM LXXII+LVII col. ii 16.	112 n.57
GEMF 15 = PGM/PDM XII	108–124
1–13	109–113
14–95	113–124
14–17	121 n.93
GEMF 15 = PGM/PDM XII 201–269	122
GEMF 18 col. viii recto 1–16 = PDM/PGM LXI 112–127	116
GEMF 30 = PGM II 64–184	123 n.104
GEMF 30 = PGM II 126–128	123–124 n. 108
GEMF 38 = SM II 82	114 n.65
GEMF 57/PGM IV	113
GEMF 57/PGM IV 1716–1870	116–117
GEMF 57/PGM IV 2145–2240	114 n.65
GEMF 74 = PGM VII 973–980	114 n.65

Heraclitus
fr. 253 Kirk/Raven 23

Herodotus
2.73 122

Hesiod
fr. 304 M–W 122

Hilarius Pictaviensis,
Tract. Ps. 136.14 (*PL* 784) 278–280

Horace
Epist.
1.16.59–62 137 n.30

Iamblichus
Myst.

5.24	117 n.76
7.4.256	110 n.45

Iuvenalis
6.542–612 141 n.57

IG

I³ 32	47
I³ 78	53
II² 1128	50
II² 1258	28
XII 3.330	32–33 (see also *LSCG* 135)

Isaeus

6.49–50	48, 54
6.64–65	54

Isocrates
17.12–14	49

Livy
7.9.8	137 n.30
7.15.2l	137 n.31
7.31.12	137 n.31
8.9.4	145 n.83
8.40.4–5	162 n.44
9.46.6	145 n.83
10.19.17	135 n.21
10.28.14	145 n.83
10.36.11	135 n.21; 137 nn.31, 32
27.27.13–14	162 n.45
27.27.13	156 n.9; 157 n.17
31.9.6–10	147 n.99
31.9.9	145 n.84
36.2.3–5	145 n.84
41.16.1–2	147 n.98
41.21.11	145 n.83
42.15–16	25
42.28.9	145 n.83
45.5	25

Longinus
De Subl.
12.1.5–7	273–274

LSCG
3	26
13	26
65	26–27
69	27
93	27
115	27
135	32–33 (see also *IG* XII 3.330)

Lysias
5.3–5	53
5.4–5	55
5.5	54
7.16	53
12.4	49
12.48	54
23.2–5, 13	49

[Lysias]
6.4	53

New Testament
Acts
10.34	177
13–28	172 n.2
15.1–21	172
19.1–7	183

Colossians
1.4	183
1.7–8	183
1.15–19	186
2.18–19	186
3.11	186
3.18–4.1	184–185
3.25b	177
4.7–9	183

1 Corinthians
1.10–17	173 n.3
1.10–13	180
1.30	177
4.14–21	173
5.1–6.20	173 n.3
5.3–5	175
6.12–14	180
7.1–40	180
7.1b–3	180
7.23	177
8.1–3	180
9.24–27	177
10.17	178
11.17–22	173 n.3
12.12–28	178
12.12–27	186
15.42–44	178

2 Corinthians
1.1–2.13	180
1.16–2.13	173 n.3
1.23–2.1	173
2.14–6.13	180
4.5	178
6.3–9	178
7.1–40	180
7.2–16	180
7.5–16	173 n.3; 180
8–9	180

10–13	181	6.6	178
10.1–13.13	180	6.16–22	177
10.1–13.10	173	7.4	178
10.1	175	7.14	177
10.9–10	175	7.25	177
11.5	180	8.10–13	178
11.21b–29	178	8.15	177
12.2–3	178	8.23	177
Ephesians		12.5	178
1.1	183	*1 Thessalonians*	
1.15	183	2.17–3.10	173
2.11–16	185	4.15–17	179
2.25–33	185	*2 Thessalonians*	
4.11–16	178	2.2	182
5.21–6.9	184–185	3.17	182
5.21–24	184		
6.4–8	185	**Old Testament**	
6.9c	177; 185	*Psalm* 136 (137)	269–288
Galatians			
1.2b	181	**Ovid**	
1.6–2.14	181 n.28	*Ars Am.*	
1.10	178	3.345–346	85
2.1–10	172	*Fast.*	
2.2	177	2.649–655	140 n.49
2.6b	177	*Her.* 9	81–83; 83–89
2.15–3.29	181 n.28	9.1–26, 47–118	85
2.19	178	9.27–45	85–86
3.6–29	172	9.139–144	86–87
3.6–14	178	9.159	87
3.13	177	*Her.* 13	81–83; 92–95
3.28	185	*Met.*	
4.1–9	177	10.1–85	80–83; 89–92
4.5	177	10.243–297	80–83; 95–96
4.21–5.1	172	10.274–276	96 n.58
4.22–31	177	15.670–680	140 n.49
5.1	177		
5.7	177	**Origen**	
5.13	177	*Fr. Jer.* (*in catenis*), 26	278–280
Romans			
1.1	178	**Paulinus of Nola**	
1.7	181	*Carmen IX*	276–283; 286–288
1.16–2.29	172		
2.11	177		
3.21–26	178	**Persius**	
3.24–28	178	2.8	137 n.30
3.24	177		
4.1–25	172		

Philippians
1.1	178
2.16	177
2.19–30	173
3.6	178

Plato
Ap.
19b	53
24b	53

Crito
54c6–8	24

Laws
11.914a	48
11.932a–d	48; 50
12.955a	47

Symp.
202a5–9	116 n.75

Pliny
Ep.
2.14.12–13	143

HN
7.139–140	157 nn.15, 16
7.139	155 n.6
28.11	140 nn.48, 49; 145 n.83, 146
28.25	144 n.75
35.4–14	154 n.5

Paneg.
1	221; 237
1.3	222; 233
1.4	233; 235
1.5	233
2.3	222
5.2–4	237
7.5	222; 233
8.2–3	234
10–11	228–230
10.3	228
10.5	228
11.1–3	225
11.2	230; 242
11.3	229
14.5	231; 232
19.1	230
24.5	241
25	239
25.5	238
30–32	238–240
30.3	238; 240
30.5	239
31.3	239
32.2–3	239; 240
35.2	229
35.4–5	229
35.4	226
40.3–4	240–241
49.1	227
52.1–7	227
52.6	235
55	227
80	237
80.3	230; 235
80.4–5	235
81–82	232
82.6–7	232
82.9	232
88	237
88.4–8	236–237
94	221
94.1	237
94.4	237

Plutarch
Alex.
2–3.4	196–203
2.1	197–198
2.3	196 n.8; 197
2.4–9	197
3.1–3	198
3.3	198–199
24.4–25.3	201
24.5–9	202
25.1–3	202
26.3–11	203
26.5	200
26.9–10	200
26.10–27	200
26.11–27.4	197
27.1–2	200
27.3–4	200
27.5–28.6	200
27.5–8	201

31.8	211	2.12.10–11	143 n.70
50.11	213	2.12.10	142 n.64, 143 n.67
54.3	202		
Ant.		2.12.11	142 n.65, 144 n.76
14.2–4	163 n.49		
14.7–8	162 n.47	3.7.2	156 n.9
Brut.		3.7.7	229
20.2–7	163 n.49	3.7.12	232
20.8–11	163 n.48	6.1.30–31	162 n.47
Caes.		8.3.63–66	283 n.50
5.2–5	157 n.12	9.3.2–3	274 n.24
68.1–7	163 n.49	10.1.27–28	38 n.30
68.3–6	163 n.48	10.5.4–11	274 n.23
Cic.		10.5.5	273
30–31	165 n.56	11.3.89	142 n.66
De superst. 3e=		11.3.150–156	139 n.46
Mor. 168a–b	137 n.36		
De Iside et Osiride		*Rhetorica ad Herennium*	
358 B	118 n.79	1.2.3	142 n.64
361 E	112 n.56	3.19–27	139 n.46
374 C–E	117 n.77	4.55.68	283 n.50
Marc. 6.5–6	144 n.75		
Quest. Rom. 14	144 n.75	**SEG**	
		30.61	42–43
[Plutarch]		27.261	43–46
Plac.			
4.19 (*Mor.* 902c–f)	136 n.25	**Seneca**	
4.20 (*Mor.* 903a)	136 n. 26	*De clem.*	
		1.19.7	145 n.84
Polybius		*De vit. beat.*	
6.53.1–54.3	153–154; 155 n.6	26.7	140 n.49
6.53.1	156 n.10	*Dial.*	
6.53.3 ff.	159 n.26	6.15.3	156 n.10
6.54.1 f.	158 n.21		
6.54.3	167 n.62	**Sophocles**	
6.54.6–15	167 n.63	*Ant.*	
		7–8	22
Porphyry		26–34	22
Abst.		446–457	21
4.9	117 n.76	282–288	22
Vit. Plot.		508–509	22
10.57–59	117 n.76	732–733	23
		736–739	23
Quintilian		745	23
Inst.		*OT*	
1.6.39–40	137 n.34	96–101	25
1.9.2	274	688–696	23

Statius
Theb.
11.503 — 137 n.30

Suetonius
Claud.
22 — 145 n.83
Dom.
13.2 — 222
Iul.
84.2–3 — 162 n.47
85.1–2 — 163 nn.48, 49
Nero
37 — 135 n.21

Tacitus
Ann.
2.73.1 — 154 n.5
3.5 — 154 n.5
3.5.1 — 156 n.10
3.76 — 154 n.5
3.76.2 — 156 n.10
4.9.2 — 154 n.5
4.38 — 245; 259–260
13.3.1 — 156 n.9; 158–159 n.25
Hist. 3.67.2 — 164 n.54

"Testament of Epicteta" (see *IG* XII 3.330 = *LSCG* 135)

Theocritus
Id.
15.94 — 109 n.42

Thucydides
6.27–29 — 53
6.53–61 — 53

Tibullus
2.2.2–10 — 140 n.49

Valerius Maximus
Praef. — 245; 248–254
2.6.8 — 245; 254
1.1.8 — 147 n.98
3.4.*ext*.1 — 245; 259
4.1.10 — 145 n.83
4.4.11 — 245; 255
4.7.*ext*.1 — 245; 255–257
6.1.*init.* — 245; 257–258
9.1.1 — 163 n.48
9.11.*ext*.4 — 245; 260–263

Varro
Ling.
5.14.80 — 147 n.92
5.16.87 — 147 n.92
6.56 — 136 n.24

www.ingramcontent.com/pod-product-compliance
Lightning Source LLC
Chambersburg PA
CBHW050515170426
43201CB00013B/1971